Philosophy After Darwin

DATE DUE			
DEC 16 86			
DEC 16 '86			

PHILOSOPHY
AFTER DARWIN

Chapters for

The Career of Philosophy

Volume III,

and Other Essays

JOHN HERMAN RANDALL, JR.

EDITED BY BETH J. SINGER

NEW YORK

COLUMBIA UNIVERSITY PRESS

1977

Library of Congress Cataloging in Publication Data

Randall, John Herman, 1899–
Philosophy after Darwin.

Includes index.
1. Philosophy, Modern—19th century.
I. Randall, John Herman, 1899–
The career of philosophy. II. Title.
B803.R25   190'.9   76-30897
ISBN 0-231-04114-4

COLUMBIA UNIVERSITY PRESS

NEW YORK   GUILDFORD, SURREY

COPYRIGHT © 1977 COLUMBIA UNIVERSITY PRESS

To
my younger son
Francis B. Randall
who knows everything
and
unselfishly shares his knowledge
with the world

Contents

Editor's Preface

THIS BOOK includes all the completed chapters for Volume III of Professor Randall's history of modern philosophy, *The Career of Philosophy*.[1] It also includes a number of other studies in the recent history of philosophy. Prevented by illness from completing Volume III, Professor Randall decided to publish the first eight chapters together with these studies. We have included another completed chapter and an incomplete one, originally written as the ninth and tenth chapters of Volume III, in the Appendix. Also in the Appendix is the most recent of several outlines of Volume III, prepared by Randall in 1969.

The first four chapters have never appeared in print. While chapters 5 through 12 have been published, none appears in any collection of Professor Randall's own writings. Chapter 8, abridged for its original publication in a journal, appears here in full.

The basis for the text of each paper published here is either the original typescript or the paper as originally published. Wherever possible, typescript and published paper have been compared in order to incorporate the latest changes introduced by Randall. As few editorial changes as possible have been made. Some stylistic and technical changes were required but these do not affect the substance of any paper.

Several footnotes and dates in the manuscripts of the first four chapters had not been completed by Professor Randall. In completing these I have made a few minor corrections in citations and quotations. For example, it is not clear which edition of Herbert Spencer's *First*

---

[1] Volume I, "From the Middle Ages to the Enlightenment" (1962), and Volume II, "From the German Enlightenment to the Age of Darwin" (1965), both published by Columbia University Press in New York and London. Parenthetical references in the chapters to the first two volumes of this work have been retained.

Principles was the source of Randall's quotations. As the wording in every case is identical or nearly so to the third edition (London, 1870), this edition is cited in the notes and, where necessary, minor verbal changes or changes in punctuation have been made for the sake of accuracy.

In general, the style of the notes conforms to that of Professor Randall's earlier works. In every chapter, after the initial citation of any work, immediately succeeding quotations from the same source are identified in the text by page numbers in parentheses immediately following each quoted passage.

At the outset Professor Randall's friends and colleagues, Professors Justus Buchler, Paul O. Kristeller, and Ernest Nagel were consulted as to the desirability of issuing such a volume. His wife, Mercedes M. Randall, as usual, worked with him at all stages. James Gutmann was helpful as always.

The editor acknowledges the assistance of Joseph L. Blau, Charles Kegley, Fred Lerner, Jonathan Singer, Joan McQuary, John D. Moore, and David Diefendorf. She especially appreciates the collaboration of Mrs. Randall.

Beth J. Singer

PART ONE

Coming to Terms with Natural Science

I

The Conflict of the Religious Tradition with Science

NINETEENTH-CENTURY PHILOSOPHIES show no such single-minded reactions to new problems as those of the seventeenth century, of the Enlightenment, or of the earlier Romantic era. They exhibit rather a great diversity of tendencies: older traditions were being continued, but becoming, as we say, more and more "academic" in the face of the new issues of the century. This was a time when philosophy was largely captured by professors of philosophy, especially in Germany with its mushrooming universities, which during the century clearly held the academic and intellectual leadership of Western civilization. The older answers were still logically defensible, but they were growing increasingly irrelevant to the central intellectual problems. And all the newer answers to the ever-growing fact of science were individual; there was no longer an accepted attitude, as there had been earlier in the modern period—unless we can say that some form of philosophic "naturalism" had been agreed upon, as it had been by all the original thinkers, and by many others, in Great Britain and America. But a vigorous dissent would be entered from Neo-Thomist priests, from the orthodox Dialectical Materialists, and from the anguished Existentialists of the German and Latin countries. It would hardly be unfair to say that the last hundred years have not seen such outstanding philosophical minds as the seventeenth century, or the classic period of German thought; the scientists have taken over the intellectual initiative. Philosophy, in an ebbing Romanticism, tended to become the expression of personal reactions. Philosophy was often held to be a matter of "temperament."

Hence the treatment of philosophical thinking in these hundred years will emphasize tendencies rather than individual "systems," which were rapidly going out of fashion anyway. These major tendencies will be illustrated by reference to certain of their leading exponents. There are at most a dozen individual thinkers who deserve extended analysis: Green and Bradley among the English Idealists, Royce the American, Nietzsche, Dilthey, and Max Weber among the Germans, Bergson in France, Croce in Italy. In our own century, one can name Dewey, Santayana, and Whitehead among the Americans, Russell in England, and Husserl and Heidegger in Germany. The increasing host of philosophical teachers and analysts need to be referred to only for particular turns of thought.

The fundamental philosophical problem, from Copernicus to Kant, was to build up, understand, and extend first natural and then social science. In the seventeenth century, it was the new science that needed justification against the reigning religious and moral tradition. This period of the assimilation of natural—largely Newtonian—science was followed by the Romantic reaction toward reasserting the claims of human personality, organizing the world of culture and human values, minimizing natural science, and concentrating on the specifically "human" experiences.

But by 1860 the scientific faith had been reestablished, and no longer stood in need of philosophic support and defense. It was now, many came to feel, religious and moral values that needed defense against the "encroachments" of science. The problem of earlier modern philosophy had been to make a mechanistic science "intelligible" in a human and social world—originally, in the Aristotelian universe. But the prestige of "science" grew, until by 1860 the problem had become rather to make man and his society and culture intelligible in a mechanistic and scientific universe.

These facts help to explain why from the beginning the "problem of knowledge" has been central in modern philosophy. "Knowledge" will always present a number of particular problems. But they will normally be either psychological problems dealing with the origin and growth of knowledge, or logical problems dealing with the structure and tests of knowledge—what we have come to call the "philosophy of science." But "knowledge in general" presents a central "metaphysical" or—as it came to be called—"epistemological" problem, only when two conflicting types of knowledge are struggling for men's allegiance. This has been the case in Western culture ever since Aristotelian science began in the twelfth century to compete with traditional Christian religious and moral truth. The struggle has lasted until the present-day acceptance of an enlarged and deepened "science" and "scientific method" as the one type of *knowledge*—though certainly not the only type of *value!* This acceptance would be denied today only by a few rather confused theologians, and by some of the heirs of the German Romantic tradition. This still leaves us with plenty of logical problems in science itself; but "*the* problem of knowledge," as such, has vanished. And to that extent, distinctively "modern" philosophy has ended.

Its epistemological problems are destined, perhaps, to a rebirth, and a kind of Indian summer, if our task of effecting a social reorganization proves to demand an absolute social faith, like Communism—or its antithesis. We should then presumably encounter again a central epistemological problem, when we try to adjust such an absolute social faith, born of the supposed needs of action, to our scientific knowledge. The attempt would create a new heritage of confusion for future philosophers to clear up.

"Modern philosophy" can be defined, in other than chronological terms, as the conflict between two types of knowledge. Such "modern philosophy" has ended when one type has won out, as science now has. Thus the whole of "modern philosophy" has been centered on "justifying" a set of facts that seemed irrelevant and unintelligible in terms of the reigning philosophy. The result has been much profound analysis, but little in the way of wisdom. Men were always committed in advance to what was bound to be an ingenious solution, which men could indeed "accept," but found it hard really to "believe." There was little time left to build from the goods at hand a really satisfying conception of the Good Life; men were too busy quarreling over whether man is "free" to do so or not. Hence we miss in modern philosophy the wisdom shared by all the philosophies of Greece, even those of the Hellenistic Age, by those of the Middle Ages at their best, including their last spokesman, Spinoza, and by those of the great Oriental civilizations. The Idealists at their best came close to it. But they could never forget they were "fighting science"; and they soon lost sight of their true mission, as the century wore on and they became the great bulwark of intellectual conservatism.

Idealism might have been a genuine attempt at exploring the new possibilities of the Good Life in the vastly richer world made possible by science and the machine process, needing an organization and adjustment incomparably more intricate than was ever possible in Athens or in Florence. But actually the Idealists made the problem insoluble by demanding a cosmic and universal sanction; by insisting that the whole possibility of the Good Life depended on finding human standards enshrined in the heart of the world process.

This task of exploring the new possibilities of man's life, of reflecting on what human excellence might mean in a scientifically known world—the turning, that is, to the issues of the Good Life and of wisdom—might have been carried through on a naturalistic basis, with a hearty welcome for the open-minded inquiry of scientific method. But it was not. It proved far easier to fall back on tradition and reinterpret the traditional values and ideals in terms of the familiar framework in which they had been embedded for two thousand years of Hebraism and Christianity. Idealism was a "theistic" interpretation of the world, that gave man and man's interests, the values man cares for, a cosmic significance. The idealistic reconstructions maintained, just as did the popular Wesleyan and Catholic religious revivals of the early nineteenth century, that there is something not improperly symbolized as "God" and "Providence," a Friend behind phenomena, who cares for man—that man's ideals are "safe" because the power behind nature is also devoted to them.

Hence, on the one hand, the Idealists have alone faced the problems of the Good Life with any adequate recognition of the complexity, richness, and variety of the factors to be organized. Compare their sense of the "problem of human freedom" with the cavalier and superficial nonchalance of the Utilitarians, like Spencer and even Mill. But on the other hand, the net result of the subtle philosophies to which the Idealists resorted to escape science was to rehabilitate a theistic, supernaturalistic, nonscientific world view. It is very difficult today even to understand the genuine insights of the Idealists, if, as the majority of the philosophically-minded are at present convinced, men can no longer take seriously this supernaturalistic frame.

The Idealists were committed to a faith in the cosmic significance of man, to a substantial God, to future immortality, to a cosmic moral order. During the nineteenth century, the scientific spirit was steadily undermining such a faith. The Idealists were committed to a "transcendental" or supernaturalistic philosophy. But such philosophies were steadily giving way to philosophies based on scientific methods. The Idealists still insisted on escaping into a realm inaccessible to scientific inquiry, despite the fact that enlarged and broadened scientific methods and concepts were making such escape impossible and, what is more important, quite unnecessary.

How deep-rooted is this craving for a cosmic guarantee of the success of our ideals—especially in days of rapid transition, when familiar and accepted values are crumbling all about us—it is not necessary to emphasize today. We are all tempted to convert passionate hopes into evidence; such, for instance, is the strength of Marxism where it is strong. If we really had to face the choice between the despair of the older "alien world" philosophies—that our most sacred ideals are inevitably doomed to defeat—and the optimism of the philosophic idealisms, few would hesitate at the leap of faith.

More recent naturalisms eliminate the need of that choice. They make clear that Nature is not irrelevant to our ideals, and does permit us to work and struggle for them. Our ideals and values are not idle dreams, but are rooted in the very conditions that Nature—and human nature—impose on us. Such a view furnishes an alternative alike to the complacent confidence of the supernaturalist, and his egotistic assumption of human powers, doomed to early disillusionment and defeat, and to the paralyzing despair of the "moral atheist," who can see no possible perfecting of "things as they are," no values implicit in Nature and in human nature that man's striving can hope to realize.

Idealism shifted men's attention from the real problems: What is the Good Life for man? How can we work to achieve it? to the very secondary problem, Is there a "Divine Force" in the universe that has commanded and will guarantee the pitifully meagre and inadequate "Christian ideals" of a thousand or two thousand years ago? The nineteenth century gave three answers: (1) There is a God, and everything will be all right; (2) There is no God, and everything is all wrong; (3) There is no God, but "Evolution" is just as good, and therefore everything will be all right. The issue was phrased as that between optimism and pessimism; the question was, Is life worth living? It can be doubted whether philosophers ever asked seriously a more foolish question. They seldom got near the real problem: What *kind* of life, individually and socially, is most worth living?

Why? Because Idealism got human values so tangled up with a theistic world view, faith in life was made so dependent on faith in God, that when science seemed to take God out of the universe, men lost their faith in life also. And to restore their faith in life, men had to deify some natural force, like "evolution." Both the antiscientific idealisms and the evolutionary philosophies were trying desperately to satisfy a religious need, to build a religious world view. And how they murdered "evolution" to do it! Only in our generation can we be said to have recovered. A wise teacher of mine remarked in 1916: "The religion of evolution has played more havoc with scientific investigation than all the Christian theologians put together." Fortunately, we have come to take our evolution less emotionally during the last fifty years.

The nineteenth century started with all human interests and values more deeply bound up with a theistic world view than at any time since the thirteenth century—and then it came to feel that such a philosophy was untenable. "Science" could hardly be disregarded. Time could not actually be "unreal"—in the world of evolution and historicism. Space was not an "illusion"—in the world of railroads, autos, and airplanes. Could science be what Fichte called it, a mere "dream world," in the civilizations of Germany, England, or America after 1870? You might be able still to "prove" it; but you could no longer "believe" it—it could not be done. It was possible, in the wooded seclusion of Jena or Heidelberg in 1800, or at Cornell in the 1890s, or in the cloisters of Oxford around 1900, to weigh "science" in the balance as a philosophy of life, as one possible if unappealing "theory" of the universe, and reject it for a more congenial humanistic "theory."

But can you do that in Columbia University in the City of New York? Or anywhere after the Manhattan Project? Science is now too deeply embedded in the basic processes of our civilization. We have got to respect it, to understand it, and hopefully even to use it. It is no longer a question merely of understanding and extending science—though much remains to be done—or of rejecting it for a more human world. Our great problem is, how to find the essential values of life *within* the world science so ably describes. We are just coming to admit it. We have have fought it tooth and nail, and explored every other possibility. Our problem, the task of the twentieth century, is to build an adequate naturalistic philosophy, to work out an adequate organization of the Good Life.

The nineteenth century tried compromise: its great problem was the *religious* problem, in the sense we can say the great problem of the seventeenth and eighteenth centuries was the *scientific* problem. Starting with a Romantic faith in an anthropocentric world, it found science swiftly and surely undermining that faith. Instead of accepting the inevitable, and seeking the Good Life in a naturalistic world, as men today have at last come to do, the nineteenth century searched frantically for a new Cosmic Companion, for an up-to-date and "scientific" God. There were apologists of hopes and aspirations, and apostles of militant denial. Most men chose compromise. None of the attempts can be said really to have succeeded. Hence, while the fundamental note of eighteenth-century philosophy is optimism, that of the nineteenth century is disillusionment and pessimism; consider the popularity of Schopenhauer at the beginning, and of Russell's "Free Man's Worship" at the end of the century. Or else it was a whistling to keep one's courage up, as in Nietzsche, Bergson, or James.

Men so much wanted to believe in God, they grasped at any straw: God was the "Unknowable," God was Evolution, God was Energy, God was the "Principle of Concretion"—somewhere, in some scientific or pseudoscientific concept, lurked the Father of mankind, exercising his Divine Providence. Men wanted to believe in God, because they simply could not order their lives if they did not. William James's early religious crisis is a good case in point. Men felt the need of a Divine sanction—even if they found it in so poor a thing as natural selection. The Idealists had staked everything on God—He must exist. Good Lord, what they raked up!

For all our own doubts, I do not think that today men feel that way. Having grown up with science, they take its world for granted. But it took a terrible struggle in the nineteenth century to give us our naturalistic temper. We can today build a human philosophy, drawing on all the techniques of science, just because men in the nineteenth century finally worked the Good Life clear of the need for a cosmic sanction.

For today, the "religious problem," as the nineteenth century felt it, has simply disappeared from all serious philosophizing. For us, the problem of religion is, not to defend against science a religion we deeply cherish, but to find a religion—if we can—that we can cherish, a religion strong enough to need no external "defense." Our criticism of the religious tradition is no longer intellectual, but moral and social. For us, "religion" is not a question of intellectual beliefs, but an organization of human life, like art, or morals, something to be used, enjoyed, and lived, something natural, and not at variance with the rest of life. We are free to work out a genuine and sustaining religious faith within the natural world, just because we no longer feel the need to defend faith in the "truth" of religion—of a particularly unscientific, poetic, and imaginative religion at that.

My own teacher once remarked that "modern philosophy" had ended in 1895. Puzzling over the date, it finally dawned upon me that that was when he saw the light. To become autobiographical, I might add that "modern philosophy" really ended in 1920. The philosophies flourishing since that date, whether imposing schemes of metaphysics, like Whitehead, philosophies of criticism, like Dewey, or the more recent efforts of the assorted analysts, simply do not take as central the cosmic religious problem. Where men used to debate the validity of religious knowledge, and its superiority to "mere science," today they carefully analyse the uses and functions of religious language.

To our way of thinking, it raises a large question: If nineteenth-century philosophers were so busy trying to adjust men's religious beliefs and moral ideals to the great new force of mechanistic and evolutionary science, why were they not equally concerned with adjusting them to the obviously still greater force of industrial society in all its ramifications? Why were not social issues more central than the intellectual issues raised by the impingement of science upon the religious tradition? It is, in fact, surprising how little the immense social changes of the nineteenth century really affected and stimulated philosophic thinking. This strikes us especially when we consider the eighteenth century, when social issues dominated even science, and the characteristic philosophies of rationalism and empiricism had so direct a social motivation and repercussion.

Of course, men in the nineteenth century had social philosophies; and social considerations did influence the adoption of general viewpoints. For us, so deeply immersed in such issues, these social philosophies of our forbears have taken on increased importance, and even seem often to push the religious issues into the background. But for their social philosophies men went mostly to the older intellectual traditions, not to the new evolutionary attitudes. Liberalism in Britain found its official philosophy in Utilitarianism, a continuation of eighteenth-century empiricism. And collectivism, in both its more conservative and its radical versions, found a congenial philosophy in some type of Idealism, especially in the Hegelian rationalism of Right or Left Wing derivation. But social values remained more or less irrelevant to the central problem of religious beliefs. And the nineteenth-century social philosophies now stand revealed as at their best woefully inadequate makeshifts for dealing with the fundamental problems of an industrial age.

For example, take the three most influential popular philosophies of the century, those of Comte, Spencer, and Marx. They developed completely divergent social philosophies. Comte's positivism stood for an enlightened despotism, for "technocracy" or rule by industrial experts. Spencer gave the classic statement of individualism and laisser-faire. And Marx was the theoretician of socialism. Yet all three were in fundamental agreement on "accepting science"; and each stood, in France, in Britain, and in Germany, as the great exponent of a negative answer to the religious problem. Or rather, each stood for finding a religious faith in science itself, for taking science—for Spencer and Marx it was "Evolution"—as a new and up-to-date Providence working for the good of man.

There are many complex reasons why it was science rather than technological society in general that furnished the main intellectual problem for the nineteenth-century thinkers. The important fact is that it did. And only after the ultimate painful acceptance of naturalism have men been free to make social problems the central impetus to philosophizing, as they were in Greece, and as they became again in the eighteenth century. It seems likely that post-"modern" philosophy will be profoundly stimulated by the problems of organizing an industrial and technological civilization, and that such social and cultural rather than purely religious problems will be the basis of twentieth-century groupings.

I

What was the actual impact of the new science? What did science actually do, that seemed in such conflict with the older religious tradition? The idea of biological evolution was the most novel and revolutionary concept in nineteenth-century science; and it came to stand as the symbol of the revitalized scientific faith. In reality, it was probably not so important in forcing on men a naturalistic philosophy as the detailed working-out of a mechanistic explanation. The latter seemed less violent a shock, for the idea had been in the world since Descartes. Science was advancing, filling in the details of the Cartesian and Newtonian program; the results were so impressive that by 1860 they could no longer be disregarded. The fundamental dogmas of the scientific faith now served to organize a vast body of facts that could scarcely be gainsaid. In the nineteenth century they took the form of sweeping generalizations: the conservation of energy, the laws of thermodynamics, the method of natural selection in biological evolution, the mechanical theory of life. Above all, there was the dogma of an unyielding mechanistic determinism. The laboratory had not yet unearthed so many facts that no single generalization could embrace them all. The breakdown in our century of traditional physical theory had not yet occurred. The idea that all such general formulations are "leading principles" of scientific investigation, in Kantian terms, "regulative principles," intellectual instruments to guide inquiry, rather than ineluctable "laws" governing the universe, had as yet received little support. The most speculative generalizations, either abandoned or drastically modified today, were seized upon after the middle of the century to complete the picture of what was called the "scientific world." Nineteenth-century science, though vastly richer than Newtonian mechanics, still clung to the same fundamental assumptions of a closed mechanical and material order of Nature. These assumptions were actually far closer to the crude and simple systems of seventeenth-century scientific enthusiasm than to the tentative, cautious, experimental science of today, with its world of radiant energy and its principle of indeterminacy. In a word, the Newtonian Mechanistic framework of thought about Nature had not yet been burst asunder. With this framework and with these assumptions and dogmas, the backbone of the scientific faith, shaken believers in the older traditions felt they had to come to terms.

The popularization of Darwin's theories came at the psychological moment to give men fighting issues. The idea of "Evolution" proved a Godsend to the religious seekers. Here obviously was the new faith needed. There *is* a Purpose in the world, man's ideals *do* matter to Nature, Heaven will be reached, in substantial form, on earth. Evolution was accepted as a new substitute religious faith, because of the great help it promised in the central religious problem. The evolutionary philosophers were so busy trying to find a new cosmic religious faith, discovering God and Providence in the evolutionary process itself, that they quite failed to recognize what evolution and a biological conception of human nature really implied. The important consequence of Darwin's theory, philosophically, the biological nature and setting of human experience, individual and social, was largely overlooked. It was obscured for fifty years, by the "philosophies of evolution." Only in the twentieth century did a few thinkers, like John Dewey and Whitehead—anticipated, to be sure, by the evolutionary voluntarism of Nietzsche—begin to realize these actual implications, and to see that if you really understood "evolution," it completely transformed the older problems, and got you into a post-"modern" age.[1]

In fact, we can now see, the idea of evolution remained throughout the nineteenth century a fundamentally Romantic conception. It started with the pioneer Romanticists, Herder, Goethe, Schelling, and Hegel. It was forced on biologists after it had long been dominant in history and the social sciences, from the time of Buffon at least (see Vol. I, Book IV, chapter 14, sec. V). It was accepted by the post-Darwinian evolutionary philosophers, not as a mere scientific theory in biology, but as a principle of cosmic explanation, as a new Primary Cause. It functioned as a new Romantic faith—the greatest and most seductive, with the possible exception of the Romantic faith in the Nation, of all the Romantic faiths. This is obvious in a pure Romanticist like Bergson; but it is just as true of the "unsentimental" Herbert Spencer. For him, Evolution was as much a religious faith as for Hegel or Marx. And his famous "law of Evolution,"

Evolution is an integration of matter and a concomitant dissipation of motion, during which the matter passes from an indefinite, incoherent homogeneity to a definite, coherent heterogeneity, and during which the retained motion undergoes a parallel transformation,[2]

[1] See John Dewey, "The Influence of Darwin on Philosophy," in *The Influence of Darwin on Philosophy and Other Essays in Contemporary Thought* (New York, 1910), lecture delivered in 1909; and J.H. Randall, Jr., "The Changing Impact of Darwin on Philosophy," *Journal of the History of Ideas*, XXII (1961), pp. 435–62.

[2] Herbert Spencer, *First Principles* (3rd ed., London, 1870), p. 396.

is as much an "idealistic" attempt to construct the world a priori as anything in Hegel; and considerably less justified, for Hegel's formula does apply, if roughly, to important phases of social development.

II

Yet—for two generations "evolution" served as the symbol of the scientific faith, before Einstein supplanted Darwin. Those who accepted it had abandoned the merely traditional ideas. It was the gateway to the scientific universe, and led men on to the fundamental assumptions of the scientific method. The men of the mid-century felt this. For them, the faith in science had become once more a living reality, in genuine conflict with their inherited faith in the cosmic importance of man. All the old problems of the eighteenth-century religious rationalists, all the old doubts raised since the days of Epicurus and Lucretius, came back to them in intensified form. Men generalized a picture of the universe from the methods, assumptions, and attitudes of nineteenth-century natural science. They thus arrived at a "scientific world view." It was a faith, of course, a negative faith, often a nightmare and an obsession. But by 1859 men were coming to feel they must accept this faith; and for such, the religious world view of the Idealists was shoved aside.

How did this picture look? Believers and nonbelievers agreed.

The human race is not capable of indefinite progress. For it to develop at all it was necessary for the earth to be in certain physical and chemical conditions that are highly unstable. There was a time when our planet was not suited to man: it was too hot and too damp. There will come a time when it will no longer be suited to him: it will be too cold and too dry. When the sun has been extinguished, an event that cannot fail to occur, men will long have disappeared. The last men will be as naked and stupid as were the first. They will have forgotten all the arts and all the sciences. They will crouch miserably in caves at the edge of the glaciers that will then roll their transparent blocks over the obliterated ruins of the cities where now we think, love, suffer, and hope. All the elms and all the lindens will be dead of cold; and the firs will reign alone on the frozen earth. These last men, deprived of all hope without even knowing the fact, will know nothing of us, nothing of our love, nothing of our genius, and still they will be our last-born children and blood of our blood. A feeble remnant of king-like intelligence, trembling in their thick skulls, will for a little time longer give them the rule over the bears crowding about their caves. Peoples and tribes will have disappeared beneath the snow and ice, with the cities, the roads, the gardens of the old world. A few families will eke out a bare existence. Women, children, old men, huddled together, will see through the mouths of their caves sadly mounting above their heads a sombre sun surrounded, like a dying ember, with a few pale rays, while a dazzling snow of stars will continue to shine all day long in the black heavens, through the glacial air. That is what they will see; but in their stupidity they will not even know they are seeing anything. One day the last of them will breathe into the alien sky the last human sigh, without hate and without love. And the earth will continue to revolve, carrying through the silent spaces the burnt-out cinders of humanity, the poems of Homer and the noble remains of the Greek marbles on its frozen surface. And no thought will ever again be launched toward the infinite from the bosom of this globe where the mind has been so daring, at least no human thought. For who can say that then another thought may not become aware of itself, and that this tomb where we shall all be sleeping will not be the cradle of a new mind? Of what mind, I do not know. The mind of some insect, perhaps.

Side by side with man, in spite of man, the insects, the bees and the ants, for example, have already done marvels. It is true that ants and bees, like ourselves, desire light and heat. But there are invertebrates less susceptible to cold. Who knows the future reserved for their labor and their patience?

Who knows whether the earth will not become good for them when it has ceased to be good for us? Who knows whether they will not some day become aware of themselves and of the world? Who knows whether in their turn they will not praise God? [3]

Anatole France was writing in the 1890s, when the full implications of the second law of thermodynamics were just being felt emotionally. But a generation later a belated sleeper, who had just found out there is no Santa Claus, an American, could still write:

What we have come to realize, then, is that the scientific optimism of which Huxley may be taken as a typical exponent was merely a new variety of faith, resting upon certain premises which are no more unassailable than those which have supported other vanished religions of the past. It had as its central dogma the assumption that truths are necessarily useful, and that the human spirit flowered best in the midst of realities clearly perceived. After the manner of all religions, it instinctively refrains from any criticism of this essential dogma, and it was left to us in an age troubled by a new agnosticism to perceive how far this first article of the scientific creed is from being self-evidently true. Experience has taught us that the method of the laboratory has its limitation, and that the accumulation of scientific data is not, in the case of all subjects, useful. We have learned how certain truths—intimate revelations concerning the origin and mechanism of our deepest impulses—can stagger our souls, and how our clear perception of our lonely isolation in the midst of

[3] Anatole France, *Le Jardin d'Épicure* (Paris, 1918), pp. 24–28.

a universe which knows nothing of us and our aspirations paralyzes our will. We are aware, too, of the fact that art and ethics have not flowered anew in the light, that we have not won a newer and more joyous acceptance of the universe, and we have come to realize that the more we learn of the laws of the universe—in which we constitute a strange incongruity—the less we shall feel at home in it.[4]

Krutch is worried, not so much by the second law of thermodynamics, like the men of the 1890s, but by recent psychological dogmas. But he returns to the same note: man is living in an "alien universe," utterly incompatible with, now, not religious but humanistic values.

The antithesis between human and natural ends is ultimately irreconcilable, and the most that man can hope for is a recurrent defiance recurrently subdued. He can deviate so far but no further from the animal norm. He can make himself into an artist or a philosopher, but there are limits set both to the perfection of these types and to the extent to which the bulk of any population can be allowed to approach either, for individuals and races alike fall victim to their humanity. In the search for human values they first lose interest in those natural virtues which serve to keep the structure of the ant-hill sound; and then when they discover that, even for them as individuals, life has no purpose which their intellects can accept, even they perish of a *taedium vitae* and leave the world to simpler peoples who have still some distance to go before they reach the end of the tether which attaches them to nature. In the drama of history barbarians are always appearing in the role of the *deus ex machina,* and the historian is always laying great stress upon "fresh blood" brought in from the provinces or infused by primitive conquerors. And yet he has seldom cared to draw the pessimistic conclusion which alone seems deducible from the facts in his possession.

Nor can it be said that to understand this paradox of humanism helps us in any way to solve it. The analysis which we perform is, indeed, itself an example of one of those exercises of the mind which is perverse because it does not serve as a means toward a natural end, and when we have admitted that the human ideal is one which the human animal cannot even approach without tending to destroy himself as he does so, we have by that very admission, both diminished our biological fitness and desolated our human feelings. Hence it is that many a man with trained mind, developed sensibilities, and even as much good will toward society as can be expected of a creature who has lost the animal's innate talent for caring more for his race than for himself, stands paralyzed in the midst of a world that has learned so many things which do not help it toward any ultimate solution of its problems, but which tend, on the contrary, rather to make him suspect that they are insoluble.

[4] Joseph Wood Krutch, *The Modern Temper* (New York, 1929), pp. 75–76.

These men cannot strive with a missionary zeal for the development and spread of pure science, philosophy, and art because they have come to believe that these things are neither ultimately satisfying or conducive to a vigorous national life, but neither can they cast their lot with the "plain man," the "sturdy citizen," or the Spartan patriot, because it is the detachment of which these are the enemies that gives human life whatever of even doubtful value it seems to the pure humanist to have. To the latter it appears that there is no choice to be made, except that between an antlike stability and an eternal recurrence which condemns humanity to a recurrent death at the top, to be followed once more by a fresh growth from the roots. (52–55)

And Krutch, in defiant despair at everything science tells him, concludes:

If Humanism and Nature are fundamentally antithetical, if the human virtues have a definite limit set to their development, and if they may be cultivated only by a process which renders us progressively unfit to fulfill our biological duties, then we may at least permit ourselves a certain defiant satisfaction when we realize that we have made our choice and that we are resolved to abide by the consequences. Some small part of the tragic fallacy may be said to be still valid for us, for if we cannot feel ourselves great as Shakespeare did, if we no longer believe in either our infinite capacities or our importance to the universe, we know at least that we have discovered the trick which has been played upon us and that whatever else we may be we are no longer dupes.

Rejuvenation may be offered to us at a certain price. Nature, issuing her last warning, may bid us embrace some new illusion before it is too late and accord ourselves once more with her. But we prefer rather to fail in our own way than to succeed in hers. Our human world may have no existence outside of our own desires, but those are more imperious than anything else we know, and we still cling to our own lost cause, choosing always rather to know than to be. Doubtless fresh people have still a long way to go with Nature before they are compelled to realize that they too have come to the parting of the ways, but though we may wish them well we do not envy them. If death for us and our kind is the inevitable result of our stubbornness then we can only say, "So be it." Ours is a lost cause and there is no place for us in the natural universe, but we are not, for all that, sorry to be human. We should rather die as men than live as animals. (248–49)

If this very quintessence of Romantic *Weltschmerz* was still possible for a sophisticated mind of the late 1920s, we need hardly judge the Victorians to be too naive when they saw their comfortable and familiar faith in danger of reconstruction. Lest this sentimental defiance be dismissed as the emotional reaction of a mere literary critic, we can cite also a man presumably endowed with the scientific spirit, Bertrand Russell.

That Man is the product of causes which had no prevision of the end they were achieving, that his origin, his growth, his hopes and fears, his loves and his beliefs, are but the outcome of accidental collocations of atoms; that no fire, no heroism, no intensity of thought and feeling, can preserve an individual life beyond the grave; that all the labor of the ages, all the devotion, all the inspiration, all the noonday brightness of human genius, are destined to extinction in the vast death of the solar system, and that the whole temple of Man's achievement must inevitably be buried beneath the debris of a universe in ruins—all these things, if not quite beyond dispute, are yet so nearly certain, that no philosophy which rejects them can hope to stand. Only within the scaffolding of these truths, only on the firm foundation of unyielding despair, can the soul's habitation henceforth be safely built. [5]

In extenuation of the philosopher Russell, it must be remembered that he wrote this burst of rhetoric at the age of thirty, and has since confessed himself thoroughly ashamed of the indiscretion of youth.

Like the astronauts, men scanned the heavens and found no trace of any Cosmic Companion for man, for any Friend who cares for human striving. Man seemed utterly alone, a cosmic accident, an unintentional mistake in the order of the universe.

The fundamental note running through these emotional expressions of the first shock was that there is no permanence for man, for the human race. Science had already destroyed the faith in personal immortality. It could of course not disprove the belief, but it could and did make it seem irrelevant to the kind of being man is. If we accept modern psychology, in any of its warring schools, there is no place for a deathless "spirit" among reflex arcs and complex habits. Indeed, belief in personal survival was the first of the old religious doctrines that seemed to go by the board, though for many it still remained fundamental. Immortality was a far more vital belief than that in God. There were plenty of discoverable substitutes for Providence, especially Evolution. There persisted a deep yearning for immortality, even if vicarious: George Eliot's "Choir Invisible" was immensely popular. For a time, the craving for permanence was satisfied by the prospect of an unlimited progress for human society. Then, in the 1880s, the second law of thermodynamics seemed to doom the human

---

[5] Bertrand Russell, "A Free Man's Worship," in *Mysticism and Logic* (London, 1918), pp. 47–48.

race itself to ultimate extinction. This proved the greatest emotional shock of all, on which we have seen Anatole France ring all the changes.

We can well ask today, why did men feel so deeply on such a highly speculative and remote matter? "Nothing remains." Why were men driven frantic by this tolling bell? The end of the world, the ultimate destruction of mankind, had been contemplated as probable—indeed, as revealed—everywhere until earthly progress became a new ideal in the seventeenth century. Why did it now appear as a high tragedy? In giving up its hope of personal survival, religious faith, even of the modernists and liberals, had staked everything on the immortality of mankind. Even eighteenth-century materialism had assumed the permanence of the universe as it is, and with it the promise of an unlimited social progress. Men still felt the need of such a cosmic guarantee of the salvation of humanity. Harald Høffding, in his popular *Philosophy of Religion* (1901), could define religion as "faith in the conservation of value." Men demanded a witness, a realm in which their interests and aspirations could be somehow registered—even the God of Whitehead, in his "consequent" function, still performs this essential service. Now, physics seemed to rob men of their faith a second time. No wonder the result for many was utter despair. We must not forget that William James sagely observed, "Pessimism is a religious disease."

Today, when our best theologians still defend God and Freedom, but not Immortality, it is difficult for us to understand this nineteenth-century cosmic disillusionment and pessimism. There is the story of the little old lady who, after a lecture in which the extinction of the race was thus dwelt upon, inquired, "Did you say man will be gone in seven million years?" "No, I said seventy million," came the reply. "Oh, I am so relieved," exclaimed the lady, contentedly. We laugh, for today the issue seems so irrelevant. For us, the second law of thermodynamics, if not exactly knocked into a cocked hat, has been so reinterpreted that its sting has been lost. Since 1890 the world has had so many ends predicted. First men foresaw the slow congealing of cosmic cold. Then radioactivity was discovered, and the world was destined to go up in smoke. Today these are all recognized for what they are—speculative generalizations of certain useful theories.

We have our own pessimisms and disillusionments, God knows;

but they are practical and human, not cosmic. They center on man's alienation from society. We can even live with the probability that we shall all blow ourselves to smithereens tomorrow. We do not any longer even want or "hope for" personal immortality: we would not know what to do if we woke up and found ourselves dead. We refuse even to speculate about the next seventy million years—unless we are cosmologists. Our problems are far more pressing.

One other alien element in the "scientific world view" awakened great emotional reactions—the mechanical determinism involved. This generated the problem of Freedom, a moral rather than a religious problem, felt especially by the anticlerical French philosophers, who made it central. William James's central emphasis on it sprang from his French training under Renouvier. Again, we can only ask, why did men find a determinism so terrible? It had been the core of the doctrine of the greatest theologians of the Church, like Augustine and Calvin, to say nothing of its position in many other religions. It was not a religious determinism, like the traditional Augustinian one. It was not a rational determinism, like that of the Stoics or Spinoza, to say nothing of Hegel. Such religious determinism meant man must act in accordance with God's will, which is perfect. Even damnation has proved emotionally tolerable, if it be taken as the decree of the All-Good. Man is still cosmically important—at worst, he is a tragic hero, like Milton's Lucifer. Rational determinism has meant, man must act in accordance with his own nature, which is in essence rational; such determinism is a promise.

But now, science seemed to hold that man must act in accordance with an alien, inhuman, callously indifferent Nature—a "Nature red in tooth and claw," Tennyson put it. Man was no longer even a tragic hero. He was rather a crawling worm on the vast cosmic stage. It is certainly a genuine problem—if man is excluded completely from Nature, as the "scientific world view" excluded him, quite inconsistently.

For many, this new form of determinism took the shape of a determination by heredity and environment. Ibsen's *Ghosts*, Gerhart Hauptmann's *Before Sunrise*—where the baby in his cradle reaches up for the whiskey bottle—emphasize the tragic implications of the former. In the hands of sociological penologists, or humanitarians like Clarence Darrow, the second form promised forgiveness, the absence of vengeance. Crime is for some an inescapable disease, to be treated by altering the environment.

Of course, aside from the Existentialists, like Sartre—who at one time believed in "absolute freedom," whatever that may be—the problem of Freedom is focused on the complex conditions of "freedom" in industrial society. Like so much else, it has become a social and practical problem.

2

Emotional Reactions to the World of
Nineteenth-Century Science

TO THE MEN brought up in the warmth of the religious and humanistic
tradition, buttressed by the thinking of the Romantic era, the universe
generalized from nineteenth-century science seemed an "alien world."
If we ask, Had the possibilities of human life actually changed, we
must answer, No—or rather, we must really answer, Yes. For science
was rapidly creating unheard of opportunities for new enjoyment and
control of the conditions of human living. Yet men despaired! They
apparently could not secure what they thought they had in their possession. Why, then, should they bother to take anything? Like Tennyson, disturbed at the threat to personal survival, they paced the
cliffs at Dover and cried out in agony, "If there is no immortality, I
shall hurl myself into the sea." To a later psychological wisdom, their
attitude seemed to partake of a certain emotional immaturity.

The dark picture of the "alien world" of science fascinated the later
Victorians. They loved to paint its alien elements as black as possible,
as our illustrations have shown, even as they shuddered in delicious
horror at the prospect. It struck terror into their hearts, for they were
just leaving the warm affection of the Christian tradition—hellfire had
been long dismissed as an idle superstition—as reinterpreted in the
optimism of the assorted Romantic faiths. Indeed, the Victorians
seem to have been able to get just as much of a kick out of it as a more
recent generation has found in waking up to the facts of human "sin."

Many believed the picture, just because it was so dreadful; they
prided themselves on their "courage" and "realism" in facing up to the
facts—even as you and I. Rather more fled from it, as from a nightmare, and took it as a springboard for faith *quand même*. It surely
needed very little of the "will to believe" to be convinced this could

not be the whole story. The picture was so obviously a work of sheer faith—like the twentieth century's faith in human Sin—an imaginative rendering of men's gloomiest forebodings. As a wise religious teacher has remarked, the defender of the faith has first to give men a great pain, and then bring out his special brand of salvation from it. The pains of hellfire had been dissolved by the acids of modernity—first by the Enlightenment rationalists, then by the Romantic idealists. The pains of the "scientific world view" were popularized just in time to save the situation for the religious leader. One wonders, indeed, how religious faith could have been kept alive through nineteenth-century social complacency if a grinning "Science" had not fortunately made its appearance; faith needs the Devil.

That alien world of the nineteenth-century dogmas has today vanished. The speculative generalizations of Victorian physics have crumbled, before further data, more adequate concepts, and above all a more just appreciation of the nature and function of scientific theories. One can only wonder whether contemporary prophets of doom—social this time—may not be similarly disappointed.

The first emotional reaction to the new world of "science" was disillusionment and despair. It was felt by those who had started with a different faith, and then had discovered there ain't no Santa Claus. Gradually, stronger souls plucked up courage. The old faith was shattered beyond saving: the universe was not going where men had expected and hoped. Where *is* it going to? At any rate, let's get aboard! If the old ideals are of no moment to Nature, what *does* Nature care about? What ends *is* she working for? If we only adopt them as our own, then we shall no longer be alone, combatting an alien universe. With pathetic eagerness, such men turned to Evolution as the new Providence. They were still interested chiefly in securing a cosmic backing for their ideals. It did not matter much *what* those ideals might be, as long as they were on the side of the universe.

And so, after a time, there followed the second emotional reaction to the new world of science: the evolutionary faiths were proclaimed, and won wide popularity, as satisfying all the old religious needs in new and up-to-date scientific form. The twentieth century has seen the end of that era of evolutionary faiths. Men are no longer disillusioned about the universe, for they have grown up without any particular illusions about it. Today few any longer feel the need of a cosmic sanction for their ends—except possibly the Marxians, the Dialectical Materialists; that faith, in its orthodox form, is the outstanding survivor into our world of the cosmically-rooted optimistic evolutionary faiths of the end of the nineteenth century. Indeed, the Marxians claim, and rightly, that theirs is the only philosophy today that really still believes in the inevitability of "progress" in the good, old-fashioned, nineteenth-century religious sense. Marxism thus betrays, in this as in so many other ways, its origin in the complacent and uncritical atmosphere of nineteenth-century "idealism." Marxism, in other words, is the last of the great Romantic faiths, lingering on in our more scientific age.

Today men feel compelled neither to see the world as "alien" and "hostile," nor as a single evolutionary process to which they must passionately and desperately cling. Today, the world appears as the "natural" if not too indulgent scene of human life, the dwelling-place of mankind, in which purposes are real, though human, and in which men can with patience and intelligence work laboriously with the materials at hand that Nature furnishes so abundantly.

As soon as men have won their way to such a "naturalistic" attitude—the third emotional reaction to the new world of science, the view that human life is a natural and intelligible consequence of cosmic forces—the problem of finding a new cosmic faith disappears, and men realize that the problem today has become to erect a human faith, to explore the possibilities of the Good Life in its natural and human setting. We are in a genuine sense back where the Greeks were—but with vastly richer possibilities, and with a much more complex and difficult problem of organizing our materials, and reducing our inevitable frictions. We have at our disposal, in fact, all the real human values men have discovered since the Greeks, together with a much greater insight into the conditions of their attainment, and much more powerful techniques of control.

There are thus discernible three main reactions to nineteenth-century science:

1. *Despair* and *disillusionment* in the face of a supposed "alien world."

2. The passionate new *faith* in "evolution" itself.

3. Gradually emerging, a frank and *critical acceptance* of natural human life and its possibilities, with a consequent shift of the center of philosophic attention from the *cosmic religious problem* of nineteenth-

century thought to the *human and social problems of industrial civilization*. These new problems involve not merely the adjustment to scientific ideas, but to all the cultural and institutional changes forced on us by our allegiance to technology and its disclosure of power over nature and over ourselves.

I

The philosophic reactions [1] to the new world of science varied with the shock felt, the resiliency of spirit displayed, and above all with the extent of emotional familiarity with the new ideas. Thus disillusionment and despair were felt by those for whom the values of human life were still completely bound up with a faith in a Cosmic Purpose. That reaction has pretty completely disappeared today, save for a few belated sleepers who have awakened rather late to the facts of life—we all of us know some, and are familiar with their literary expression. Alexandre Koyré has remarked that it was not till the rise of atheistic existentialism that French thinkers faced seriously the problem of how to get along without God: the idealistic tradition lingered on longer in Germany and France.

This reaction took the form mainly of a cosmic religious pessimism. But it was strengthened during periods of social disillusionment, as after the failure of the revolutions of 1848 to bring the millennium. This shift took place as the religious faith in social progress tended to subordinate the earlier cosmic faith. It was widespread after 1890, when the full impact of the new "science" began to be felt, and coalesced with the beginnings of disillusionment with industrial society. Poets brought up in Romantic Idealism found it gone—men like Matthew Arnold, Tennyson, Arthur Hugh Clough, and James Thompson. This pessimism found its deepest philosophic expression in the writings of Arthur Schopenhauer, whose *World as Will and Idea*, though issued in 1819, first began to be widely read at this time. It was all the stronger in coming from the heart of Idealism itself. Schopenhauer's disciple, Eduard von Hartmann, carried it still further, and held that if all men could only agree to take their lives together, the Will would finally be terminated. Von Hartmann lived happily to the age of 95. In English literature, this view is familiar in Thomas Hardy, for

---

[1] For literary expressions of these attitudes, see J.H. Randall, Jr., *The Making of the Modern Mind* (50th Anniversary Ed., New York, 1976), Book IV, Chapter 21, pp. 563–74.

whom the universe was not merely "alien," but an actively hostile antagonist: in *Tess of the d'Urbervilles*, the "President of the Immortals" is positively diabolical, justifying the charge of Kent: "As flies to idle boys, so are we to the Gods: they kill us for their sport." Such an attitude is easily pushed into an exhilarating combat with the universe, as in Nietzsche: man's life becomes not meaningless but tragic. Hardy ended in seeing pure indifference, and futility, in *Jude the Obscure*.

II

For those with such feelings, there were revived all the characteristic philosophies of refuge and consolation, first worked out in classic form and given their historic names in the Hellenistic Age: Epicureanism, Stoicism, Scepticism. In twentieth-century moods of social disillusionment with industrial society—in the 1920s, with its crudities, standardizations, and ugliness; in the 1930s, with its breakdown and inefficiencies; more recently, with its follies, brutalities, and urge to suicide—many have been thrown back again on the same moods of Hellenistic society. The world has seemed to be too much for them. But in our century it has been our human, industrial, and nationalistic world from which sensitive men have been "alienated." Since the 1920s all the compensatory philosophies have been strong once more, just as in the 1890s, from the millennial idealism of the Marxians in the 1930s to the sheer endurance of Stoicism, this time as the escape primarily from an "alien society" rather than from an "alien universe."

It seems quite likely that these compensatory philosophies will wax in strength with the cultural tensions and conflicts of the near future. Instead of facing patiently the exacting task of working out some measure of human security, many will doubtless seek escape into some transcendentental realm of "absolute security" above the battle, and find that kind of emotional strength usually called "salvation" in the confident possession of the "word of God," or in some exclusive insight into the "unconditioned." There are already many signs of such an emotional reaction on the part of sensitive religious leaders today.

This all points to the probability that we shall see much religious concern with the problem of emotional adjustment to the tensions and hardships of rapid social transition—the problem of achieving emotional stability in the midst of rapid cultural change. This is surely a valuable measure for many. And it is not necessarily a "failure of nerve." For such men, it may well be the best way of regaining their "nerve"; history records the immense power of religious vision. But it would be a pity were it to mean also a failure of intelligence. One may well hope that it will not result merely in the provision of a religious refuge and consolation. That seems a real danger today. One may hope as well that it will not turn religion itself, with all its genuine sources of spiritual power, into a mere form of amateur psychotherapy, as it sometimes threatens to do in our discontents.

The existential philosophy, in its more Kierkegaardian and pathological moments, often seems to suggest such a failure of intelligence. The social function it performed in Germany as a "crisis philosophy," before the Federal Republic achieved prosperity and sanity once more, seems now clear. Fortunately, German thinkers have been recovering from its initial excesses, and returning to a broader and less emotional Phenomenology. The function of existentialism in France, where it originally expressed the emotions and the ideas of the resistance movement, and supported the emphasis of the French resistance to the Nazis on action rather than on the increasing "historicism" of the older traditional philosophies, seems today more confused. With Merleau-Ponty the French philosophers also seem to be returning to a Phenomenology. The possible function of German and French existentialism in the United States is the most dubious of all. So far, it has appeared mainly as a new fashion in religious apologetics, along with a certain vogue as the *dernier cri* among literary journalists. In view of its fundamental opposition to the underlying American temper, it seems doubtful whether existentialism in America can ever appeal as much more than a passing "fashion."

The irony of the situation, which we now see clearly when we contemplate the emotional reactions of the nineteenth century, is that men were despairing of the universe at the very time when they were just beginning through science to gain some measure of satisfaction and control in it. The lack of wisdom of the disillusioned Victorians is now apparent to us. But one wonders, will not the present wave of literary despair at the revolutionary changes forced by industrial society, when it is just beginning to fulfill its great promise of offering genuine possibilities for the Good Life, now not just for a privileged class, but for all, seem to the next generation equally paradoxical? Considering the world in broad perspective, the human race never had greater justified grounds for optimism than today. All over the world, for the first time, men—common men—are beginning to have hope that they can somehow escape the agelong social oppression, starvation, and poverty they have hitherto taken for granted. This fundamental revolution will undoubtedly involve the pangs of many sharp pains of transition; revolutions are not pretty things to contemplate. But throughout Asia, Africa, and Latin America—if not in literary circles in Western Europe—there is for the first time an immense surge of hope. Philosophy could—and will, even though the philosophers be not academic teachers—play an important role in analyzing and spreading understanding of what is happening and what it means for the human race.

III

The specific philosophies to which men turned to secure release from this first emotional reaction were, in traditional terms, Epicureanism, Stoicism, and Idealism. This was the age of the appeal of the cult of Omar Khayyam: eat, drink, and be merry, for tomorrow we die. Intelligent hedonism always leads to some form of aestheticism; and men now took refuge in the ivory tower of Beauty, as the one sure good life offered. The "new Cyrenaicism" of Walter Pater had a wide appeal: burn with a hard, gem-like flame; "not to discriminate every moment some passionate attitude in those about us, and in the very brilliance of their gifts some tragic dividing of forces on their ways, is, on this short day of frost and sun, to sleep before evening." [2] The joys of aesthetic appreciation were the nearest thing left to the emotional satisfaction religion had given in the past; and for many religion itself now became a branch of aesthetics. Pater, Ernest Renan, Anatole France, Santayana all found beauty in the religious tradition. This cult of beauty, of course, is apt to be individualistic, antisocial, and passive.

Other ivory towers, newer and more up-to-date, made their appeal during the 1930s to intellectuals. There was symbolic logic, aiming at beauty and not at use. There was a nonpious Neo-Thomism, directed toward security without faith. There was dialectical materialism, bringing, to intellectuals in the United States at least, certainty with-

[2] Walter Pater, Conclusion to *The Renaissance* (London, 1893; ed. 1913), p. 237.

out responsibility. Whatever the original intention of these various cults, they have in the recent past certainly functioned as philosophies of consolation and irresponsibility—as the opiate of the intellectuals.

Others turned to forms of Stoicism, shorn of its faith in Nature, of its traditional religious side, and turned into a mood of sheer Stoic resignation and acceptance. Such an attitude has been widespread among young men for a generation. In the nineteenth century, this Stoicism meant the sheer maintenance of traditional ideals in the face of the "alien world." It was expressed in Clough's " 'Tis better to have loved and lost, than never to have loved at all." T.H. Huxley, in a famous essay,[3] held that ethics, indeed the whole of human civilization, is a total reversal of the evolutionary course of Nature. Men are struggling and fighting against great odds to maintain their human values. The young Bertrand Russell expressed a *fin de siècle* attitude of Promethean defiance. Even then Russell was a conscientious objector against Power, and against the greatest power of all, Nature. The world, Nature, is wholly bad. Let us defy it! Let the free man "sustain alone, a weary but unyielding Atlas, the world that his own ideals have fashioned despite the trampling march of unconscious power." [4]

This sounds noble, exalted, the stuff of which martyrs are made. But the reaction of the present-day mind is apt to be, Why the heroics? Is it very intelligent? Such Promethean defiance strikes men today, even young men, as Romantic rhetoric. Stoicism has always been strong on Duty, but usually rather weak on brains. Does not this attitude abandon the real and insistent problem, What can we do with the materials we do have available? Is the world after all wholly bad? Is it not as meaningless to make such a wholesale emotional judgment, as with the Idealists, to say the world, despite appearances, is wholly good?

[3] T.H. Huxley, *Evolution and Ethics* (London, 1892; New York, 1896).
[4] Bertrand Russell, "A Free Man's Worship," in *Mysticism and Logic* (London, 1918), p. 57.

3

The Romantic Faith in Mechanistic Evolution

THE COMING of Darwin and the ideas for which he stood as a symbol initiated a fundamental intellectual revolution, like those associated with the names of Copernicus, Galileo, Newton, Freud, Planck, Einstein, and Franz Boas. To these must be added that of the great intellectual revolutionary of the thirteenth century, Aristotle. For the coming of Aristotelian science at the end of the twelfth and the beginning of the thirteenth centuries set off the first of the great intellectual revolutions through which our Western culture has passed.

All these successive intellectual revolutions in our cultural tradition illustrate a rather similar pattern of cultural change. First, there appears a group of partisans of the new idea, who see its promise, what illumination and suggestive further ideas it can afford. In reaction against their one-sided enthusiasm for the new idea, the partisans of the old, of tradition, consolidate their forces. This is usually accomplished too late for them to fight more than a rearguard action. By this time there has appeared a third group, the adjusters—the compromisers and mediators—who interpret the new idea in the light of the traditional notions with which men are already familiar. They take it as really confirming in a new way the older and familiar ideas.

These three stages of cultural adjustment to a novel conception have in our tradition normally taken a generation or so to be worked out. Only then do men begin to suspect, and far-seeing thinkers to realize, that the new idea has been more disruptive and subversive than it at first seemed. For when taken seriously it has really been transforming the problems completely. And certain pioneer thinkers begin to perceive implications of that novel conception which the vast majority even of intelligent men were at first, and for about a generation, prevented from seeing by their inability to loosen the hold of older preconceptions upon their minds and imaginations.

With the assimilation of the ideas of Darwin, the sharp battle between the partisans of the old and the new has long been a familiar story. The classical account is to be found in Andrew D. White's *History of the Warfare between Science and Theology in Christendom* (1896). Today, that battle has been won, and for the present generation belongs to the dim, far-off remembered things that amused the late Victorians. That battle is won, though there linger doubts as to whether the war may not have been lost—through the intervention of the Danish warrior king, Kierkegaard. (Once before, a Danish king, Christian IV, changed the religious face of Western civilization by intervening in the Thirty Years' War, followed up, as more recently, by the Swedes under Gustavus Adolphus—in the second generation of the twentieth century it was the Swedish crisis theologians.)

But we can now see that this battle, violently as it raged in its day, over the acceptance of biological evolution, was ultimately of little philosophical moment. The doughty warriors and protagonists of Darwin's ideas were hardly philosophically significant. Thomas Huxley in England, Asa Gray in America, Ernst Haeckel in Germany, were scarcely profound philosophical minds. And the leaders on the other side were philosophically beneath contempt. For philosophy, all the important figures inspired by the impact of Darwin fall into what have just been distinguished as the third and fourth groups, the "adjusters" and the "transformers." The third group, the adjusters, took evolution as merely confirming in a new way the older, traditional ideas. The fourth group, the transformers, took it as rather transforming the whole problem, and as suggesting further novel ideas.

Those who have lived through the heyday of the evolutionary religious faiths, of the philosophies of cosmic evolution, have seen them come, and have seen them recede into the limbo of indifference—though Teilhard de Chardin still has devotees. But we are still in the midst of the work of the fourth group, of the transformers. Even when, like so many philosophers today whose eyes are focused on new and quite different intellectual problems, we do not very clearly realize it, all our present-day philosophizing is still profoundly influenced by the intellectual consequences of accepting Darwinian evolution.

Under the third group, the adjusters who used evolution to bolster up pre-Darwinian ideas, may be included three subgroups. First, there are the original advocates of a mechanistic evolution, men like Herbert Spencer, John Fiske, and Ernst Haeckel. Secondly, there are those who originally interpreted evolution in idealistic terms, including in Germany men like Karl Marx and Nietzsche, and in France, Durand de Gros, Alfred Fouillée, Jean Marie Guyau, and Henri Bergson. In America this group is represented by the "dynamic idealists" at Ann Arbor, Alfred Lloyd, George Herbert Mead, James Hayden Tufts, and John Dewey in his earlier phases, together with evolutionists like John Elof Boodin at U.C.L.A. After about a generation, the mechanistic interpretation of evolutionary philosophy broke down, leaving cosmic evolution identified with the creative evolution group, men like Bergson, William James, and F.C.S. Schiller. As a result of analytic criticism applied to their conceptions, there appeared a third subgroup, the philosophers of "emergent evolution," Conwy Lloyd Morgan, Samuel Alexander, A.N. Whitehead, and in America, Roy Wood Sellars. Here belong certain aspects of John Dewey's thought.

Here too, along with the third group of adjusters, would belong the three most influential popular philosophies of the nineteenth century, those of Auguste Comte, Herbert Spencer, and Karl Marx. All three were in fundamental agreement on "accepting science" and its novel ideas. They stood, in France, England, and Germany, respectively, as the great popular exponents of a negative answer to the dominating religious problem of nineteenth-century thought. Or, more exactly, they stood as the great exponents of finding a new religious faith in scientific ideas themselves, and of taking "evolution" as a new and up-to-date Providence working for the salvation of men.

These three popular enlighteners also brought "evolution" to the support of completely divergent social philosophies, to which they had each been committed long before they heard of Darwin.

Comte, who died in 1857, and put out his *Positive Philosophy* from 1830 to 1842, developed his own "evolutionary" Law of the Three Stages out of eighteenth-century rationalism and empiricism, out of the faith in the progress of reason of Voltaire and Condorcet. He saw the course of history culminating in the enlightened despotism of the

Age of Reason, as transformed to suit an industrialized society in the technocracy of Henri Saint-Simon. Darwin, when he came to France, brought the tinge of biological evolution to an evolutionary philosophy fully worked out, especially in sociological evolutionists like Émile Durkheim and Lucien Lévy-Bruhl.

Herbert Spencer developed his "synthetic philosophy" out of Utilitarianism, a continuance of eighteenth-century British empiricism, which had become the ideology of the British Liberal tradition. The whole synthetic philosophy is already present in Spencer's essay, "Progress: Its Law and Cause," written in 1857. And when Spencer became the most popular British evolutionary philosopher, he bent evolution to the service of *laisser-faire* and a very individualistic Liberalism. The outstanding figure in nineteenth-century British empiricism, John Stuart Mill, included biological evolution in the later editions of his *System of Logic* as an interesting example of an hypothesis. British empiricism has remained pre-Darwinian in its basic assumptions pretty much down to Bertrand Russell and A.J. Ayer.

Karl Marx developed his historical materialism out of left-wing Hegelianism, which he never really reconstructed, and his socialism out of the idealistic collectivism of men like Fichte (see his *Closed Commercial State* of 1800) and like Hegel himself, as well as of his fellow-Hegelians of the 1840s. When the *Origin of Species* came out, Marx was at first very suspicious of its reliance on the archconservative, Malthus. Later, Engels tells us, he said, "Fritz, study Darwin, and see if there is anything there we can use."

There have been listed the major groups and figures among the third set of philosophical assimilators, the adjusters, who tried to harmonize Darwinian ideas with the pre-Darwinian faiths already in them. We shall here examine the initial impact of Darwin in generating these mediating philosophies of the late nineteenth and early twentieth centuries, these cosmic evolutionary faiths which have now been superseded by other philosophical fashions in what we like to boast of as our own "Age of Anxiety." In further chapters we shall examine the later philosophic impact of Darwin during the fourth stage, in which evolution has transformed the problems themselves, set new conditions for philosophizing, and suggested ideas undreamed of during the period of the dominance of these cosmic evolutionary faiths.

I

Darwin's ideas came into an intellectual world admirably prepared to welcome them. Alfred Russell Wallace's anticipation would alone make clear that in considering the idea of the evolution of biological species we are not dealing with the brilliant hypothesis of a single man of genius, but rather with an idea for which men's intellectual experience was ready and prepared. The great problem of cultural assimilation in the nineteenth century was the religious problem. With such a central cultural experience, the men of the nineteenth century were looking desperately for a new religious faith, a new Cosmic Companion, an up-to-date "scientific" God. The popularization and speedy establishment of Darwinian evolution came at the psychological moment. Evolution was a genuine godsend to the religious seekers after escape from the alien world. Here, in the very heart of "science" itself, was obviously the new faith needed and so greatly yearned after. There is a purpose in the world, man's ideals do matter to nature, heaven will be reached, in substantial form, on earth. As Edward Rowland Sills put it,

> Some call it evolution,
> Others call it God.

But not only did Darwin's ideas come as the answer to the central cultural problem of the times, the religious problem. For about a century evolutionary notions had been enjoying a growing popularity. In biology itself, after the eighteenth-century explorations of such ideas by Buffon, Robinet, Diderot, and Lamarck, they had indeed been losing ground. The opposition of Cuvier, and the lack of any plausible explanation of the method of evolution, before Darwin's natural selection, seemed to create an impasse. That is why they had such an impact when they irrupted into biology.

But in most other fields, evolution was becoming an increasingly popular idea. It took two major forms, which actually constituted the faiths which the adjusters took Darwin as supporting from biology. On the one hand was the notion of a liberal, "rationalistic" evolution, bound up with the idea of "progress" in human history. On the other was the cosmic Evolution of Romantic idealism. This form, starting with the evolution of man's religion, in Lessing and Herder, culminated in the full temporalizing of the great chain of being in Schelling—still in a religious interest.

The first form was French and British. Its classic statement is in Condorcet's *Progress of the Human Mind* (1794), written in prison in the shadow of the guillotine, yet expressing a magnificent faith. Condorcet summed up a half-century of French analysis of man's perfectibility. Condorcet's English disciple was William Godwin, who, ironically, provoked the Malthus who was to suggest to Darwin natural selection as the mechanism of evolution, and thus reinstate Godwin's own views. This is also the background of Spencer's pre-Darwinian "Progress: Its Law and Cause," as well as of Saint-Simon, also inspired in prison, and through him of Comte's Law of the Three Stages.

The second form was primarily German. It began in religion, in Lessing's *Education of the Human Race* (1780); in Herder's *Philosophy of History* (1774) and *Ideas for the History of Man* (1784). It was made cosmic in Schelling's evolutionary metaphysics; his *Philosophy of Nature* displays Nature as the evolutionary manifestation of the Absolute. Oken develops the same general conception. Hegel did not temporalize his own philosophy of nature: there is in Hegel no biological evolution of species, as in Schelling. But Hegel has a chain of being, a series of levels, easily made temporal by later Hegelians after Darwin. And, as the great idealist of social experience, Hegel made fundamental the evolution of human society, institutions, and culture—everything he called *Geist*. In fact, the later cosmic evolutionary philosophers were overwhelmingly Hegelian in character, with a change only in the new biological terminology adopted. Alexander Humboldt in his *Kosmos* (1845–58) offered an impressive evolutionary system of scientific knowledge. With these men must be grouped those who pursued the Hegelian idea of social evolution, the left-wing Hegelians of the forties, including Feuerbach and Marx.

These varieties of evolutionary ideas in philosophy, as distinguished from biological theory, which has its own story, were prevalent for a century before 1859. This fact explains why Darwin had so immediate a welcome from scholars in history, the social sciences, and philosophy. It also explains why they pretty uniformly misunderstood him, why they took him as merely reinforcing their own ideas, long familiar, and why they failed to see the real significance of his thought. In the last analysis, it explains why they were adjusters, harmonizers of old and new, and not transformers. These were the cosmic evolutionary faiths Darwin was at first taken as substantiating.

II

How biological evolution would be speedily brought to the support of faiths already worked out in the pre-Darwinian era, especially of the faiths of Romantic idealism, was, however, not immediately recognized in 1859. This was especially the case in England and America, where religious orthodoxy, the heritage of the great religious revivals of the first half of the century, was still strongly entrenched.

Its hold had long been broken in Germany, where religion was now dominated by the great idealistic and humanistic reinterpretations of the nature and function of religion itself that were the German heritage from Romantic idealism. These included the three main forms of nineteenth-century "liberal" religion, of the theology of Divine immanence. The first was the Hegelian interpretation, making religion a form of philosophical knowledge expressed in religious symbols. The second was the Ritschlian, making it a form of moral action, of ethical idealism. The third was that of Schleiermacher, making it a form of religious feeling and experience, of religious "consciousness." To these three German religious currents, Darwinian or biological evolution was quite congenial. It reinforced their own philosophy of monism, and of the immanence of the Divine. They had all been long accustomed to viewing God as the force behind a cosmic evolution, and to finding purpose and values in nature. Thus later American representatives of these German theologies, the modernists and "liberal" theologians of the end of the century, became in the U.S.A. the strongest champions of Darwin—men like Lyman Abbott, Henry Churchill King, and other Schleiermacherians and Ritschlians. But to these German religious currents, Darwin seemed also rather irrelevant: he offered little of novelty in the way of ideas that interested them.

In France, Darwin did not appear too disruptive either. There anticlerical and secular thought was strong. It took two main forms. There was first the evolutionary "spiritualism" of Victor Cousin, based largely on Schelling. Cousin's school produced imposing works on historical evolution. Secondly, there was the cultural evolutionism of the Positivists. Both welcomed and interpreted Darwin. The former developed a strong school of idealistic evolutionists, culminating in the next generation in Bergson's creative evolution.

In England and America, there had been little reinterpretation of religion before 1859; that had to wait for the next generation. The only exceptions had been Coleridge and the still small party of Broad Churchmen, and the American Transcendentalists, among the tiny minority of New England Unitarianism. So in America there was no large religious party to welcome Darwin; the full shock of the naturalization of man was felt there. Darwin was taken as completing the picture of the "scientific universe"; he became for two generations the symbol of the scientific faith, till he was superseded by Einstein. Accept evolution, and you had abandoned mere tradition. Darwin was the gateway to emancipation, to freedom from a literal orthodoxy. Such liberation brought the freedom to embrace one of two alternatives: the religion of science, in one of its nineteenth-century mechanistic versions, or an idealistic reinterpretation of both religion and science. The first alternative had great popular appeal. The second made by far the wider appeal to those with religious and humanistic interests, to the academic class, who teach and support American philosophy.

In other words, the impact of Darwin was to foster simultaneously the popular philosophies of evolutionary materialism, and the academic philosophies of idealistic reinterpretation and reconstruction. Thus in England and America it was Darwinian evolution that provoked the idealistic protest against the "scientific" universe and the alien world, and the idealistic reconstructions of the religious tradition; philosophic idealism was dominant in academic circles till about 1900. In Germany, the idealistic protest and reconstruction had been accomplished in the first half of the century, long before Darwin. There idealism already possessed its own version of evolution, in Hegelian or Schellingian forms. Hence it found Darwin either irrelevant, or else a mere additional support. In France, Darwin either strengthened the existent Positivistic evolutionism, or else it supported the secular ethical idealism in its opposition to mechanistic Positivism, on what was the central philosophical problem in France from 1870 to 1914, the issue of determinism vs. freedom. French ethical idealism worked out a philosophy of "creative evolution" in which evolution was made to tip the scales for freedom.

III

Thus in Anglo-American philosophizing, Darwin initiated two simultaneous movements: the religion of science, and the idealistic reinterpretations. In the religion of science, Thomas Huxley was the great popularizer of Darwin, and the mighty battler against the orthodox. His ideas were fused in the popular mind with Herbert Spencer's synthetic philosophy, known then as "evolutionary naturalism." This was in spite of the fact that Spencer himself was not a "naturalist," but an agnostic materialist, and Huxley was an epiphenomenalist, an agnostic, and in the end a British empiricist and phenomenalist. The works of Darwin, Huxley, Spencer, and Tyndall, a popularizer of physics, in Appleton's International Library of Science,[1] stood in stately rows on library shelves at the turn of the century. This was true science! In addition, there were W.K. Clifford and George J. Romanes, who were mechanistic panpsychists. So was Ernst Haeckel, the German popularizer of Darwin, who combined in himself the functions performed in England by Huxley and by Spencer. He called himself a "monist"—of atoms and consciousness, of God and matter. Here too belongs Marxism, though it is hardly a "religion of science," and owes little to Darwin. It was interpreted in Engels's *Dialectics of Nature*, which the more scientifically-minded German Social Democrats refused to publish, as a Hegelian version of emergent evolution.

Just a word about so-called "Darwinian ethics." Some early *laisser-faire* individualistic Liberals, like Spencer in England and William Graham Sumner at Yale, pressed their Darwinian arguments to a deterministic conclusion. Sumner took the struggle for existence as a contest between individuals, ruling out any altruism as disserviceable. For him, the sole function of government is to protect the property of those fit to survive. The struggle is economic, and fitness is determined by financial success. This is clearly the rationale for a predatory and completely competitive nineteenth-century capitalism. It is also an interesting interpretation of the catch-phrases of evolution to be offered by a Christian clergyman. But Sumner was a Republican who bitterly attacked any protective tariff, so his influence was very

---

[1] Professor Randall's reference is to the *International Scientific Series*, published by D. Appleton and Co. (New York, 1872–1909). This series included works by or about each of the figures Randall mentions here. (Ed.)

small, except on his Yale students. It was just as easy for Lester F. Ward to take the struggle as between species, and thus to justify the welfare state as necessary for the survival of mankind: by raising the quality of its inferior members, it can enable man to become fitter to survive over other species.

This is the beginning of a realization of the implications of evolution for ethics, that takes us from the adjusters to the transformers. It was carried further in the group of social scientists at the turn of the century, many of them at the new University of Chicago: Albion W. Small, W.I. Thomas, Charles H. Cooley, Veblen, Dewey, Tufts, Mead, and Angell. They all emphasized the dynamic character of social organization, the new direction to evolution given by the coming of man. Before, evolution was the record of the adaptation of organisms to their environment. Man's rôle is to adapt the environment to the needs of the human animal. Social science should study a great variety of social arrangements to better adapt the environment to man.

The truth is that "social Darwinism," "Darwinian ethics," was never popular or influential. Such ideas were indignantly repudiated by Darwin himself, and by Huxley, in his famous lecture of 1892, "Evolution and Ethics." Much more Darwinian is the generous humanistic ethics of men like Sir Julian Huxley.

The other movement Darwin initiated in England and America was the late nineteenth-century wave of idealistic reinterpretations. In Anglo-American philosophy we should have to distinguish: (1) T.H. Green and Liberal idealism; (2) Bernard Bosanquet and Conservative idealism—here would belong also Creighton and Thilly at Cornell; (3) Royce and Howison, and pluralistic idealism—the currents of personalism and cultural pluralism; (4) F.H. Bradley, and the transformation of idealism into instrumentalism.

It is to the point to say a word about the cultural function of this idealistic reaction to Darwin. It is conventionally taken as a religious apologetic, the defense of religious and humanistic values against an "alien world." This function is surely involved; though whether the particular values of so humanized a religion are worth defending, has been doubted by many more recent theologians. But more important is the fact that Darwin forced on English and American religious thinking that reinterpretation of the nature and function of religion which Germans had faced some fifty years earlier. That is, Darwin is directly responsible for the modernism and liberal theology of the late nineteenth and early twentieth century—the pre-Barthian era. This reconstruction of the religious tradition was far more important philosophically than any conservative opposition by the orthodox.

Darwinian evolution also reinforced the strong evolutionary element in the Hegelian form of idealism. This, among other reasons, is why Dewey, for example, found Darwin's thought so congenial. It had a lesser influence on the Kantian forms of critical idealism or neocriticism, for which time is ultimately merely a form of sense intuition. But even there it led outstanding neo-Kantians to undertake lengthy histories of "pure reason." The most imposing of these works, tracing the historical development of schemes of understanding, are Ernst Cassirer, *Das Erkenntnisproblem* (1906), and Léon Brunschvicg, *Les Étapes de la Philosophie Mathématique* (1912), *L'Expérience Humaine et la Causalité Physique* (1922), and *Le Progrès de la Conscience dans la Philosophie Occidentale* (1927).

IV

It remains here only to comment on the philosophies of cosmic evolution, from Herbert Spencer to Sir Julian Huxley and Teilhard de Chardin, the philosophies of the two generations before the mid-century, which interpreted evolution as the greatest of the Romantic cosmic faiths. It did not take long for seekers after a new religious faith to realize that evolution was really the answer for which they had been so long looking. For, like the faiths of the earlier forms of Romantic idealism, it too emphasized the categories of life: organism, functioning, adaptation, fitness, survival. It too was concerned with time and growth, as against all static concepts. It too pointed to directions in nature, to a process easily identified with progress in human affairs. Darwin himself might have offered an analysis of the method of evolution that was in its details mechanistic. But that explanation did not, and could not, deny the facts of novelty, of creativity, of the achievement of natural ends. And clearly the "chance" to which Darwin himself attributed the source of variations cried aloud for further interpretation. For all these reasons, the theory of evolution made a strong emotional appeal to those brought up in the idealistic faiths. Above all, it proved very congenial to liberal and modernistic religious thinking. And in responding to the central religious problem some men drew equally on the new German theology and on the new evolutionary ideas. Thus John Fiske, in his *Outlines of Cosmic Philosophy* (1874), easily transformed Spencer's "Unknowable" into the more familiar "God." And Henry Drummond had no difficulty in reading Darwin's "descent" of man as the *Ascent of Man* (1894).

The philosophies of cosmic evolution went through a discernible series of stages. First, there was simultaneously a generalization of a mechanistic interpretation of the evolutionary process, as in the examples of Spencer and Haeckel; and an idealistic interpretation, in the French versions of Durand de Gros, Alfred Fouillée, and J.M. Guyau. Corresponding to these French thinkers would be Nietzsche and the forms of voluntaristic idealism in Germany.

Secondly, under the impact of Weismann and his theory of mutations, and of Mendel and his careful analysis of genetics and the ordinary processes of inheritance, mechanistic evolution broke down. This left the enterprise of generalizing evolution into a cosmic philosophy identified with what Bergson in 1907 called "creative evolution." This movement had literary repercussions in Samuel Butler and G.B. Shaw; it is found in the more speculative sides of William James and F.C.S. Schiller.

Thirdly, there was a sharp reaction against "creative evolution" from the developing philosophies of mathematical physics. Thus Russell, in his Platonic mood of 1914 (*Our Knowledge of the External World*), denied all importance to time: it is a mere accident of the human organism that we do not remember the future and painfully try to predict the past. These physical philosophies emphasized a realm of essences, of mathematical structure, of logical forms. Here also would belong Santayana, despite the Hegelian model he followed in *The Life of Reason;* and Edmund Husserl, who, in sharp reaction to logic as against psychologizing, to "thought" as against "thinking" and "judgment," kept a generation of German philosophers from "taking time seriously," until the appearance of Heidegger's *Sein und Zeit* in 1927.

Fourthly, aware of these analytic criticisms from the philosophers of mathematics and physics, men began to work out illustrations of the final stage of cosmic evolutionary philosophizing, the philosophy of emergent evolution. This led directly to the fourth major group, the transformers. Emergent evolution is still the most plausible form of a generalized philosophy of evolution, and is still advocated with great vigor by Sir Julian Huxley, as well as by Teilhard de Chardin. The term itself, and most of its representatives, are English. Here belong Conwy Lloyd Morgan, *Emergent Evolution* (1923); Samuel Alexander, *Space, Time, and Deity* (1920); and A.N. Whitehead's "philosophy of organism," *Process and Reality* (1929). In America there appeared Roy Wood Sellars, *Evolutionary Naturalism* (1929); and John Dewey's *Creative Intelligence* (1917) and *Experience and Nature* (1925).

The basic idea of emergent evolution is that new configurations produce new behavior, so novel as to be a qualitative change. The idea goes back at least to Aristotle's *De Generatione et Corruptione*. To faithful mechanists it has always seemed to deny the validity of analysis, especially in its classic nineteenth-century formulation by Hegel, for whom quantitative changes, accumulating, are transcended in a qualitative change. This basic idea is associated with the new critical naturalism of twentieth-century thinking, with its opposition to reductive analysis. It is part of the reflection of the breakdown in our age of the mechanistic theories of nineteenth-century physics.

Thus Dewey emphasized that there is no ultimate "givenness" of the environment, dictating "adaptation" as an inevitable end. Rather, with man, the environment can be reconstructed by "creative intelligence." Whitehead emphasized the evolution of structures as systems of activity. There can be no genuine "evolution" if only the rearrangement of matter is involved. Evolution demands as its necessary condition the presence of organic systems and selective activity, the creativity of organisms with respect to their environment; and this depends on cooperation with a multitude of other organisms (*Science and the Modern World*, 1925, Chapter 6).

This suggestive analysis of Whitehead, the greatest of the philosophers of emergent evolution as a cosmic faith, points on to the more penetrating if more modest evolutionary philosophers who have tried to express what they represent as the real implications of evolution for philosophy—to the transformers.

V

Herbert Spencer (1820–1903) is the very paradigm of an adjuster, of one who used the new idea of evolution to support his preconceived gospel. As Dewey says, "The point that seems to me so significant . . . is this sitting down to achieve a preconceived idea,—an idea, moreover, of a synthetic, deductive rendering of all that is in the Universe. . . . Spencer and his readers are committed in advance to a definitely wrought out, a rounded and closed interpretation of the universe." [2] Spencer's gospel was the evangel of individualism, absorbed from his father, a Quaker and a philosophical radical, and from the spirit of the times. Spencer was quite devoid of historical sense, and had no intellectual roots in the British tradition stemming from Locke. As Dewey puts it,

> Spencer is the heir not of the psychological individualism of Locke direct, but of this individualism after exportation to and reimportation from France. It was the individualism of the French Encyclopedist, with its unwavering faith in progress, in the ultimate perfection of humanity, and in "nature" as everywhere beneficently working out this destiny, if only it can be freed from trammels of Church and State, which in Spencer mingles with generalizations of science, and is thereby reawakened to new life. . . . Spencer's work . . . carries over the net result of that individualism which represents the fine achievement of the seventeenth and eighteenth centuries. It preserves it in the only way in which it could be preserved, by carrying it over, by translating it into the organic, the systematic, the universal terms which report the presence of the nineteenth century spirit." (52)

By fusing the faith in an inevitable and automatic progress with the new idea of evolution, Spencer identified the two great ideas of Liberalism.

"To Spencer is certainly due the immense credit of having been the first to see in evolution an absolutely universal principle. . . . He is the philosopher whom those who have no other philosopher can appreciate." [3] Spencer was the great popularizer in Britain and America of the conviction that Evolution answered all the answerable questions. For Spencer made his peace with traditional religion by insisting that there is an absolutely Unknowable which religion takes as its province. All religions agree there is an ultimate mystery. Here Spencer's argument "consists chiefly of a rehash of Mansel's rehash of Hamilton's 'Philosophy of the Conditioned,' and has hardly raised its head since John Mill so effectively demolished it." [4]

Spencer, a self-educated civil engineer, wrote his first papers at the

[2] John Dewey, "Herbert Spencer" (1904), in *Characters and Events*, Vol. I (New York, 1929), p. 46.
[3] William James, "Herbert Spencer's Autobiography," in *Memories and Studies* (New York, 1911), pp. 124, 126.
[4] *Ibid.*, p. 128.

age of twenty-two upon "The Proper Sphere of Government," intended to show the restrictions upon governmental action required in the interests of the individual. He had already, through reading Lyell in 1839, decided on the correctness of the theory of natural development. In his first major work, *Social Statics* (1850), he combined the two ideas, and conceived social development on the analogy of organic. The perfect development of life he takes as a divine idea awaiting realization.

A theory of life developed by Coleridge has prepared the way for this generalization. "By life," says he, "I everywhere mean the true idea of life, or that most general form under which life manifests itself to us, which includes all other forms. This I have stated to be the *tendency to individuation;* and the degrees or intensities of life to consist in the progressive realization of this tendency. . . ." Yet must this highest individuation be joined with the greatest mutual dependence.[5]

Actually, Spencer seems to have started from his convictions as to society, and generalized them.

In fact, he makes use of the idea of division of labor, originally worked out in political economy, in his biological speculations, and then in his cosmological, in very much the same way in which Darwin borrowed the Malthusian doctrine of population. The social idea first found biological form for itself, and then was projected into cosmological terms. I have no doubt that this represents the general course of Spencer's ideas.[6]

VI

Spencer had the same ideas, which he expanded but did not change, from his days as a young writer seeking his fortune in London till he ended his life, "an old-maidish personage, inhabiting boarding-houses," in Brighton. Those ideas appear in "The Development Hypothesis" of 1853; they are set forth in detail in the "Progress: Its Law and Cause" of 1857. The scheme of what was to be his comprehensive system was drawn up in the first week of 1858; the rest of his life was to be a reading for support and a filling-in. Spencer had already, in 1855, published his *Principles of Psychology*, judged by James his most original work. For in it he had put forth the two ideas that separate

[5] *Social Statics*, Abridged and Revised (New York, 1892), pp. 255–56, 260. In a note (p. 256) Spencer adds: "At the time I wrote this I was not aware that Coleridge was indebted to Schelling for this idea."

[6] Dewey, "Herbert Spencer," p. 61n.

him most sharply from the assumptions of British empiricism. All ideas come from experience, but the most fundamental ones from the experience of the race, which are biologically inherited. Here was an evolutionary basis for the a priori. After sixty Spencer was involved in a long controversy with Weismann, who presented evidence against this inheritance of acquired characteristics. Spencer's second idea was happier: it places him with the transformers rather than the adjusters. He defines experience as "the adjustment of internal to external relations." Here indeed was a new conception of experience from those of Locke or Hume, a conception that began to bear fruit with James and his twentieth-century successors.

"Progress: Its Law and Cause" starts by distinguishing the fruits of progress, the heightening of human happiness, from its nature in itself. He turns to embryology:

In respect to that progress which individual organisms display in the course of their evolution, this question has been answered by the Germans. The investigations of Wolff, Goethe, and Von Baer, have established the truth that the series of changes gone through during the development of a seed into a tree, or an ovum into an animal, constitute an advance from homogeneity of structure to heterogeneity of structure.[7]

This is the law of all progress:

Whether it be in the development of the Earth, in the development of Life upon its surface, in the development of Society, of Government, of Manufactures, of Commerce, of Language, Literature, Science, Art, this same evolution of the simple into the complex, through successive differentiations, holds throughout. From the earliest traceable cosmical changes down to the latest results of civilization, we shall find that the transformation of the homogeneous into the heterogeneous, is that in which Progress essentially consists. (3)

This law Spencer proceeds to illustrate in the Nebular Hypothesis, in the geology of the earth, in the growth of the forms of Life, in Humanity as socially embodied, in the division of labor, in Language, in all the Arts.

We believe we have shown beyond question, that that which the German physiologists have found to be the law of organic development, is the law of all development. (29, 30)

[7] Spencer, "Progress: Its Law and Cause," in *Illustrations of Universal Progress* (New York, 1864), p. 2.

Does not the universality of the *law* imply a universal *cause?* Can we not transform this empirical generalization into a rational generalization, by deducing it from some universal principle, some law of change? We can—"We pass at once to the statement of the law, which is this:— *Every active force produces more than one change—every cause produces more than one effect*" (32). And with living organisms, "there must arise. . . . also a tendency to the occasional production of a somewhat higher organism" (48). After a long consideration of industrial production, Spencer concludes, we do not know what force is; we do not conceive how sensations are possible.

Inward and outward things he thus discovers to be alike inscrutable in their ultimate genesis and nature. . . . He learns at once the greatness and the littleness of the human intellect—its power in dealing with all that comes within the range of experience; its impotence in dealing with all that transcends experience. . . . He alone *knows* that under all things there lies an impenetrable mystery. (59, 60)

In 1862 there came out *First Principles*, an elaboration of the earlier essay on progress; in 1896 the Synthetic Philosophy was concluded with the last volume of the *Principles of Ethics*. Spencer had worked out his ideas and illustrated them copiously. In 1884 he brought out his last popular book on individualistic freedom, the four essays in *The Man Versus the State*. In social theory, he serves as the model of Victorian Liberalism pushed almost to anarchism. The state should be limited to keeping the peace, internally and externally. As a young Quaker he had maintained that all war is wrong. Throughout his life he had an abhorrence of everything that savored of militarism, contrasting it most unfavorably with industrialism. He saw only an infringement of liberty in public education, in a government post office, and in health and sanitary regulations.

Dewey, an evolutionary transformer if there ever was one, puts the judgment:

Spencer is a monument, but, like all monuments, he commemorates the past. He presents the achieved culmination of ideas already in overt and external operation. He winds up an old dispensation. Here is the secret of his astounding success. . . .

Spencer's conception of evolution was always a confined and bounded one. Since his "environment" was but the translation of the "nature" of the metaphysicians, its workings had a fixed origin, a fixed quality, and a fixed goal.

Evolution still tends in the minds of Spencer's contemporaries to "a single, far-off, divine event,"—to a finality, a fixity. . . . A thoroughgoing evolution must by the nature of the case abolish all fixed limits, beginnings, origins, forces, laws, goals. If there be evolution, then all these also evolve, and are what they are as points of origin and of destination relative to some special portion of evolution. They are to be defined in terms of the process, the process that now and always is, not the process in terms of them. But the transfer from the world of set eternal facts and of fixed ideal values to the world of free, mobile, self-developing, and self-organizing reality would be unthinkable and impossible, were it not for the work of Spencer, which, shot all through as it is with contradictions, thereby all the more effectually served the purpose of a medium of transition from the fixed to the moving. A fixed world, a world of movement between fixed limits, a moving world, such is the order.[8]

VII

Spencer's *First Principles*, after his 125 pages on the Unknowable, proceeds to define philosophy. "Philosophy seeks for wide and deep truths, as distinguished from the multitudinous detailed truths which the surfaces of things and actions present." [9] It is "knowledge of the highest degree of generality" (131). "Science is partially-unified knowledge; Philosophy is completely-unified knowledge" (134). Its method is that of the sciences:

[The conceptions] which are vital, or cannot be severed from the rest without mental dissolution, must be assumed as true *provisionally*. The fundamental intuitions that are essential to the process of thinking, must be temporarily accepted as unquestionable: leaving the assumption of their unquestionableness to be justified by the results.

How is it to be justified by the results? As any other assumption is justified—by ascertaining that all the conclusions deducible from it, correspond with the facts as directly observed—by showing the agreement between the experiences it leads us to anticipate, and the actual experiences. (137–38)

Now, all manifestations of the Unknowable are divided into the object and the subject, the not-self and the self, the non-ego and the ego, the world of consciousness and the world beyond consciousness.

In brief, our postulates are: an Unknowable Power; the existence of knowable likenesses and differences among the manifestations of that Power; and a resulting segregation of the manifestations into those of subject and object. (157)

[8] Dewey, "Herbert Spencer," pp. 59, 60–61.
[9] *First Principles* (3rd ed., London, 1870), p. 129.

Spencer thus does not question Cartesian dualism. This Power or Force he recognizes as an ultimate symbol, and its persistence is the fundamental premise of all knowledge. He rejects "conservation" as connoting a Conserver, and "energy" as but one kind of Force.

All motion is rhythmical, all phenomena undergo a process of development and dissolution. From this follows universal Evolution. At first he took the psychical to be a transformation of the material, like that of motion into heat. But in the second edition he adopted the identity view, that the two are phenomenal and mutually irreducible forms of the Unknowable Force. Spencer works out his law of Evolution, as integration, differentiation, determination, leading to a state of equilibrium. Then a new process of dissolution ensues, since all motion is rhythmical.

He follows out the physiological law of differentiation and the economic law of the division of labor. He disagrees with Comte in maintaining the autonomy of psychology: there must be some unknowable underlying substance to hold the series of impressions and ideas together and preserve its unity. This left an easy opening for T.H. Green.

Epistemology hardly fascinates Spencer, but he tries to accord their due to both rationalism and empiricism. In the hereditary nature of the individual and in the logical principle underlying all inference, there is an a priori element: something which cannot be deduced from experience. But what is a priori for the individual is not so for the race. The a priori is inherited experience. Man is born with those psychical connections that form the substrata of "necessary truths." In the long run, all knowledge and all forms of thought spring from experience. Thus Spencer sought to escape from Mill's circle as to induction.

Spencer's sociology is dominated by the struggle between militancy and industrialism in societies; freedom depends on the triumph of the latter. Ethics is divided into an *Interimsethik*, relative ethics, and absolute ethics, which states the future goal, a perfect human life in a perfect society, whose first characteristic is the freedom of the individual, in so far as this involves no encroachment on the right of all others to equal freedom. In it man will be perfectly adapted to the social environment, and the social environment to man. No man will want what every other man does not also want. This end is hardly imminent, but

by the Law of Evolution it is inevitable. Man's chief duty is not to try
to hasten it by State interference.

VIII

In Germany, Ernst Haeckel (1834–1919) performed the same function Spencer served in England—he created a generalized philosophy
of cosmic Evolution, scornful of the academic "metaphysicians" and of
the spokesmen of traditional religious ideas. He had the advantage
that he was a trained professor of zoology at Jena, and prefaced his
philosophical writings with a two-volume *Generelle Morphologie der
Organismen* (1866). "It was," he said, "the first attempt to apply in detail the newly established theory of evolution to the whole science of
organic forms." [10] To popularize Darwinism, he issued in 1868 his
Natural History of Creation. Darwin judged this fully anticipated his
own *Descent of Man.* In 1874 came out Haeckel's *Anthropogenie,* on
man's ancestry. He announced his philosophy of "monism" in *Der
Monismus als Band zwischen Religion und Wissenschaft* in 1893, and followed it with his most popular work, *Die Welträtsel* (tr. as *The Riddle of
the Universe*) in 1899.

Reality displays no gulf between matter and mind; it is absolutely
unified. There are no separate substantial souls. The world space is
infinite and completely filled with substance. World time has no
beginning or end. Substance is everywhere, in continuous motion and
change; the quantity of matter and of energy remains constant. Motion is cyclical, as in Spencer: there are phases of evolution and dissolution, of "pyknotic" condensation and break-up. The earth is a ball of
condensed dust from the sun. Man is a placental mammal, a transitory
aggregate of matter and energy.

On the relation of mind and matter Haeckel wavered. Now he
seems to make mind the product of the brain, now he calls himself a
hylozoist and a parallelist. In *Kristallseelen* (1917) he puts it, "All substance possesses life, inorganic as well as organic; all things have souls,
crystals as well as organisms" (viii). In *Die Welträtsel,* he says matter
cannot exist without spirit, nor can spirit without matter. In *Die Le-
benswunder* (1904) he taught the threefold character of substance—matter, energy, and soul—in all inorganic and organic bodies.

[10] Ernst Haeckel, *The Riddle of the Universe at the Close of the Nineteenth Century,* tr.
Joseph McCabe (New York and London, 1900), p. vii.

Though he repudiated God, freedom, and immortality, Haeckel tried to found a new monistic religion. God and world are identical; man worships the true, the good, and the beautiful. The golden rule holds in ethics; complete virtue is the right equilibrium between love of neighbor and self-love. Monistic religion culminates in appreciation of the beauties of nature. Monist societies were set up, related to the earlier societies for ethical culture: both aimed to give morality a foundation independent of any religious creed. Friedrich Jodl represented this tendency in Vienna; Paul Carus brought the idea to America and founded *The Monist* journal. Haeckel's monism was popularized in the United States by Carus and by the sociologist Lester F. Ward, who freed "Darwinian ethics" from its identification with a purely competitive egoism in William Graham Sumner.

IX

It is interesting that all of the doubts expressed about cosmic extensions of evolution, like those of Spencer and Haeckel in our twentieth-century disillusionment, found utterance in 1865 in a long criticism of Spencer [11] by Chauncey Wright (1830–75). Wright was a member of the Harvard group that included Charles S. Peirce and William James; like Peirce, he was a mathematician, and trained in biological and physical research.

Spencer's cosmic evolution Wright rejects rather contemptuously. It misconceives physics, it goes far beyond the evidence, above all it is metaphysical, it deals with laws of physics as abstract elements from which to draw a picture of the universe. But this is part of religion and of poetic myth-making. It is not science. The scientist uses "laws" to extend his knowledge of concrete fact, not to describe the cosmos. Such laws are the eyes with which to see nature, not the elements of the nature discovered; they are finders, not summaries of truth. Wright was a leading spirit in the group in which pragmatism was born. Science arises from rational curiosity—not, like metaphysics, from the desire to defend our emotional preferences, which are a matter of character.

For Wright, nature is not a progression to a single end, but, as for Aristotle, an endless succession of changes, constant in their elements,

[11] Chauncey Wright, "The Philosophy of Herbert Spencer" (1865), in *Philosophical Discussions*, ed. posth. by C.E. Norton (New York, 1877), pp. 43–96.

though infinite in their combinations, without beginning or end. Hence he could combine belief in the universality of physical causation with an Aristotelian belief in accidents. Actual laws are inductive and empirical; hence accidents are unpredictable by finite human knowledge. The emergence of consciousness, the development of the voice into language, the properties of new chemical combinations, are all subject to law, but unpredictable. Life is subject to the law of the conservation of energy, but nothing characteristic of life can be deduced from that law.

Mr. Spencer's law is founded on examples, of which only one class, the facts of embryology, are properly scientific. . . . To us Mr. Spencer's speculation seems but the abstract statement of the cosmological conceptions, and that kind of orderliness which the human mind spontaneously supplies in the absence of facts sufficiently numerous and precise to justify sound scientific conclusions. Progress and development, when they mean more than a continuous proceeding, have a meaning suspiciously like what the moral and mythic instincts are inclined to—something having a beginning, a middle, and an end—an epic poem, a dramatic representation, a story, a cosmogony. It is not sufficient for the purposes of science that the idea of progress be freed from any reference to human happiness as an end. . . . Plato's astronomical speculations were teleological in this artistic sense. . . . Aristotle exhibited the characteristics of scientific genius in no way more distinctly than in the rejection of this idea, and of all cosmological speculations.(73, 74)

Nothing justifies the development of abstract principles in science but their utility in enlarging our concrete knowledge of nature. The ideas on which mathematical Mechanics and the Calculus are founded, the morphological ideas of Natural History, and the theories of Chemistry are such working ideas—finders, not merely summaries of truth. (56)

X

Whereas Wright was the first major critic of Spencer's cosmic philosophy, the great critic of his social philosophy—called "social Darwinism," but much more accurately "social Spencerianism"—was Lester F. Ward (1841–1913). Ward was a minor government official in Washington who in 1883 published the first comprehensive sociological treatise written in the United States, *Dynamic Sociology*. This technical work sharply distinguished social evolution from biological evolution, emphasized purposive direction in society, and refused to take "nature" as a guide to human policy. It influenced the pioneers of sociology in academic America, Albion W. Small, Richard T. Ely, and

E.A. Ross—Ward himself became professor at Brown only in 1906. When founded on a more adequate psychology—Ward's own *Psychic Factors of Civilization* (1893) was quite traditional—his social Darwinism proved very influential in the Progressive era.

For Ward social principles do not depend on simple biological analogies. Sociology is an autonomous discipline dealing with a novel and unique level of organization. "There is no necessary harmony between natural law and human advantage." *Laisser-faire* was a useful criticism when government was in the hands of an oligarchical class; but when it has become really representative, the popular will can be exerted through governmental action. Genetic progress must be supplanted by telic progress:

Thus far, social progress has in a certain awkward manner taken care of itself, but in the near future it will have to be cared for. To do this and maintain the dynamic condition against all the hostile forces which thicken with every new advance, is the real problem of Sociology considered as an applied science.[12]

Ward was contemptuous of Sumner's social Spencerianism.

The whole book is based on the fundamental error that the favors of this world are distributed entirely according to merit. Poverty is only a proof of indolence and vice. Wealth simply shows the industry and virtue of the possessors. The very most is made of Malthusianism, and human activities are degraded to a complete level with those of animals. Those who have survived simply prove their fitness to survive; and the fact which all biologists understand, viz., that fitness to survive is something wholly distinct from real superiority, is, of course, ignored by the author because he is not a biologist, as all sociologists should be.[13]

Ward debunked nature as a model, pointing out its wastefulness; then he destroyed belief in the continuity between process in nature and process in society, showing the importance of human purposive action.

---

[12] Lester F. Ward, *Dynamic Sociology*, 2 vols. (New York, 1883), Vol. I, p. 706.
[13] Ward, *Glimpses of the Cosmos*, 6 vols. (New York, 1913–18), Vol. III, pp. 303–4.

4

The Idealistic Protest

PARTLY THROUGH the sheer persistence of the assumptions of the preceding Romantic era, and partly because it seemed the surest way out of the distasteful conclusions of the new faith in mechanistic evolution, the philosophy to which most thinkers, especially those in academic communities, turned to escape the new world of nineteenth-century science was some version of the now traditional philosophical Idealism. In the background was the admitted preeminence of the German universities, with their roots in the great achievements of classical German philosophy, which still made some form of that tradition central in their organized intellectual life. From France, to strengthen the academic tradition of Cousin's spiritualism; from England, and especially Scotland, to bolster the defenses against Mill's empiricism and Spencerian evolutionary "naturalism," and to replace the declining philosophy of Common Sense as the answer to irreligion; from the new American colleges, just burgeoning into universities, and anxious to go for inspiration to the now classic land of the mind, Germany; from the Italy of the finally united *Regno;* to say nothing of the lands further East: a stream of students set in to the German seats of academic wisdom.

In each of these countries the story of the introduction of philosophical Idealism into the academic institutions is the story of what was brought back from a fruitful sojourn in Germany. Sir William Hamilton (1788–1856; from 1836 professor at Edinburgh; "Notes and Dissertations" in *Works of Thomas Reid*, Edinburgh, 1856, Vol. II, pp. 742–991; *Discussions on Philosophy*, Edinburgh, 1852, esp. "Philosophy of the Unconditioned") and James Frederick Ferrier (1808–64; from 1845 professor at St. Andrews; *Institutes of Metaphysic*, Edinburgh, 1854) brought idealism into the Scottish tradition. James Hutchinson

Stirling (1820–1909; *The Secret of Hegel*, London, 1865), John Grote (1813–66; *Exploratio Philosophica*, Vol. I, 1865, Vol. II, 1900), and above all T.H. Green (1826–82) began to divert the waters of the Rhine into the Isis and the Cam. Jean Ravaisson (1813–1900) and Jules Lachelier (1832–1918) under the Empire and the early Third Republic established the curriculum of the French universities as idealism. Francis Bowen (1811–90) brought idealism to Harvard Common Sense, and Noah Porter (1811–93) installed it at Yale, leaving James McCosh (1817–94) to fight a losing battle for common sense at Princeton; Alexander T. Ormond (1847–1915) and John Grier Hibben (1861–1933) soon conquered there in the name of idealism. In England the last generation of the century saw great teachers of idealism— William Wallace (1844–97), Bernard Bosanquet (1848–1923), and above all Francis Herbert Bradley (1846–1924). There were lesser lights from Scotland: John Caird (1820–98) and his brother Edward Caird (1835–1908), and Benjamin Jowett (1817–93). Cambridge saw J. McTaggart Ellis McTaggart (1866–1925; *Some Dogmas of Religion*, 1906; *The Nature of Existence*, 1921, 1927), James Ward (1843–1925; article, "Psychology," in *Encyclopedia Britannica*, 11th ed.; *Naturalism and Agnosticism*, London, 1899; *The Realm of Ends*, 1911; *Psychological Principles*, 1918), and G.F. Stout (1850–1944; editor of *Mind*, 1896–1920; *Analytic Psychology*, 1896; *Manual of Psychology*, 1898; *Mind and Matter*, 1931; *God and Nature*, 1952). By that time there were few dissenters in the English, Scottish, or Irish universities.

In America, after popular movements like the New England Transcendentalists, the St. Louis Hegelians (Henry Brokmeyer, William Torrey Harris, editor of the *Journal of Speculative Philosophy*, 1867–93, and Denton J. Snider), and the Concord School of Philosophy of Bronson Alcott, which brought to the fore Thomas Davidson (1840–1900), the first academic idealist was Laurens Perseus Hickok (1798–1888) of Union College, whose students Julius H. Seelye (1824–1905) and Charles Edward Garman (1865–1907) brought the doctrine to Amherst. The beginnings of the academic teaching of philosophy in America came from this band of German-trained idealists. George Herbert Palmer (1843–1933) took it to Harvard; George Holmes Howison (1834–1916), starting in St. Louis, taught first at M.I.T. and after 1884 at Berkeley, spreading to his students a pluralistic personal idealism. Borden P. Bowne (1847–1910) taught a Meth-

odist personal idealism at Boston University, leaving pupils like Edgar
S. Brightman (1884–1953), A.C. Knudson (1873–1953), and Ralph T.
Flewelling (1871–1960), who transferred its seat to the Mudd School
of Philosophy at the University of Southern California. A.C.
Armstrong (1860–1935) taught at Wesleyan, George Trumbull Ladd
(1842–1921) at Yale—still the seat of American idealism—George Ful-
lerton (1859–1925) at Pennsylvania and then at Columbia; all made
philosophical idealism a genuine cultural force. Hopkins started with
George Sylvester Morris (1840–89), who carried his dynamic idealism
to Michigan, where he was soon joined by John Dewey and James H.
Tufts (1862–1942). The two latter left for the newly-founded University of Chicago in 1892, leaving Alfred H. Lloyd, R.M. Wenley, and
Dewitt H. Parker to hold the fort at Ann Arbor. Nicholas Murray
Butler (1862–1947), returned from Germany, established Kantian idealism with the founding of the graduate Faculty of Philosophy at
Columbia in 1890. Jacob Gould Schurman (1854–1942), a Scot who
long taught at Dalhousie in Halifax, set up the Sage School of Philosophy at Cornell in 1892, together with the organ of idealism, the
Philosophical Review, gathered about him James Edwin Creighton
(1861–1924), a pupil from Dalhousie, Frank Thilly, William A. Hammond, and Ernest Albee, and trained a generation of teachers of philosophy. And in 1882 Palmer and James called the greatest American
idealist, Josiah Royce (1855–1910), to Harvard.

It is not our intention to go into the differing shades of opinion of
this galaxy of near-great teachers of philosophy in Britain, France, or
the United States. We want to point out something about the social
and cultural function of the whole movement, and how it differed in
Britain, the United States, France, and Italy. Something must be said
about Royce, and about the schools of personal, pluralistic, objective,
and dynamic idealism in America, as well as about figures like Croce
and Gentile in Italy. But the main analysis of the whole movement,
from the time Green took over English philosophy from Mill to that
in which Bradley handed it on to the naturalists of the twentieth century, will be undertaken in connection with the three major English
idealists, T.H. Green (1836–82), and Bosanquet (1848–1923) and
Bradley (1846–1924) in the next generation. We can then turn to the
somewhat different developments of the idealistic tradition in Germany itself, where the Neo-Kantian philosophy of natural science and

the working out of an idealistic philosophy of the *Geisteswissenschaften* had significant consequences. Whereas British and American idealism started as the defense and reconstruction of the religious tradition in the face of nineteenth-century science, French idealism was primarily a defense of moral freedom. In both cases, the tradition grew more and more secular. But only in Germany did idealism push on to philosophies of the natural and the social sciences. Side by side with these issues, idealism criticized the laisser-faire of nineteenth-century individualism, and supported the theories of the welfare state and of the social democratic movement.[1]

I

The philosophic idealism to which these varied thinkers in different lands turned for diverse purposes was, by the 1860s, no longer a novel and revolutionary philosophy: it had become the older established conservative tradition. And it was to the great figures of the beginning of the century that men had recourse—above all to Kant or Hegel. The trouble was that while men could still repeat the arguments, outside the enthusiasm of the Romantic movement, in the saner and soberer atmosphere in which they now seemed to offer help, it was much, much harder to believe them. Thus idealism could easily "accept" the doctrines of the new science—in their proper place, as after all merely "phenomenal" and "mere appearance." God was still there, a witness who records and preserves all man's struggles. Philosophy became a way of giving men "what they want when they say God," as Bosanquet put it, a way of "proving" God, freedom, and immortality, in the face of negative scientific evidence. The impact of idealism

---

[1] On English and American idealism in general, see Thomas M. Forsyth, *English Philosophy: A Study of its Method and General Development* (1910); James Seth, *English Philosophers and Schools of Philosophy* (1912); Rudolf Metz, *A Hundred Years of British Philosophy* (1928), Part II, Chapter I, "The Neo-Idealist Movement"; John Passmore, *A Hundred Years of Philosophy* (1957), Chapters 1, 2, 13; Herbert W. Schneider, *A History of American Philosophy* (2nd ed., 1963), Chapter 7, "Idealisms"; Arthur K. Rogers, *English and American Philosophy Since 1800: A Critical Survey* (1923), Chapter 5, "Absolute Idealism," Chapter 6, "Personal Idealism, etc."

See also G.P. Adams, *Idealism and the Modern Age* (1919); R.F. Alfred Hoernlé, *Idealism as a Philosophy* (1927); G. Watts Cunningham, *The Idealistic Argument in Recent British and American Philosophy* (1928); R.G. Collingwood, *Speculum Mentis* (1924), *An Essay on Philosophical Method* (1933), *An Essay on Metaphysics* (1940); G.R.G. Mure, *The Retreat from Truth* (1958); Brand Blanshard, *The Nature of Truth*, 2 vols. (1939); M.J. Oakeshott, *Experience and Its Modes* (1933); A.C. Ewing, *Idealism: A Critical Survey: The Idealist Tradition from Berkeley to Blanshard* (1957).

grew more and more conservative: in countless classrooms, men used it to show that there really is a God, though science cannot find Him, and that society is really working for the highest ends, though it certainly does not seem to be.

German idealism never became divorced from the scientific currents, as happened in England and America. Neo-Kantianism was a genuine philosophy of the natural sciences, and it also developed an ethical and social philosophy giving an idealistic foundation to the program of the Social Democrats. Another strain was vitally concerned with the philosophical creation of the social sciences, the *Geistes-* or *Kulturwissenschaften*, and its foremost minds, Wilhelm Dilthey, Max Weber, and Ernst Cassirer are still living ferments in that developing field, whose influence in England and America dates largely from the thirties. Lotze was the sanest and most scientifically minded of the idealists: it is not without significance that Dewey's more technical analysis sets out from Lotze. There was also an ethical and religious idealism, of which Windelband and the popular Rudolf Eucken are the best known exponents. And there is the social criticism of Nietzsche and the movement known as *Lebensphilosophie*, to say nothing of the currents which in the twentieth century developed into phenomenology and existentialism—a kind of radical offshoot of idealism, though the Germans usually make a careful distinction.

Neo-Kantianism and what is usually called "Hegelian" absolute idealism were imported into England around 1870, having already been abandoned by the Germans as a useful instrument in facing the nineteenth-century religious problem. Ferrier established it at St. Andrews, T.H. Green at Oxford, and Cambridge soon followed suit with McTaggart. In Britain, as distinguished from America, idealism also played a function in social thinking. It gave scope for a mild collectivism on fundamentally Liberal principles, continuing the development we have traced (Vol. II, Book VI, chapter 10) in Stuart Mill's working out of his initial Philosophical Radicalism. Through its influence on the upper class and intellectuals at Oxford and Cambridge, it furnished the background for the social faith of the Neo-Liberals, the Neo-Conservatives, and the Labour Party, after the dam broke in 1906. Green himself led in assimilating more collectivistic ideas into the tradition of political Liberalism, and later social philosophers like Lord Haldane and Harold J. Laski, as well as a number of academic professors in the Scottish universities—J.S. Mackenzie, J.H. Muirhead, Sir Henry Jones, etc.—laid the foundations for the modern British welfare state.

In America, though the St. Louis Hegelians developed a social philosophy—Denton J. Snider especially, who followed Hegel's admiration for the Greek *polis*—idealism was used primarily as an instrument for rationalizing the religious tradition, and in the colleges and seminaries became the bulwark of religious liberalism—bringing in the humanistic values and the theology of the Divine Immanence to which Germans, faced by a similar problem, had turned in the early 1800s. Hegel, primarily, but Schleiermacher and Ritschl as well, attracted a wide following for their respective reinterpretations of the religious tradition: Hegel and Ritschl in particular supported the rising Social Gospel.

In the United States the persisting Puritan—or, as Santayana called it, "genteel"—tradition led American idealism to display a stronger tinge of moral struggle than was appropriate in the more decorous idealists of the Church of England. Josiah Royce had a profound realization of finite evils; he saw life as tragic, involving a genuine confrontation with Evil. For him, the "Absolute" became a society of spiritual selves bringing good to pass out of evil. At times, it appeared like the last act of a play, in which everything is explained, the hero and heroine are reunited, and the villain turns out to be the hero's father engaged in developing his son's character. Royce himself pushed on to other things, to a philosophy of cultural pluralism and to an interest in symbolic logic. Borden P. Bowne, from Boston University, taught a much more conventional and conservative "personal idealism," insisting that the Absolute must be personality. He created the official philosophy of Liberal Methodism, and Methodist denominational colleges began concentrating on a sound personalism and a winning football team.

English idealism, while it served as the bulwark of Anglican modernism and the Broad Church movement, started by Coleridge and his disciples, developed a strain that grew more secular and less religious, especially in contrast with contemporary American idealism: perhaps Butler was the foremost user of idealism to undergird a secular and humanistic culture in the U.S. In England, when the premises were logically worked out by acute critics like Bradley and McTaggart, the

Absolute turned out to be not identifiable with "God," but beyond good and evil, a total intelligible universe of human values. The outcome was the "idealistic atheism" of Bradley, and its counterpart in McTaggart at Cambridge. The Anglican clergy, acknowledging Bradley as the greatest of the Idealists, not unnaturally preferred the more accommodating religious views of Bosanquet. Bosanquet had marked social interests: he was secretary of the Charity Organization Society in London. He urged men to "cooperate with the real forces in society," and treated idealism as a means of showing how everything had to be as it was, and why it should not be interfered with. However, he was an early supporter of the Labour Party. Bosanquet and his brother between them owned half the coal fields of Northumberland. Under Kantian influence, time had dropped out of Hegel during the trip across the Channel, and the dialectic became a "philosophical logic" rather than a pattern of social and historical development. It was the Cornell school in America that stood closest to Bosanquet; but, partly because of its marked interest in historical development, it never became so closely identified with a philosophy of wholesale social justification.

Yet—while idealism in both Britain and America was deeply entangled in these vital social and cultural problems, its working out, in Bradley most clearly but even in Bosanquet as well, led on into the interests and the positions of later twentieth-century philosophizing. If the position is followed out, honestly, and without undue religious bias, and in an objective and "scientific" spirit, it leads easily to the naturalistic metaphysics of the next century; and such philosophic naturalism can be characterized as the more critical and scientific treatment of the total subject matter of the idealistic metaphysics of the turn of the century.

In its more technical aspects, philosophical idealism did manage to overcome the dualism of modern philosophizing since Descartes. It envisioned a world with a *logos*, a logical structure in it once more, a structure that became intelligible and accessible again to the mind of man. The subjectivistic and observational assumptions Locke transmitted to subsequent empiricists were gone. It was an easy step—as Bosanquet himself pointed out in his *The Meeting of Extremes in Contemporary Philosophy* (London, 1921), his valedictory—from "objective idealism" to the later philosophies of logical realism, like Samuel Alexander, or Morris R. Cohen: Green's great critical insistence was that "reality" is a logical system. If, like Bradley, men emphasized the Hegelian logic of contradiction, they ended up remarkably close to the instrumentalism of John Dewey, with a functional position.

Moreover, for idealism, especially that with a Hegelian background, the world was once more also a system of values. Idealism overcame the second major dualism of modern philosophy, that between existence and value. For it, values were no longer "subjective," or "inside the head," but objective once more as in Greek thought. Sensitivity to values had of course always been the strong point of the idealistic thinkers, as contrasted with the crudities of the contemporary scientific philosophies. Idealism was "conservative" in the best sense of the term, in its discriminating preservation of traditional values in the face of a doctrinaire assault. No one has ever made a better defense of the Christian values of rejection, of sacrifice, than T.H. Green; and, in more Hegelian language, Bosanquet's argument for the values of "negativity." Then, too, the idealists all continued the Hegelian notion of socialized liberty, of a human freedom to be achieved, not through individualism, but through social action. This became the great weapon in Britain and to a lesser extent in the United States, against the laisser-faire of the classical economists and the individualistic Liberals. First Green himself, and in the next generation (despite the conservatism of Bosanquet) the Scottish Liberal Idealists, J.H. Muirhead, J. Stuart Mackenzie, and Henry Jones, managed to transform the historic British conception of personal freedom into something to be achieved only in a rationally organized society.

At the same time, Hegelian forms of idealism were apt to overcome also the moral dualism between the Ideal and the Actual. They emphasized the "immanence of God," the "Divinity" of human nature, and tended toward a secularism and an optimism—toward what the Neo-Orthodox in their reaction have called the "humanistic" impact of the idealistic reconstruction of religion. This formed an admirable intellectual expression for that era of sentimental, benevolent, and mildly humanitarian religion. The "modernistic" acceptance of the world, the flesh, and the devil, tempered with a high-minded and hopeful plea for more "good will," more of the "spirit of Jesus," is apt to strike us today as the very quintessence of the middle-class security and complacency of that era in the late nineteenth century and before

1914 from which, for better or worse, we seem to have been delivered in our own Age of Anxiety.

Hegelian idealism, especially in the popular Bosanquet version, emphasized the ideal worth of present institutions, the value of private property as necessary for "developing one's personality," the ideal functions of the State and of patriotism. During that era of Kipling, the British idealists in particular often seemed incapable of distinguishing between the Absolute and the British Empire.

The Kantian ethical dualism between man's actual moral experience and the moral or "spiritual" ideal strikes most of us today as more radical, more inspiring, and—blessed word!—more "realistic." No one, in fact, who ever listened to Felix Adler's harsh condemnation of "empirical man"—of man and human nature as they actually are encountered in our experience—needed to learn anything about "Sin" from those Neo-Orthodox who awakened rather late to the facts of life and of the human predicament.

Nevertheless, as we can realize today, idealism did keep alive a concern with man's spiritual life when it could find little place in the scientific philosophies. And an enlarged naturalism would attempt a more critical and scientific treatment of the values and the conception of the world of the Idealists. Their range of interests, in the light of our present-day subtle analyses of human experience, stands out in marked contrast to the often myopic limitations of our own specialized and penetrating analyses.

PART TWO

British and American Idealism

5

T. H. Green and Liberal Idealism

THOMAS HILL GREEN (1836–82),[1] the keenest critical mind to appear in Britain since Hume, stood for three main critical endeavors. In the first place, he was the major nineteenth-century critic of the reigning Utilitarian philosophy represented by Mill and those he had influenced. Utilitarianism he criticized in the interests of Liberal Religion—of the type of religious life represented by Maurice, Kingsley, and earlier by Wordsworth and Coleridge. He thus figures as the "Mr. Gray" of Mrs. Humphry Ward's novel, *Robert Elsmere*. In this criticism in religious interests, he gave an excellent modern defense of the characteristically Christian moral ideals of selection, renunciation, and moral struggle. In this Green is the analogue of the great religious liberals who in the earlier twentieth century criticized the orthodox tradition, playing a rôle in the religious life of England and America that had been earlier played by the great modernistic critics of the religious tradition in nineteenth-century Germany.

Originally published as "T. H. Green: The Development of English Thought from J.S. Mill to F.H. Bradley," in *Journal of the History of Ideas*, XXVII, no. 2 (April–June 1966), pp. 217–44. Reprinted by permission.

[1] *Works of Thomas Hill Green*, ed. R.L. Nettleship, 3 vols. (London, 1885–88; 4th impression, 1899). *Prolegomena to Ethics*, ed. A.C. Bradley (Oxford, 1883; 5th ed. with preface by Edward Caird, 1906). *Memoir* by R.L. Nettleship in *Works*, III, pp. xi-clxi.

W.H. Fairbrother, *The Philosophy of Thomas Hill Green* (London, 1896). T.M. Forsyth, *English Philosophy*, Chapter 7 (London, 1907). L.T. Hobhouse, *The Theory of Knowledge*, Chapter 1 (London, 1896). John MacCunn, *Six Radical Thinkers* (London, 1907). Edward Caird, "Professor Green's Last Work," *Mind*, VIII (1883), pp. 544–61. Henry Sidgwick, "Green's Ethics," *Mind*, IX (1884), pp. 169–87; "The Philosophy of T.H. Green," *Mind*, X, N.S. (1901), pp. 18–29. John Dewey, "The Philosophy of T.H. Green," *Andover Review*, XI (1889), pp. 337–55; "Some Current Conceptions of the Term, 'Self,' " *Mind*, XV (1890), pp. 58–74; "Green's Theory of the Moral Motive," *Philosophical Review*, I (1892), pp. 593–612; "Self-Realization as the Moral Ideal," *Philosophical Review*, II (1893), pp. 652–64. By far the best study of Green as critic is Howard Selsam, *T.H. Green: Critic of Empiricism* (New York, 1930).

Secondly, Green stood in Victorian England as the great intellectual critic of the social philosophy of laisser-faire individualism. He was a mildly collectivistic Liberal—like the later John Stuart Mill, whose social philosophy he virtually carried forward. Through his position at Oxford he had an extraordinary influence in molding the ideas of a generation of English political leaders—those who triumphed in 1906 with the "Neo-Liberalism" of Henry Campbell-Bannerman and Herbert Asquith, including their philosophical leader, Viscount Haldane. His social criticism had far wider repercussions, however, on the leaders of more radical movements. It is hardly too much to say that his social thought dominated the British Labour Party, in its non-Marxian divisions, down through G.D.H. Cole and Harold J. Laski; and Green was the chief influence in the early social philosophy of John Dewey in America. Green was a democrat, an advocate of social intervention to correct injustices in economic life, a Little Englander on the issue of imperialism. He is comparable to the more intellectual leaders of the movements, like the New Freedom, and the New Deal, that have transformed the United States into a "welfare state."

Thirdly, and philosophically most important, Green was the major late-nineteenth-century critic of the tradition of British Empiricism, a philosophy and an intellectual method he saw as the foundation of both Utilitarian moral philosophy and the social philosophy of individualism. Just as Stuart Mill's fight was all his life against the *a priori* intuitionism of the impressive German thinkers, so Green's great fight was against "empiricism," from his earliest essays to his posthumous *Prolegomena to Ethics*. This meant that Green confronted the same intellectual problems as the men he was consciously combatting: he was trying throughout to "refute" them. He was not attempting, like F.H. Bradley in the next generation, to restate and transcend those problems. Green liked to regard himself in the revealing light of a "Plato refuting the Sophists."

In his criticisms, he drew upon the ideas of German philosophy; it was in his day that the Rhine began to flow into the Isis at Oxford. He used German ideas especially to formulate his own alternative positive position, which is by far the weaker side of his thought. In his own metaphysics he drew primarily upon Kant: Part I of the *Prolegomena*, stating his own position, is definitely "Neo-Kantian."

The reason why he used Kant more than Hegel is clear: Hegel was not enough of an empiricist, his "sublimations" did not give sufficient leverage to attack the empiricists, they were not fighting weapons. Kant, in contrast, was—to Green at least—an empiricist with the insight to add what the empiricists had omitted, intelligible structure.

Green did not need to conduct his criticism in terms of German ideas, in terms of Kant. He could, for instance, have used Aristotle, as is clear from his long study of "The Philosophy of Aristotle" of 1866. Had he done so, he would have avoided the Kantian language, problems, and dualisms, and gained a more naturalistic form of discourse. He could then have put his main criticism of the empiricists, "Being has an intelligible structure," in less idealistic language. Green's constructive philosophy, his own Neo-Kantian metaphysics, is clearly not essential as a basis for his criticisms. In it he displays little originality: his greatness is as a critic, not as a system-builder. This is another reason why he preferred to use Kant rather than Hegel, and why he preserves such continuity with the British critical tradition, and appears today as the inevitable next stage after Mill.

Green was fundamentally opposed to the reduction to other terms of actually experienced wholes and aggregates, in the moral life, in political life, in the construing of knowledge. Explanation does not come from a reductive analysis of wholes into their elements. There can hence be no valid "natural history," no genetic method. Green opposed both the empiricists and the evolutionary naturalists, like Spencer and George Henry Lewes. There is, in fact, no discoverable "origin" of experience, moral, social, or intellectual, in terms derived from it and presupposed by it. Green opposed both reductionist analysis and the evolutionary "creationist" analysis. Now these are all basically Aristotelian ideas. There is in Green the suggestion of the conception of "process" as fundamental, of the actualization of what is potential. The suggestion is couched, to be sure, in the language of "experience"; this caused the empiricist assumptions, which Green is sweeping out through the front door, to come constantly creeping in again through the back door.

The only possible analysis of experience consists in making distinctions within it, not in reducing it to other terms or to its "elements." It must be the analysis of what are recognized to be organized wholes; it must be a *factorial* analysis. There is nothing "outside" experience:

experience is not to be "explained" in terms either "inside" or "outside" itself. Experience is a given fact. Analysis can reveal its anatomy, the relations obtaining in it. But there is no "real world" outside experience.

Green hence opposed "phenomenalism," "subjectivism," the "false idealism" of Berkeley and Hume. "A true idealism trusts, not to a guess about what is beyond experience, but to the analysis of what is within it." "Experience" is the only reality, and everything in experience is real, in some sense. The intellectual problem is to find, in just what sense—to find its relations to other realities. For Green, therefore, "experience" is equivalent to what the Idealists call "reality," and naturalists, "nature"—the all-comprehensive term.

From this viewpoint, Green undertakes a critique of all dualisms—just as have done the later naturalisms of our century. There is first the dualism between "ideas" and "things." In point of fact, Green holds, the world of things is actually a world of "ideas," a logical order: the relations obtaining between things are in fact logical relations. Thus causation is not mere succession of events—as Mill was proclaiming—but itself a logical relation. The simplest experience has what can be called a "logical structure."

The term "logical structure" is used to state, in more neutral terms, what Green himself calls an "ideal order" or an "order of thought." Both of Green's terms demand analysis to determine just what he meant by them. Green is himself of course a logical realist: for him the structure of experience and of knowledge is a discovery, not a human invention or "interpretation," in the Kantian sense. It is a "discoverable" structure, an "accessible" structure. Green's can hence be called a "structural idealism," as against other forms of "functional idealism," like Hegel's or Bradley's. In traditional terms, Green is a Platonist, almost literally in the great tradition of Augustinianism. This aspect of Green is precisely the object of Bradley's criticism: Bradley was trying to work out a functional idealism.

What this discoverable logical structure in things means is perhaps clearer in the naturalists of the twentieth century. Thus Morris R. Cohen holds, "we discover implications in things"; he is a structural naturalist. John Dewey prefers to say, "we construct inferences on the basis of natural relations"; he is a functional naturalist. Frederick J. E. Woodbridge, speaking as a structuralist, holds, "Nature has a logical structure." Dewey the functionalist preferred to say, "Nature has a 'logiscible' structure." On this issue, Green would have sided strongly with Cohen and Woodbridge.

The second dualism Green attacked was that between the "particular" and the "universal." For him, the relation is not a problem but a fact. Individuals are "real" only in virtue of their universal relations; particulars are real because of the structure in which they are embedded. This is what Green made out of Hegel's "concrete universal." He contended for, "not the admission of an ideal world of guess and aspiration alongside of the empirical, but the recognition of the empirical as itself ideal."

All these views are naturalistic, and Aristotelian. Green might have developed them consistently. His aim is to interpret all "experience"—that is, all the facts—and to use categories that are not merely analytic, but organic. He insists the concepts of valid analysis must be functional. The dualisms he seeks to break down he sees in the context of "experience"—man is a dweller in a human world. It was in fact just the intellectual function of Idealism to destroy the two-world (ultimately Cartesian) view that sundered man from his world.

But the language of experience Green employed interfered with his real aim: Green was, in other words, not thoroughgoing enough in his criticisms. The factors in experience and knowledge which Green brings in, and which had been neglected by the empiricists (see especially James Mill, the champion neglector), were in that language all identified with "mind" as a substance distinct from bodies or "things," and for Green they retained this "mental" character—though on his own principles the difference between "mind" and "body" was now a meaningless distinction. It remained for the next generation of Idealists, notably Bradley, to work itself out into a consistent "naturalism"—to put it concretely, to lose its "mind."

But for Green the world of things is not merely a "logical" order, it is an order of "thought." The simplest experience not only has a logical structure, it is a "work of thought," the "product" of judgment. That is, the order or structure on which Green is rightly insisting against the empiricists is not something found, an encountered fact; it needs a "source," it is not "natural," but must come from "outside" the facts.

In the empiricist tradition—in James Mill, for instance—structure is not found in observations. The Idealists insist: "but the structure is there!" Since they also accept the empiricists' assumption that particulars are given without relation, mere structureless "feelings," they are driven to hold that the structure must come from somewhere else, from "mind"—it is supernatural, or at least superexperiential.

There can be admitted a certain truth in the contention of the Idealist: the order or structure discovered in the experienced world *is*, in an important sense, the product of intelligence working on natural materials, and building up systems of science, of religion, of "values." The "discovery" of this structure is the actualization of what in the materials remains merely potential. The structure there is, as Dewey has called it, "logiscible"—though when produced, it is produced *in* the materials as well as in the "mind"—the process is a natural production. The *expression* and *statement* in knowledge of this potentially discernible structure is certainly an addition to the world unexpressed, even though it is a natural addition.

Aristotle stated this situation, "Knowledge and the thing known [the structure] are one and the same thing." Knowledge is thus an actualization of what was originally merely potential—it is something produced, something set "in operation." Dewey has stated it, Knowledge of this structure is a process of "verification," of "making truth." The process of knowing is "creative," *changing* nature by adding to it; and the expression of this structure by intelligence is a social product, selective and emphasizing. That is, knowing is "creative," like any art.

The more recent linguistic emphasis has followed up and elaborated this position of Dewey's, that communication and language "create" whole new sets of structures that are genuine additions to nature or experience unexpressed. Dewey's own emphasis on "inquiry" as the context within which "new forms accrue" to the situation keeps this "art" an art of "discovery." Certain linguistic views seem to make it pure invention, a creation *ex nihilo*—not an art working with natural materials, but something completely artificial. These views are then caught in the traditional empiricist difficulties: there is assumed to be no discoverable structure in the world; all structure is a human contribution—not of "mind," as Mill and the Idealists had it, but of Language. Such views retain a supernaturalistic and dualistic conception of the functioning of language.[2]

[2] This is why the working out of a naturalistic conception of language and communication seems so important a task for present-day Anglo-American philosophizing.

In this sense, truth can be admitted in the contention of the Idealist that knowing *adds* something to the world not known. But the Idealist theory forced the Idealist to make the work of intelligence something magical and wholesale—something hardly "intelligent" at all, but rather "mental"—and something not amenable to criticism and revision. Hence the Idealistic construing of knowing has been upset at every change in the way science expresses the structure realized in the experienced world. The classic illustration is Kant's "pure" and unchanging structure of "Reason," which turned out to be only the structure of Newtonian science, and has today been passed beyond by the progress of scientific formulation.

Green himself, despite his keen criticism of historic intellectual dualism, retains nevertheless two major dualisms in his thought: that between a "timeless Self" and the experienced world; and that between "Thought" and "Feeling."

1. Green takes the unity of experience, abstracts it from experience, and sets it over against experience as the "source" of the structure encountered in experience. In his ethics, the "Self" is set over against desires and impulses as their antithesis; it is not taken as their organization and progressive realization. And since obviously neither you nor I make the world order, Green is driven to set up a further "Eternal Selfconsciousness" as its source, "constituting" Nature by its presence to Nature.

From the Kantian point of view, the dualism of nature and knowledge is disposed of in a different way. . . . It is not that first there is nature, and then there comes to be an experience and knowledge of it. Intelligence, experience, knowledge, are no more a result of nature than nature of them. If it is true that there would be no intelligence without nature, it is equally true that there would be no nature without intelligence. Nature is the system of related appearances, and *related appearances are impossible apart from the action of an intelligence* [emphasis mine]. They are not indeed the same as intelligence; it is not reducible to them nor they to it, any more than one of us is reducible to the series of his actions or that series to him; but without it they would not be, nor except in the activity which constitutes them has it any real existence. Does this then imply the absurdity that nature comes into existence in the process by which this person or that begins to think? Not at all, unless it is necessary to suppose that intelligence first comes into existence when this person or that begins to understand—a supposition not only not necessary, but which, on examination, will be found to involve impossibilities analogous to those which prevent us from supposing that nature so comes into existence.

The difference between what may be called broadly the Kantian view and the ordinary view is this, that whereas, according to the latter, it is a world in which thought is no necessary factor that is prior to, and independent of, the process by which this or that individual becomes acquainted with it, according to the former it is a world already determined by thought, and existing only in relation to thought, that is thus prior to, and conditions, our individual acquaintance with it. The growth of knowledge on our part is regarded not as a process in which facts or objects, in themselves unrelated to thought, by some inexplicable means gradually produce intelligible counterparts of themselves in thought. The true account of it is held to be that the concrete whole, which may be described indifferently as an eternal intelligence realized in the related facts of the world, or as a system of related facts rendered possible by such an intelligence, partially and gradually reproduces itself in us, communicating piece-meal, but in inseparable correlation, understanding and the facts understood, experience and the experienced world.[3]

Green is thus taking the subject-object distinction in experience out of its context, generalizing it, making it absolute, and the "source" of all structure in experience. He is hence left with the same problem as the empiricists he is combatting: how to get from my experience to the world conceived as the structure of this "eternal experience"? Green's new dualism is not between sensations and the Newtonian world order, but between empirical "experience" and this eternal "experience," between the experienced order and the "real" order, or "Absolute"—the dualism between appearance and reality.

This idealistic dualism of Green's is certainly reinforced by Green's moral and religious interests. These are not the cause of his going so far in criticizing empiricism and evolutionary naturalism, but rather the cause of his not going further—of his not seeing the full implications of his own principles; the "Self" in the moral life must be taken as an ideal to be set over against moral experience; the "Eternal Self" as God must be set over against mere Nature. Thus Green's own dualisms come, as all such dualisms normally do, from practical motives. Distinctions practically important in experience are made absolute. Even intellectual dualism—that between the ideal of the perfect or the "real" order, and our present meager knowledge—comes from such a practical motive. "Truth" is then taken not as the existent system of the sciences, but as an aim leading beyond them, as an ideal limit to knowledge. Such distinctions seem indeed necessary for

[3] T.H. Green, *Prolegomena to Ethics*, Book I, Chapter I, Section 36 (Oxford, 1883; 5th ed., 1906), pp. 40–41.

"practice," even for the practice of intellectual inquiry; but unless they are seen in their context, they lead to metaphysical confusion—as in the case of T.H. Green.

2. Green's second remaining dualism is that between "feeling" and "thought." Events and particulars, as "feelings"—Green follows the empiricist terminology started by Thomas Brown—are in themselves relationless. The structure we find them in must come from another "source"—"mind" or "thought" contributes all relations.

No feeling, as such or as felt, is a relation. We can only suppose it to be so through confusion between it and its conditions, or between it and that fact of its occurrence which is no doubt related to other facts, but, as so related, is not felt. . . . A feeling can only be felt as successive to another feeling, but the terms of a relation, even though the relation be one of succession, do not succeed one another. In order to constitute the relation they must be present together; so that, to constitute a relation between feelings, there must be something other than the feelings for which they are equally present. The relation between the feelings is not felt, because it is only for something that distinguishes itself from the feelings that it can subsist. . . . Facts, we are sure, are in some way permanent. They are not "like the bubble on the fountain," a moment here, then "gone and forever." But if they were feelings as we feel them, they would be so. They would not be "stubborn things"; for as each was felt it would be done with. They would not form a world to which we have to adapt ourselves; for in order to make a world they must coexist, which feelings, as we feel them, do not. (41–42)

"Feelings" are the mere raw material, transitory, relationless, without structure; they are multiplicity, plurality, change, the brute material or "data" of experience and knowledge. All unity, all order, all structure must come from "thought," magically injected.

Green holds, there is either an inexplicable preestablished harmony between feeling and thought; or else, in the act of knowing itself, relations are "established"; feelings are transformed into relations that form an "order of thought." In the next generation, Green's great critic, F.H. Bradley, held that this "act of thought" is disruptive and illicit: it distinguishes and picks apart what is originally together in a whole. The problem for him is, how can the disrupted factors be got together again? His answer runs, only by a superrational "Feeling of the Whole": "Knowledge arises out of what is *akin* to knowledge, but never *like* knowledge." Knowledge *ought* to be just *like* its original in feeling, it really *ought* to make *no difference* in the situation. Bradley is here clearly continuing the empiricist assumption, that the "original" of knowledge is the criterion of the certainty and extent of knowledge. Fortunately, later in life Bradley learned better.

But for Green, the act of thought is not disruptive but synthetic, in the Kantian sense "constitutive." For him, knowledge arises out of what is so unlike knowledge that it can never be known. We can, in the end, hope to know only the "knowing," or "thought." We cannot "know" feelings or particulars at all.

For Bradley, we must try to know what knowing has already destroyed. For Green, we can know only what knowing has itself created. This dualism between Feeling and Thought was something Green tried desperately to overcome. He denied explicitly that knowledge arises out of feelings existing independently of knowing. Every "experience" is something given, a subject matter containing both feeling and thought, both particulars and their relating structure. "Neither is the product of the other." "Each in its reality involves the other." But the hold of the empiricist assumptions he was criticizing was too strong for him—even as those assumptions had been taken over by Kant himself (see Vol. II, Book V, chapters 5 and 6).

Green might have been more successful if he had followed up his early use of Aristotle as a critical instrument—if he had taken knowledge as a process of actualizing the structure potential in particulars—instead of using the Kantian position, that knowing contributes a structure of its own to particulars that are in themselves wholly relationless and without structure. To bring out Green's fundamental criticism, we shall start with his use of this Aristotelian instrument of criticism.

I

Green's study of Aristotle [4] involves a certain Kantianism, especially in its language: Self-consciousness appears as the "source" of the structure found in the world.

The truth is, that the elements into which Aristotle resolves the intelligible world, are not fully conceived of by him as determinations of a creative spirit, which reflects itself in things. To him they are rather fixed elements in a world presented from without. Hence the sequence and dependence of one on

---

[4] "The Philosophy of Aristotle," a review of Sir Alexander Grant's edition of the *Ethics*, in *North British Review* (Sept. 1866); *Works*, III, pp. 36–91.

the other are not clearly seen. The thread of spiritual unity on which they all hang escapes his grasp. (III, 69)

This Kantianism is certainly present; and there are certain strange interpretations of Aristotle, especially of the logic, with references to "a crudity in Aristotle's philosophical digestion"—he had not studied Kant. But these elements are hardly essential; and in fact Green is carried far by Aristotle's realism.

Plato and Aristotle agree: "The real is the intelligible, the intelligible is the real." Aristotle, in fact, is more of an "idealist" than Plato: he has no "false dualisms" in his thought:

If Plato is "idealist," Aristotle is more . . . he less frequently lapses into the false dualism of soul and body, mind and matter, ideas and things, which made Plato, against his principles, a mystic, and which has clung like a body of death to Platonising philosophy ever since. (47)

In other words, what Green calls "idealism" we should today call "naturalism."

The Greeks found structure or "meanings" to be the object of knowledge, and therefore "real," by criticizing "the sensible." Green here distinguishes "the sensible" from "sensation" or "feeling," his later term for particulars; his language is here less subjectivistic than later—an important point in understanding his criticism.

For Heraclitus, the object of sense is unknowable and indeterminate, "becoming." The knowable must be definable and describable. The properties of "the sensible" are not themselves sensible, but intelligible, universals. Take "this bed" (Green takes as his example of a particular an "object of sense," not a "sensation" or "feeling," as he does later). This bed is not a *tode ti*, but a *toionde:* the attempt to know "the sensible" at once transforms it into something intelligible. "The object of sense is ever becoming an object of 'thought' " (Green has read Hegel). What *is*, is what is known, a "form"; the object of knowledge and "true reality" coincide. What we *know* is "the real." (Green's emphasis makes clear the vehemence of both Bradley and Dewey in denying this in the next generation.) Why was this truth ever lost? "The more complex knowledge becomes, the harder it is to 'begin at the beginning' and analyze its elements."

Plato is a combination of Heraclitus' position with Socrates' notion of definition. Plato asks, "What can a thing be *said* to be?" He is seeking a definition. The answer will be, not something sensible, but a "form," the thing itself *as known*, the sum of its properties. The thing is the unity of its properties, a center of relations, structures, and interests.

Green's criticism of this Platonic position is: (1) It is too rigid and limited a scheme of "attributes." Things are *all* their intelligible relations; the universal is not merely a class corresponding to the name or definition, but "any knowable relation." (2) It is too empirical: in it sense objects are made real entities in themselves, and contrasted with universals or classes, as the determinate subject of properties, instead of being taken as "merely individual," with no determinate reality, and hence in themselves as nothing, "which becomes universal as soon as it is known." That is, for Green, "the sensible," the particular or individual, is in Aristotle's terms "matter," not "substance."

Green therefore criticizes Aristotle's logic of real independent substances, using the views of the *Metaphysics* and the *De Anima*. (1) The logic of Aristotle is barren, and produces nothing new. (2) Because it is a logic of "abstraction" from rich particulars to barren abstractions, and follows the Tree of Porphyry to bare "being," it reverses the actual process of knowing, which actually begins with the most general, and becomes more and more determinate.

The futility of this view . . . supposes the process of thought to begin where it actually ends, and end where it really begins. It supposes it to begin with a knowledge of the thing, as a complex of determinate attributes, for unless the attributes are there, they cannot be abstracted; and to end with the simple predication of being, which, as excluding all definite attributes, is virtually nothing. As the Platonic "criticism of the sensible" implied, the real process is just the reverse. The first act of thinking or knowing is the judgment "something is," and the predicate of this judgment, "being," or the simple relation which it expresses, becomes gradually a subject of more and more determinate properties, as in successive judgments it is brought into new relations. The syllogism or deduction, moreover, is simply the induction, so to speak, upside down. It adds on again the attributes which the induction had taken away. The induction having abstracted from "this, that, and the other" magnets all particular properties but that of attracting iron, the syllogism, or series of syllogisms, by dividing the "*summum genus*" in which this abstract property is envisaged, brings it again into connection with the complex particularity of "this, that, and the other." (59–60)

One might remind Green of the process of thinking described in the Proemium to the *Physics*. But if we ask whose criticism of the *Organon*

Green is here reflecting, it is clearly Mill's: Green had read the *Logic*, and repeats it with Hegelian overtones.

The sensible is unreal; nothing is predicable of it. It *becomes* "real" only when it is fixed in relation to other things. The universal is real, and is "in" things. The individual thing is real, and an object of knowledge, but only in virtue of its universal relations, without which no intelligible propositions could be formulated about it. "The thing is a unity only relative to a multiplicity." Aristotle makes the universal a class, not a relation, while in fact the properties connoted by the name are superficial; and he abstracts to a point where no propositions are at all possible. Aristotle's logic is thus not "idealistic" enough. He admits sensible things which are "not an idea, not intelligible through and through."

We cannot know by abstraction, for properties must be known before they can be abstracted. If thought, then, is a process of abstraction—as it is according to the Aristotelian logic—we think by other methods than we know. Thought, therefore, cannot give us knowledge, but only lead us away from it. (61–62)

Aristotle's logic, understood as Mill understands it, has this "vicious abstraction"; it remains Platonic and "unidealistic."

The *De Anima* and *Metaphysics* represent "a more thorough and therefore truer idealism" (we should say "naturalism"), especially in the polemics against the Platonists. Here, the most general and indeterminate genus is matter, which is "formed" by differentiae.

The place which the conception of "matter" fills in this theory is inconsistent with its place in the theory of induction. According to the latter, "matter" is constituted by the individual things which "are nearest the sense," and from which thought abstracts the properties which constitute the "form" or species. . . . In the Metaphysics, on the other hand, the "summum genus" itself appears as the "matter" which is *formed* by successive *differentiae* till the most determinate complex of attributes has been reached. Here we see that matter has changed places. It appears itself as that abstraction of being which was most remote from matter according to the theory of induction. We are now on the traces of a true theory of knowledge as a process of definition. "Matter" with Aristotle is a relative term. It may either be the simple negation of all form, the absolutely unknown, or it may be the less completely formed or known in contrast with the more completely. Matter, if of the former kind, may be called, in Aristotle's phraseology (with an unessential variation of its meaning), "matter as an object of sense," *hylē aisthētē;* if the latter, "matter as an object of thought," *hylē noētē*. It is in the latter sense that the "summum genus," being, is matter in relation to the formative process of definition. It is the predicate in the judgment "something is," which is itself determinate or formed in relation to the absolutely formless matter of sense, but which has the minimum of form consistent with its being an object of knowledge at all. It is as yet void of all the qualities which will attach to it, as the process of differentiation, in which, according to Aristotle, definition consists, goes on. . . .

Matter and form, then, are related to each other respectively as the more abstract and more concrete, and as the less or more perfectly or definitely known. The process of thought appears as one not of abstraction but of concretion. . . .

Such a theory of the process of thought does away with the false antithesis between experience and reasoning, between induction and deduction, between relations of ideas and relations of things. (62–63)

The process of thought goes from matter to form; it is "concretion," not abstraction. Such a view destroys false antitheses. All experience is a combination of induction and deduction, it involves interpretation, it brings ideas to bear on new instances. All relations are in a sense "logical": there is no antithesis between "relations between ideas" and "matters of fact." "The world of experience is a world of ideas"—of intelligible things; its order is an intelligible order, an "order of thought." Universals are not apart from things, but are "in" them and are "real."

That which can be predicated of the sensible thing, in other words, that which can be known about it, is the essence, and an object not of sense but of thought. (68)

Substance is individual, but not merely individual; and Green criticizes the sharp dualism between matter and form. Substance is "an individual universalized through its particular relations or qualities." (70)

Thus we see that the *prōtē ousia*, or individual substance, and the *deutera ousia*, or essence constituted by general attributes, are not to be placed, as Aristotle placed them, over against each other, as if one excluded, or even could be present without, the other. They are as necessarily correlative as subject and object, as the self and the world. . . . Each, taken by itself, is matter, as the indeterminate and negation of the knowable. Each, again, so taken, is matter, as the "subject" (*hypokeimenon*), receptive of form—of a form, however, not imposed from without, but projected from within. Each, lastly, may be regarded either as a void "substratum," or as a complex of attributes, according as it is isolated or regarded in the realization which it only attains by passing into its opposite.

The crudity in the philosophical digestion of Aristotle, which prevented the due fusion of the correlative meanings of *ousia*, was the notion—our old enemy—that the individual substance, as matter, was given by sense, and yet had determinate properties. This brings him into collision with his own principle, that the matter of sense, as indeterminate, was unknowable. The "object of sense" and the "individual" he constantly uses as equivalent terms. . . . The *aistheton* with him, as the qualified object of knowledge presented in limits of space and time, thus corresponds to the object of intuition, as distinct from sensation, of Kant. (70–71)

Thus placing ourselves outside the process by which knowledge is developed, we see that its sensuous conditions are only knowable under categories which sense itself does not supply. . . . We learn to know things "piecemeal," and inevitably mistake the piece for the whole. Each object, as known, is indeed in relation to all other things; the divine ether which permeates the world is also in it; but the relation is to us at first potential, not actual, and must always remain so in proportion to the limitation of our knowledge. . . . Finally, the matter, which attaches to it as a supposed object of sensuous perception, unknowable because indeterminate itself, can only be described by its relation to the knowable as that which makes knowledge imperfect. (72–74)

The process of knowing thus proceeds from sense to thought.

It is as the element of imperfection that "matter" appears in the Aristotelian definition of the form or essence as the proper object of knowledge. This, he says, is "substance without matter" (*ousia aneu hyles*). . . . This definition involves a contradiction in terms. . . . In his definition of the essence, however, or thing so known, Aristotle attains the true view of matter, as simply the negation of the knowable. (74)

This true view is clearest in Aristotle in the distinction between the potential and the actual. "Essence" is then not only a "substance dematerialized," but also a potentiality actualized. The sensible is pure potentiality, nothing in itself, determined only in knowledge.

The "potentiality" is nothing apart from that which it becomes. Thus the sensible is nothing by itself, but determined as being, i.e., as an object to a thinking subject, it is the primary *dynamis* of which all knowledge and reality is the gradual actualization. This actualization is not a process of abstraction but of addition. . . . (76)

When we describe our knowledge, therefore, as dependent on matter, because developed through sensuous impressions, all that we really do is to describe it as beginning with what is actually nothing, as becoming what it is not, in short, as progressive. . . . (82–83)

In his later writing, "the sensible" and "the universal" are replaced by "feeling" and "thought," to introduce subjectivistic confusions.

What is Green's problem here? As against the empiricists, he is insisting that "the real is intelligible," not merely sensible—that "the empirical is ideal." He is driven by this emphasis to say, "the intelligible is the real"; it is the object of *knowledge* that is real, and the object of knowledge consists in intelligible relations. Therefore, he concludes, "reality" is synonymous with intelligible relations. In substance the intelligible aspect is "form"; therefore form is alone known, and the sole reality. What then is "matter"? The unknown aspect of substance, the unintelligible aspect—though it is experienced in various nonrational ways. How is it to be *known?* How can we know "matter," if by definition the only knowable aspect of substance is form? How can we know the intelligible relation of form to matter, of intelligibility to that of which it is the expression? Putting the problem in logical terms: how can we know the relation of relations to the terms they relate? We are landed squarely in the fundamental problem of Bradley, with which he wrestled so long, and so futilely. What is "real" is experienced; but what is known is not the same as what is experienced. It somehow ought to be. How can it?

What is the trouble with these dialectical problems in which both Green and Bradley, in different ways, landed themselves? "Reality," we can say, is the world in which we mortals *participate*. Knowing is clearly one form of "participation." "Reality," then, will be the known world in its setting within the experienced world. How do we "participate" in the world at once experienced and known? Bradley's answer was, through the mystic experience, which brings all together. Dewey's answer is, through the experience of art, intelligently reconstructing natural materials. For the one, the ultimate participation is *theoria*; for the other, it is *technē*.

If we consult Aristotle, rather than a modern philosopher of experience, we learn, things are experienced and things are known: both processes take place through *nous*. They can be analyzed by *dianoia* and *logos*. The relation between the intelligible expression of the world and that of which it is the intelligible expression is for Aristotle not a problem to be wrestled with, but a fact to be noted—because Aristotle starts with substance, with what is encountered. Green starts with matter; for him substance becomes identical with intelligibility, with form. That is, for all his polemics, Green started precisely where the empiricists started: he started without intelligibility, without structure, and had to find it elsewhere. Thus does Green illustrate the all-permeating influence of the empiricist tradition on English thinkers. Clearly, this is why he could not accept intelligibility and structure as encountered, but had to go on to discover its "source"—Kant's "reason."

For Green himself, of course, this epistemological position was closely bound up with the most practical moral and religious issues. "It should follow from this that a knowledge of the divine and eternal is not to be attained by turning away from the world of experience, but by understanding it" (84). The great religious principle of the Immanence of God, so fundamental for the nineteenth-century liberal religious thinking that relied on German philosophy, is thus involved in the very structure of all experience. What Neo-Orthodox critics called the "humanism" of that liberal religion, its faith in the potential divinity of man, was precious to Green. He opposed the transcendence involved in Platonistic theology, even that of the Church Fathers.

When, as in the later Alexandrian stage, Platonism became a religion, this defect in its logic appeared as a limitation on the spiritual life of man. It is not a mere paradox to say that its antagonism to Christianity was the reflex of its metaphysical insufficiency. The philosopher could not accept the idea of God, who realized himself in the particularities of nature and man's moral life. . . .

For the false dualism, the Aristotelian formulae go far to provide a substitute. (78–79)

Aristotle's Unmoved Mover ought, in fact, to be an immanent God indwelling the world.

The divine reason, says Aristotle, moves the world as an object of "intellectual desire." Now, as such desire implies a complete reciprocity between the subject and object of it, this properly conveys the idea that God is in the world, "desiring" his own realization, and that this desire underlies its process of development. (85–86)

In fact, of course, Aristotle keeps his God out of all relation to the world, and hence makes him no true actualization of its potentialities.

God with him, as *choristos*, is not merely distinct from the world, but virtually out of relation to it; not the perfect actuality of which the world is the *dyna-*

mis, but an actuality absolutely *aneu dynameōs*. His own conception of substance might have shown him a more excellent way, for substance is *choristos*, as individual and separate from all things else, yet known through relations which are the negative of this mere individuality. (88)

Thus the highest thought with Aristotle—the thought of God, and of the philosopher in his moments of divine abstraction—is either thought about nothing, or thought about the barest and emptiest of sciences. We are here again on the track which leads to a "religion of annihilation." (89)

II

Not Aristotle but Kant, however, was the system and the language Green accepted and used in his later criticism. And with Kant, in spite of his efforts, he took over the elements of "empiricism" there embedded: Kant's strain of psychological subjectivism, and Kant's assumption that particulars—the "sense manifold"—are presented to us without any structure or intelligibility in themselves.

In his *Lectures on the Philosophy of Kant* [5] Green accepts certain of the Kantian positions in epistemology and ethics as "true."

1. He accepts the doctrine of the noumenon as ego: the "timeless self" as a member of the intelligible world and as the "source" of the intelligible order in experience and in our knowledge of it.

2. He agrees that this structure has its "source" in "the unity of the self-conscious subject, present to all intuitions."

3. He accepts the categories as logically *implied in* all experience, but not psychologically derived *from* experience.

4. He accepts the transcendental deduction of the categories, as the objectively necessary conditions of all experience; that is, as logical postulates, as objectively necessary relations in experience.

5. He agrees that objects are laws of relation between phenomena; as such, they need a "source," to be found in the self, not in independent substances.

6. He accepts time and space as necessary logical systems of objects, as real relations between them; they are psychologically learned, but they are logically prior to the learning.

Green tried to make Kant consistently a logical analysis of the "necessary conditions" of the experienced world, of the structure there implied; he tried to take all Kant's presuppositions as necessary logical

[5] *Works*, II, pp. 2–155.

conditions of all cognitive experience. In this, he resembled the contemporary German Neo-Kantians, especially the Marburg School. He was not wholly successful in this endeavor: he still felt these conditions, this structure, needed a "source": it was not enough that they are found in experience by analysis. Green was still caught in the problem, "how the mind comes to be furnished with ideas"—the Lockean problem. Structure and relations need a "substratum," the Self; they cannot really be "*in*" particulars, they must come from somewhere else.

Green's conscious aim, he states, is to remove the "empiricism" from Kant: to remove all traces of a psychological analysis of knowledge, and leave a purely logical analysis of its assumptions—to remove the Locke and Hume from Kant. Green had the insight to recognize this remnant of empiricism left in Kant's transcendental analysis; he thought of himself as "developing his meaning," as "removing the survivals of a way of thinking, it was the true result of his philosophy to set aside," and thus to make Kant a "true idealist." In other words, Green saw clearly the difficulties in Kant's analysis, and the way out.

Green saw as these Lockean elements left in Kant, and as interfering with the statement of a "true idealism"—or naturalism:

1. Kant's dualism between "form" and "matter," between the structure found and the "data" of sensation. The "twofold origin of knowledge is unsatisfactory"; it leads in Kant to the need for "unifying schemata" to put the two together. The categories are really different types of unified structure discovered—Green found this view admirable. This dualism appears as the dualism between "intuition" and "conception"; objects are taken as independently given, actually as "feelings." Really, says Green, there is no separate "intuition" of reals, independent of structure—of Locke's "substances that operate on us whether we will or no."

Kant has in fact, says Green, two views of objects: the first, of objects as presented; the second, of objects as connected into an intelligible system by the categories: i.e., as individual, and as related, corresponding to Locke's "ideas of sensation" and "ideas of reflexion." But individuality, to be given "here and now," already implies structure and relations. There can be no real separation between the two, save in analysis. There is no such thing as "mere thought" or "mere feeling."

We hold that these phrases represent abstractions to which no reality corresponds, either in the facts of the world or in the consciousness to which those facts are relative. (*Prolegomena*, sec. 51)

This notion of an independent "intuition" leads to the notion of a "*Ding-an-sich*," a pure particular without determination, and hence never experienced, but quite unknowable. It leads to the opposition between two sources of knowledge, "an opposition between the source of our experience, *qua sensation*, and the source of it, *qua order* of sensations" (*Works* II, 28). Actually, there is no opposition between subject and object, which is a distinction *within* experience, not *between* experience and an unknown *X*—an insistence common to naturalisms as different as those of Dewey and Heidegger.

The [true] cause of any phenomenon, on its material as well as on its formal side, as sensation no less than as conceived, lies in its relation to all phaenomena, in the system of nature, and this the unchangeable subject renders possible. (II, 30)

2. The second Lockean dualism in Kant is that between judgments as universal and necessary, and as particular and contingent, as *a priori* and as *a posteriori*—Hume's "relations between ideas" and "matters of fact." All experience is in fact universal, revealing permanent relations. Hence universals can be said to come "from experience."

3. There is the dualism between synthetic and analytical judgments, corresponding to Locke's "instructive" and "trifling" propositions. This is really a matter of the mere degree of complexity.

(a) "All bodies are extended," is an analytical judgment according to Kant; (b) "All bodies are heavy," a synthetical judgment. This cannot mean that "extension" is included in the meaning of the term "body," while "heaviness" is not. Such inclusion is relative to the individual's state of mind. To educated men both predicates, to uneducated neither, are included in what they understand by "body." . . .
Both judgments are synthetical, in the sense that in them thought goes beyond the *subject-conception*, . . . Both are analytical as implying an analysis of that mere consciousness of "something there" with which our knowledge begins.[6] (II, 61–62)

[6] Green thus anticipates the controversial views of Willard V. Quine. Selsam summarizes Green's argument: "Green's doctrine of judgment, and his difference from Kant, thus stand out quite clearly. A consistent idealism cannot distinguish between *a posteriori* and *a priori* judgments, since it recognizes in the beginning no distinction between intuition and conception, or that which is given and that which the mind adds of itself. Since nothing is given apart from thought, there is nothing to which thought can

4. There is the dualism between the inner and the outer sense, with time and space as the "forms" respectively of each. This is based on the Lockean assumption of an "external world" and "mind." Kant's trouble was that he never really gave up the notion that the sensuous or determinable is given to the understanding as a manifold in space and a manifold in time.

Though considering it merely determin*able*, he yet assigns to it such actual determinations as relation in space and relation in time constitute. (II, 69)

The true difference between outer and inner sense Green finds to lie

in the relation of the object as an object of consciousness, not in consciousness as apart from the object. [It is a distinction] between the consciousness of objects as related to each other, not to the conscious subject, and the consciousness of objects as changes in the state of the conscious subject. Thus it is really a distinction not between two sorts of sense as such, but between two sorts of intellectual interpretation of sense, two functions of the understanding in the connection of phaenomena. (II, 65–66)

Externality is a relation of body to body, not of body to mind. The world is "external" to the organism, not to "mind"—it is accessible to mind. Green thus avoids both phenomenalism and subjectivism—and what he calls a "false realism." The "external world" is "real"; but what is it? the relations existing only "for thought"—relations that are accessible and knowable to mind. For Green, *esse est intelligi*.

In all his criticisms of Kant, Green is opposing Kant's absolute dualisms, between matter and mind, sense and thought, perception and conception, outer and inner, etc.; which all go back to the assumption that something is furnished "*to* experience" from outside, on which the experiencing subject works. Against Kant, he insists that these are all distinctions found *within* experience, by logical analysis; they are not psychological or physiological distinctions between experience and some presumed "source" of experience.

The long wrestling with Kant's compromises has shown that there are two ways of escaping them. The first is that of a frank realism: we

---

add something of its own, and the dichotomy falls. Likewise with synthetical and analytical judgments, no absolute distinction can be made, for synthesis and analysis are but two facets of every judgment. This is the beginning of that complete revolution in English logic, represented especially in the work of Bradley and Bosanquet, which was the result of the development of idealism away from Kant, and in which Green's work was largely instrumental." Howard Selsam, *T.H. Green*, p. 37.

are dealing throughout with an experienced world, our observations of which are discovered to be embedded in a structure of relations that is directly accessible to mind. The second is the way of "idealism": we are dealing throughout with the experiencing subject, and the system of nature of our knowledge is "rendered possible by an unchanging subject." The logical structure in it will then be a "structure of thought." But it will not be "rendered possible" by man's individual knowing, but by an Eternal "Subject."

In both cases, of realism and idealism alike, the human mind is learning to know an objective system, either of "nature" or of "Eternal Thought." What is the real difference between these two views—granted the language is different? If everything is "natural," "nature" ceases to have meaning as a *distinctive* category, and becomes the most inclusive category of all, equivalent to what the Greek tradition called "being." If everything is "thought," then "thought" likewise ceases to have meaning as a *distinctive* category, and is equally equivalent to "being."

What, then, is the ultimate difference between "naturalism" and "idealism"? If the logic of the two positions is followed out, the answer seems to be, nothing. In any case, the intellectual problems faced by both turn out to be identical. Why, then, did Green oppose "naturalism"? Because for him a system of "thought" seemed accessible to the human mind in a way that a system of "nature" did not. Why this difference? Because "nature" and "thought" are still divorced for Green. Man's "mind" is a part, not of "nature," but of "Eternal Thought"—though on his own view Eternal Thought is itself the constitutive part of nature. Green maintained that nature is not "logical," or intelligible, without a structure contributed by "thought." Yet there could be no "nature" apart from this "thought." If this is true, how could it be "not logical" apart from it? This seems self-contradictory.

Thus Green, by his acute critical and analytic procedure, seems to make clear that "idealism" is either identical with "naturalism" or else self-contradictory. Of course, the human mind being held back by practical considerations as it is, preventing it from following out the full implications of its own assumptions, idealism has ended by being mostly self-contradictory.

III

We have said that when its logic is pushed idealism turns out to be either identical with naturalism or else self-contradictory. Now, the major reason why Green himself objected to "naturalism" was that nineteenth-century science entertained so inadequate a conception of "nature." The "nature" of the nineteenth-century scientific philosophies offered a "nature" without any logical structure. These philosophies Green undertook to criticize in terms of their popular exponent in England, Herbert Spencer.[7] He did so in the only popular articles he published his lifetime, three pieces in the *Contemporary Review* for December 1877, and March and July 1878; a fourth was left unpublished because of Lewes' death in 1878.

Green's main criticism is that Spencer and Lewes stand for an evolutionary empiricism. Spencer is an "empiricist"; and not a consistent empiricist, like Hume (Green had written the long three-hundred-page Introduction to his edition with Grose of Hume's writings, in 1874), ending in a world still accessible to mind; but ending without either a world (without structure) or mind. Spencer is a Lockean empiricist, operating with an "external world" opposed to "mind." But for him mind, as for Locke, can know only its own contents; so he ends in the same contradictions as Locke.

The one novelty in Spencer is his attempt to sketch the evolutionary *genesis* of mind and its categories. Now, empirical psychology, thinks Green, is bad enough; empirical psychogeny is worse! It brings in all the confusions of the genetic fallacy Green always opposed. Spencer tries to derive the system of knowledge with its logical order from an alogical "nature." But for knowledge, nature must be at least potentially "logical." It must at least be "logiscible." Now, Locke could not derive knowledge from sensation alone, from "feeling," for the simplest feeling presupposes already a logical system. Mill could not derive the uniformity of nature from "induction," for induction presupposes it. These points of Green are all well taken: empiricism did operate with an alogical, meaningless world, in which the experience of logic was unintelligible. Green puts it, "Given a world of in-

---

[7] "Mr. Herbert Spencer and Mr. G.H. Lewes: Their Application of the Doctrine of Evolution to Thought," *Works*, I, pp. 373–520.

telligible relations, it is easy to account for knowledge." Naturalism of course has taken it as given. Why did not Green? In point of fact, he did. Green's problem is, not how "the cosmos arises in consciousness," but "how the consciousness for which the cosmos eternally exists becomes partially ours." Why can Green not take his "Eternal Consciousness," the "Absolute," as the intelligible system of nature? Because for Green nature is still distinct from mind, it has no intelligible system of itself, its system or structure needs a "source." Thus Green himself remains a Lockean, and commits the same genetic fallacy.

Green begins with his first principle: "Locke showed, once and for all, that the object of knowledge is 'in' consciousness"—that is, it is accessible to mind. "Beginning with a doctrine which, if it means anything, means that only as an element in a world of consciousness can any material relation be known, we are asked to explain consciousness itself as one sort of material relation; which is as if a physiologist should explain the vital process by some particular motion of a muscle which it renders possible" (I, 377f.). "Mind" is an objective logical order. It must be determinate: nature can be called a "realm of mind." This seems sound; but Green confuses this objective "mind" with the human mind. Evolution involves the physical genesis of "mind." Green counters, the human mind can have a genesis only in the logical sense, in which Spinoza in Book II of his *Ethics* calls the order of nature the "origin and genesis of the human mind." The genesis of the human mind cannot be "evolution," which Spencer brings in like "a magic charm." Evolution implies a continuity, an identity in difference; and there is none between a sequence of feelings, as physiological products, and the unity of consciousness, or knowledge. Green here assumes, of course, as usual, that natural processes are in themselves alogical: an assumption he shares with Spencer. Green is denying the appearance of novelty, of what was to be called in the twentieth century "emergence." "Naturalism," as it was in that later generation worked out, holds that prehuman nature is indeed not "logical," but is "logiscible," not understood, but intelligible. Green, however, can find no potentiality in Kant: this suggests how different his mature view might have been had he continued to use Aristotle instead of Kant.

Both Spencer and Lewes hold that "the real is what is given in feeling," in the feeling of resisting force. Green denies that feeling or sensation is "knowledge" of the real at all. "Real objects are given only in judgment, in thought." Sensation is not knowledge at all, holds Green—taking a position Dewey was to continue. Feeling is not even an element in the perception of a "fact." For feelings are always particulars, and perception, holds Green—with Aristotle—is of universal relations. "Facts" are elements in a system of universals, of structure. A sensation cannot be an element of a perceived "fact," only the fact that a sensation is felt.

We shall find reason for holding that, whereas perception in its simplest form is already a consciousness of relation, a sensation neither is so, nor, remaining a mere sensation, can become one of the related elements of which in every perception there is a consciousness. . . .

That all perception is consciousness of relation, will probably find general acceptance. Perception is of facts—a perceived object is resoluble into certain facts—and facts consist in relations. But upon what ground can we doubt that a sensation may—not to say must—enter into such a relation as one of its constituents? When, feeling a pain or pleasure of heat, I perceive it to be connected with the action of approaching the fire, am I not perceiving a relation of which one constituent, at any rate, is a simple sensation? The true answer is, No. That which is perceived to be related to the action mentioned is not a sensation, but the fact that a sensation is felt—a fact to which the designation "vivid," appropriate to the sensation, is inappropriate. If, in order to make sure of the existence of the relation, I try walking backwards and forwards, out of the range of the fire's heat and into it again, the related facts are equally before my mind all the time. It is not the case that one of them vanishes from consciousness and returns again, as would be the case if one of them were the sensation which ceases when I have withdrawn to a certain distance from the fire. On the contrary, the consciousness of it as a related fact becomes most clear just when, with a last step backward from the fire, the feeling of warmth passes away—clearness of perception increasing as vividness of sensation grows less. We conclude, then, that "facts of feeling," as perceived, are not feelings as felt; that, though perception presupposes feeling, yet the feeling only survives in perception as transformed by a consciousness, other than feeling, into a fact which remains for that consciousness when the feeling has passed. (I, 411–12)

Sensations, as Dewey later put it, are "had," while perceptions "know" facts. Sensations to be sure precede and accompany perception.

To feel warm, then, is not the same as to perceive that I am warm, or that my body is so. The perception is of something qualified by the feeling, or of the feeling as a *change* from a previous state. . . . In the perception the feeling is no longer what it is as a feeling, but takes its character from a relation to something else. . . . The contrary persuasion is the result of our having no words to express sensations proper, except those already assigned to the perception of sensible objects. . . .

The affection of the retina by rays of light proceeding from certain points is not in itself a recognition of the points from which the rays proceed, or of relation between them. Yet, from speaking of the affection as an image, we are apt to think of it as if it were such a recognition. Hence our habit of overlooking the essential difference between the "phenomenon" as it issues from the process of attention—the proper object of perception—and the sensation which precedes, or any of the sensations which accompany it, including the last. The sensation has no parts, or related elements, as the phenomenon has. . . . A plurality of objects is a plurality for consciousness only in virtue of a twofold intellectual act. In the first place, upon the simple visual sensation there must have supervened successive acts of attention, in which what by anticipation are called the parts of the luminous area are traversed (we say "by anticipation" because it is only through the process of attention that for consciousness they become such parts); and, secondly, upon these successive acts there must have supervened a synthesis by which the elements, successively detached in the acts of attention, are held together in negation of the succession as coexisting parts of a whole. . . .

It appears, then, that perception in its simplest form . . . neither is nor contains sensation. This is true of it in each of its stages. It is true of that original interpretation of the sensation as a *change*, which excites the attention necessary to discover what the change or thing changed is, and which must be other than the sensation so interpreted. It is true again of that process of attention itself in which momentarily changing sensations become facts determined by comparison with other experience. (I, 413–16)

In other words, there can be no "perception" without conception, or "meaning." One detects the influence of this view of Green's in Dewey's position that sensations are not knowledge at all, but rather the stimulus to knowledge. It is to be noted that Green here still takes sensations as relationless or structureless in themselves; the relations or "meaning" must come from outside, from "thought." Yet of course there is in Green's world no intelligible place for such isolated particulars; for that world is "real" only as held together by the Eternal Consciousness.

I V

Green's analyses reach their focus in his Lectures on Mill,[8] which exhibit his keenest criticism, more devastating than Mill on Hamilton.

[8] *Works*, II, pp. 195–306.

It is based on the idea of nature as a system of related particulars. Green opposes, first, Mill's observationalism, his view that the system of science comes from relationless and structureless particulars, or feelings. Green contends that the system can come only from particulars already related through an intelligible structure. Secondly, Green opposes Mill's nominalistic logic, his "Scholasticism"; that is, his position that the function of thought is to "abstract" attributes from the given, springing from his assumption, shared with Locke and Hume, of the sharp contrast between the sensible thing and the work of thought. Nominalism, Green suggests, is the legitimate offspring of the syllogistic logic; it recognizes that the function of logic is merely to analyze the meaning of "names," as contrasted with Green's own logic of relations, in which thought is no mere "abstraction."

Mill takes logic as the science of intellectual method. But, Green observes, every method implies a metaphysics. Mill, however, tried to avoid one, with the result that he made the metaphysical presuppositions of the empiricist tradition. Mill's metaphysical errors are:

1. His acceptance of the Lockean "idea," as alone known, but at the same time the effect of the real. For him, a phenomenon is both a feeling and the thing felt; he wavers between the "false idealism," in which "everything is a state of consciousness," and a "true idealism," in which "everything is related to consciousness," and hence accessible to mind.

2. Mill's false antithesis between thought and things. Mill is at times a realist, holding that propositions have existential import, and state the real relations of things—as that "gold is yellow." But Mill denies real things have any knowable relations. Only the coexistence of impressions in the mind is knowable. Green's alternative is, the system of nature is quite "objective," but it is not "external" to mind, and hence inaccessible to it.

3. Mill is confused on the categories. He should have started with propositions, and classified names according to their function in propositions.[9] From propositions we can then derive the "primary relations, without which there can be no system of nature at all." The categories are really the logical presuppositions of experience. Mill goes from names to things to propositions, and identifies the "origin"

[9] Green's doctrine that the proposition or judgment is primary is of course derived from Hegelian logic. It was anticipated by Thomas Reid (see Volume II, Book VI, chapter 6, section I).

of the categories, which is actually logical, with the psychological process of learning. Mill takes the categories as the "summa genera of things," the outcome of knowledge; for him they come at the end. Green takes the categories as really presupposed in all knowledge, the "relations of formal concepts." For him, they come, not at the end, but at the beginning of knowledge: they must be used in knowing anything at all.

4. Mill retains the abstraction of the "thing-in-itself," because he views cause and substance, not as relations *in* experience, but as causes *of* experience. Green maintains that mind and things are "real" only as parts of a single system of relations. Yet is not Green's own view pretty much like Mill's? What is the difference between saying that relations need a "cause," and that they need a "source"? Mill sums up his view in the antithesis between reality and theory: things are first real, and then we formulate a theory about them.

Upon Mill's doctrine, that things really exist quite independently of thought or conception, and that the latter merely results from impressions that things make on us through sensation, neither the Copernican nor any other theory can be accounted for, for every theory corrects sense, or rather (since mere sense gives nothing to correct), the inferences from sense. In truth the reality of things is their determination by each other as constituents of one order, a determination which only exists for thought. It is not that there is first the reality of things, and then a theory about it. The reality *is* a theory. No motion is properly a phaenomenon, but a relation between phaenomena constituted by a conceiving mind; a way of holding together phaenomena in thought. Just as the motion of a planet is a way of holding together certain phaenomena, the only possible mode of holding these phaenomena together as one, so the Copernican system is the only way of holding the planetary motions together as one, as changing appearances of one principle. It is a reality (not a mere theory *about* reality). (II, 268–69)

Green concentrates his fire on Mill's nominalistic logic. Mill has two different views of propositions, that they state the relation of attributes, and that they state the relation between phenomena, or feelings. Green counters, every proposition states the relation between an object and its attributes; it is "the thought of an object under relations." A proposition does not relate an idea by means of the copula with another idea; there is only one idea, "the conception of the real relations between the attributes." Green here foreshadows the view of judgment Bradley was to elaborate.

Green attacks Mill's view of the nature of inference and generalization. There are three views, all to be found in Mill:

The question at issue concerns the nature of "generalization." Is it (a) a process from concrete individuals, by omission of their distinguishing attributes, to a class; or (b) a process from a constantly observed sequence of one sensible event on another to the involuntary expectation of one upon the recurrence of the other; or (c) a process from a multitude of separate events to their uniform conditions (relations) or single cause? (II, 273)

Is the right view that of the Schoolmen, of Hume, or of Kant?

Mill has (a) in his theory of the syllogism, and (b) in his theory of induction. Green states (c):

The inference to the mortality of Socrates rests on the observation neither of all the particulars nor of many particulars, as all or as many; it is neither an *epagogē dia pantōn*, which is no inference at all, nor an *epagogē dia pollōn*, which can yield no scientific certainty; it has nothing to do with the quantity of the particulars, but only with their kind; nothing to do with how often an event happens, but only with the question, what it really is that happens in each event. Inference is a process from the "*ordo ad nos*" or "*ad sensum*" to the "*ordo ad universum*," from the phaenomenon in its proper sense to its conditions, a process to which the mere repetition of occurrences in *ordine ad sensum* contributes nothing. The inference to all possible cases of a like event, so far as made at all, is made in the first complete discovery of the conditions of the single event. Once know what death really is in the case of a single man, i.e. the conditions on which it depends, then I learn no more by seeing any number of men die, I do not become any more certain that Socrates will die. Whatever uncertainty there may be as to the mortality of Socrates consists in the uncertainty whether the ascertained conditions of mortality are present in his case or no; whether the resemblance of Socrates to the men who have died (or, it may be, to single men who have died, for the number of cases makes no difference) is a resemblance in respect of the conditions on which mortality depends. No doubt, in the process of ascertaining what these conditions are, a great number of cases may have to be observed in order to the exclusion of unessential circumstances. (II, 275)

Inference lies, not (as Mill says) in the generalization from observed instances to all, but (a) in the discovery of the real conditions of the observed instances, (b) in the discovery whether other apparently like instances are really like. Given the real similarity of the other instances, there is no inference to them. (II, 277)

Hence there is no difference between inference in mathematics and in natural science.

The inference in natural science no less than in geometry is to a universal, to an eternal and unchangeable relation; and in natural science it may be from a single phaenomenon, just as in geometry from a single construction. The difference lies in the dependence of the ascertained conditions upon other conditions in the one case, their independence in the other. (II, 278)

The *nous* of Plato and Aristotle just sees the structure there!

This brings Green to Mill's theory of induction and of the uniformity of nature. The latter axiom is

an assumption that things resembling each other in a great many points will resemble each other also in others, or that what has happened often will happen always, that the future will resemble the past. If we ask [Mill] for the ground of such an assumption, we are referred to *induction per enumerationem simplicem*. A rule which is to enable us to dispense with such *enumeratio* is itself founded on it. . . . But how do we know that the instances, with the examination of which we are always dispensing on the strength of the rule, might not be just what would invalidate it if they were examined? . . . A bundle of expectations has nothing in common with the ground of inductive reasoning, as it actually exists. This ground is more fitly expressed as the conception of "the unity of the world" than as that of "the uniformity of nature," at any rate if the latter is supposed to be equivalent to the assumption that the future will resemble the past. The future might be exceedingly unlike the past (in the ordinary sense of the words) without any violation of the principle of inductive reasoning, rightly understood. If the "likeness" mean . . . that different experiences of the future will be part of one system with the present, the result of conditions that now are, it is true; but to such a system and conditions the distinction of past and future does not apply; they are eternal. (282)

Green has his own answer:

If, then, the principle of induction—call it the conception of the unity of the world, or what you will—is neither derived from observation, as Mill says, nor born ready-made with every man, how (it may be asked) do we come by it? The answer is, that it is implicit in the simplest act of knowledge (When the human animal begins to know, I do not pretend to say). (II, 284)

Green sums up:

The business of induction . . . is to find a true and adequate description of the single case, to find the sum of its conditions. This done, everything is done. . . . The only sense in which generalization, as a process from the observed to the unobserved, has a place in knowledge, is as an anticipation of what results from the combination of conditions already known in their separate, but not in their joint, action, i.e. as the process which Mill calls "deduction." (II, 293–94)

The consequences for Mill's doctrine of causation are clear.

In this lies the difference between "a cause" and "a reason," in the confusion between which the great error of ancient philosophy lay (though Aristotle distinguishes *aition gnōseōs* and *aition genesiōs*). From a reason you can infer the consequent, from a cause you cannot infer the effect. . . . So Hume said, "No idea or object considered in itself can give a reason for drawing a conclusion beyond it. . . ." We reply, that "no idea or object" *can* be "considered in itself"; and just because it cannot, every "idea and object" (every experience in the way of feeling, every object to which we refer such experience) compels a conclusion beyond it. (II, 300–1)

Causation is in itself a "logical" or intelligible relation; Green means by "cause" as the sum of the conditions of a phenomenon a *formal cause.*

The absolute antithesis between the relation of reason and consequences and that of cause and effect is part of the false antithesis between thought and reality. . . . Once apprehend (what is implied in all the teachings of science) that there are no isolations or separations in nature, that "individuals" are mere logical fictions, that no event happens which is not determined by, and does not contribute to determine, the whole system of nature . . . the notion that the relation of cause and effect is fitly described as that of an invariably preceding to an invariably following event must be given up. Any effect in its reality is its cause. What is the cause of water? . . . The cause of water is the combination of hydrogen and oxygen in certain proportions. . . . There is no antecedence in time of cause to effect. . . . The view of cause as an event uniformly preceding another event, is incompatible with the definition of it as the sum of the conditions of a phaenomenon. (II, 302–3)

V

Green is preeminently the critic of empiricism and its relationless world. He insists, the real world is the world experienced; and the experienced world is a world of intelligible relations, a "logical order," a "system of thought." In the simplest bit of the experienced world, in a "perceived fact," logical relations enter in.

He starts (like Kant) with the empiricist position: "the experienced world is a mere series of feelings." He then insists, there are no "mere feelings," but only feelings related in a logical system. Then he arrives at the position, that strictly speaking there are no "feelings" at all—they form no part of the intelligible world, which is alone "real." The experienced world is the known world, and the object of knowledge must be a system of universals. The particulars (in the language of experience, the "feelings") have dropped out, and are left hanging. Where can they go? Even perception is of universals, not of sensations or feelings.

At times Green says, the real world is the world of related particulars, experience is of related feelings: "feeling and thought are mutually dependent, and imply each other." But his whole emphasis is, feelings include relations; do relations imply feelings? No! Feelings are not "real" as felt, but only as a meaning, a universal—only "in their relationships." Green's argument runs: there is something in experience "other than" thought, feeling; but the "reality" of feeling lies in its "otherness" to thought, in its relations. Green is most consistent when he says, sensations are not elements in "experience" at all, but are part of a physical, organic process, certain *changes* in the body; and the body is a system of relationships.

In other words, Green takes "experience" as itself identical with thought; the real world is the intelligible world. Matter, *hylē*, has dropped out completely: it is merely the potentially intelligible, the less known. Aristotle held, all knowledge is of universals, but only related particulars exist. The object of knowledge is hence not an "intelligible world," but the intelligible aspect of the natural world of particular individuals. St. Thomas, interestingly, faced the same problem as Green (in *De Veritate*, V): particulars are never known directly, but only "felt." They can be known only by a "certain reflection"; and St. Thomas concludes, there "must have been" particulars to start the process of perceiving universals going.

In other words—traditional in character—Green is a Platonist and an Augustinian: for him the human mind in knowing establishes relations with the Eternal Mind. Green is offering a Victorian version of the Augustinian theory of knowledge as a Divine Illumination. The parallel is fascinating to work out. Against Green, the next generation saw the greatest of the English Idealists, F. H. Bradley, start by vindicating the reality of "feeling" or particulars; for him the "real world" must include feeling as well as thought.

6

Idealistic Social Philosophy and Bernard Bosanquet

ASIDE FROM his keen criticisms of empiricism, in Hume and Mill, of the evolutionary naturalism of Herbert Spencer, George Henry Lewes, and of Kant himself, T.H. Green's chief influence on the broader currents of thought of his day was as the first major critic of Utilitarian libertarianism—the laisser-faire individualism associated with the classical economists and with the Victorian Liberals. In this Green was beginning at the point where Stuart Mill had arrived after 1848, and continuing his reconstruction of the tradition of political liberalism into a rather more collectivistic form. In both ethics and political theory Green was as devoted to human freedom as the Mill of the *Essay on Liberty* of 1859; but he drew upon certain Hegelian ideas to introduce a more socialized conception of the nature of human freedom. The moral ideal for him was self-realization, the development of the moral capacities of one's true self; and this implied institutional arrangements that would foster man's moral self-realization. Green returns to the classical conception of human freedom as the freedom to act rationally, and he follows Hegel in determining what "rationality" is concretely in the moral life from the institutions of a rationally organized society.

In this conception, Green was followed by the young Bradley of the *Ethical Studies* of 1876, especially in "My Station and its Duties"; and by William Wallace, in his *Lectures and Essays* (1898). Finally, the chief work of Bernard Bosanquet's *The Philosophical Theory of the State* (1899), drew the threads together in a social philosophy of a definitely Hegelian and much more conservative stamp. It is hardly too much to say that, aside from its function in the reconstructing of the religious

Originally published in *Philosophy and Phenomenological Research*, XXVI, no. 4 (June 1966), pp. 473–502. Reprinted by permission.

tradition, the cultural impact of Idealism in Britain came from this continuance of the socializing of the cherished conception of freedom which Stuart Mill had already begun. Aside from its contribution to the working out of the new twentieth-century naturalisms, the enduring contribution of Idealism to the intellectual life of Britain was to furnish rational justification for the restrictions on laisser-faire practical men were demanding, and for the beginnings, modest as they were at first, of the present British welfare state. This was the function of its social and political philosophy.[1]

I

T.H. Green's major work in political philosophy is the lectures he delivered in 1879–80 on *The Principles of Political Obligation*, following those on Kant's moral theory. It is significant Green developed his liberal social theory, like his ethics, out of Kant rather than directly out of Hegel, like Bosanquet. Green considers first "The Grounds of Political Obligation," treating the moral function served by law and the rational justification for obeying the law. He examines the theories of Spinoza, Hobbes, Locke, and Rousseau. He rejects both the Utilitarian rationale of the service of happiness, and the Kantian abstract reason of duty. Finally he examines in detail the chief rights and obligations enforced in civilized states, considering their justification in terms of his theory.

Bosanquet remarks, of his more Hegelian views, "the essence of the theory here presented is to be found not merely in Plato and in Aristotle, but in very many modern writers, more especially in Hegel, T.H. Green, Bradley, and Wallace." [2] This underlines the Greek foundation of much of Green's view, already clear from chapter 5, section 1. Indeed, the whole moral ideal of self-realization of the Idealists, combined with a secondary recognition of the place of self-in-

---

[1] T.H. Green, *Lectures on the Principles of Political Obligation*, in *Works*, II, pp. 334–549. F.H. Bradley, *Ethical Studies*, Essay V, "My Station and its Duties" (1876; revised ed., Oxford, 1927). William Wallace, *Lectures and Essays* (London, 1898), esp. "Our Natural Rights," p. 213, and "The Relation of Fichte and Hegel to Socialism," p. 427. Bernard Bosanquet, *The Philosophical Theory of the State* (London, 1899; 2nd ed., 1910; 3rd ed., 1920). See L.T. Hobhouse, *The Metaphysical Theory of the State* (London, 1917). On the social philosophy of the Idealists, see Frederick P. Harris, *The Neo-Idealist Political Theory: Its Continuity with the British Tradition* (New York, 1944); A.J.M. Milne, *The Social Philosophy of English Idealism* (London, 1963).

[2] Bosanquet, *Philosophical Theory of the State*, Preface to 1st ed., p. viii.

terest and pleasure, is fundamentally Aristotelian, however filtered through Hegel's adaptation.

Moral goodness is an attribute of character.

But it is impossible that an action should be done for the sake of its goodness, unless it has been previously contemplated as good for some other reason than that which consists in being done for the sake of its goodness. It must have been done . . . irrespectively of being done from this which we ultimately come to regard as the highest motive. . . . A prior morality, founded on interests which are other than the pure interest in being good, and governed by rules of conduct relative to a standard of goodness other than that which makes it depend on this interest, is the condition of there coming to be a character governed by interest in an ideal of goodness. Otherwise this ideal would be an empty one.[3]

The morality of goodness, when achieved, criticizes the morality of other interests. The other interests are not rejected as of no moral value; they become elements in a character governed by the ideal of goodness. Thus Green brings together formal and material elements in his ideal. The latter consist of (1) rules embodied in positive law and enforced on the individual by a political superior, and (2) rules subject only to a "law of opinion"—moral rather than political obligations.

What then is of permanent moral value in the institutions of political life? Now the condition of a moral life is the possession of will and reason. "All moral ideas have their origin in reason, i.e., in the idea of a possible self-perfection to be attained by the moral agent." All particular moral ideas "arise, as the individual's conception of the society on the well-being of which his own depends, and of the constituents of that well-being, becomes wider and fuller; and they are embodied in the laws, institutions, and social expectation, which make conventional morality" (337–38).

The value then of the institutions of civil life lies in their operation as giving reality to these capacities of will and reason, and enabling them to be really exercised. In their general effect, . . . they render it possible for a man to be freely determined by the idea of a possible satisfaction of himself, instead of being driven this way and that by external forces . . . and they enable him to realize his reason, i.e., his idea of self-perfection, by acting as a member of a social organization in which each contributes to the better-being of all the rest. (338–39)

[3] *Principles of Political Obligation*, in *Works*, II, p. 336.

Certain rights and obligations *should* be enforced; some are actually enforced. The former have been known as *jus naturae*, which is thus a standard for criticizing positive law.

There is a system of rights, and obligations which *should* be maintained by law, whether it is so or not, and which may properly be called "natural"; not in the sense in which the term "natural" would imply that such a system ever did exist or could exist independently of force exercised by society over individuals, but "natural" because necessary to the end which it is the vocation of human society to realize.

The "jus naturae," thus understood, is at once distinguished from the sphere of moral duty, and relative to it. It is distinguished from it because admitting of enforcement by law. Moral duties do not admit of being so enforced. . . . When obligations are spoken of . . . as part of the "jus naturae" correlative to rights, they must always be understood not as moral duties, not as relative to states of will, but as relative to outward acts, of which the performance or omission can and should be enforced. . . . There is a moral duty in regard to [legal] obligations, but there can be no [legal] obligation in regard to moral duties. (339–40)

Green sums up the relation between moral duties and legal obligations:

We begin the ethical criticism of law with two principles: (1) that nothing but external acts can be matter of "obligation"; and (2) that . . . the question what should be made matter of [legal] obligation . . . must be considered with reference to the moral end, as serving alone law and the obligations imposed by law have their value. (340–41)

Green quotes Henrici in his fundamental principle: "Right is that which is really necessary to the maintenance of the material conditions essential to the existence and perfection of human personality" (341*n*). "What sort of outward acts *should* be matter of legal obligation?" Green asks. His answer runs:

Those acts only should be matter of legal injunction or prohibition of which the performance or omission, irrespectively of the motive from which it proceeds, is so necessary to the existence of a society in which the moral end stated can be realized, that it is better for them to be done or omitted from that unworthy motive which consists in fear or hope of legal consequences than not to be done at all. . . . We hold that those actions or omissions should be made [legal] obligations which, when made obligations, serve a certain moral end; that this end is the ground or justification or rationale of legal obligation. (344)

Green is attacking the prevalent view, which he calls "a one-sided view of the function of laws; the view, viz., that its only business is to prevent interference with the liberty of the individual." This theory, he holds, has done its work. It "now tends to become obstructive, because in fact advancing civilization brings with it more and more interference with the liberty of the individual to do as he likes, and this theory affords a reason for resisting all positive reforms, all reforms which involve an action of the state in the way of promoting conditions favorable to the moral life."

The true ground of objection to "paternal government" is not that it violates the "laissez-faire" principle and conceives that its office is to make people good, to promote morality, but that it rests on a misconception of morality. The real function of government being to maintain conditions of life in which morality shall be possible, and morality consisting in the disinterested performance of self-imposed duties, "paternal government" does its best to make it impossible by narrowing the room for the self-imposition of duties and for the play of disinterested motives. (345–46)

Green is very clear that "all rights are relative to moral ends or duties."

The claim or right of the individual to have certain powers secured to him by society, and the counter-claim of society to exercise certain powers over the individual, alike rest on the fact that these powers are necessary to the fulfillment of man's vocation as a moral being, to an effectual self-devotion to the work of developing the perfect character in himself and others. (347)

Individual rights have generally been asserted as deduced from certain prior "natural rights"; on this ground political obligation was presented through the seventeenth and eighteenth centuries till Hume began to apply the "utilitarian" theory. The latter is right in holding that "these powers are necessary to the fulfillment of man's vocation as a moral being." But "Utilitarianism proper recognizes no vocation of man but the attainment of pleasure and the avoidance of pain." Green agrees with this view in opposing natural rights. Granted all rights can be derived from such primitive rights; what is their obligation?

From his moral theory Green takes the notion:

The conception expressed by the "should be" is . . . the conception of an ideal, unattained condition of himself, as an absolute end. Without this conception the recognition of a power as a right would be impossible. A power on the part of anyone is so recognized by others, as one which should be exercised, when these others regard it as in some way a means to that ideal good of themselves which they alike conceive; and the possessor of the power comes to regard it as a right through consciousness of its being thus recognized as contributory to a good in which he too is interested. (350)

All rights are social, and come from membership in society.

No one can have a right except (1) as a member of a society, and (2) of a society in which some common good is recognized by the members of the society as their own ideal good, as that which should be for each of them. (*Ibid.*)

There ought to be rights, because the moral personality—the capacity on the part of an individual for making a common good his own—ought to be developed; and it is developed through rights; i.e. through the recognition by members of a society of powers in each other contributory to a common good, and the regulation of those powers by that recognition. (351)

The capacity for being determined by a good so recognized is what constitutes personality in the ethical sense. (350)

Rights, as the Utilitarians and Mill held, are teleological and social; but the end for Green is self-realization, the development of one's capacities and powers—or, rather, self-realization in and through the realization of the powers of one's society. Green has got beyond "natural" or "primitive" rights, and beyond mere happiness as pleasure and pain. First in time come customary rights; then legal rights; and finally rights as due to moral personalities.

Historically the conception of the moral person . . . is not arrived at till after that of the legal person has been thus disentangled and formulated; and the abstract conception of the legal person, as the sustainer of rights, is not arrived at till long after rights have been actually recognized and established. (352–53)

[Such rights] are "innate" or "natural" in the same sense in which according to Aristotle the state is natural: . . . they arise out of, and are necessary for the fulfillment of, a moral capacity without which a man would not be a man. (353)

There can be no right without a consciousness of common interest on the part of members of a society. (354)

Green sums up the "ground" of political obligation:

The capacity on the part of the individual of conceiving a good as the same for himself and others, and of being determined to action by that conception, is the foundation of rights; and rights are the condition of that capacity being realized. No right is justifiable or should be a right except on the ground that directly or indirectly it serves this purpose. (353)

In his *Essay on Bentham*, Stuart Mill had reached the point where he held the end of man to be "the pursuit of spiritual perfection." (See Vol. II, Book VI, chapter 10, sec. I.) Beginning at this point, Green gives it a much more concrete meaning as the final good of man. And he has an answer to the problem with which Mill wrestled: how is my good involved in the good of others? How is the good of the individual inherently social? This is what Green made out of Aristotle, Hegel, and Stuart Mill. Suggestions came from the earlier thinkers, to be sure; but it is hard not to feel that for Green the greatest of these was Mill—the "Utilitarian" whose views he thought he despised. And yet Green is commonly called a "Hegelian" in his moral and political theory!

Green criticizes the classics of modern political theory—Spinoza, Hobbes, Locke, and Rousseau—for being unhistorical-minded, for not considering the development of society and of man through society. The state they see as supreme coercive power, not as ultimately my own "will."

To ask why I am to submit to the power of the state, is to ask why I am to allow my life to be regulated by that complex of institutions without which I literally should not have a life which I can call my own, nor should be able to ask for a justification of what I am called on to do. For that I may have a life which I can call my own, I must not only be conscious of myself and of ends which I present to myself as mine; I must be able to reckon on a certain freedom of action and acquisition for the attainment of those ends, and this can only be secured through common recognition of this freedom on the part of each other by members of a society, as being for a common good. (428)

The exercise, manifestation, expression of this consciousness [of having life and ends of one's own] through a freedom secured in the way described is necessary to its real existence, just as language of some sort is necessary to the real existence of thought, and bodily movement to that of the soul. (429)

Social institutions are necessary to the development of man's powers; to say that the rights of government are founded on the consent of the governed is a confused way of saying "that the institutions by which man is moralized, by which he comes to do what he sees that he must, as distinct from what he would like, express a conception of a common good" (429–30). This is what Rousseau really meant: like

Hegel, Green is building on Rousseau's "general will." Actual social institutions, of course, are the expression of private interests; Green has Hegel's realism. "Is it not certain that private interests have been the main agents in establishing, and are still in maintaining, at any rate all the more artificial rights of property?" (434).

Is it not an unproved assumption that the state is in an institution for the promotion of a common good?

How can the state be said to exist for the sake of an end, or to fulfil an idea, the contemplation of which, it is admitted, has had little to do with the actions which have had most to do with bringing states into existence? (437)

But neither are living bodies conscious of their complex functions.

The pure desire for social good does not indeed operate in human affairs unalloyed by egotistic motives, but on the other hand what we call egotistic motives do not act without direction from an involuntary reference to social good. (439)

Consider Napoleon. "It is thus that actions of men, whom in themselves we reckon bad, are 'overruled' for good. There is nothing mysterious or unintelligible in such 'overruling.' There is nothing in the effect which we ascribe to the 'overruling,' . . . which there was not in the cause as it really was" (440). This is what Green makes out of Hegel's *"List der Vernunft."* The social good as realized in existing states is their function, not the *motive* for their formation.

Green explains how rights and obligations arise in all social relations, of which the state is merely the capstone, not the creator. "A state presupposes other forms of community, with the rights that arise out of them, and only exists as sustaining, securing, and completing them" (445). "Rights are made by recognition. There is no right 'but thinking makes it so'; none that is not derived from some idea that men have about each other. Nothing is more real than a right, yet its existence is purely ideal, if by 'ideal' is meant that which is not dependent on anything material but has its being solely in consciousness" (446).

Green's social and teleological foundation of rights and obligations is more important, certainly philosophically, than any of his particular applications, where he continues Mill's process of recognizing the need of more and more regulation of the "freedom" of the individual. He inevitably reflects the social needs and conditions of the sixties and seventies—of the period of the American Civil War, whose moral issues figure largely in his analyses. Thus he asks, "Has the citizen rights against the state?" It is contradictory, he points out, to hold that the right of the sovereign power depends on the consent of its members, and that these members have only such rights as are conferred on them by the sovereign—Hobbes's view. The sovereign presupposes rights and exists to secure them; but these rights belong to individuals only as members of society. A right to act "unsocially" is thus a contradiction in terms.

The state then presupposes rights, and rights of individuals. It is a form which society takes in order to maintain them. . . . In analyzing the nature of any right, we may . . . consider it as on the one hand a claim of the individual, arising out of his rational nature, to the free exercise of some faculty; and on the other, as a concession of that claim by society, a power given by it to the individual of putting the claim in force. (450)

A citizen must always act as a member of his state. But what does this assertion amount to? "Does it mean that he has no right to disobey the law of the state to which he belongs, whatever that law may be?"

So far as the laws anywhere or at any time in force fulfil the idea of a state, there can be no right to disobey them; or, there can be no right to disobey the law of the state except in the interest of the state; i.e., for the purpose of making the state in respect of its actual laws more completely correspond to what it is in tendency or idea, viz., the reconciler and sustainer of the rights that arise out of the social relations of men. (452–53)

Green is here more interested in attacking laisser-faire, in justifying governmental "interference," than in stating abstract freedoms.

On this principle there can be no right to disobey or evade any particular law on the ground that it interferes with any freedom of action, any right of managing his children or "doing what he will with his own," which but for that law the individual would possess. (453)

Powers long allowed, men incline to regard as permanently their rights. But it does not remain their right when a law has been enacted that interferes with it. Green grows concrete:

A man e.g. has been allowed to drive at any pace he likes through the streets, to build houses without any reference to sanitary conditions, to keep his children at home or send them to work "analphabetic," to buy or sell alcoholic drinks at his pleasure. . . . But he only possessed these powers as rights through membership of a society which secured them to him, and of which the only permanent bond consists in the reference to the well-being of its members as a whole. . . . If upon new conditions arising, or upon elements of social good being taken account of which had been overlooked before, or upon persons being taken into the reckoning as capable of participation in the social well-being who had previously been treated merely as means to its attainment—if in any of these ways the reference to social well-being suggest the necessity of some further regulation of the individual's liberty to do as he pleases, he can plead no right against this regulation. (453–54)

For all these "rights" have been allowed only as conducive to social well-being, a judgment now reversed.

"The assertion by the citizen of any right which the state does not recognize must be founded on a reference to an acknowledged social good" (454). There must be some common consciousness of [social] utility shared by the person making the claim and those on whom it is made, "He must be able to point to some public interest, generally recognized as such, which is involved in the exercise of the power claimed by him as a right" (455).

As a general rule, no doubt, even bad laws, laws representing the interests of classes or individuals as opposed to those of the community, should be obeyed. There can be no right to disobey them, even while their repeal is urged on the ground that they violate rights, because the public interest, on which all rights are founded, is more concerned in the general obedience to law than in the exercise of those powers by individuals or classes which the objectionable laws unfairly withhold. (456)

A tariff in private interests does not justify smuggling.

The cardinal case in point for Green was the American Fugitive Slave laws. No state law can neutralize the claim of the slave himself to be free. "The obligation to observe the law, because it is the law, does not exist for him" (458). But how about the citizen?

It does not necessarily follow that the duty of befriending the slave is necessarily paramount to the duty of obeying the law which forbids his being befriended. If it is possible for the latter duty to be paramount, it will follow, on the principle that there is no right to violate a duty, that under certain conditions the right of helping the slave may be cancelled by the duty of obeying the prohibitory law. It would be so if the violation of law in the interest of the slave were liable to result in general anarchy, . . . [in] the disappearance of the conditions under which any civil combination is possible; for such a destruction of the state would mean a general loss of freedom, a general substitution of force for mutual good-will in men's dealings with each other, that would outweigh the evil of any slavery under such limitations and regulations as an organized state imposes on it. (459)

Moral dilemmas could be as perplexing in the nineteenth century as in the twentieth.

In his chapter on "The Right of the State over the Individual in War," Green deals with another problem that has not grown less acute since his day. War is not, literally, "multitudinous murder"; for murder, morally, is killing a man "to gain his private ends" and with "malice" against the person killed. "It does not follow from this, however, that war is ever other than a great wrong, as a violation on a multitudinous scale of the individual's right to life" (467–68).

What *is* important to bear in mind (being one of those obvious truths out of which we may allow ourselves to be sophisticated), is that the destruction of life in war is always wrong-doing, whoever be the wrong-doer, and that in the wars most strictly defensive of political freedom the wrong-doing is only removed from the defenders of political freedom to be transferred elsewhere. If it is difficult in any case to say precisely where, that is only a reason for more general self-reproach, for a more humbling sense (as the preachers would say) of complicity in that radical (but conquerable, because moral) evil of mankind which renders such a means of maintaining political freedom necessary. (471)

For Green it was wars for "political freedom" that could most plausibly be defended morally; in the fifties and sixties they ostensibly abounded. But—"of the European wars of the last four hundred years, how many could be fairly said to have been wars in which either or any of the parties were fighting for this end?"

Our conclusion, then, is that the destruction of life in war (to say nothing of other evils incidental to it) is always wrong-doing, with whomsoever the guilt of the wrong-doing may lie; that only those parties to a war are exempt from a share in the guilt who can truly plead that to them war is the only means of maintaining the social conditions of the moral development of man, and that there have been very few cases in which this plea could be truly made. (473)

In the chapter on "The Right of the State in Regard to Property," Green is a more moderate critic of the Victorian economic system than the later Mill. He follows the Hegelian and Idealistic justification of private property: "the foundation of the right of property lies in the will, property is 'realized will' " (523).

Just as the recognized interest of a society constitutes for each member of it the right to free life, just as it makes each conceive of such life on the part of himself and his neighbor as what should be, and thus forms the basis of a re-straining custom which secures it for each, so it constitutes the right to the in-struments of such life, making each regard the possession of them by the other as for the common good, and thus through the medium first of custom, then of law, securing them to each. (522–23)

The rationale of property is that everyone should be secured by society in the power of getting and keeping the means of realizing a will, which in possibil-ity is a will directed toward social good. Whether anyone's will is actually and positively so directed, does not affect his claim to the power. This power should be secured to the individual irrespectively of the use which he actually makes of it, so long as he does not use it in a way that interferes with the exer-cise of like power by another, on the ground that its uncontrolled exercise is the ground of the condition of attainment by man of that free morality which is his highest good. . . . Only then is property held in a way inconsistent with its idea, and which should, if possible, be got rid of, when the possession of property by one man interferes with the possession of property by another; when one set of men are secured in the power of getting and keeping the means of realizing their will, in such a way that others are practically denied the power. In that case it may truly be said that "property is theft." (526)

This view requires that every man should have at least the chance to acquire property. And Green follows the logic of this ideal of uni-versal proprietorship. "Is the requirement that every honest man should be a proprietor compatible with any great inequalities of pos-session?"

In order to give effect to it, must we not remove those two great sources of the inequality of fortunes, (1) freedom of bequest, and the other arrangements by which the profits of the labor of several generations are accumulated on persons who do not labor at all; (2) freedom of trade, of buying in the cheap-est market and selling in the dearest, by which accumulated profits of labor become suddenly multiplied in the hands of a particular proprietor? Now clearly, if [such] an inequality of fortunes . . . necessarily results in the exis-tence of a proletariate, practically excluded from such ownership as is needed to moralize a man, there would be a contradiction between our theory of the right of property and the actual consequences of admitting the right according to the theory. (526–27)

Green concludes, property must be unequal. Equal inheritance among children is for the social good. The right of bequest is more doubtful, as Mill had recognized. Green inclines to favor it: "there may be special reasons for limiting it in regard to land" (529). The accumula-tion of capital does not keep laborers from being small-scale capitalists themselves, and thus educating themselves in the responsibilities of ownership. Green foresees the direction the "capitalism" of England and America was actually to take. Ownership of land has been mismanaged, leading to a rural "proletariate." It is the landlords of England, not the "capitalists," who are to blame for keeping ownership from all. "The question in regard to land stands on a different footing from that in regard to wealth generally, owing to the fact that land is a particular commodity limited in extent. . . . These reasons . . . necessitate a special control over the exercise of rights of property in land, and it remains to be seen whether that control can be sufficiently established in a country where the power of great estates has not first been broken, as in France, by a law of equal inheritance" (534–35).

That Green is basically a Gladstonian Liberal is clear, trying to urge the beginnings of social regulation. It is not surprising, either, that in writing in "The Right of the State in Regard to the Family," he comes out, in those pre-Hollywood days, for monogamy as against polygamy, and for divorce for infidelity only. The important point is the effect of his principles, so influential at Oxford, in transforming Victorian Liberalism into Edwardian Neo-Liberalism, with all it was to lead to.

II

Francis Herbert Bradley wrote his essay, "My Station and its Duties," as a young man, in 1876, at the age of thirty, while Green was still alive. The whole volume contains what the editor of the second edition calls "a brilliant and incisive criticism of what the author held to be false in the reasoning and conclusions of the prevailing English philosophy [the Utilitarian school]." This essay examines its doctrine of "individualism," stemming from Hobbes and Locke, and is a brilliant rephrasing in English of the socialized concepts of Hegel. "Individualism" Bradley defines as the view holding:

That the state was prior to the individual, that the whole was sometimes more than the sum of the parts, was an illusion which preyed on the thinkers of Greece. [It is really Aristotle Bradley is rehabilitating.]. . . . The family, the society, the state, and generally every community of men, consists of individuals, and there is nothing in them real except the individuals. Individuals have made them, and make them. . . . The individuals are real by themselves.

. . . The whole is the mere sum of the parts, and the parts are as real away from the whole as they are in the whole. . . . [In short], the community is the sum of its parts, is made by the addition of parts.[4]

These views are offered by the individualists as "facts." But what are the "facts"? They are human communities, the family, society, and the state. "Historical science has rejected and entirely discredited the individualistic origin of society, and, if we turn to practice, we find everywhere the state asserting itself as a power which has the right to make use of and expend the property and person of the individual without regard to his wishes. . . . Both history and practical politics refuse to verify the 'facts' of the individualist" (164–65).

Bradley starts with the Idealistic—and Aristotelian—conception, that the end of conduct is self-realization. But what self? Happiness, as the addition of particular pleasures, is a futile and bastard product. "If we want morality, it is something like a universal that we want" (160). But if we take the universal as the end, "the supposed pure will or duty for duty's sake," this Kantian view is also an "unreal conception." So is asceticism:

The self can not be realized as its own mere negation, since morality is practice, is will to do something, is self-affirmation. (161)

Morality implies a superior, a higher self, a universal something which is above this or that self, and so above mine. . . . Self-realization is left as the end, the self so far being defined as neither a collection of particular feelings nor an abstract universal. . . . The end is the realization of the good will which is superior to ourselves. . . . The good will (for morality) is meaningless if it be not the will of living, finite beings. It is a *concrete universal.* . . . It is an organism and a moral organism. . . . It is the realization of the whole body, because it is one and the same will which lives and acts in the life and action of each. It is the self-realization of each member, because each member cannot find the *function*, which makes him himself, apart from the whole to which he belongs. (161–63)

Here is a universal which can confront our wandering desires with a fixed and stern imperative, but which yet is no unreal form of the mind [Kant], but a living soul that penetrates and stands fast in the detail of actual existence. . . . We have found the end, we have found self-realization, duty, and happiness in one—yes, we have found ourselves, when we have found our station and its duties, our function as an organ in the social organism. (163)

[4] Bradley, *Ethical Studies* (revised ed.), pp. 163–64.

The "individual" of individualism is an abstraction; no such individual men exist. "What we call an individual man is what he is because of and by virtue of community, and communities are thus not mere names, but something real, and can be regarded only as the one in the many" (166).

Even Mill admits that without general conceptions general language would be impossible. "If I wish to realize my true being, I must realize something beyond my being as a mere this or that; for my true being has in it a life which is not the life of any mere particular, and so must be called a universal life."

What is it then that I am to realize? We have said it in "my station and its duties." To know what a man is you must not take him in isolation. He is one of a people, he was born in a family, he lives in a certain society, in a certain state. What he has to do depends on what his place is, what his *function* is, and that all comes from his station in the organism. (173)

Bradley defends his Hegelian—and Aristotelian—view against that of Kant. That made the universal abstract, it made it "subjective," and it left a part of ourselves outside it. In contrast, the "my station and its duties" view holds "(1) the universal is concrete; (2) it is objective; (3) it leaves nothing of us outside it" (176). It is concrete: "it is an obvious fact, that in my station my particular duties are prescribed to me, and I have them whether I wish to or not." It is not merely "subjective" or "objective": "it is that real identity of subject and object, which is the only thing that satisfies our desires." And thirdly, "the universal which is the end . . . gets rid of the contradiction between duty and the 'empirical' self; it does not in its realization leave me forever outside and unrealized" (177–81). Not only what ought to be in the world is, but I am what I ought to be. Bradley grows rhapsodic quoting Hegel:

Yes, the state is not put together, but it lives; it is not a heap nor a machine; it is no mere extravagance when a poet talks of a nation's soul. It is the objective mind which is subjective and self-conscious in its citizens: it feels and knows itself in the heart of each. It speaks the word of command and gives the field of accomplishment, and in the activity of obedience it has and bestows individual life and satisfaction and happiness.

First in the community is the individual realized. (184–85)

"Once let us take the point of view which regards the community as the real moral organism, . . . there is no need to ask and by some scientific process find out what is moral, for morality exists all round us, and faces us, if need be, with a categorical imperative, while it surrounds us on the other side with an atmosphere of love" (187)

In 1876 Bradley did not hesitate to draw out all the "conservative" implications of his Hegelianism. He opposes "the common error that there is something 'right in itself' for me to do, in the sense that there must be some absolute rule of morality the same for all persons without distinction of times and places." " 'My station and its duties' holds that *unless* morals varied, there could be no morality; that a morality which was *not* relative would be futile" (189).

Morality is 'relative,' but is none the less real. At every stage there is the solid fact of a world so far moralized. There is an objective morality in the accomplished will of the past and present, a higher self worked out by the infinite pain, the sweat and blood of generations, and now given to me by free grace and in love and faith as a sacred trust. It comes to me as the truth of my own nature and the power and the law, which is stronger and higher than any caprice or opinion of my own. (190)

Morality is always developing, though in the end the process is a "contradiction." Evolution means that "history is the working out of the true human nature through various incomplete stages towards completion, and 'my station' is the one satisfactory view of morals. Here all morality is and must be 'relative,' because the essence of realization is evolution through stages" (192).

How do I get to know in particular what is right and wrong? Certainly not from moral philosophy.

There cannot be a moral philosophy which will tell us what in particular we are to do, and also it is not the business of philosophy to do so. All philosophy has to do is "to understand what is," and moral philosophy has to understand morals which exist, not to make them or give directions for making them. . . . Ethics has not to make the world moral, but to reduce to theory the morality current in the world. If we want it to do anything more, so much the worse for us; for it cannot possibly construct new morality . . . In short, the view which thinks moral philosophy is to supply us with particular moral prescriptions confuses science with art, and confuses, besides, reflective with intuitive judgment. (193)

Bradley turns Aristotelian: "that which tells us what in particular is right and wrong is not reflection but intuition." In a note he adds: "If the reader dislike the word, he may substitute 'perception' or 'sense,' if he will." He adapts Aristotle: "To the question, How am I to know what is right? the answer must be, By the *aisthesis* of the *phronimos*; and the *phronimos* is the man who has identified his will with the moral spirit of the community, and judges accordingly." Particular moral judgments depend on insight into the circumstances, which is seldom discursive or reflective. "What is moral *in any particular given case* is seldom doubtful." Almost fifty years later Bradley adds the note: "This is too optimistic." At the time, he added: "Collisions of duties are avoided mostly by each man keeping to his own immediate duties, and not trying to see from the point of view of other stations than his own"—Plato's "minding one's own business."

Bradley's Hegelian complacency comes out most clearly in his criticism of "conscience" and private judgment in morals—what Hegel called *"Moralität."* Speaking of the insight or intuition that decides particular cases, he says:

This intuition must not be confounded with what is sometimes mis-called "conscience." It is not mere individual opinion or caprice. It presupposes the morality of the community as its basis, and is subject to the approval thereof. Here, if anywhere, the idea of universal and impersonal morality is realized. For the final arbiters are the *phronimoi*, persons with a will to do right, and not full of reflections and theories. If they fail you, you must judge for yourself, but practically they seldom do fail you. Their private peculiarities neutralize each other, and the result is an intuition which does not belong merely to this or that man or collection of men. "Conscience" is the antipodes of this. It wants you to have no law but yourself, and to be better than the world. But this intuition tells you that, if you could be as good as your world, you would be better than most likely you are, and that to wish to be better than the world is to be already on the threshold of immorality. (198–99)

This glorification of customary morality "is intolerable to those mainly who, from inexperience or preconceived theories, can not see the world as it is" (199).

Those who have seen most of the world . . . know most also how much good there is in it. They are tolerant of new theories and youthful opinions that everything would be better upside down, because they know that this also is as it should be, and that the world gets good even from these. They are intolerant only of those who are old enough, and should be wise enough, to know better than that they know better than the world; for in such people they cannot help seeing the self-conceit which is pardonable only in youth. (*Ibid.*)

To make the world better is near immorality when it disregards the world of existing laws, institutions, social usages, moral opinions, and feelings, in which the young have been brought up. "It is not wrong, it is a duty, to take the best that there is, and to live up to the best. It is not wrong, it is a duty, standing on the best of the existing, to try and make not only oneself but the world better."

But it is another thing, starting from oneself, from ideals in one's head, to set oneself and them against the moral world. The moral world with its social institutions, etc., is a fact; it is real; our "ideals" are not real. "But we will make them real." We should consider what we are, and what the world is. We should learn to see the great moral fact in the world, and to reflect on the likelihood of our private "ideal" being anything more than an abstraction, which, because an abstraction, is all the better fitted for our heads, and all the worse fitted for actual existence.

We should consider whether the encouraging oneself in having opinions of one's own, in the sense of thinking differently from the world on moral subjects, be not, in any person other than a heaven-born prophet, sheer self-conceit. (199–200)

The community is thus the real moral idea, stronger than all private criticisms of it. "There is nothing better than my station and its duties, nor anything higher or more truly beautiful" (200). Yet the community is not ultimate. Bradley admits: "the community in which he is a member may be in a confused or rotten condition, so that in it right and might do not always go together" (*ibid.*). "You cannot confine a man to his station and its duties." "A man cannot take his morality simply from the moral world he is in." That moral world is itself "in a state of historical development." The world is not altogether as it should be: this leads to a process of trying to make it better. The content of the ideal self does not fall wholly within any community, is not *merely* the ideal of a perfect social being. And Bradley leaves us with the final contradiction: the morality of the community must develop historically, but the individual must not depart from customary morality as it is.

III

Bernard Bosanquet (1848–1923),[5] the most popular and influential of the English Idealists, was a man of very different stamp from the

[5] Bernard Bosanquet, *Logic* (London, 1888; 2nd ed., 1911); *The Philosophical Theory of the State; Implication and Linear Inference* (London, 1920); *History of Aesthetic* (London, 1892); *The Principle of Individuality and Value* (London, 1912); *The Value and Destiny of the Individual* (London, 1913); *The Meeting of Extremes in Contemporary Philosophy* (London, 1921).

searching critic Green or the relativistic and functional Bradley. A man of extensive private means, he was not a university don, but officially the secretary of the London Charity Organization Society, in the best tradition of Tory paternalism. He was closer to Green's emphasis on logical structure than to Bradley's long search to include feeling and immediate experience. But he was much more of a Hegelian than the neo-Kantian Green, and made the most of the systematic side of Hegel: he took literally, in his Gifford lectures, the Hegelian conviction that Truth is found only in the Whole, and he insisted that the Absolute—the total system—is the only ultimate individual. He wrote extensively on the Hegelian—or "philosophical"—logic; on religion, in which he followed Green rather than Bradley in "not sharply distinguishing between God and the Absolute," and on aesthetics, producing what served long as the standard history of aesthetics in English. And at the end of his life he welcomed the convergence between a structural Absolute Idealism and the philosophic realism of Samuel Alexander and the American Neo-Realists, even as Bradley was approaching the more functional instrumentalism of Dewey. But aside from his *logic*, which for a generation taught the Idealistic position to students, Bosanquet's best known and most influential book was his *Philosophical Theory of the State* (1899), which became a byword for the Hegelian glorification of the State, rephrased in terms of modern nationalism and the British Imperial destiny of the Kipling era. As Green became the Bible of British Neo-Liberalism and the Labor welfare state, so Bosanquet was the "ideal" expression of the Tory *noblesse oblige* of the Disraeli-Joseph Chamberlain-Unionist tradition. And where Green expressed nineteenth-century liberalism in religion, Bosanquet appealed rather to the "modernists" who wanted to preserve continuity with older forms while reinterpreting their meaning. All in all, it is not hard to see why the Oxford clerical graduates coming up to Convocation freely acknowledged Bradley as the ablest English Idealist, but preferred to follow the safer and sounder teachings of Bosanquet.

Bosanquet's popular appeal is clear from a passage in the preface to his first series of Gifford Lectures, for 1911, *The Principle of Individuality and Value.*

I am persuaded that if we critically consider what we really want and need, we shall find that it can be rationally established by a straightforward argument.

In thus maintaining that philosophy gives us the quintessence of life, I am not suggesting that the best thing in life is the pursuit of philosophy. What I mean is that the things which are most important in man's experience are also the things which are most certain to his thought. And further, I should urge, this is not an accident but inevitable, because importance and reality are sides of the same characteristic.[6]

Where Bradley was perversely urging that the things most important in experience, like personality and God, were ultimately self-contradictory, Bosanquet was proclaiming them to be most real. No wonder he appealed to those Idealists taught to say, "On earth there is nothing great but man, in man there is nothing great but mind." [7] And no wonder Bosanquet, along with the other British Right Wing Hegelians, John and Edward Caird, and A.E. Taylor (*Elements of Metaphysics*, London, 1903), was eagerly read in American colleges and seminaries, where the more original thought of Royce proved meat almost as strong as Bradley's.

Bosanquet's thought is a philosophy of the social organism, and his "metaphysics"—or "logic": for the Hegelian there is no distinction—is a metaphysics of organism. Totality, self-completion, organism, individuality, are all different terms for the same social Whole. "What really matters is not the preservation of separate minds as such, . . . but it is logic, the spirit of totality or effort to self-completion, which, being the principle of individuality, is the key to reality, value, and freedom." [8] In detail, the "whole" is the "concrete universal." "Thought has always the nature of a system of connected members, and is an effort to take that form, which we may call a 'world.' This is the only sort of thing which can satisfy the logical law that contradiction is a mark of unreality, or—the same law—that the truth or the real is 'the whole' " (xix).

An experience which throws light on something beyond itself is called "universal." . . . What is really universal—i.e., what expresses the work of thought in throwing light on experience—is always of the nature of "a world." . . . Logical completeness or universality is not a deadening but a vitalizing quality, and thought is not a principle of reproducing reality with omissions,

[6] Bosanquet, *Principle of Individuality and Value*, p. v.
[7] Bosanquet, *Meeting of Extremes in Contemporary Philosophy*, p. vi. Bosanquet is quoting S. Alexander (*Proceedings of the British Academy*, 1913–14, p. 279), who is contrasting this temper of the Idealist with that of the Realist: "to order man and mind to their proper place among the world of finite things."
[8] Bosanquet, *Principle of Individuality and Value*, p. xviii.

but of organizing worlds and investing their detail with fresh significance.
. . . The essence of thought is this nisus towards a whole—to adjustment, to
seeing things as harmonious. . . .

Thus we arrive at the idea of the logical universal as a living world, complete
and acting out of itself. This, so far as complete, is "the individual," and ultimately must be one only, and perfect [the Absolute]. It is not, therefore, an
atom, which is its extreme opposite. (xix–xx)

Such system or organism is not inconsistent with uniformity or "general law."

What is meant when individuality is contrasted with general law is that the
laws, e.g., of space and time, do not explain the conduct of a person. This is
not because they are too universal, but because they are not universal enough.
They have too little in them. So Laplace's "calculator" could not predict everything, unless he knew much more than the position of all physical elements. He would not be a true type of intelligence. What is repugnant to man
is not prediction of his conduct, but reduction of himself to a different kind of
existence. (xxii–xxiii)

Individuality or completion is the ultimate criterion of value.

Things, acts, feelings, have "value" in as far as they are completely organized,
do not break down, have parts or members which confirm and sustain one
another. Art is only one case; the principle extends to everything within experience.(xxxi)

So the Greek theory of the State expressly says you cannot value the individuals separately, and then find the value of the social whole by adding up those
of the individuals, because each individual only has his full and real nature
and value in the whole life of the community. (xxxiii)

The Self is the extension of Nature, not opposed to it, and both are completed in the Whole.

It is very difficult to draw the line between Nature and the Self. Nature as
regarded by mathematical physics is not a reality, but merely a way of representing certain characters of the world which are convenient for calculation.
Nature as we really experience it, with primary, secondary, and tertiary (aesthetic) qualities, can only be distinguished from ourselves as fragmentary experiences from conscious centres of experience. . . . It is actually real; but
. . . its being physical cannot exclude its being continuous with what is
psychical. . . . It seems better to accept it frankly as complementary to mind,
i.e., as an external system, continuous with our minds, through which the
content and purposes of the universe are communicated. . . . Nature is not
the slave of man. Nature, then, lives and is complete in the life of our minds,
each of which draws its content from some particular range of Nature, so that

all the detail of the universe is elicited into mental foci, and "external" conditions are held together in such foci, and pass, through them, into the complete experience which we call the whole or the Absolute. (xxxvi)

Bosanquet illustrates his conception of this all-inclusive Whole or "world" by the world of a poet's vision.

We might compare the Absolute to, say, Dante's mind as uttered in the *Divine Comedy*. In it external nature, say, Italy, becomes an emotion and a value, not less but more than spatial; each self, say, Paolo or Francesca, while still its real self, is also a factor in the poet's mind, which is uttered in all these selves taken together; and the whole poetic experience is single, and yet includes a world of space and persons. (xxxvii)

With his drive toward an all-inclusive system as the goal of the urge to self-completion, Bosanquet better than Bradley represents the tendency of all Hegelianisms to include all so-called different points of view at some place in his intellectual "organism." Where Hegel was concerned to embrace all past philosophies, and to include them in a drive toward intellectual imperialism, Bosanquet at the end tried to swallow up all the contemporary tendencies in philosophizing in his vision, to come to terms with the Realists, Alexander, Neo-Realism, and Critical Realism, with the New-Idealists of Italy, Croce and Gentile, with the Whitehead of the *Concept of Nature*, and the Haldane of the *Reign of Relativity*, with McTaggart's a priorism, and Bradley's experientialism, even with the Husserl of the *Logische Untersuchungen*. He saw reconciliation between "the ontological mode of statement and reasoning" of McTaggart and "the attempt at a critical survey of experience in which my work has mainly consisted. It seems to me almost fundamental to our respective standpoints that I hold no experience, however empirical *prima facie*, to be destitute of metaphysical implication." [9] These are all further examples of the way in which man has used "the technical language of thought to embody his overwhelming sense of his unity with and in a universe which excelled himself" (lx). Again, "you find . . . in all quarters of the philosophical world, the insight that truth, value, and a common possession of externality, affirm themselves as a solid meeting-point of minds in social intercourse, so that the identity and universality of mind [objective mind], if you doubt it in one sense, returns upon you as a granite-hard fact in

[9] Bosanquet, *Meeting of Extremes in Contemporary Philosophy*, p. xi.

another" (ix–x). Bosanquet can even assimilate the ideas of relativity, in Bradley's dialectical version or in Haldane's more "scientific" construing.

My view would be that the absolutist, to whom a perfectly thoroughgoing relativity has always been of the essence of the real, has played an effective part in forcing philosophy to the more concrete standpoint from which it treats such experiences today. In space-time, change, and relation, it now deals with the relational wholes, relational arrangements, unities comprising and sustaining relations, apart from which absolutism has always maintained both relations and terms to be inconceivable. Unities contain relations, but unities are not relations, nor constituted by relations. "The universe contains change, but the universe itself cannot change." (xii–xiii)

Even in Whitehead, "you find the connection of one member with another in the universe to have all sorts of characteristics of inevitable complementariness. . . ."

With more careful and less controversial modes of approach, you find you can get below these first obvious answers in the common-sense catechism, and pursue, as Hegel pointed out, in the higher walks of thought *modifications* of a common basis [emphasis added], rather than tumble this way and that between crude contradictories. (x)

Even in religion he finds agreement with Alexander. It is true, "God is not, as such, of the nature of mind or spirit, and therefore He cannot be united with men in any such kind of being. . . ."

One cannot but note that our leading thinkers are more and more inclined to insist on the metaphorical character of the phrases in which we express the identity of consciousness between God and men. . . . The account of the universe as it is an actual object of worship—as a whole straining towards deity—goes far to compensate for the rejection . . . of such special terms as mind and spirit. (171)

"Alexander gives full weight to the special religious experience, the emotion towards a something which demands our worships, and in which we come to feel a greater than ourselves with which we are at one. This gives us a deeper view of the universe than that which treats the religious experience as mythical"(172).

Here Alexander . . . has emphasized another experience. In religion we find "saving experiences"—he quotes the phrase from William James—in continuity with a wider self. We are one with the whole by faith and not in works. Here our inadequacy is done away. This is the very meaning of "saving experiences." We throw ourselves upon the grace of the universe and find in oneness with it an adequacy which is self-contradictory for us as finite agents. (173)

"Religion . . . is . . . a special differentiation in experience addressed to and uniting the finite being with the universe in a special aspect and character—that of a unity which thrills and grasps the finite soul"(174).

IV

Since Bosanquet's whole philosophy is a drive towards self-completion through unity with a higher inclusive Whole, it is easy to see how he works out the Greek, Rousseauian, and Hegelian social philosophy of the community and State as the higher, inclusive social organism.

Bosanquet offers his work as "an attempt to express what I take to be the fundamental ideas of a true social philosophy." [10] He has found this true philosophy in Plato and Aristotle, in Hegel, Green, Bradley, and Wallace, especially in Hegel and Bradley. He hardly expects to improve on such thinkers; and in fact his views are not fundamentally new, after Green and Bradley had already adapted Hegel to the British political tradition. He claims two points of originality. The first is his "attempt to apply the conceptions of recent psychology to the theory of State coercion and of the Real or General Will, and to explain the relation of Social Philosophy to Sociological Psychology." The second is "the conviction that the time has gone by for the scrupulous caution which Green displayed in estimating the value of the State to its members" (ix). There does run through Bosanquet an emphasis on the "ideality" of existing social arrangements. "Our growing experience of all social 'classes' proves the essentials of happiness and character to be the same throughout the social whole" (ix). "The poor" are generally just as good as other people. There is no larger proportion of bad homes among the poor than among the rich. The social student should shun mere optimism, but most of them take up an attitude of indifference, if not of hostility, to existing society. They hardly "believe" in it. Except for Hegel and Bradley, "they partly fail to seize the greatness and ideality of life in its commonest actual phases. . . . Those who cannot be enthusiastic in the study of society

---

[10] Bosanquet, *Philosophical Theory of the State* (2nd ed.), p. vii.

as it is, would not be so in the study of a better society if they had it" (xi).

Now a philosophical theory is "the study of something as a whole and for its own sake. . . . It may be compared to the gaze of a child or of an artist. It deals, that is, with the total and unbroken effect of its object. It desires to ascertain what a thing is, what is its full characteristic and being, its achievement in the general act of the world" (p. 1).

Everything, and in this case more particularly the political life of man, has a nature of its own, which is worthy of investigation on its own merits and for its own sake. . . . The philosophical problem is to see our object as it is and to learn what it is, to estimate, so to speak, its kind and degree of self-maintenance in the world, rather than to trace its history or to analyze its causation. (2)

This study implies that its object will reveal its true position and relations with reference to all else that man can do and can know.

This position and these relations constitute its rank or significance in the totality of experience, and this value or significance—what the form of life in question enables man to do and to become—is just what we mean by its nature "in itself," or its full and complete nature, or its significance when thoroughly studied "for its own sake" from an adequate point of view. (2–3)

Sociology since Comte is concerned with laws, causes, and effects. The social philosopher asks rather, "what is the completest and most real life of the human soul?" The latter began with the ancients, was revived by modern idealism from Rousseau to Hegel, and has found a second home in Britain. The former flourishes more especially on French and American soil. Social philosophy is "ethical."

Society for it is an achievement or utterance of human nature . . . that can answer the questionings which are suggested by the scrutiny of human life from the point of view of value and completeness. . . . In what way through society, and in what characteristics of society, does the soul lay hold upon its truest self, or become, in short, the most that it has in it to be? How does the social life at its best compare with the life of art, of knowledge, or of religion, and can the same principle be shown to be active in all of them? (50–51)

Now, philosophy gives a significance to sociology; sociology vitalizes philosophy; they supplement each other. But philosophy is teleological and functional; it considers the values the individual finds in the whole.

It is Bentham who represents the antithesis of Bosanquet's political thinking. He describes law as a necessary evil, and government as a choice of evils. Every law is contrary to liberty, and hence gives pain. "For him then liberty has the simplest and apparently widest meaning, which includes liberty to do evil, and is defined, we must suppose, purely as the absence of restraint. And he therefore has no doubt whatever that the citizen can acquire rights only by sacrificing part of his liberty" (57).

The same opposition between freedom and law dogs Mill as well. "Having so deep a sense, as he has, of social solidarity, he nevertheless treats the central life of the individual as something to be carefully fenced round against the impact of social forces" (60).

Mill's idea of Individuality is plainly biassed by the Benthamite tradition that law is an evil. . . . Thus we find concentrated in a few pages of the "Liberty" all those ideas on the nature of Individuality, Originality, and Eccentricity, which are most opposed to the teaching derived by later generations in England from the revival of philosophy and criticism. . . . That the individuality or genius, the fulness of life and completeness of development which Mill so justly appreciates, is not nourished and evoked by the varied play of relations and obligations in society, but lies in a sort of inner self, to be cherished by enclosing it, as it were, in an impervious globe, is a notion which neither modern logic nor modern art criticism will admit. (60–61)

It is not that Mill's demarcation of the sphere of liberty and that of law, as applying where liberty would harm others, would unduly curtail social interference. "We should rather anticipate that it would leave an easy opening for a transition from administrative nihilism to administrative absolutism; and some such transition seems to have taken place in Mill's later views" (63).

Every act that carries a definite damage to any other person belongs to the sphere of law, and every act that can be supposed likely to cause such a damage, to that of morality; and individuality has what is left. (63)

If strictly pressed, [this demarcation] excludes individuality from every act of life that has an important social bearing. . . . The demarcation between individuality and society, contrived in defence of the former, has pretty nearly annihilated it. (64)

Moreover, Mill's criterion is useless. "For every act of mine affects both myself and others; . . . It may be said that no demarcation between self-regarding and other-regarding action can possibly hold good"(64). In practice, Mill objects to trying to prevent immorality or irreligion by punishment, on the ground that it interferes with liberty in purely self-regarding actions. On the other hand, he holds the existence of a moral obligation to educate one's children is a ground for enforcement by law of universal State-enacted examinations. "Sheer compulsion," Bosanquet remarks, "is not the way to enforce a moral obligation." Mill suggests it might be just to interdict marriage for those who cannot support a family. "This is a case in which authoritative interference must inevitably defeat its object."

Throughout all these objections to authoritative interference we trace the peculiar prejudice that the criterion of its justifiability lies in the boundary line between self and others, rather than in the nature of what coercive authority is and is not able to do towards the promotion of the good life. (64–65)

Mill appeals to a quite different criterion when he remarks, of slavery, "It is not freedom to be allowed to alienate his freedom," just as it is not freedom to be allowed to walk over a bridge which is certain to break down and cause his death. Here Mill appeals from momentary wishes to what freedom really demands, and approaches the sound doctrine of the "real" will and "being forced to be free."

Bosanquet exposes even worse contradictions in the less subtle Herbert Spencer. Even T.H. Huxley, who speaks of "self-restraint as the essence of the ethical process," while "natural liberty" consists in "the free play of self-assertion," illustrates the confusions of making the opposition.

The idea that assertion and maximization of the self and of the individuality first becomes possible and real in and through society, and that affirmation and not negation is its main characteristic: these fundamental conceptions of genuine social philosophy can only be reached through a destructive criticism of the assumptions which erect that paradox into an insoluble contradiction. (73)

From these criticisms of contemporary "individualists" Bosanquet's own positive position has become pretty clear. In developing it, he relies heavily on Rousseau—more heavily than Bradley—and on Hegel. He accepts Rousseau's distinction between the Will of All and the General Will: the essential difference for him is that the will of all is a sum of particulars, even when unanimous, while the General Will appeals to something common or general in its nature. Rousseau con-

tradicts his own sound conception when he affirms the absolute supremacy of the popular will, which can only be the will of all. Bosanquet prefers to speak of the Real Will of a community.

In order to obtain a full statement of what we will, what we want at any
moment must at least be corrected and amended by what we want at all other
moments; and this cannot be done without also correcting and amending it so
as to harmonize it with what others want. . . . Such a process of harmonizing
and adjusting a mass of data to bring them into a rational shape is what is
meant by *criticism*. And criticism, when applied to our actual will, shows that
it is not our real will; or, in the plainest language, that what we really want is
something more and other than at any given moment we are aware that we
will, although the wants which we are aware of lead up to it at every point.
(119)

"To obtain something which approximates to a real will, then, involves a process of criticism and interpretation, which may be either
natural or intellectual; that is to say, it may proceed by 'natural selection,' through the method of trial and error, or it may be rapidly advanced at favorable moments by the insight of a great mind" (119–20).

Hegel Bosanquet defends against the charge of being a reactionary
defender of the Prussian bureaucracy of 1820. His philosophy of right
long antedates the Wartburg protest: it appears in the *Encyclopedia* of
1817, and in fact started in 1802 not with Prussia but with the Greek
polis. Moreover, Hegel was not sketching an "ideal state," but analyzing existing states: "the object of political philosophy is to understand
what a State is," as Hegel made very clear.

If there is taken to be an absolute opposition between the self and
others, liberty becomes a wholly negative idea. But this endangers the
fundamental principle, "according to which self-affirmation is the root
of morality." It is assumed by "individualism" that the self in society
is something less than, if it could so exist, it would be out of society,
and liberty is taken as "the arrangement by which, at a sacrifice of
some of its activities, it is enabled to disport itself *in vacuo* with the
remainder" (125).

But actually the average individual is not the real self or individuality. "The centre of gravity of existence is thrown outside him."

It is true that to feel your individuality is to feel something distinctive, which
gives you a hold and substance in yourself and a definite position among
others. . . . But this substance and position are always sustained by some

kind of determinate achievement or expansion on the part of the self. It always comes from taking hold of the world in some definite way; which, just because it is definite and affirmative, is at once a distinct assertion of the self, and a transition from the private self into the great communion of reality. (125–26)

Our real self or individuality may be something which in one sense we are not, but which we recognize as imperative upon us. Liberty, to be sure, is the essential quality of human life. But it cannot be simply something which we have, still less something which we have always had—a *status quo* to be maintained. "It must be a condition relevant to our continued struggle to assert the control of something in us, which we recognize as imperative upon us or as our real self, but which we only obey in a very imperfect degree" (127).

It is possible for us to acquiesce as rational beings in a law and order which on the whole makes for the possibility of our asserting our true or universal selves, at the very moment when this law and order is constraining our particular private wills in a way which we resent, or even condemn. Such a law and order, maintained by force, which we recognize as on the whole the instrument of our greatest self-affirmation, is a system of rights; and our liberty, or to use a good old expression, our liberties, may be identified with such a system considered as the condition and guarantee of our becoming the best that we have it in us to be, that is, of becoming ourselves. And because such an order is the embodiment up to a certain point of a self or system of will which we recognize as what ought to be, as against the indolence, ignorance, or rebellion of our casual private selves, we may rightly call it a system of self-government or free government; a system, that is to say, in which ourselves, in one sense, govern ourselves in another sense; not as Mill has said, by each one of us being subject to all the "others" (taking "others" in the same sense in which each of us is "one"), but by all of us, as casual private units, being subject to an order which expresses, up to a certain point, the rational self or will which, as rational beings, we may be assumed to recognize as imperative. (127–28)

We have thus arrived at the true view of liberty. As rational beings, we are subject to the imperative claim on us of a will which is real or rational. "Any system of institutions which represents to us, on the whole, the conditions essential to affirming such a will, in objects of action such as to constitute a tolerably complete life, has an imperative claim upon our loyalty and obedience as the embodiment of our *liberty*" (149). "The imperative claim of the will that wills itself is our own inmost nature, and we cannot throw it off. This is the ultimate root of political obligation" (*ibid.*). Here is the classical "freedom of reason," combined, as in Kant, with autonomy—in obeying reason we are obeying our true selves, and are hence free. Finally, here is the Hegelian locus of "reason" in a system of social institutions. "It is such a 'real' or rational will that thinkers after Rousseau have identified with the State. In this theory they are following the principles of Plato and Aristotle," as well as Rousseau (149–50).

The State so conceived is not merely the political fabric. The term does emphasize the political aspect of the whole.

But it includes the entire hierarchy of institutions by which life is determined, from the family to the trade, and from the trade to the Church and the University. . . . The State, it might be said, is thus conceived as the operative criticism of all institutions—the modification and adjustment by which they are capable of playing a rational part as the object of human will. . . . It follows that the State, in this sense, is, above all things, not a number of persons, but a working conception of life. (150–51)

Secondly, the State as the operative criticism of all institutions is necessarily force, and in the last resort is the only recognized and justified force. "For the force of the State proceeds essentially from its character of being our own mind extended, so to speak, beyond our immediate consciousness" (152).

We make a great mistake in thinking of the force exercised by the State as limited to the restraint of disorderly persons by the police and the punishment of intentional lawbreakers. The State is the flywheel of our life. Its system is constantly reminding us of duties, from sanitation to the incidents of trusteeship, which we have not the least desire to neglect, but which we are either too ignorant or too indolent to carry out apart from instruction and authoritative suggestion. We profit at every turn by institutions, rules, traditions, researches, made by minds at their best, which, through State action, are now in a form to operate as extensions of our own minds. (152)

The ultimate end of Society and the State as of the individual is the realization of the best life. "By the State we mean Society as a unit, recognized as rightly exercising control over its members through absolute physical power" (185). The distinctive attribute of the State is to be ultimate arbiter and regulator of claims, of a workable system in the bodily world.

It is in its ultimateness *de facto* that the differentia lies which separates it from the innumerable other groupings and associations which go to make up our complex life. This is shown in the fact that each of us must belong to a State, and can belong to only one. It is because the authority is ultimate that it must be single. Now, authority which is to be ultimate in a sphere including the world of bodily action, must be an authority which can use force. And it is for this reason that force is involved in the distinctive attributes of the State. (188–89)

Like Green, Bosanquet limits the power of the State to securing the performance of external acts. It cannot secure any motive save hope of reward or fear of punishment; it cannot determine that the action be done from the motive which alone would give it immediate value or durable certainty as an element in the best life. What it can effect is to remove obstacles, to destroy conditions hostile to the realization of the end. "When force is opposed to freedom, a force that repels that force is *right*" (191).

Rights are claims recognized by the State, i.e., by Society, acting as ultimate authority, to the maintenance of conditions favorable to the best life. "All rights, as claims which both are and ought to be enforceable by law, derive their imperative authority from their relation to an end which enters into the better life. All rights, then, are powers instrumental to making the best of human capacities, and can only be recognized or exercised upon this ground. In this sense, the duty is the purpose with a view to which the right is secured" (210).

Bosanquet concludes by appraising the ethical value of the great institutions, the Family, Property, the Neighborhood, class, the Nation-State, humanity. Where Green's limited horizons are revealed mainly in his treatment of property, Bosanquet's come out when he deals with the Nation-State. "The Nation-State is the widest organization which has the common experience necessary to found a common life. This is why it is recognized as absolute in power over the individual, and as his representative and champion in the affairs of the world outside" (320). Is State action to be judged by the same moral tests as private action? No; the State as such can have no ends but public ends.

The State, then, exists to promote good life, and what it does cannot be morally indifferent; but its actions cannot be identified with the deeds of its agents, or morally judged as private volitions are judged. Its acts proper are always public acts, and it cannot, as a State, act within the relations of private life, in which organized morality exists. It has no determinate function in a larger community, but is itself the supreme community; the guardian of a whole moral world, but not a factor within an organized moral world. Moral relations presuppose an organized life; but such a life is only within the State, not in relations between the State and other communities. (324–25)

A public act which inflicts loss, such as war, confiscation, the repudiation of a debt, is wholly different from murder or theft. It is not the act of a private person. It is not a violation of law. It can hardly be motivated by private malice or cupidity. . . . We deny that States can be treated as actors in private immoralities which their agents permit themselves in the alleged interest of the State . . . we deny that the avowed public acts of sovereign powers, which cause loss or injury, can be imputed to individuals under the names of private offences; that someone is guilty of murder when a country carries on war, or of theft when it adopts the policy of repudiation, confiscation, or annexation. (326–28)

One intellectual consequence of Bosanquet's political philosophy was the rise in opposition of various forms of political pluralism. Another was the attempt at Versailles to create a moral community of States. In the Introduction to the second edition (1910) Bosanquet tries to answer the criticisms that his "classical theory of the State" was "too narrow and rigid, too negative, and too intellectualist."

It is "too narrow, because the analysis which applies easily to the City-state, and with some reinterpretation to the Nation-state, is held to be inapplicable to the varied gradation of communities with which modern life makes us acquainted—to a man's membership in the Empire composed of free dominions, or in the European concern of nations, or in the Parliament of man, the federation of the world; not to speak of the hierarchy of societies in which we are involved within the boundaries of the Nation-state itself" (p. xxi).

Bosanquet can freely admit the Maitland and Gierke view of institutional pluralism, defended in England by John Neville Figgis.

We are thus led to see more plainly the true character of the State as a source of pervading adjustments and an idea-force holding together a complex hierarchy of groups, and not itself a separable thing like the monarch or the "government," or the local body with which we are tempted to identify it. . . . The position sketched by [Maitland], according to which the real or general will is present in its degree in every co-operating group of human beings, is one with which the theory of the State is fully in accord. Where two or three are gathered together with any degree of common experience and co-operation, there is *pro tanto* a general will. (xxiii)

Bosanquet still insists on "the State as the ultimate and absolute power of adjustment, and therefore single in respect to every individual."

The uniqueness of the general will of the State, and the necessity that it should be unique, is an additional and peculiar feature, depending on the necessity that an absolute power should be single in reference to each individual. (*Ibid.*)[11]

Bosanquet, like Hegel, found it hard to understand federalism. But he bravely makes the attempt.

How far even the absolute power of any one group in relation to individuals within it may be interfered with by constitutional tradition or by a conflict of authorities (as, e.g., the conflict between a State and the Federal Government in the U.S.A.), or by International Courts or Leagues, is a question of degree and detail. It must be remembered that our theory does not place Sovereignty in any determinate person or body of persons, but only in the working of the system of institutions as a whole. There is therefore no technical difficulty in the modification of the Nation-state towards larger forms of authoritative co-operation, so long as it is made clear to what system of authorities every separate human being is subject in respect of the ultimate adjustment of claims upon him. And it would seem that there must always be a machinery for making this clear (like the Court which interprets the constitution of the U.S.A.), if civilized life is to be possible. The all-important point is that the recognition of the Real or General Will should be maintained. (xxiii–xxiv)

As to his theory being "too negative," Bosanquet reiterates:

It is absolutely certain that morality and religion cannot be enforced by the State. The thing is a contradiction in terms. . . . It means that the most powerful of all social and human motives cannot be directed, controlled, or moulded by the public power as such. (xxix)

There is a necessary opposition between the nature of the power of the State and the nature of the good life which is its ultimate end.

The content of legislation and administration with a view to the public good, the inventive, experimental, creative element, is almost entirely supplied by one or other of the forms of social action which are not due to the initiative of the State. . . . The work of the State is *de facto* for the most part "endorsement" or "taking over"—setting its *imprimatur*, the seal of its force, on what more flexible activities or the mere progress of life have wrought out in long

---

[11] See, however, J. Muirhead, ed., *Bernard Bosanquet and his Friends: Letters Illustrating the Sources and the Development of his Philosophical Opinions* (New York and London, 1935), p. 163: "Bosanquet lived to become an ardent supporter of the League [of Nations] which was formed in 1919." In a letter to R.F.A. Hoernlé, then at Harvard, Sept. 14, 1919, Bosanquet wrote: "We hope it is to be all right about the treaty and League. If America really stood out, I presume the bottom would fall out of the whole thing. . . . I am never very uneasy about our labour movements, except when the government either yield or bluff unseasonably. I should like a labour government with one or two good liberals in it. It is madness to go slow just now." *Ibid.*, pp. 218–19.

years of adventurous experiment or silent growth. True social work, independent of the public power, is the laboratory of social invention. The taking over of social inventions by the State is something like the taking over of a private business by a limited company, and there are analogous results for good and evil. The introduction of State socialism would be a gigantic taking over of this kind. (xxxii–xxxiii)

Bosanquet concludes: "The end of the State is assuredly good life or the excellence of souls; but for a power which deals primarily with a compulsory arrangement of externals, and for all of us so far as in our degree we have power over externals affecting others, the only path to that end lies in very fine adjustments directed to eliciting what *ex hypothesi* they cannot produce." (xxxiv)

As to the charge of being "too intellectualist," Bosanquet is quite unregenerate. He deplores the movement, that has not grown less since his day, that holds that life, novelty, creativeness are incompatible with the principle of abstract intelligence.

We are thus brought into the presence of a curious form of agnosticism. Life, volition, immediate experience become, as it were, a Kantian thing-in-itself. For in as far as mind finds articulate utterance or expression it departs—so the argument runs—from its self-complete and concrete being. And like all agnosticism, this readily turns to pessimism. For pessimism is at hand whenever we are led to suppose that the determinate is the derivative and the secondary, and that the best experience and the true inwardness of life are unutterable. (xxxvii)

Bosanquet voices the faith of Idealism in rationality when he concludes:

Views of the type here advocated not only give the truest interpretation of social forces and processes, but have in the recent past proved the most fruitful guide and inspiration of social improvement. . . . The ancient theory of the State can only be strengthened and amplified by the wealth of modern experience. . . . I believe that, resting on a tradition derived from thinkers who have been the sanest and profoundest students of civilized life, it affords a serviceable clue to the interpretation of such developments. (xxxix–xl)

7

Josiah Royce and American Idealism

AMERICAN philosophic idealism was usually classified into four main "schools," with their seats at different universities where outstanding personalities gathered bands of disciples about them: (1) absolute idealism: Harvard University, Josiah Royce; (2) speculative or objective idealism: Cornell University, James E. Creighton; (3) personalism: Boston University, Borden P. Bowne; and (4) dynamic idealism: University of Michigan, George Sylvester Morris. In addition, there were two significant pluralistic idealists: Felix Adler of the New York Ethical Culture Society and George Holmes Howison of the University of California.[1]

Originally published in *The Journal of Philosophy*, LXIII, no. 3 (February 3, 1966), pp. 57–83. Copyright © 1966 by Journal of Philosophy, Inc.

When this paper appeared in *The Journal of Philosophy*, Ignas Skrupskelis wrote an extensively documented critique of certain parts of it. This critique was never published but was sent to Professor Randall. In a letter dated August 28, 1966, Randall replied, "I must say that your comments on the Royce chapter are by far the most valuable I have yet received on any of these chapters, and I shall make full use of them in revising it." The letter goes on to say that Randall "had hoped to have [the chapter] checked by Joseph Blau before printing," but that he was unable to do so.

I have not found any copy of the paper in which Professor Randall has embodied Skrupskelis' criticisms. Following Professor Randall's stated intent, I have changed several incorrect dates and corrected a small number of straightforward factual errors which Skrupskelis identified and which could be remedied by a simple verbal change. But I have made no other changes in the text. Instead, I have taken Skrupskelis' comments into account in several editorial footnotes. Professor Blau generously helped in the preparation of these notes and provided additional factual corrections. (Ed.)

[1] H.W. Schneider, *A History of American Philosophy* (2nd ed., New York, 1963; 1st ed. with full bibliographies, 1946), sec. VII. W.H. Werkmeister, *A History of Philosophical Ideas in America* (New York, 1949). Harvey G. Townsend, *Philosophical Ideas in the United States* (Cincinnati, 1934). I. Woodbridge Riley, *American Thought from Puritanism to Pragmatism and Beyond* (1915; 2nd ed., New York, 1923). More general intellectual history: Merle Curti, *The Growth of American Thought* (New York, 1943); Morris R. Cohen, "A Brief Sketch of the Later Philosophy," *The Cambridge History of American Literature*, Vol. III (Cambridge, Mass., 1933), pp. 225–65; Morris R. Cohen, *American Thought: A Critical Sketch* (Glencoe, Ill., 1954); Joseph L. Blau, *Men and Movements in*

I

Easily the foremost American idealist is Josiah Royce (1855–1916) of California, who from 1882 to 1916 taught at Harvard. Royce resembles his great English contemporary, F.H. Bradley, in that his thought was constantly growing, and the final phase, embodied in his Hibbert Lectures, *The Problem of Christianity* (1913), represents by far the most interesting and original stage of his thinking. He had reached the notion of the Absolute as "the Beloved Community," loyalty to which was religion at its best, and called his final philosophy a "philosophy of social loyalty." In Volume II of these lectures, *The Real World and the Christian Ideas*, he worked out certain novel metaphysical ideas, based on a theory of interpretation derived from Peirce, which are his enduring deposit. Hence we shall emphasize this final philosophy of Royce's, rather than his starting point in the *tour de force* of the chapter in his dissertation on "The Possibility of Error," embodied in his first book, *The Religious Aspect of Philosophy* (1885).

Royce [2] regarded his later phase as beginning with *The Philosophy of Loyalty* (1908); though he believed his *Problem of Christianity* "to be in essential harmony with the bases of the philosophical idealism set forth in various earlier volumes of my own, and especially in the work

---

American Philosophy (New York, 1954); John E. Smith, *The Spirit of American Philosophy* (New York, 1964).

Collections of American Idealists: Clifford Barrett, ed., *Contemporary Idealism in America* (New York, 1939); personal sketches in G.P. Adams and W.P. Montague, *Contemporary American Philosophy*, 2 vols. (New York, 1930); H.M. Kallen and Sidney Hook, *American Philosophy Today and Tomorrow* (New York, 1935).

[2] Royce, *The Religious Aspect of Philosophy* (Boston, 1885); *The Spirit of Modern Philosophy* (Boston, 1892); *The Conception of God* (Berkeley, Cal., 1895; 2nd ed., with an additional essay by Royce, 1897); *Studies of Good and Evil* (New York, 1898); *The World and the Individual:* Gifford Lectures, Vol. I (New York, 1899), Vol. II (New York, 1901); *The Conception of Immortality* (Boston, 1900); *The Philosophy of Loyalty* (Boston, 1908); *The Sources of Religious Insight* (Boston, 1912); *The Problem of Christianity* (New York, 1913); *Lectures on Modern Idealism*, ed. J. Loewenberg (Cambridge, Mass., 1919); *Fugitive Essays*, ed. J. Loewenberg (Cambridge, Mass., 1925); *The Hope of the Great Community* (New York, 1916); *War and Insurance* (New York, 1914).

On Royce, see: *Papers in Honor of Josiah Royce*, ed. J.E. Creighton, in *Philosophical Review*, 25, (1916); *The Journal of Philosophy*, centenary number, LIII, no. 3 (Feb. 2, 1956); John E. Smith, *Royce's Social Infinite* (New York, 1950); Stuart G. Brown, ed., *The Social Philosophy of Josiah Royce* (Syracuse, 1952); James Harry Cotton, *Royce on the Human Self* (Cambridge, Mass., 1954); Harold N. Lee, "Royce as Logician," *Tulane Studies in Philosophy*, IV (1955); Gabriel Marcel, *Royce's Metaphysics* (Chicago, 1956).

See also J.H. Muirhead, *The Platonic Tradition in Anglo-Saxon Philosophy* (London, 1931), Part III, Chapters 4–8; G.W. Cunningham, *The Idealistic Argument in Recent Brit-*

entitled *The World and the Individual*." ³ What is most novel in his later philosophy he attributes to Peirce:

As to certain metaphysical opinions which are stated, in outline, in the second volume of this book, I now owe much more to our great and unduly neglected American logician, Mr. Charles Peirce, than I do to the common tradition of recent idealism, and certainly very much more than I ever have owed, at any point of my own philosophical development, to the doctrines which, with technical accuracy, can be justly attributed to Hegel. (xi)

In fact, Royce continues, in his former position, that taken in *The Spirit of Modern Philosophy*, he "came nearer to being a follower of Schopenhauer than a disciple of Hegel. As far as it went this statement gave a just impression of how I then stood. I have never, since then, been more of an Hegelian than at that time I was. I am now less so than ever before" (xii).

Royce states his social idealism in contrast to James. He thinks highly of the *Varieties*.

Yet in one very important respect the religious experience upon which I most depend, differs very profoundly from that whose "varieties" James described. He deliberately confined himself to the religious experience of individuals. My main topic is a form of *social religious experience*. . . . This social form of experience is that upon which loyalty depends. James supposed that the religious experience of a church must needs be "conventional," and consequently must be lacking in depth and in sincerity. (xv–xvi)

Royce specifies:

This, to my mind, was a profound and a momentous error in the whole religious philosophy of our greatest American master in the study of the psychology of religious experience. All experience must be *at least* individual experience; but unless it is *also* social experience, and unless the whole religious community which is in question unites to share it, this experience is but as sounding brass, and as a tinkling cymbal. This truth is what Paul saw. This is

ish and American Philosophy (New York, 1938), Chapter 10; George Santayana, *Character and Opinion in the United States* (New York, 1920), Chapter 4; G.H. Mead, "The Philosophies of Royce, James, and Dewey in Their American Setting," *International Journal of Ethics*, 40 (1929–30), pp. 211–31, reprinted in *George Herbert Mead: Selected Writings*, ed. Andrew J. Reck (Indianapolis, Ind., 1964), pp. 371–91.
  [Since the publication of Professor Randall's paper, a major addition to Royce studies has been provided by the publication of Bruce Kuklick, *Josiah Royce: An Intellectual Biography* (Indianapolis, 1972). This book has been used in rechecking Professor Randall's data. (Ed.)]
  ³ *Problem of Christianity*, Vol. I, p. x.

the rock upon which the true and ideal church is built. This is the essence of Christianity. (xvi)

Royce states the core of his message: "It must be my Community that, in the end, saves me. To assert this and to live this doctrine constitute the very core of Christian experience, and of the 'Religion of Loyalty'. . . . We are saved, if at all, by devotion to the Community. . . . This is what I mean by loyalty. . . . I now say that by loyalty I mean the *practically devoted love of an individual for a community*" (xvi–xvii).

Historically speaking, the Christian Church first discovered the Christian ideas. The founder of Christianity, so far as we know what his teachings were, seems to have defined them adequately. They first came to a relatively full statement through the religious life of the Pauline Churches; and the Pauline epistles contain their first, although still not quite complete, formulation. Paul himself was certainly not the founder of Christianity. But the Pauline communities first were conscious of the essence of Christianity. . . . Those [Catholic modernists] are right who have held that the Church, rather than the person of the founder, ought to be viewed as the central idea of Christianity. (xx–xxi)

Royce is therefore uninterested in the efforts of religious liberals like Harnack to recover the "personality" of Jesus.

If Christianity is, in its inmost essence, the "religion of loyalty," the religion of that which I have called "The Beloved Community," and if Pauline Christianity contained the essence of the only doctrine by which mankind, through loyalty, are to be saved, then Buddhism is right in holding that the very form of the individual self is a necessary source of woe and of wrong. In that case, no individual human self can be saved except through ceasing to be a *mere* individual.

But if this be so, Harnack's view and the usual "liberal" view, to the effect that there was an ideally perfect human individual, whose example, or whose personal influence, involves a solution of the problem of human life, and is saving—this whole view is an opinion essentially opposed to the deepest facts of human nature, and to the very essence of the "religion of loyalty." Not through imitating nor yet through loving any mere individual human being can we be saved, but only through loyalty to the "Beloved Community." (xxiv–xxv)

But did not the Founder found the Church? Was the early Christian community its own creator? Royce has no hypothesis as to how the Church began. "The historical evidence at hand is insufficient to tell us how the church originated."

On the other hand, regarding the essence of the Christianity of the Pauline churches and concerning the actual life of those churches, we possess, in the Pauline epistles, information which is priceless, which reveals to us the religion of loyalty in its classic and universal form, and which involves the Christian ideas expounded . . . in what here follows. (xxix)

This statement makes clear not only the central religious thread of Royce's philosophy of social experience; it explains also why Santayana could take Royce as the exemplar of the "genteel tradition," the fusion of philosophic idealism and American Calvinism.

II

"With recent idealism," Royce remarks, "the 'father of Pragmatism' [Charles S. Peirce] has always felt only a very qualified sympathy, and has frequently expressed no little dissatisfaction. Some twelve years ago, just after I had printed a book on general philosophy [*The World and the Individual*], Mr. Charles Peirce wrote to me, in a letter of kindly acknowledgment, the words: 'But, when I read you, I do wish that you would study logic. You need it so much.' " Royce adds: "By a small and grateful company of philosophical students, Mr. Peirce is prized, not solely, and not, I think, mainly for his part in the early history of Pragmatism, but for his contributions to Logic. . . . Those ideas of Charles Peirce about Interpretation to which I shall here refer, never, so far as I know, attracted William James's personal attention at any time. I may add that, until recently, I myself never appreciated their significance. In acknowledging here my present indebtedness to these ideas, I have to add that, in this place, there is no room to expound them at length" (II, 115–117).

What the study Peirce recommended taught Royce was two major ideas: the mathematical notion of an infinite series, and the notion of a community of interpretation. The first is set forth in the Supplementary Essay to Volume I of *The World and the Individual*, Royce's answer to Bradley: "The One, the Many, and the Infinite." The second is elaborated in Volume II of *The Problem of Christianity*.[4]

---

[4] The Supplementary Essay appears in the first edition of *The World and the Individual*, Vol. I (1899). Clearly, since Peirce's recommendation was made after the publication of this volume, Randall's statement that this recommendation influenced the essay is in error. However, Randall provides the correct information concerning Peirce's influence at the beginning of section V of this paper (p. 146 below). By 1899 Royce already admitted Peirce's impact on his thought concerning infinite series; cf. the long footnote in *World and Individual*, Vol. I, pp. 511–12 and, in the same work, Vol. I, p. xix and Vol. II, p.

Royce had long loved the Infinite, and had found in it the ground for certainty. But he had been held back by the traditional fear of an infinite regress. In mathematical logic he found proof that the infinite is not a sign of indeterminacy or irrationality, as the Greeks had believed, but rather a sign of "perfect order," of "a well ordered series." With the existence of the infinite thus established, Royce could at last work out his central insight, that man finds salvation in devotion to an infinite Community, a community, he learned from Peirce, of interpretation. He was prepared for the Beloved Community of interpretation, devotion to which he makes central in his final philosophy.

Bradley's *Appearance and Reality* argued that the Absolute is a merely ideal conception. The *existence* of an infinite multitude is a self-contradictory notion. Dissenting, Royce aims to establish an analogy between the determinate infinite of the mathematician and the actual many-in-one world. A mathematical series is infinite when it stands in a one-to-one correspondence with a constituent part of itself—when the whole can be correlated with a part. The relations between finite members resemble the structure of the series as a whole. Such a relationship of whole series and individual members is perfectly definable, even though there be infinite series, such as the sets of even numbers, of odd numbers, of squares, etc. A determinate infinite is mathematically possible, as against Bradley.

Is it actual? Royce illustrates by maps upon which the map itself is depicted, with a further map on the depiction, *ad infinitum*. [5] So also is the thought of a thought, the consciousness of consciousness of self, loyalty to the ideal of loyalty, the oughtness of oughts, and many others. These are all existing examples of mathematically well-ordered series, of perfectly determinate infinites. Royce has shown that particular ideas are intelligible only as they are fitted into ordered systems or connected series. Either, then, the Absolute exists, or there is no knowledge, no truth, no reality, no finite things.

---

xvi. There are additional references to Peirce in the main body of the work, e.g., Vol. I, pp. 254, 255, 514*n*, 562*n*, and Vol. II, p. 195.

Another source for Royce's doctrine of the infinite was Dedekind's *Was Sind und Was Sollen die Zahlen*, which Royce liberally quotes. (Ed.)

[5] Santayana puts the argument and his comments on it: "Imagine an absolutely exhaustive map of England, spread out upon English soil. The map would be a part of England, yet would reproduce every feature of England, including itself; so that the

The existing Absolute is thus a determinate, infinite whole, the series of self-representative series, the self represented in endlessly different persons. The Absolute is the melody; we are the notes. God knows and appreciates the composition as a whole, and also pays attention to each note or phrase in the contrapuntal harmony of the universe. But we mortals can hear only stray notes, or now and again snatches of the divine music. The infinity of intercommunicating selves constitutes one body, one community, the Absolute Self. God can be one only by being many, an infinite series. The finite parts depend on the whole; the whole is the sum and complete unity of all the parts. Thus are the many one, and the one many. Royce insisted this was a rational theism; to the unregenerate it seemed more like pantheism.

Royce thus proved the Absolute in 1899, with the aid of the determinate infinite of the mathematicians. Between the publication of his Gifford Lectures in 1899 and his death in 1916, he published two monographs [6] and six articles on mathematical logic, serving as the American pioneer in introducing that discipline to English readers. Like the Russell of that time, Royce was a Platonic realist: concepts, laws, numbers, are perfectly objective and "real," not as spatiotemporal, but as objective relations between ideas and systems of ideas. He was a Platonic logical realist, rather than a "Hegelian," and took

---

map would reappear on a smaller scale within itself an infinite number of times, like a mirror reflected in a mirror. In this way we might be individuals within a larger individual and no less actual and complete than he.

"Does this solve the problem? If we take the illustration as it stands, there is still only one individual in existence, the material England, all the maps being parts of its single surface; nor will it at all resemble the maps, since it will be washed by the sea and surrounded by foreign nations, and not, like the maps, by other Englands enveloping it. If, on the contrary, we equalize the status of all the members of the series, by making it infinite in both directions, then there would be no England at all, but only map within map of England. There would be no absolute mind inclusive but not included, and the Absolute would be the series as a whole, utterly different from any of its members. It would be a series while they were maps, a truth while they were minds; and if the Absolute from the beginning had been regarded as a truth only, there never would have been any difficulty in the existence of individuals under it. Moreover, if the individuals are all exactly alike, does not their exact similarity defeat the whole purpose of the speculation, which was to vindicate the equal reality of the whole and of its *limited* parts?" *Character and Opinion*, pp. 135–36.

[6] "The Relation of the Principles of Logic to the Foundations of Geometry," *Transactions of the American Mathematical Society*, 24 (1905), pp. 353–415; "Principien der Logic," *Enzyklopädie der philosophischen Wissenschaften* (1912), Vol. I, tr. by B.F. Meyer in *Encyclopedia of the Philosophic Sciences* (1913), Vol. I, pp. 67–135.

the mathematician as dealing as much with given "facts" as the engineer or the farmer. This was the root of his long quarrel with James's version of pragmatism. Logic is "the general science of order, the theory of the forms of an orderly realm of objects, real or ideal." [7] Order is not an arrangement introduced by the mind into the amorphous facts of nature; it is a discovered scheme of valid relationships. Reality is found always in verified, ordered series of ideas; anything less is a senseless fragment. Nothing can be understood in isolation. The clue to reality is the connectedness of things. Will and purpose are central in individuals and in the cosmos, but without knowledge of the order of things there can be no fulfillment of purposes. How, then, are purposes and the world order connected?

This is the question Royce sets himself in Volume II of *The Problem of Christianity*, "The Real World and the Christian Ideas." It is an interpretation of meaning in social and teleological, functional terms, culminating in the construction of the Absolute as the great community of intercommunicating, mutually interpreting spirits—in religious terms, that spiritual community which is the ideal Church, the "Beloved Community." Rationally interpreted, the Divine is an ideal spiritual community. This brought Royce close to pluralistic idealists like Howison or Felix Adler.

To work out this conception, Royce seized on the second great idea he found in Peirce, Peirce's theory of signs. Signs for Peirce are symbols invested with meaning by the experience of a community. When any object acquires a meaning, it is "interpreted." This is a social process involving three terms: the sign, the interpreter, and the interpretee. The interpreter interprets the sign to the interpretee, who may be himself or another. Interpretation is an unending process, for the interpretation may function as a sign in further interpretations, and so on without end. The world of interpretation is thus inexhaustible and ever growing, ever being enriched with new interpretations. Interpretation is the foundation of "community," of our fellowship with fellow spirits: it is the Kingdom of Heaven of the Christians. Individuals are linked triadically into a community of interpretation: A interprets B to C. Royce has abandoned the dyadic relation of epistemology— between idea and object—for the triadic relations of language, of the

---

[7] *Encyclopedia of Philosophic Sciences*, p. 69.

social use of symbols. Knowledge is essentially social; if it is real "knowledge," its subject matter, "reality," must exhibit the same structure and be itself "social."

Royce took over Peirce's doctrine of the community of scientists engaged in the cooperative search for ultimate truth and made out of it a metaphysics:

A process of interpretation involves, of necessity, an infinite sequence of acts of interpretation. It also admits of an endless variety within all the selves which are thus mutually interpreted. These selves, in all their variety, constitute the life of a single Community of Interpretation, whose central member is that spirit of the community whose essential function we know. In the concrete, then, the universe is a community of interpretation whose life comprises and unifies all the social varieties and all the social communities which, for any reason, we know to be real in the empirical world which our social and our historical sciences study. The history of the universe, the whole order of time, is the history and the order and the expression of this Universal Community. (II, 272-73).

In *The Philosophy of Loyalty* (1908) Royce states the ethical implications of the Great Community of interpretation. This ideal community, existing in aspiration rather than as yet in fact, is the true object of love and loyalty. The true moral maxim becomes "loyalty to loyalty," which expresses devotion to the whole community, the source of being for the individual. Royce sees the beginnings of such a community in the community of scientists cooperating in the search for truth, and also in the Christian community of love modeled on the Pauline Church. Political states or nations are not communities in the true sense, since they foster a spirit of partisanship, exclusiveness, and animosity toward one another. They breed individualism, and that is the sin against the Holy Ghost. Taken by himself, the individual is a lost soul; to be a real individual, one must be a loyal member of the Great Community, for only through the community comes the grace that makes salvation or selfhood possible. God is the spirit of the community; the love of God is loyalty to loyalty. The Great Community is "real," not as actually embodied in existence, but as the eternal moral basis of all order.

At this point in Royce's philosophical development, World War I broke out. Royce rose to the occasion and, in *The Hope of the Great Community* (1916), dramatically denounced the Germans as aggressors, as evil rampant, as disloyal to the Great Community. Together with his heroic zeal, he proposed a scheme of insurance against war (*War and Insurance*, 1914). Insurance involves the triadic relation between insured, insurer, and beneficiary; insurance is the tangible embodiment of interpretation, enabling all to bear one another's burdens. By insurance "we are saved through community." Church and insurance company together form the hope of the great community.

III

By what path did Royce reach this philosophy of loyalty to the Great Community? From the beginning his thinking was dominated by the single theme: his conviction that we are all members of one body, one great community, the infinite, eternal, divine Whole, which is the source of all the meaning and purpose that can be embodied in our finite individual experience. All his life Royce was searching for arguments to support this basic insight, arguments that would give it precise logical articulation. His is, like Hegel's, an idealism of man's social experience. But he was, as we have seen, no facile repeater of Hegel's thinking. He started with an original but paradoxical dialectical argument of his own, which made his philosophic reputation. Pursuing the difficulties in his formulation, he was led, mainly by Schopenhauer, to an "absolute voluntarism" or "absolute pragmatism" that brought him close to the Cornell school of Creighton and to Bosanquet; this second period of his thinking is expressed in his Gifford Lectures, *The World and the Individual.* Then he discovered Peirce and mathematical logic, and proceeded to work out his most original formulation of the idealism of social experience. Thus, like Bradley, Royce exhibits three main periods.

Royce was born, in 1855, in Grass Valley, California, the son of forty-niners who had come West seeking gold. His mother was a pious Christian of strong character, who gave him his first teaching, secular and religious. In 1866 the family moved to San Francisco, and Josiah was schooled there and in Oakland. In 1873, two years after its opening, he entered the University at Berkeley.[8] He read Spencer and

[8] The University of California was originally located in Oakland and moved to Berkeley in 1873. Royce enrolled on September 23, 1871, while the university was still in Oakland, and continued his studies in Berkeley. See William Warren Ferrier, *Origin and Development of the University of California* (Berkeley: The Sather gate book shop, 1930), pp. 279, 412. (Ed.)

Mill on his own, and studied under the geologist Joseph Le Conte and the poet Edward Rowland Sill. Graduating in 1875 with a thesis on the theology of Aeschylus's Prometheus, he was given some money to study in Germany, by a group of prosperous pioneers. There he heard Lotze, read Schopenhauer, Schelling, Kant, and Pfleiderer—he became profoundly erudite in German philosophy—and allowed his Romantic feelings to blossom. He got one of the first fellowships at Johns Hopkins, just opened, and received his degree in 1878 with a thesis "On the Principles of the Interdependence of Human Knowledge." At Hopkins William James had assured him that "a young man might rightfully devote his life to philosophy if he chose." With no opening at Hopkins, Royce returned to teach logic and rhetoric at Berkeley, studying and writing on logic and mathematics.[9] In 1882 James and Palmer called him to Harvard, where he was an immediate success, rising eventually to become Professor of the History of Philosophy. In 1885 President Eliot invited him to give the Lowell Lectures. But when Mr. Lowell explained he would have to sign a creed, he refused to do so for money, and instead wrote a book on *California: A Study of American Character*.[10] He closed with a prophetic paean to society:

It is the State, the Social Order, that is divine. We are all but dust, save as this social order gives us life. When we think it is our instrument, our plaything, and make our private fortunes the one object, then this social order rapidly becomes vile to us; we call it sordid, degraded, corrupt, unspiritual and ask how we may escape from it forever. But if we turn again and serve the social order and not merely ourselves, we soon find that what we are serving is simply our own highest spiritual destiny in bodily form. *It* is never truly sordid or corrupt or unspiritual; it is only *we* that are so when we neglect our duty.[11]

Royce wrote his first philosophical work, *The Religious Aspect of Philosophy* (1885), in a style modeled on Fichte's *Vocation of Man*—it was

[9] According to the Register of the University of California for 1878–79 and 1879–80, Royce's title was "Instructor in English Language and Literature." However, he did teach logic to some of his students. (Ed.)

[10] Randall should not be construed to imply that Royce's *California* was in some way connected with his refusal to give the Lowell Lectures. He merely used the time he might have spent preparing the lectures to write a book which Horace E. Scudder of Houghton-Mifflin had suggested to him two years earlier. (This is mentioned in a letter to Bernard Moses, dated September 7, 1883. This letter is now in the Bancroft Library of the University of California.) (Ed.)

[11] *California: A Study of American Character* (Boston, 1886), p. 501.

often asked who translated Royce's prose from the German. Thus
Royce started his long series of attempts to demonstrate logically the
object of religious faith. He changed his ideas of what that object is,
but never his conviction it could be proved rationally and that such
proof was the crucial task of philosophy. To reinterpret religious faith
into something that could be demonstrated—this was Royce's life-long
quest. Amidst the Harvard galaxy of the turn of the century, he was
in this sense the traditionalist. Santayana wanted to understand religious faith, but he did not dream of "demonstrating" such poetry
and imagination. James the experimentalist was always looking for a
new faith; he defended the right to believe it—if you could find one.
This was Harvard's contribution to what may be called the idealistic
protest against mechanistic science.

Armed with Christian training—but no orthodox beliefs—and with
post-Kantian German Romantic idealism, especially Fichte, Schelling,
Goethe, and Schopenhauer, from whom he learned the importance of
evil, but with sympathy for little in Hegel save his system-building,
Royce in his first book set out to prove the Absolute. He tried to do it
with an unconvincing but clever and original bit of dialectic, whose
form he was for some time reconstructing. He tackled two problems:
the moral problem of pessimism and the theoretical problem of truth.
No moral ideal can be established, since each rests on the physical fact
of liking or disliking, and none can be proved obligatory. But "the
truth of the matter is concealed in the doubt." The very fact that man
fails to find any particular binding "ought" implies that he is inspired
by the moral will that all such particular ideals *ought to be harmonized.*
The good of such harmony is self-evident. Therefore pessimism as to
any discoverable ideal asserts an absolute ideal of harmony. Royce
formulates this, in Kantian terms: "In so far as in thee lies, act as if
thou wert at once thy neighbor and thyself. Treat these two lives as
one life." [12] Do not try to be happy as an individual—nothing particular can be final. And organize life, and be loyal to the organization.
Man in his aloneness is a meaningless fragment; to have meaning and
content, his life must be interpreted in the light of the community of
purposes and ends all men ought to share. Such an organized community of ends is found imperfectly in science, more perfectly in the

[12] *Religious Aspect of Philosophy*, p. 149.

state, but best of all in the spiritual community of the Church. Art is but an imperfect agency of organization, since artists cultivate not community but individuality. As has been remarked, Royce talks about the state with the fervor of a Prussian or a Californian.

Secondly, Royce takes up the logical problem of judgment. Men err; how is error possible? Borrowing a chapter from his thesis, he argues that the recognition of error implies the existence of an absolute truth. An error could never be ascertained unless there are in fact a more inclusive truth. Thomas has an erroneous idea of John. This means that Thomas' idea of John does not agree with the true idea of John. But Thomas' error could never be found out unless there were in fact a more inclusive thought that included both Thomas' erroneous idea and also the true idea of John; for the error of Thomas' idea can be detected only by comparison with the whole truth about John, and that truth must be present to some mind. In short, error becomes possible as one moment or element in a higher truth, that is, in a consciousness that makes the error a part of itself, while recognizing it as error.

Either there is no such thing as error, which statement is a flat self-contradiction, or else there is an infinite unity of conscious thought to which is present all possible truth (424).

Santayana points out the missing link in this argument:

Here again Royce slipped into a romantic equivocation which a strict logician would not have tolerated. Knowledge of the truth, a passing psychological possession, was substituted for the truth known, and this at the cost of rather serious ultimate confusions. It is the truth itself, the facts in their actual relations, that honest opinion appeals to, not to another opinion or instance of knowledge; and if, in your dream of warm sympathy and public corroboration, you lay up your treasure in some instance of knowledge, which time and doubt might corrupt, you have not laid up your treasure in heaven. . . . To personify the truth is to care less for truth than for the corroboration and sympathy which the truth, become human, might bring to our opinions. It is to set up another thinker, ourself enlarged, to vindicate us; without considering that this second thinker would be shut up, like us, in his own opinions, and would need to look to the truth beyond him as much as we do. (*Character and Opinion*, 104–5)

Royce's argument runs: an idea cannot be true or false to itself, but only to another idea, and this to a third, *ad infinitum*. Therefore, if any thought is an error, it is so only because there is an infinite judge of truth. This judge must be actual, if error is actual. "Infinite error and evil are actual and are eternally so judged by an inclusive infinite thought. In this religious insight the mind can rest." This is the "religious aspect of philosophy." The actuality of error and evil establishes the necessary existence of absolute truth and good. Royce's cleverness is apparent.[13]

The completed whole of thought is the infinite perfection of the real. "The world, then, as a whole, is and must be absolutely good, since the infinite thought must know what is desirable, and knowing it, must have present in itself the true objects of desire" (444). Hence the goal of action is "the progressive realization by men of the eternal life of an Infinite Spirit."

Finite evils exist: Royce was a realist, and his ethics heroic. How can they exist in a perfect universe? Evil is an episode, a fragment, which in the total scheme of things is conquered by good. But its existence is morally necessary, for it is in the struggle against evil that good is realized. Evil can never be removed completely from the finite world. Virtue, for Royce as for Fichte, is to battle heroically for the good. It is not ends attained or goods enjoyed, but fighting the good fight.

I V

Were this *tour de force* the best Royce could do, he would be dismissed as a clever run-of-the-mill nineteenth-century idealist, with a strong dash of Calvinistic theology. In his second stage, he raised himself to the level of the objective idealism of the Cornell School and of Creighton and Bosanquet—that is, to a sound if unoriginal idealism.

James praised Royce's book extravagantly, and was greatly influenced by him during the eighties and early nineties; James reached his own distinctive positions slowly. But in their frequent arguments, James became more and more anti-monistic, pluralistic, and empiri-

[13] Santayana states Royce's famous argument from the existence of error: "Error exists, he tells us, and common sense will readily agree. . . . But if error exists, Royce continues, there must be a truth from which it differs; and the existence of truth (according to the principles of idealism, that nothing can exist except for a mind that knows it) implies that someone knows the truth; but as to know the truth thoroughly, and supply the corrective to every possible error, involves omniscience, we have proved the existence of an omniscient mind or universal thought; and this is almost, if not quite, equivalent to the existence of God." *Character and Opinion*, pp. 100–1.

cal. Unlike some of the British idealists, Royce also took experience and the reality of persons seriously, and James in turn forced him to a more empirical grounding of the Absolute and to greater justice to the reality of the finite world. How *can* separate minds or persons be unified, as his imperative demanded? How can God experience individual existences? And how can man act as a person, if he be merely a "thought" of God? Royce fell back on Schopenhauer's voluntarism. From the point of view of the world of idea, which Royce called "the world of description," there is no answer. Two minds cannot unite; two ideas cannot be compounded. But from the point of view of will, which Royce called "the world of appreciation," unification is possible. Two wills can unite. By love or mutual appreciation men can transcend their individual selves, and "two lives can become one life." Likewise, God, by an act of love or appreciation, can single out an individual for his attention. We men can share in the "reflective publicity" of a common light or will. God looking down can *see* us at once, all together; but he is more than thought, he is a will, a self that can *attend* to us one by one.

To answer the pluralistic idealists like George H. Howison, Royce turned, in *The Conception of God* (1897), to a closer examination of finite human experience. Its very nature, he argues, implies an absolute experience. Our human experience is passing and fragmentary, but it always contains in itself more than we see at first glance. We interpret the fragmentary facts of the immediately given by fitting them into organized systems of science. So organized, experience "fulfills" the fragmentary perceptions by revealing how they fit into the community of facts and ideas. Absolute truth and reality would then be absolutely organized experience fulfilling all possible finite facts and systems of facts.

Every intelligent interpretation of an experience involves the appeal from the experienced fragment to some more organized whole of experience, in whose unity this fragment is conceived as finding its organic place. . . . There is an Absolute Experience, for which the conception of an absolute reality is fulfilled by the very contents that get presented to this Experience. This Absolute Experience is related to our experience as an organic whole to its own fragments.[14]

[14] *Conception of God*, 2nd ed., pp. 42–44.

Royce has landed with Bosanquet and Creighton in objective idealism; Howison still asked, how is individual freedom possible for the
mere "fragment" of an "absolute experience"? Is this not "oriental
pantheism"? Royce then made the principle of individuation finite
purpose or will. God is not merely the all-knower; he is cosmic purpose, the end upon which converge all finite purposes. God's loving
purpose differentiates and individuates the world out of his cosmic
thought. Finite individuals can find fulfillment only in exemplifying
self-transcending purposes and in loyalty to more and more inclusive
ends. Individual freedom comes only through conscious participation
in the life of the Absolute. "A world of individuals more separate than
this . . . would be a world of anarchy . . . a moral hell" (275).

All this is little more than a restatement of classic German idealism
of the more voluntaristic type, combined with James's doctrine of
selective attention applied to God to form a theology.

V

Royce needed new ideas. Invited to give the Gifford Lectures for
1899 and 1900, he proceeded to work them out in terms of a new doctrine of "meaning." And just at this time Peirce urged him to study
mathematical logic, with startling effects on Royce, who had long
been interested in mathematical thought. The results are embodied in
the first statement of his final position, in his supplementary essay to
Volume I of *The World and the Individual*, on "The One, the Many,
and the Infinite," and worked out in detail in Volume II of *The Problem of Christianity*.

The Gifford Lectures are the only place where Royce treats the
philosophic problems of his position in their own terms without making them subsidiary to his religious faith. Unfortunately, in the process he changed his position radically, and so his most original philosophic views are not found in what was intended to be his systematic
and definitive utterance. Hence the relation of *The World and the Individual* to Volume II of *The Problem of Christianity* is something like that
of Kant's *Critique of Pure Reason* to his *Critique of Judgment*—the former
is more systematic, but the latter far more suggestive.

Royce summarizes his "Idealistic Theory of Knowledge":

The contrast between these two types of human knowledge, the "descriptive"
and the "appreciative," has been made to depend solely upon the difference

between the "social" and the "individual" points of view. I still defend, and
. . . expound afresh, the thesis that the contrast between our "descriptive"
knowledge of the *physical world* and our "appreciative" knowledge of the facts
of finite life, is determined precisely by this difference between our social consciousness of what is "valid for all individuals" and our personal consciousness
of what is valid for the Self. But it is true that one must still seek *within* the
consciousness of the individual Self for the motives that make it logically possible for this Self to regard the abstraction called "a view valid for all individuals" as a possible abstraction. We must show how the Self can make such a
view the object of its own contemplation in any sense whatever. For the
human Self, although it comes to be aware of itself in terms of its social contrast with other Selves, still (in so far as it has become self-conscious at all) acknowledges its objects as valid, in the first place, from *its own* point of view,
and not from the point of view of another Self. How comes it, then, to interpret the world of facts as such that *another* Self could find *these same facts*, or
some aspect of them, to be also its own facts? [15]

Royce, seeking the "logical roots" of this power to make impersonal
abstractions in the consciousness of the Individual, finds it in "a certain contrast between two aspects of the inner personal consciousness
of any intelligent individual whose relations to the world are such as
are our human relations" (ix).

The World of Description is essentially a world of abstractions, valid for the
Self only in so far as it conceives itself as at present unable to find how the
facts express its own conscious purpose, and, consequently, valid for the Self
only in so far as the Self, in its submissiveness, conceives these facts as also
valid for an indefinite number of *other* points of view, which it has not yet
made its own. Thus, *within* the individual consciousness, I point out one of
the roots from which the more abstract interpretation of the world that is
"valid for all" the members of a society grows. (ix)

Royce found the idea of "meaning" the key to uniting these two
dimensions of reality: will and idea, or appreciation and description.
'Meaning' has a double significance. It can signify what I "mean" or
intend to do, or it can signify what I "mean" or refer to as an external
object. In Lecture VII of Volume I, the act of intention or purpose he
calls an "internal meaning," and the act of referring, an "external
meaning." They are but two phases of a single purpose. Our internal
meanings, that is, our wills and purposes, demand objectification or
external realization; our external meanings, or ideas, demand to be ap-
propriated as satisfactions or fulfillments of our internal meanings.

[15] *World and Individual*, Vol. II, pp. vii–ix.

What we call the external world is thus the end or objective toward which our purposes are directed. Reality is the objective fulfillment of individuated aims. This view is of course close to Fichte's voluntarism.

And Royce was willing to call his view "absolute pragmatism." The internal meaning of ideas is their purposive, teleological character. The test of true correspondence of idea with outer facts is the degree to which these facts fulfill or embody the purpose that is the core of the idea in its internal meaning. A thing is real only if and to the extent that it thus fulfills the internal meaning of ideas. In the perspective of the cosmos, "purpose" determines "reality." For what we find as outer fact, imperfectly relevant to our individual purposes, is an expression of the completely determinate and absolutely fulfilled purpose of the Absolute. To the extent, therefore, that our own purposes become broader and more inclusive, more self-transcending, to that degree our ideas are more adequately fulfilled; we come to possess more and more truth and reality, and we become more truly individuated and, hence, truer "individuals." Ideas are true only if they work. But the only ideas that will work are those in harmony with the inclusive purpose of the Absolute. This is "absolute pragmatism."

Royce could not follow Spinoza in taking reality to be beyond good and evil. In absolute reality, all is for the best; but men are not mere pawns of the Absolute. The perfection of the whole requires that every deed be atoned for. The imperfection of the human will is the source of evil and suffering; but the world order will neutralize your evil deeds: other finite agents will overcome the evil you have done. Yet the imperfection of the will is the very condition of good, which is just the perpetual struggle against evil. The sorrows of finite man are God's sorrows also, for he knows and experiences all.

Royce's theodicy accepts a tragic sense of life, the religious demand that God's will be holy, and the human need to struggle against sin. This paradoxical double sense that man is wicked but the universe perfect outraged James, the melioristic pluralist with a finite God struggling against evil. He would not admit original sin, the *necessary* existence of evil in a perfect universe. James remarked that Royce wanted "not the absence of vice, but vice there, and virtue holding her by the throat." [16] Santayana, still less sympathetic, observed, "Virtue

[16] *The Will to Believe* (New York, 1897), p. 169.

consisted (as Royce often put it) in holding evil by the throat; so that the world was good because it was a good world to strangle, and if we only managed to do so, the more it deserved strangling the better world it was" (116). "What calm could there be in the double assurance that it was really right that things should be wrong, but that it was really wrong not to strive to right them?" (126). To Royce, James's view was lack of faith in a successful outcome and moral anarchy in criticizing the universe. Royce continued to glorify God and enjoy him forever.

Royce can thus be regarded as the sublimation of the Calvinistic and Puritan tradition; so he appeared to the Latin Santayana and to sensitive, sophisticated, and enlightened students of his, like Wendell T. Bush. Or, in the present fashion, he can be taken as an early Existentialist, viewing man as alienated from his essential being in the social community of persons, as he appears to the perceptive John E. Smith. Perhaps most judicious of all was the judgment of George Herbert Mead, that Royce is the expression of the American democratic ideal of a plurality of divers persons united in devotion and loyalty to the construction of an ideal community in which every individual's differences would be preserved and would contribute to the richness of the whole. From any of these twentieth-century perspectives, Royce's long and futile attempt to "demonstrate" the ideal he saw so clearly as the necessary implication of thought is a hang-over from the historically limited assumptions of the nineteenth-century idealism he imbibed at the German fount. Royce's dialectic is of mere historical interest. His vision and his faith—his loyalty to loyalty, to the spirit of cooperation—is of enduring worth.

VI

Royce ended with a fundamentally social ideal, a community of intercommunicating selves united in love. Two other American idealists arrived at a somewhat similar pluralistic spiritual ideal: the one academic, George Holmes Howison, who initiated and long taught the study of philosophy at Berkeley; the other the founder of his own religious institution, Felix Adler, who after 1903 taught also at Columbia. Felix Adler (1851–1933),[17] son of the rabbi of Temple Emanu-El in New York, himself a German Reform rabbi, was reared as his

[17] *An Ethical Philosophy of Life* (New York, 1918); *The Reconstruction of the Spiritual Ideal* (New York, 1924).

father's successor. In Germany he studied with Hermann Cohen and Albert Lange, the neo-Kantians, where he imbibed the neo-Kantianism of the Marburg School; and with Trendelenburg, the Aristotelian. He found also the notion of a free and universal religion of right and duty. This he founded on the "ethical experience," the "nonempirical" experience of the inalienable worth of every individual. Returned from Germany, he made a dramatic recantation of the limitations of Judaism from his father's pulpit, and set up the New York Society for Ethical Culture in 1876. Thereafter he was a leader in the Free Religious Association, a participant in Thomas Davidson's school at Glenmore in the Adirondacks, and a civic prophet of political and educational reform—the Ethical Culture schools were a natural development of his program. A leader of an expanding religious institution, which appealed especially to those German Jews who found Reform Judaism too restricting and not Gentile enough, Adler always wanted to be taken seriously as a philosopher and was delighted when friends set up a chair of social ethics for him at Columbia in 1903. After 1920 he preferred to develop his ideas in a group that met at his own meetinghouse, which he could limit to those he judged receptive.

Fundamentally a neo-Kantian in ethics,[18] he tried to socialize the individualistic moral ideal of the Kantians and thus provide an idealism that would be not only liberal but also democratic. Reason, as he saw it, does not merely formulate a rational ideal of Newtonian universality. Starting with the experience of moral worth, it constructs the spiritual ideal of an organic society of ethical selves, which he at one time called "the Metorganism," or the "ethical manifold," and regarded as the rational formulation of *Göttheit*, divinity. This spiritual ideal is transcendent and is to be distinguished sharply from man the empirical being as he is. Adler distrusted the idealizations of human nature of contemporary Hegelians and used to urge students to study Kant and beware of Hegel:

The disparateness of the physical world and the ethical universe should ever be kept in the foreground. Every effort to solve the riddle by somehow identifying the two has failed. To account for the existence of a finite world of indefinite extensibility side by side with a universe *ex hypothesi* infinite is impossible. Instead of seeking to explain let effort go toward utilizing. Let the *world*

[18] See *Essays Philosophical and Psychological in Honor of William James* (New York, 1908), pp. 303–65.

be used instrumentally for the purpose of verifying the existence of the universe.[19]

Adler thus escaped the paradoxes of Royce's Hegelian thought by denying that the problem of evil could be solved intellectually: evil is to be *used* for spiritual purposes, not explained or explained away. Though his language was Kantian, Adler had little to learn about Sin.

This same practical attitude led him to be suspicious of any attempt at a rational theology or theodicy:

Ethics has lain in the lap of theology, which was itself corrupted by the attempt to apply to ethical problems the inadequate principle of causality in the form of creation theories, while again in recent times, by way of reaction against theology, the solution of ethical questions is sought for in the empirical disciplines where a measure at least of objective certainty has rewarded the investigators. Even Kant, who asserted the independence of ethics, actually made it dependent on Newtonian science [Adler here followed the critiques of Hermann Cohen]. The great task now is, strictly to carry out the idea of the independence of ethics, not indeed as if its principles were unrelated to those of science and art, but in the sense of independently investigating the problems *peculiar* to ethical consciousness. (132–33)

In Adler is no clever Roycian dialectic, but rather the appeal to ethical experience:

For the average man, and indeed for all men, the test of the truth of a theory is the practice to which it leads. Abstract metaphysical arguments appeal only to a few, and even for them the formula in its abstract guise is unconvincing. . . . And so with respect to conduct: look at the ways of human behavior traced out in accordance with the plan of the ethical manifold, and see whether such behavior wins the approval of the spiritual nature implicit within you. This is not a transcendental derivation of ethics. The ideal of the infinite society is a fulguration *out of* ethical experience, to be ever renewed *in it*. We build not only our world, but our [spiritual] universe. (134)

The ethical maxim Adler read: "Endeavor always to elicit the best in others, and thereby in yourself also." The ethical manifold is a society in which this maxim is practically embodied. Use the empirical as an instrument for realizing the spiritual. Only thus can we hope to solve our most pressing problems—such as the labor problem, the problem of the family, the problem of patriotism and international relations:

[19] *Ethical Philosophy of Life*, p. 134.

If Kant has failed at this point, as I believe he has, his usefulness as a guide in the reconstruction of modern life is seriously diminished. What he had set out to demonstrate, the inalienable worth of man, remains: but foundations other than his must be found. For the formula "not merely as a means but also as an end" I would substitute: "Treat every man as a spiritual means to thine own spiritual end and conversely . . . treat the extent and the manner in which we are to use one another as means as being determined by the criterion that our exchange of services shall conduce to the attainment of each other's ends as ethical beings conjointly." (138–39)

Kant was the great spokesman of eighteenth-century individualistic liberalism and democracy. Adler expresses a more socialized democracy. Thus he seeks to go beyond the individualistic morality of the face-to-face group assumed in the Gospels and to create a group ethics, an ethics of group relations. He tried to work out an ethical theory of the functions of the various vocations, and suggested an interesting educational program based on this functional conception.

Adler had his blind spots: he found it difficult to expand his theory of the function of the nation into a genuine international community, and, like Royce, he was caught by the pressures of World War I—though he insisted any justification of that war must hold good for the Germans as well as the Allies. But his idealism of a pluralistic social experience has a reality and a genuineness often lacking in the dialectic of a Royce—or a McTaggart. And his scorn for the idealization of finite evil is refreshing after Hegelian disquisitions on the immanence of the Divine.

VII

George Holmes Howison (1834–1916),[20] who installed philosophy at Berkeley in 1884 and founded its famous Philosophical Union, like Adler criticized Kantian individualism and worked out a somewhat similar ethical pluralism. A teacher of mathematics in St. Louis, he was a member of the Kant Club that went over Brokmeyer's translation of Hegel's *Phenomenologie;* he taught logic and the philosophy of science at M.I.T. from 1872 to 1878; then enjoyed two years' study in Germany under Michelet the Hegelian, and began to expound "the

[20] Howison, *The Limits of Evolution* (New York, 1901; rev. ed., 1904). See John Wright Buckman and George Malcolm Stratton, *George Holmes Howison, Philosopher and Teacher* (Berkeley, 1934); Thomas O'Brien Hanley, "George Holmes Howison," *Pacific Historical Review*, 30 (1961), pp. 271–78.

'Absolute Idea' as a Reason eternally personal, and the ground and source of the personality in man, instead of a mere bond of Logical Energy, coming first to consciousness in human nature." [21] Howison preached a personalistic pluralism, and saw the Ideal as the "eternal republic of God."

Howison lists his theses:

I. All existence is either (1) the existence of *minds*, or (2) the existence of *the items and order of their experience:* all the existences known as "material" consisting in certain of these experiences.

II. Time and Space, and all that both "contain," owe their entire existence to the essential correlation and coexistence of minds.

III. These many minds, being in this mutual recognition of their moral reality the determining ground of all events and all mere "things," form the eternal (i.e., unconditionally real) world; and by a fitting metaphor, consecrated in the usage of ages, they may be said to constitute the "City of God." . . . God, the fulfilled Type of every mind, the living Bond of their union, reigns in it, not by the exercise of power, but solely by light.

IV. The members of the Eternal Republic have no origin . . . no source in time whatever. They simply *are*, and constitute the eternal order. . . .

VII. This Pluralism held in union by reason, the World of Spirits, is thus the genuine *Unmoved One that moves all Things.* Not the solitary God, but the whole World of Spirits including God, and united through recognition of him, is the real "Prime Mover." . . . Its oneness is not that of a single inflexible Unit, leaving no room for freedom in the many, for a many that is really many, but is the oneness of uniting harmony, of spontaneous cooperation, in which every member, from inner initiative, from native contemplation of the same Ideal, joins in moving all things changeable toward the common goal.

VIII. The movement of things changeable toward the goal of a common Ideal is what we have in these days learned to call the process of Evolution. (128–39)

Howison's "eternal Republic of God" is a democratic, pluralistic type of community of human minds.

Howison was a pluralistic personalist. Borden P. Bowne (1847–1910) [22] was a personalist also, but, far from being a pluralist, he was a Methodist, expounding Methodist liberal theism. Attacking

[21] Buckman and Stratton, p. 69.

[22] Borden P. Bowne, *Studies in Theism* (1879); *Metaphysics* (1882); *Philosophy of Theism* (1887); *Immanence of God* (1909); *Principles of Ethics* (1893); *Theory of Thought and Knowledge* (New York, 1897); *Personalism* (1908). See Edgar S. Brightman, *Person and Reality* (New York, 1958); Ralph T. Flewelling, *The Person, or the Significance of Man* (Los Angeles, 1952); Francis J. McConnell, *Borden P. Bowne* (Cincinnati, 1909).

Spencer as a student at New York Univeristy, Bowne studied with Lotze in Germany, and absorbed the doctrine of the empirical reality of the self, as a substitute alike for the substantial soul of tradition and for the congeries of impressions of the empiricists. The self is an ultimate empirical reality; following a "transcendental empiricism" and reconstructing the Kantian categories, he showed, by the principle of sufficient reason, that persons can be caused only by persons and that the ultimate cause or creator must therefore be "at least personal." He had thus to defend the validity of speculative hypotheses, which he insisted were fruitful and led to new facts. The many disciples of Bowne have tended to shift their arguments from Bowne's own cosmology to the theory of value, holding that "the only world-view in which values and meanings can have a permanently real status is one for which minds, personalities, and their values are supreme."

VIII

Pluralistic and personal idealism, which we have treated in terms of their outstanding American representatives, had doughty defenders in England as well. John McTaggart Ellis McTaggart (1866–1925), the contemporary of Bradley at Cambridge, taught a pluralistic idealism with many features resembling that of Howison and of the "Great Community of social experience" phase of Royce's thought. Though he long taught his views to a select few at Cambridge—the curriculum restricted the philosophical tripos much more narrowly than Greats did at Oxford—his writing was mostly in the form of commentaries on Hegel (*Studies in the Hegelian Dialectic*, Cambridge, 1896), and was sharply critical of rational theology (*Some Dogmas of Religion*, Cambridge, 1906); so he won little influence among either the humanists or the theologians. His major theoretical work, *The Nature of Existence* (Vol. I, 1921; Vol. II, 1927), developed a high apriorism, and was hardly appreciated until it evoked the elucidation of the critical mind of his devoted student, C.D. Broad (*An Examination of McTaggart's Philosophy*, Cambridge, 1933–38). Perhaps McTaggart's major influence was exerted through long personal discussion with Alfred North Whitehead, who seems to have absorbed his "Hegelian" elements from him.[23]

---

[23] There is an inimitable portrait of McTaggart in Leonard S. Woolf's *Sowing*.

G.F. Stout (1860–1944), who conducted *Mind* from 1896 to 1920 and made it the house organ of English Idealism, was known chiefly as a psychologist who elaborated on William James (*Analytic Psychology*, 1896; *Manual of Psychology*, 1898); he was largely responsible for the abandonment of the older association psychology in Great Britain and cleared the ground for Freud and Jung, who have had few more academic rivals in England. Toward the end of his life he set forth a pluralistic version of idealistic metaphysics.

In this endeavor his chief companion was James Ward (1843–1925), who wrote the influential article on "Psychology" for the 11th edition of the *Encyclopedia Britannica* and in 1899 wrote the most popular of all statements of pluralistic Idealism in England, *Naturalism and Agnosticism*, anticipating C.D. Broad with its keen analysis of scientific thought.

As early as 1887 the Scotsman Andrew Seth Pringle-Pattison (1856–1931) defended personal idealism against Hegelian absolutism in his lectures *Hegelianism and Personality*. In 1917 was issued his Gifford Lectures, *The Idea of God in Contemporary Philosophy*. But in 1920 Henry C. Sturt (1863–1946) gathered together the more theistic critics of the "atheistic" Absolutes of Bradley and McTaggart in *Personal Idealism: Philosophical Essays by Eight Members of the University of Oxford*, inspired in part by Bowne's American personalism, but less sectarianly Methodist in character. In 1908 Sturt continued the attack with *Idola Theatri*.[24]

IX

With such pluralists as Adler and Howison abroad and with Royce himself verging toward a more and more social ideal, there was room in America for the defense of a cultural idealism closer to the Hegelian tradition. This was worked out in the philosophy of spirit, or objective and speculative idealism, which found its seat at the Sage School of Philosophy at Cornell after 1892. Started by Jacob Gould Schurman (1854–1942), a Scot imported from Dalhousie University in Halifax, this was carried on, when he became president in 1892, by a former pupil of Schurman's at Dalhousie, James E. Creighton

[24] *Personal Idealism: Philosophical Essays by Eight Members of the University of Oxford*, ed. H. Sturt (Oxford, 1902); A. Seth Pringle-Pattison, *Hegelianism and Personality* (Edinburgh, 1887); H. Sturt, *Idola Theatri* (Oxford, 1908).

(1861–1924), who remained the leader of an able group of trainers of humanistic teachers of philosophy. Minimizing psychology, this group examined "objective mind" in its historical development and its institutional form. It combined a critical analysis of the categories, in the Kantian spirit, with an emphasis on the historical growth of the human spirit, in Hegelian fashion. Critical logic was combined with a philosophy of history to form a theory of experience as an organic whole, in both individual and society. The outcome was expressed in works on "philosophical logic" (by Creighton himself and Harold N. Smart) and studies in the history of philosophy (Frank Thilly, disciple of Friedrich Paulsen; William A. Hammond; Ernest Albee, historian of utilitarianism). Schurman started the *Philosophical Review* in 1892 as the organ of Cornell idealism, and Creighton in 1902 founded the American Philosophical Association.

Schurman himself saw Kant as the mediator between Hume's empiricism and Leibniz's rationalism, founder of the science of the necessary forms of empirical reason. Philosophy itself goes on to mediate between the sciences and the arts, just as America is the mediator among the nations:

If the favoring aspects of Greek civilization are not today reproduced in the American love of independence and the American respect for law, in the American union of half a hundred "sovereign" commonwealths with all their county and town governments under the federal head, in the American churches with their democratic organization and their multifarious and plastic creeds, in American freedom of thought and speech which has always tended to build and not merely to destroy; then one can scarcely imagine where they are to be found, even in approximation, among the peoples of the earth. . . .

The new birth of Philosophy amongst ourselves will be the final outcome of devotion to special philosophical interests and of cultivation of special philosophical domains. . . . It is fortunate, indeed, that the spirit of specialization has taken possession of philosophy, and we may congratulate ourselves on the special investigations and special publications conducted by Americans. But division of labor is profitless without cooperation.[25]

Creighton continued the emphasis on cooperation in the building up of a genuine *Geisteswissenschaft* and an influential *Lebensphilosophie*:

In every department of investigation the conviction seems to be growing that intellectual companionship and coöperation are essential to real progress. . . . We have learned that to isolate oneself intellectually is to render one's work

[25] "Prefatory Note," *Philosophical Review*, 1 (1892), pp. 3–5.

unfruitful; that there is in every generation a main drift of problems within which we must work, if we wish to contribute anything to the common cause.[26]

Thought must be social, and it must be historical: the continuity and unity of experience must become a conscious possession. Cornell idealism was humanistic in method as well as in objective. Nature was to be interpreted as man's environment, the scene of human experience, neither external nor central. Nature, society, and individual together form a community of thought and culture—of "spirit," in Hegelian terms. The whole program was an attempt to integrate philosophy as intimately as possible with human society and culture. All experience is an absolute, coherent, organic whole: Creighton and Cornell strove mightily to make it so.

Philosophical science is not "natural" science, and cannot "accept its facts" from the latter. To do so would be to put "psychologism" and "naturalism" in place of philosophy. But philosophy, to be philosophy at all, has to *humanize* its facts, that is, to look at them from the standpoint of complete and self-conscious human experience, for it is only from this standpoint that a meaning for them can be found. The philosopher is thus essentially a humanist rather than a naturalist, and his closest affiliations are with the sciences that deal with the products of man's thought and purposive activity. In his relation to natural science, he is less concerned with the facts regarded objectively than with the thinking operations by which these facts were obtained. . . . Similarly, the abstract view of nature as a whole which the physical naturalist furnishes, has to be humanized by philosophical interpretation, *which construes the facts differently*, finding in nature the congeniality with the mind of man through which alone it is intelligible. And, on the other hand, the philosophical standpoint necessitates a different account of the facts of mind from that given by the psychological "naturalist." . . . Just as philosophy humanizes the physical facts by viewing them in relation to mind, so it also objectifies subjective facts by viewing them as functions through which the individual realizes his unity with nature and with his fellow men. (23)

Obviously, from such an "objective idealism" it was but a short step to twentieth-century naturalism.

X

The most forward-looking of the various American types of philosophic idealism was the "dynamic idealism" that Morris taught for a

[26] *Studies in Speculative Philosophy* (New York, 1925), p. 7.

few years at the new university of Johns Hopkins and then transferred
to its seat at Ann Arbor. It was forward-looking in that for a time it
included John Dewey and James Hayden Tufts. In a deeper sense, it
was forward-looking because, unlike the Hegelians, it emphasized the
biological as well as the cultural and social aspect of human experience, and led easily into the biological naturalisms of the early twentieth century. The leader was George Sylvester Morris (1840–1889),[27]
a student from Union Seminary who continued his studies in Germany under Ulrici at Halle and Trendelenburg at Berlin, who had advanced from Hegel to Aristotle. Morris started teaching at Michigan
in 1870, and in 1878 moved to Hopkins, to teach a scientific philosophy among the other sciences there fostered.

Trendelenburg taught Morris an activistic view of the Kantian categories and the importance of the Aristotelian notions of movement,
development, growth, and actualization. Morris, in fact, is something
like what T.H. Green might have become had he followed up his
early use of Aristotelian ideas. Acts of thought are literally motions;
hence the science of mind can be assimilated to the science of the
other forms of natural energy. The creative powers of mind can be
understood as natural energies, free and spontaneous. Morris, like
Trendelenburg, took this as a criticism of the Hegelian emphasis on
logic and dialectic. The historical movement of thought has been not a
march of dialectic, but a growth of living activities. Morris criticized
the identity philosophies of Spinoza, Leibniz, and Hegel, and contrasted philosophical method with mathematics and logic. Philosophy
was to him an independent experimental science, radically different
from both mathematics and mechanics. It was the science of the life or
psyche of the body, the science of experience as lived.

Like Green, Morris is a critic of the assumptions and methods of
British empiricism.

The search for a fundamental, spiritual, living, and absolute reality, like that
of Self, by psychological inquiries pursued under the limitations, and determined by the presuppositions, of the method of purely physical science, must
necessarily be fruitless. . . . The theoretical sensationalist (as Locke, Mill, *et
al.*) and the critical idealist (Kant), who start with the express or implicit as-

[27] Morris, *Philosophy and Christianity* (New York, 1883). See Marc Edmund Jones,
George Sylvester Morris: His Philosophical Career and Theistic Idealism (Philadelphia, 1948);
Evelyn Urban Shirk, *Adventurous Idealism: The Philosophy of Alfred Lloyd* (Ann Arbor,
1952).

sumption of the mechanical relation as the fundamental one between subject and object, come quickly to the conclusion that the true object is an unknown and unknowable substrate or thing-in-itself, which the subject-forms of intelligence never reach. The conclusion is a *reductio ad absurdum* of the premise on which it rests. The science of knowledge has nothing to do with unknowable objects. It has no ground on which to posit their existence. It has positive ground for absolutely denying their existence, for *knowing* that they do not exist. . . . The phenomenal object is not a veil or screen effectually to shut out from us the sight of the noumenal object. Nor is the former separated from the latter by an impassable interval. On the contrary, to thought it instrumentally reveals the true object. . . .

In other words, that *is* which is *known*. Knowledge and being are correlative terms. When we know therefore what is the true *object of knowledge*, we know what is the final and absolute significance of the terms *being* and *reality*. (287, 44–45, 70)

Thus combining Aristotelian realism and voluntarism, Morris tried to put philosophy on a strictly scientific basis. But he could not convince either President Gilman or G. Stanley Hall that he was a scientist: the latter insisted he was a moral philosopher. Hall had come to Hopkins from the laboratory of experimental psychology of Wundt; the metaphysics of Morris and his colleague Charles S. Peirce he regarded as too speculative to be soundly biological. John Dewey appeared from Vermont in 1883, to study under Morris. He worked at his own "philosophical biology" or "psychology," which came out in 1887; he began with a thesis under Morris on Kant's "psychology," emphasizing the third Critique. He tried to prove that Kant's theory of judgment as mediating "made reason or spirit the center or organic unity of the entire sphere of man's experience"; in assigning the central position and function to man's "intelligence" (as Morris called Kant's "reason"), Kant was the founder of true philosophic method, and "so far as he was false to it he fell into his own defects and contradictions."

Dewey joined Morris, who, disillusioned with Hopkins, had returned to Michigan, at Ann Arbor in 1884. Morris spent the summer of 1885 in England, meeting the British idealists, especially Bradley, Wallace, and Edward Caird. Morris saw Hegel with new eyes: Hegel was really an objective empiricist, trying to integrate experience through intelligence. It was Dewey who set forth this Hegelian version of dynamic idealism, which he called "psychology" in the broad sense of philosophical anthropology, and outlined it in his *Psychology* of 1887. He pushed it further in his *Outlines of Ethics* of 1891. Just at this time Dewey discovered James's *Psychology*, and abandoned his earlier idealistic terminology for James's more biological language, and was lost to dynamic idealism.

Morris's ideas were taken up by another man at Ann Arbor, Alfred H. Lloyd, who came to Michigan in 1891 and taught there till 1927. Lloyd set forth his version of Morris's conception in his *Dynamic Idealism* of 1898. But Lloyd was an early practitioner, as a writer, of the cult of unintelligibility: his four books are all abstruse, subtle, and ironical. He also claimed to be stating the "metaphysics of psychology" and promised "to give a distinct explicit doctrine of the soul." Casual readers thought him a reactionary; closer inspection revealed an unconventional scorn of religious comfort. Doubting was the surest approach to idealism: the aim was to live critically. To think meant to see a problem as a problem.

Matter as organic is intelligent, and mind as dynamic is material or substantial. . . . Soul . . . is the fulfilling organic activity, or the substance in which an organic matter and a dynamic mind are one.[28]

Lloyd was particularly attracted by the Hegelian struggle of opposites in history (*Philosophy of History*, Ann Arbor, 1899), and developed a view of history as centering in problems and conflicts, usually unsolved.

Morris, Dewey, and Lloyd illustrate dynamic idealism in the double sense: thinking is the most active form of living, and each of them in his own person united energy and thought.

We have seen the various forms idealism took, especially in America, where it developed in relative freedom from its Hegelian heritage. We must now return to Bradley, in whom idealism genuinely transcended its limitations.

[28] *Dynamic Idealism* (Chicago, 1898), p. 159.

8

F. H. Bradley and the Working-out of
Absolute Idealism

FRANCIS HERBERT BRADLEY (1846–1924) [1] agreed with the other English idealists that the real world is the experienced world. But he started with the fundamental conviction that "experience" is more than "thought," as Green had maintained. Bradley's basic drive is the refusal to abolish "feeling" in favor of knowledge and intelligibility. "Feeling" is a fundamental and ineradicable aspect of "reality"—more fundamental, in fact, than thinking.

In the immediately experienced world, all intelligible distinctions and relations are merged in a "whole of feeling" which is the ultimate subject matter of philosophy. "Thought" arises out of feeling, out of "immediacy," as an interpretation of immediate experience by distinguishing relations and aspects in it. "Knowledge" is only one aspect of the experienced world; it needs blending with "feeling" and will to include all the experienced aspects.

"Feeling" starts for Bradley, in his *Principles of Logic* (1883), in pretty much the empiricist sense, as isolated sensations; and as subjective (in

---

Originally published in abridged form in *Journal of the History of Philosophy*, V, no. 3 (July 1967), pp. 245–67. Copyright © 1967 by Journal of the History of Philosophy, Inc. Reprinted by permission.

[1] F.H. Bradley, *Ethical Studies* (Oxford, 1876; 2nd ed., revised, with additional notes by the author that categorically reject many of the earlier positions, Oxford, 1927). *Principles of Logic* (Oxford, 1883; 2nd ed., revised, 1924). *Appearance and Reality: A Metaphysical Essay* (London, 1893; 2nd ed., with an Appendix, 1897). *Essays on Truth and Reality* (Oxford, 1914). *Collected Essays*, 2 vols. (Oxford, 1935).

See *Mind*, XXXIV, N.S. (1925), A.E. Taylor, "I—F.H. Bradley"; J.H. Muirhead, "Bradley's Place in Philosophy." See also T.M. Forsyth, *English Philosophy* (London, 1910), Chapter 7, second part; Rudolf Kagey, *F.H. Bradley's Logic* (Ph.D. dissertation, Columbia University, 1931). The best philosophical analyses of Bradley are Robert D. Mack, *The Appeal to Immediate Experience* (New York, 1945), and Richard Wollheim, *F.H. Bradley* (London, 1959).

flavor at least). It then becomes neutral: "feeling" is identified with "the felt"; and it grows richer, attempting to include the whole wealth of immediate experience. Thus Bradley gets very close to Dewey's conception of "direct experience," "nonreflective experience," without, however, Dewey's biological analysis. It is through this conception of experience that Bradley approaches the naturalism to which his thinking almost arrived at the end. Thought, that is, has a setting in experience: it is relational, and by its analysis breaks up experienced and felt wholes.

There is a double insistence in Bradley. On the one hand, reality is experienced, but is not adequately expressed in thought. On the other, reality *is* accessible to knowledge. What has often been called Bradley's "scepticism" is really an objective relativism. Thought, logical structure, is not ultimate. In *Appearance and Reality*, he insists it is really self-contradictory; then later he emphasizes rather that it is always relative to its particular subject matter. The real, experienced world is never identical with the intelligible world, yet it is also never "extraneous" to it. The relation of the two can be said to be, in Aristotelian terms, that of substance to form, that of *what is* to its intelligible aspect.

The intelligible world, the system of science and knowledge, thus fundamentally needs *criticism* in the light of its setting in the experienced world. This is not only the entire drive of Dewey's *Experience and Nature;* it is the expression of that whole current of thought on the Continent which began with the criticism of Hegel's "panlogism" in the 1840s, and is today called "Existentialism." Bradley is the British counterpart of all those who have criticized philosophies of logical structure like T.H. Green's, or like the other contemporary forms of Neo-Kantianism in Germany and France. The "known world" is a world of relations distinguished in the richer "real world." These distinctions are ultimately relative to their particular setting, but in that setting they are valid enough.

Bradley's celebrated doctrine of the "degrees of truth and reality" means that practically knowledge is "true": any idea which fulfills its purpose of rendering some portion or aspect of experience intelligible and significant and meaningful, and which is not ousted by a better idea, Bradley is willing to say is "so far true." It is valid, in its own sphere and purpose, despite its ultimate inconsistency; the wave theory of light would be an example, before it was incorporated fully into quantum mechanics as a more inclusive intellectual system. And Bradley accepts a functional or instrumental test for these relative truths. Yet, he reminds us, they are hardly "the Truth"—of Spinoza, for instance. Knowledge is the search for unity in difference, for the structure embedded in the whole of experienced "reality." And this ideal remains ultimately unrealizable, for thought is not the same as reality. "Reality" is that "completion of thought beyond thought, that remains forever an Other."

Reality *is* experienced, and reality is *not fully known;* it is intelligible, but not merely a logical system—in Aristotelian terms, it is Substance, not Form alone. Yet the effort to know reality is necessary to a fuller "participation in reality." The "real" world is the world we "participate in," in all kinds of experience. Knowing is only one kind. Reality is thus the known world in its setting in the experienced world, the "unity in difference" of all experience. For Bradley, what he calls "Absolute Experience" (corresponding to T.H. Green's "Eternal Thought") unites all these aspects. Bradley emphasizes their unity, but this is not essential to his position—the "unity" seems to be largely polemical, like Green's emphasis on "thought" and structure. Knowing, the intelligible world, is an expression of "reality," of "the Absolute." But it is an incomplete and inadequate expression of it: it appears to us always *in* some particular setting. The Absolute is not apart from the known world—there is no negative theology in Bradley—it is always expressed in it; but the Absolute is *what* is expressed, it is not reducible to the *expression* alone, as in Green.

Now these ideas of Bradley, though given a Romantic tinge—after all, the great Germans had lived—are at bottom all Aristotelian ideas, with the single exception of the emphasis on Unity, which is Spinozistic and of course Hegelian. And, being expressed in the language of experience, they also sound very much like the ideas of another functional Left Wing Hegelian, John Dewey. For both Bradley and Dewey, everything encountered through experience is "real"; the problem is to find how it is real, just what its status is, just what are its causes and conditions and relations to other things or aspects of experience that are equally "real." (To be sure, Bradley uses the term "real," where Dewey prefers the term "natural"; but, for the one, "reality" is the all-embracing comprehensive term, just as, for the other, "nature" serves the same function).

As is appropriate for the teleological and functional thinker like Bradley, he reaches his clearest statement at the end of his intellectual development, in the "Concluding Remarks" that close the *Essays on Truth and Reality*.

> Everywhere on behalf of the real Absolute I have been warning the reader against that false absolutism which in philosophy is to me another name for error. And it is an error which results in a twofold mistake. It takes some distinction within the whole and asserts it as being real by itself and unconditionally, and then from this misconceived ground it goes on to deny or belittle other complementary aspects of the same whole. But, as against such absolutism, the very soul of the Absolute which I defend is its insistence and emphasis on an all-pervasive relativism. Everything is justified as being real in its own sphere and degree, but not so as to entitle it to invade other spheres, and, whether positively or negatively, to usurp other powers. The absolute right owned by every side of life is, in other words, conditional on its service, and on its acceptance of limited value and reality. And it is the true Absolute alone that gives its due to every interest just because it refuses to everything more than its own due. Justice in the name of the Whole to each aspect of the world according to its special place and proper rank—Reality everywhere through self-restriction in claim and in denial—this may be said to be the principle which unites these Essays. And this principle throughout conflicts with what we have condemned as the vice of abstractionism and absolutism.
>
> My opponents for the most part, it seems to me, have failed here to understand. Where the absolute reality of some feature of the whole is rejected, they too often interpret this as the denial that such a feature exists.[2]

Thus change is found throughout the world; but is it ultimate—is that which changes itself to be called "change"? Personality possesses an eminent reality—does this mean there is nothing "more inclusive, more concrete and real"? Is the Whole to be identified with "a Personality"?

> I have insisted upon the absolute, the unassailable right of every aspect of life to its own place, function and liberty. . . . The attempt to lower science and art to the rank of mere instruments springs, I urge, once more from this propensity to mistake some perverted distinction for a separate Power, and to sentence whatever is excluded from this to unreality or mere subservience. . . .

[2] F.H. Bradley, *Essays on Truth and Reality*, pp. 47–71.

On the one side the creations of the intellect everywhere are real. The substantial terms and relations, into which analysis breaks up the continuity of the given, are no mere errors or simple instruments. . . . And the idea that by disregarding these figments of the understanding we are to gain reality, is a mistake now long since refuted [since Hegel]; for it is only through such distinction and dissection that it is possible to reach knowledge progressively more living and individual. On the other side these constructions, however inclusive, are not independent truths. They are real only so far as subordinate and as relative to individual totality. And even in life it is only when I forget higher experience that I can anywhere accept for all purposes as final the partial and abstracted products whether of science or of a presumptuous "common sense."

On the one hand it is the entire Reality alone which matters. On the other hand every single thing, so far as it matters, is so far real, real in its own place and degree, and according as more or less it contains and carries out the indwelling character of the concrete Whole. But there is nothing anywhere in the world which, taken barely in its own right and unconditionally, has importance and is real. And one main work of philosophy is to show that, where there is isolation and abstraction, there is everywhere, so far as the abstraction forgets itself, unreality and error. (472–73)

The overtones of Hegel in this objective relativism are apparent. But it *is* an objective relativism, that points equally to the more pluralistic Dewey.

I

Bradley is one of those few British philosophers who could learn from experience; and in the discussions and polemics that followed his *Appearance and Reality* in 1893, especially with William James and John Dewey, he learned enough to modify significantly his views there expressed. There are thus three main stages in Bradley's thinking: the initial stage before his great metaphysical essay, in which he carried on many of the assumptions of the empiricists he was criticizing, just as T.H. Green had done; the stage represented by *Appearance and Reality*, which is best known of the three, and which usually identifies him with a kind of Hegelian "scepticism"; and the stage represented by his replies to critics, collected in *Essays on Truth and Reality* in 1914, and dominating his drastic revisions of his earlier writings in the last decade of his life. This final stage of Bradley's thinking is best called an "objective relativism," a genuinely functional position; it is very close to Dewey's "instrumentalism" of the same period, and even made too many concessions to the "pragmatism" of James. This final objective relativism is by far the most philosophically significant of Bradley's periods, both for itself, and because it illustrates so clearly how the self-criticism of Hegelian idealism could lead British and American thought in the twentieth century, as it had already led German philosophizing in the 1840s, into the position generally called "twentieth-century naturalism"—as distinguished from the materialistic and nonfunctional "naturalism" that took that name during the nineteenth century.

Hence we shall here set forth Bradley's final position in his later writings, and then return to the path by which he arrived at it, through his long paradoxical search to get all of immediate experience into intellectual expression, into "thought." That final position is most clearly stated in the introduction [3] written in 1906 for a book never completed:

Every aspect of life may in the end be subordinated to the Good, if, that is, we understand the Good in a very wide sense. Everywhere in life we seem forced, sooner or later, to ask the question Why. And the answer to that inquiry seems everywhere to be found in the fact of contentment and absence or suppression of unrest. We may appeal from one thing to another thing, but it is to this aspect of things, and it is to things as more or less possessing this aspect, that we are brought at last. And we are led to conclude that, so far as anything in the above sense is good, there is nothing else in the world which can pretend to stand above it.

The claim of reason and truth to be an exception here will not hold. For, if you ask what is truth, you are led to answer that it is that which satisfies the intellect. The contradictory and the meaningless fail to be true because in a certain way they do not satisfy. They produce a special kind of uneasiness and unrest; and that on the other side which alters this unrest into an answering contentment, is truth. It is truth, we may say, where the intellect has found its good.

Whatever a man is engaged in, whatever he feels or does or apprehends or pursues, this, so far as it satisfies him, is good in itself.[4] It possesses what you may call, if you please, the ultimate quality of goodness. So far as anything satisfies, there is no possible appeal beyond it, and nothing has any rational

---

[3] Chapter 1, "Introductory," in *Essays*, pp. 1–18.

[4] Note by F.H.B.: "Goodness, worth, and value, are of course all the same thing. The definition of the Good given in my *Appearance* I have now for some time ceased in one point to consider correct. I do not think that desire should be included in the definition [Bradley has moved away from empiricism]. Wherever, and so far as, I feel myself positively affirmed, there, so far, is goodness. Desire, at least in the ordinary course, will necessarily supervene, but it is wrong to take it as being from the first essential."

claim against that which in itself is fully satisfied. With regard to philosophy, for example, it is now an old saying that it must presuppose the will to think, and that if one is ready to contradict himself, philosophy can have no concern with him.

All thinking, in brief, rests on the agreement, tacit or expressed, to accept a certain test. It consists, in other words, in the pursuit of one kind of satisfaction, and its arguments appeal to no one except so far as he is engaged in this pursuit. And, as in philosophy, so everywhere throughout life the same principle holds. Whether it is an affair of mere enjoyment and liking, or a matter of moral and religious conviction and preference, or again of aesthetic perception and taste, throughout these differences we find everywhere in one point the same thing. So long and so far as that which occupies you is able to give you rest and contentment, that thing, whatever it is, has goodness. And there is nothing which from the outside has against this thing any claim upon you. So long as remaining there, wherever you are, you find yourself satisfied and at one with your own being, so far, apart from mere violence, you are secure in yourself. Here, if in the camp there is no division, the enemy will not penetrate. A man, we all know, should not be shamed out of his reason, and he cannot rationally, we all know, be argued out of his feelings.

But on the other hand it is an old experience that nowhere is perfect good. Goodness does not really reside where perhaps we tend first to place it. There is nothing, in other words, in life which, taken in and by itself, completely satisfies. Our life has several main aspects, and, even within each aspect, we are led forever in some point to desire something better and beyond. And we find in the end that no one aspect by itself can have goodness and be unmixed good. Everything in life is imperfect and seeks beyond itself an absolute fulfillment of itself. And thus everything in life, we may say in the end, is subordinate, and subordinate to the Good. . . .

On the one hand every side of life, so far as it is good, is justified in itself, while on the other hand the perfect good is found in none of them. We are hence mistaken when we attempt to set up any one aspect of our nature as supreme, and to regard the other aspects merely as conducive and as subject to its rule. (1–3)

This supremacy of "the Good" may be compared with its equally Platonic ultimacy for Dewey: for him too "truth is the good in the way of beliefs." And for Bradley all special activities, important as they are, are incomplete and inadequate: he has the same Romantic drive as Dewey for all-inclusiveness. He puts this search for "totality," for ultimacy:

There certainly are other aspects of life, where satisfaction and the Good are no less to be found. The perfect Good resides in each, but in each it exists imperfectly, and none therefore is supreme. On the one hand we can experience and feel our nature as a whole, and, as against this whole, we can realize the inadequacy of any one side of life. And, because this is so, we cannot identify our whole being with one of its aspects and take everything else as subject to a one-sided supremacy. On this point the verdict of those who know most of life has been passed long ago and, later or sooner, this finding must at some time have come home to us as true. We can feel that life has failed if it is all inactive pleasure, or contemplation, or if it consists solely in moral struggle or religious emotion, or again in mere labor or in any activity without rest and enjoyment. We can be sure that our truth is not the full possession of reality, we can know that there are ends beyond aesthetic achievement and joy, and something again of value beyond life in society or in the family. Such things, we feel, are good, but there is not one of them which includes all the rest. There is none of them which possesses unqualified goodness, and hence there is not one of them to which all the others can be subject. (4)

Take pleasure. Mere pleasure is clearly not "the Good"; and then there is nothing which cannot on occasion be pleasant. Take practical activity, the mere quantity of doing. Such activity demands some end, some idea, which is itself "real."

Practice I take to imply and to depend on an unrealized idea. It contains the idea of a "to be" and a "not yet," a something which has to be carried out in fact, but which, as soon as it is carried out, has ceased forthwith to be practical. Practice is the perpetual undoing of the condition which is implied in its own existence, and it cannot therefore offer by itself a satisfaction which is ultimate. . . . This difficulty is brought out in a striking form by the postulate made in religion, in any religion, that is, which is not perfect. The Good, which in religion is the complete Good and the supreme Reality, must be carried out in practice, and yet, in order to be made real, it is presupposed. The Good, that is, cannot in religion be taken as unreal, or as merely real elsewhere; for, if so, the Good would no longer be supreme. The Good therefore must be taken by faith as already real here. But, with this, it has become clear that, while practice consists in alteration, the alteration which it makes does not, as such, qualify the reality. In other words, if you regard the Good as entire or supreme, the Good ceases before your eyes to be merely practical. (6–7)

The Good cannot be merely activity, it must be the End of activity.

Likewise, the beautiful entails a pursuit, and is thus lost in practice. Besides, there is much ugliness in the world. Knowing, science, is also a pursuit.

Science in its widest sense is a pursuit, and it never becomes wholly an attained object. It is but one side of life which is entangled with other sides, and again, as a pursuit, it has a practical aspect and it therefore itself is burdened with the inconsistency of practice. In any case, its object, even so far as that is attained, is the world of mere truth, and does not include all reality. To understand, as it is given to us, or given to anyone, to understand is not wholly to possess even in apprehension, and still less is it the same as to enjoy and to do. (8)

Science is instrumental, in the Hegelian sense, "mediate."

Even the higher totality of common life—the social ideal of Josiah Royce's "Beloved Community," or Dewey's "shared enjoyment of meanings"—is not ultimate.

Though in this position there is much truth, it seems impossible to accept it as final. For, if we judge by what we can perceive, the individual members, in whatever higher unity, are more or less the sport of change and accident. And the whole, in which they are united, has itself the defects of finitude. . . . Hence our common life and our supreme good escapes once more to take its place in an invisible world. It is in some city of God, in some eternal church, that we find the real goodness which owns and satisfies our most inward desire. But on the other side such a reality exists only for faith. This does not mean that we cannot know at all the supreme good and reality. It means that we are ignorant as to the variety of those forms of finite soul which may take part of its life, and it means that in the end we do not know how they, together with all their inward and outer diversities, reach harmony within it. I am therefore forced to deny that the chief good is merely social. (9)

Yet each aspect of goodness has a relative independence, with its own terms and its own structure.

You may choose or not choose to philosophize or to paint, but you certainly cannot altogether paint or philosophize as you choose. Whether and how far you will do these things, you may from the outside determine according to what you think moral. But it is only from the inside that you are able to learn the right method of doing them, and that method is independent of anything which may count as right outside. My will and my conscience can in short no more tell me how I ought to pursue truth, than they can show me how to ride a horse or how to play on a piano. (11)

Thus morality and religion have no rights within philosophy, or within art:

Philosophy aims at intellectual satisfaction, in other words at ultimate truth. It seeks to gain possession of Reality, but only in an ideal form. . . . Now among the various aspects of our nature . . . not one is supreme, but each within its own limits has a relative supremacy. And hence you cannot carry over conclusions and results from morality and religion which, as admitted results, are to be received and accepted by philosophy. These results for philosophy can be no more than material. . . . I do not think, myself, that a true philosophy will conflict with a sound morality or religion. In my opinion, a true philosophy certainly does not contradict the postulates required for conduct. It will or it may understand them otherwise—as to this I do not doubt—but I cannot admit that to understand otherwise is necessarily to deny. . . . There are two questions which it is common but most dangerous to confound. The first asks about the sense of a doctrine as a working belief, while the second investigates the ultimate meaning and theoretical guarantee of that doctrine. The second inquires into the position of something in the universe at large, while the first asks merely how it stands in my heart and conscience. . . .

Philosophy at its best is but an understanding of its object, and it is not an experience in which that object is contained wholly and possessed. (11–13)

A true philosophy cannot justify its own apotheosis. Nay, from the other side the metaphysician might lament his own destiny. His pursuit condemns him, he may complain, himself to herd with unreal essences and to live an outcast from life. It is three times more blessed, he may well repeat, to be than to think.[5] But in such a mood the man would so far fall away from philosophy. A true philosophy must accept and must justify every side of human nature, including itself. Like other things it has its place in that system where at once every place and no place is supreme. The mastery of that system in thought, however far we carry it, leaves philosophy still the servant of an order which it accepts and could never have made. (13–14)

Bradley sums up his vision of all-inclusiveness with relative independence:

Philosophy like other things has a business of its own, and like other things it is bound, and it must be allowed, to go about its own business in its own way. Except within its own limits it claims no supremacy, and, unless outside its own limits, it cannot and it must not accept any dictation. Everything to philosophy is a consideration, in the sense that everything has a claim and a right to be considered. But how it is to be considered is the affair of philosophy alone, and here no external consideration can be given even the smallest hearing. (15)

Bradley regarded this as a warning to religious and moral "pragmatists" who allowed nonphilosophical considerations of the needs of "life" to interfere with philosophic analysis. But his statement can equally be taken as the manifesto of a naturalistic metaphysics which

[5] Note by F.H.B.: "I may perhaps illustrate this by transcribing one of those notes which, some twenty years ago, I used to attempt to fix my passing moods. 'The shades nowhere speak without blood, and the ghosts of Metaphysic accept no substitute. They reveal themselves only to that victim whose life they have drained, and, to converse with shadows, he himself must become a shade.' "

is resolved to leave nothing significant out. It shows how easy was the transition from Bradley's "Hegelian" idealism to twentieth-century naturalisms like Dewey's or Whitehead's, possessed of the same Romantic urge to take account of all the facts of human experience.

Bradley concludes his Introduction with a statement of his faith:

Philosophy demands, and in the end it rests on, what may fairly be termed faith. It has, we may say, in a sense to presuppose its conclusion in order to prove it. . . . And its conclusion, further, is not, and never could be, carried out in detail actually and completely. . . . Philosophy is a search, a search for that which in the end is true. So far as a man stands outside this pursuit, it cannot in the end justify its existence against him. . . . A man may enter on the pursuit of truth, or he may abstain from that pursuit; but, if he enters on it, and so far as he enters on it, he commits himself inevitably to a tacit assumption. . . . His action has no sense unless he does assume, or, if asked, would assume, that, when he has got propositions, he is able to judge of them, and can then tell whether they do or do not put him in ideal possession of reality. . . . Hence the only scepticism in philosophy which is rational must confine itself to the denial that truth so far and actually has been reached. (15–17)

This is Bradley's answer to the charge that his *Appearance* is wholly "sceptical." The scepticism of "metaphysics" is, like that of science, cumulative and provisional. This is the faith of all Hegelianisms—of Dewey and other naturalists as well.

II

What this intellectual vision of Bradley meant concretely and specifically comes out clearly in his Chapter XV, "On God and the Absolute," [6] his discussion of the issues in the conflict between philosophy and religion so central in his day. Bradley's critique of religious ideas reveals both his genuine sensitivity to religious values and the intellectual integrity exhibited in the manifesto of the last section.

A.E. Taylor, in his article in the Bradley issue of *Mind*,[7] writes revealingly about the religious experience and attitude of his teacher. Taylor's own interest, of course, is to show that Bradley was really, like Taylor himself, a Christian Platonist.

Bradley had the reputation of being hostile to Christianity, and was known to Oxford graduates as an "idealistic atheist," like J.E. Mc-

---

[6] Chapter 15, *Essays*, pp. 428–59.
[7] A.E. Taylor, "I—F.H. Bradley," *Mind*, XXXIV, N.S., pp. 1–12.

Taggart at Cambridge; idealism took both leading English idealists far beyond ordinary Christian thinking. Really, insists Taylor, he possessed a genuinely religious nature. He called himself a Christian and an Anglican, and felt an increasing need of a really "spiritual" religion. He hated "Bibliolatry," and preferred the Living Spirit. He liked the Roman Catholic refusal to allow the laity to wander through the Bible unaided: he felt, in fact, they did not go far enough. Bradley had had an Evangelical upbringing which did not endear the Church to him.

Bradley's own religious experience was of a deeply personal religion, unmediated by any church, bringing him into direct contact with what he called "Reality"; he was by temperament a mystic. He despised the historical and institutionalized rituals. Like so many in the wake of the Romantic movement, he insisted on the unity of the Divine and the human: he felt the "Absolute" present in man. He had little historical interest in the religious tradition: he held the Incarnation, the core of Christianity, was no historical event, single and unique, in Jesus of Nazareth alone. This sense of the Incarnation in all mankind was of great importance for Bradley: it leads, he thought, to the attempt to achieve "Deiformity" in one's own personality.

On the other hand, he opposed the liberals' doctrine of the mere "immanence" of God, with its temptation to a resulting humanism, and faith in secular social progress; he disliked the Christian humanitarianism of Tolstoi, and similar aberrations. "The wrath of God is as real as the Love of God," he insisted; he was thus hard-boiled, and no sentimentalist, a religious "realist" in the present fashion. He wrote an attack on "Christian ethics," which he asserted to be "injurious to good citizenship." In many ways he foreshadowed in his attitude the Reinhold Niebuhr of the twentieth century. He opposed taking the "teachings of Jesus" as a final code of morals, the authoritarianism of treating the Gospel ethics as ultimate.

Theologically, he held that the idea of a "personal God" is self-contradictory. We must indeed use anthropomorphic concepts, but we should recognize that they are inadequate and misleading. He came too early to view religious language as symbolic and mythical, but he had reached the same idea. "A God comprehended is no God at all," he insisted. Taylor concludes, Bradley stood religiously "in the great tradition," with the Augustinians—like T.H. Green. He was, in other words, a Christian Platonist—like Taylor himself. But if this be so, he certainly emphasized the Augustine of varying human experience, rather than merely the logical Platonism that Green concentrated upon.

In his own critique of religious ideas, Bradley starts by denying that his Absolute Totality—"Nature" for the naturalist—can be identified with God.

God for me has no meaning outside of the religious consciousness, and that essentially is practical. The Absolute for me cannot be God, because in the end the Absolute is related to nothing, and there cannot be a practical relation between it and the finite will. When you begin to worship the Absolute or the Universe, and make it the object of religion, you in that moment have transformed it. It has become something forthwith which is less than the Universe. . . .

There is a fundamental inconsistency in religion. For, in any but an imperfect religion, God must be perfect. God must be at once the complete satisfaction of all finite aspiration, and yet on the other side must stand in relation with my will. Religion is practical, and on the other hand in the highest religion its object is supreme goodness and power. We have a perfect real will, and we have my will, and the practical relation of these wills is what we mean by religion. And yet, if perfection is actually realized, what becomes of my will which is over against the complete Good Will? While, on the other hand, if there is no such Will, what becomes of God? The inconsistency seems irremovable and at first sight may threaten us with ruin. (*Essays*, 428–29)

Interestingly, this is the same criticism that Dewey makes of the traditional concept of God. Bradley is restating St. Augustine's problem: How can God be at once the Great All and Holy Will?

Thinkers have tried to escape this inconsistency by proposing the notion of a finite God, like Stuart Mill and William James. This is indeed a possible religion.

Such a religion even in one sense, with the lowering of the Deity, may be said to have been heightened. To help a God in his struggle, more or less doubtful and blind, with resisting Evil, is no inferior task. And if the issue were taken as uncertain, or if even further the end were known to be God's indubitable defeat and our inevitable disaster, our religion would have risen thereby and would have attained to the extreme of heroism. (429)

But such a Romantic version of Manichaeism would leave out assurance and spiritual peace. The strength gained by the fear of possible defeat would encourage men to follow the Leader blindly.

But, in order to function, does religion have to be theoretically consistent? Bradley's answer is, No.

Is there any need for our attempt to avoid self-contradiction? Has religion got to be consistent theoretically? Is ultimate theoretical consistency a thing which is attainable anywhere? And, at all events, is it a thing attainable in life and in practice? . . .

All truth must be imperfect. . . . The idea that in the special sciences, and again in practical life, we have absolute truths, must be rejected as illusory. We are everywhere dependent on what may be called useful *mythology*, and nothing other than these inconsistent ideas could serve our various purposes. . . .

The ideas which best express our highest religious needs and their satisfaction, must certainly be true. Ultimate truth they do not possess. . . . What we have to consider is the relative importance of that purpose which the ideas serve, and how well, viewed from all sides, they aid and express its satisfaction. (430–31)

Does this mean that Bradley has succumbed to James's pragmatism in practice? No—for there *is* a Beyond. But Bradley approaches the more recent notion of the symbolic character of all religious ideas and language.

On the personality of God, Bradley undertakes an acute criticism, bringing out all the logical difficulties; and he rejects the idea literally. He asks instead, what *is* God for the "religious consciousnss"? There can certainly be religion without a personal God; but is it the highest form? The Divine Immanence is more important than God's "personality."

The real presence of God's will in mine, our actual and literal satisfaction in common, must not in any case be denied or impaired. This is a religious truth far more essential than God's "personality," and hence that personality must be formulated, no matter how inconsistently, so as to agree with this truth and to support it. (433)

Yet is the Divine to be found merely in man? Is it merely individual? Is such a humanism satisfactory? No; for the religious consciousness must transcend the individual. Is any individual independently "real"? No; he is always an individualization.

Apart from the community, what are separate men? It is the common mind within him which gives reality to the human being, and taken by himself, whatever else he is, he is not human. When he opposes himself to the community it is still the whole which lives and moves in discord within him, for by himself he is an abstraction without life or force. . . . For religion, if the one indwelling Spirit is removed, there are no spirits left. . . . If anywhere the community is real, the reality of God in religion seems a matter of course. . . . The question you can go on to ask, is whether and in what sense the reality of the immanent Will is also personal. (434–35)

Bradley plumps for a "necessary pantheism."

The highest Reality, so far as I can see, must be super-personal. At the same time to many minds practical religion seems to call for the belief in God as a separate individual. And where truly that belief is so required, I can accept it as justified and true, but only if it is supplemented by other beliefs which really contradict it. And these other beliefs are more vital for religion. But how this necessary "pantheism" is to be made consistent with an individual Creator I myself do not perceive. (436)

At the end Bradley states his final answer.

If now, passing onwards, I am asked if the personality of God is required for religion, . . . I can answer at once No. . . . If without that belief religion remains imperfect, the belief is true and in a sense even necessary for religion. . . . Whether the conclusion is true or false is a question of fact. The answer depends on the interpretation of actual religious experience, in the present, in the past, and, I should be inclined to add, in the future. (449–50)

Yet if we adopt the personality of God as a working idea, we should realize what we are letting ourselves in for. Bradley quotes a Christian:

"It is not merely one of the doctrines of religion, but the central doctrine, the motive for all religious exercises, that God cares for every one of us individually, that he knows Jane Smith by name, and what she is earning a week, and how much of it she devotes to keeping her poor paralyzed old mother." (Hamerton, in *Essays*, 450)

Bradley's analysis of the idea of immortality is equally devastating. Here too he starts with the demands of the religious consciousness, and subjects them to sceptical analysis: this is what the dialectic of *Appearance and Reality* means concretely. Both are important, mysticism and logic, living and knowing. He sets forth a Platonic conception of immortality, and demonstrates the futility for religion of any idea of a "future existence." He mocks the presumption of the "hope" to see loved ones again.

The main demand of religion is for the assurance that the individual, as one with the Good, has so far conquered death, and that what we call this life with its before and after is not the main reality. . . . But for myself I feel the gravest doubt with regard to the necessity [of a "prolonged existence."] (438–39)

Bradley is caustic on psychical research:

Mere personal survival and continuance has in itself absolutely nothing to do with true religion. A man can be as irreligious (for anything at least that I know) in a hundred lives as in one. . . . And if you are to treat the evidence scientifically, you must divest your mind of preconceived ideas. . . . When we are satisfied that we converse with beings other than living men, the question as to what these beings are at once becomes formidable. The old reply, still given, I believe, by orthodox Catholicism, has at least to be considered. The inquiry which is opened is not altogether a pleasant one. (440n)

"Modernistic" ideas of immortality, an "impersonal" immortality, are only a sign of "mental confusion."

I should wish to survive if my future life were to be desirable, and I on my side to remain much what I am now. But, if my future life is to be undesirable, I am of course averse from it. And, if I am not to continue to be what I am, the future life, being the life of another man, does not personally concern me. (452)

Finally Bradley considers the relation between religion and morality.

From the point of view of mere duty, . . . I find no difference at all between religion and morality. . . . In morality proper the moral ideal is, so far, not viewed as existing. . . . The moral idea is a 'to be' which is 'not yet.' But in religion the ideal good must be taken as real, though . . . as also in part not realized. Where for us there is only an idea, I do not see how it is possible to have religion. Morality, it is true, can make a religion of morality. It can contemplate its ideal, . . . and can entertain towards its ideal those emotions which we call religious. But so far as it does this, it necessarily regards its object as somehow real. It has so far ceased to be mere morality and has passed into an imperfect form of religion. (441–42)

Religion emerges when the Ideal is taken as the real thing. "But for morality the object is not real" (442n). Religion is a need, but it cannot be based on metaphysics.

I think that any positive metaphysical doctrine must remain 'esoteric,' while a religion condemned to be esoteric is but a refuge amid general destitution. Therefore, a religious belief founded otherwise than on metaphysics, and a metaphysics able in some sense to justify that creed, seem to me what is required to fulfill our wishes. (446–47)

Bradley's whole application of his final position is thus a kind of relativism plus.

Life as a whole is liveable because we select arbitrarily those ideas which seem best to suit the occasion, while all the rest of our sound sense and clear thinking is for the occasion ignored. . . . For myself I must confess that I see no way, whether now or in the future, by which the clear thinking which calls itself "Common Sense" and is satisfied with itself, can ever be reconciled to metaphysics. By metaphysics I mean . . . all speculation which is at once resolved to keep its hold on all sides of fact, . . . and to push, so far as it can, every question to the end. (443–44)

Is this conclusion to be called "scepticism"?

Such a scepticism . . . may serve at the least as a deliverance from spiritual oppression. For it may free us . . . from the tyranny of intellectual prejudices, and in our own living concerns from the superstitious idolatry of abstract consistency. For such a scepticism all our truths without exception are mere working ideas. And this of course does not mean that all truths are "practical." It means that our ideas are there to serve our living interests, of whatever kind these may be, whether practical or otherwise, and that our ideas are to be subject to those interests which they serve. (445)

III

F.C.S. Schiller called Bradley's final position "the last halting place before Pragmatism." At this point it may be well to compare that position with the functional naturalism (or "pragmatism") of John Dewey. Bradley is in the great tradition of the "Knowers"—of Aristotle, Plotinus, Spinoza, and Hegel. For him, experience reveals a *Logos*, an intelligible structure in the world. But he is also in the great tradition of the critics of this vision of the Knowers—of Aristotle again, of the Romanticists, of John Dewey himself. For these critics, the intelligible system of the world is not the world as experienced; it is rather the "system" of that world, the "form" of substance, the "meaning" of experienced nature. Bradley regarded his efforts as seeking to free the "intelligible world" of the last taint of the "intellectualism" of men like T.H. Green. For him, the world is experienced on at least three different levels: (a) it is "felt" without being "known"; (b) it is "known" in terms of its logical structure; (c) it is "apprehended as an encompassing presence with which the whole man is at one."

The aim of knowledge is to find a harmonious, logically consistent "system" of the experienced world. All actual "knowledge" is relative to its subject matter, to its particular field; it must interpret its own particular aspect of the experienced world, and is to be tested by whether it *does* so interpret its subject matter, whether it does find a logical structure there. In this process of interpreting, it must be continually confronted by the experienced world it is interpreting. Bradley has thus arrived at an "instrumental" or functional theory of actual knowledge, of relative truths. But knowledge is not "instrumental" to something else—to the needs of "practice," as James was insisting. It is "instrumental" to interpreting its appropriate subject matter. Bradley does not emphasize the "experimental method of verification," like Dewey. He can be said to have an "instrumental logic," but not a "scientific method."

Yet all relative knowledge of specific structures is ultimately "instrumental" to "the direct grasp of the experienced world in its fulness." The ideal of the search for Truth is "to possess and enjoy Reality, to participate in the experienced world, to gain a sense of immediate oneness with the whole rich experienced world." The ultimate aim of philosophy is thus, in traditional terms, to become One with True Being. Relative truths, as interpretations of aspects of the experienced Whole, are means to absolute Truth, to identification with the Whole. In a word, Bradley shares the mysticism of the Knower—a mysticism which is the culmination of the rigorous thinking of Aristotle, Plotinus, Spinoza, and Hegel.

Bradley has given a classic statement of this mysticism of the Knower.

There is a further reason which, with myself perhaps, has even more weight. All of us, I presume, more or less, are led beyond the region of ordinary facts. Some in one way and some in others, we seem to touch and have communion with what is beyond the visible world. In various manners we find something higher, which both supports and humbles, both chastens and transports us. And with certain persons, the intellectual effort to understand the universe is a principal way of thus experiencing the Deity. No one, probably, who has not felt this, however differently he might describe it, has ever cared much for metaphysics. And, wherever it has been felt strongly, it has been its own justification. The man whose nature is such that by one path alone his nature will reach consummation, will try to find it on that path, whatever it may be, and whatever the world thinks of it; and if he does not, he is contemptible. Self-sacrifice is too often the "great sacrifice" of trade, the giving cheap what is worth nothing. To know what one wants, and to scruple at no means that will get it, may be a harder self-surrender. And this appears to be another reason for some persons pursuing the study of ultimate truth. . . .

I will end with a word of warning. I have been obliged to speak of philosophy as a satisfaction of what may be called the mystical side of our nature—a satisfaction which, by certain persons, cannot be as well procured otherwise. And I may have given the impression that I take the metaphysician to be initiated into something far higher than what the common herd possesses. Such a doctrine would rest on a most deplorable error; the superstition that the mere intellect is the highest side of our nature, and the false idea that in the intellectual world work done on higher subjects is for that reason higher work. Certainly the life of one man, in comparison with that of another, may be fuller of the Divine, or, again, may realize it with an intenser consciousness; but there is no calling or pursuit which is a private road to the Deity. And assuredly the way through speculation on ultimate truths, though distinct and legitimate, is not superior to others. There is no sin, however prone to it the philosopher may be, which philosophy can justify so little as spiritual pride.[8]

IV

Bradley is thus an instrumentalist whose functional knowledge of particular areas of experience all leads to the ultimate experience of mysticism. A comparison with his companion functional Left Wing Hegelian, Dewey, will be illuminating. For Dewey, the end of knowledge is to possess and enjoy experienced values, to participate in "shared experience." But for Dewey, this "participation" is not identified with "thought," it is not "Truth" with a capital "T," it is not a cognitive experience. For him, thought is one aspect of experience, of the process of enriching experience by making other and further experience possible. The name Dewey gives to the creative process involving thought, feeling, and will, is "Art"—*techné* in the Greek and Romantic sense. "Art" in Dewey corresponds to Bradley's "Absolute experience," as the ultimate and all-inclusive experience.

If Bradley is an instrumentalist and a mystic, Dewey is an instrumentalist and an artist. For him, knowledge has its setting in the artistic experience—in man dynamically interacting with Nature, and thus realizing all Nature's characteristic traits. For Bradley, knowledge has its setting in the mystic experience—in man achieving Oneness with Reality (which Dewey calls "Nature"), realizing identity with all its traits. For both, "science," "thought," what the Greeks

---

[8] *Appearance and Reality*, 2nd ed. (London, 1897), pp. 5–6.

called *dianoia* and *epistēmē,* is not ultimate. Beyond lies what the Greeks called *nous,* the "immediate apprehension of the fulness of Reality," as Bradley puts it, which is "more than knowing." This ultimate experience Bradley identifies with the Greek *theoria,* and takes, with Aristotle, as superrational, as above discursive thinking. Dewey identifies it with *technē,* and takes it, with Plato, as being "other than" rational. Hence Bradley distinguishes between relative truths and "the Truth," Dewey between scientific truths or warranted assertibilities and "enjoyed meanings." Obviously, more confusion is possible with Bradley's rendering, for his "truths" turn out in the end not to be "True," while Dewey's "truths" are true: they are "verified" or "warrantedly assertible."

Yet—Bradley is full of statements like: "When we say, 'Not only *that,* but so much *more:* that you must not merely say *that,*' critics take this as a denial of *that.*" "There is no reality anywhere except in appearances, and in them we can discern the main nature of Reality." "Though my experience is not the whole world, yet that world does appear in my experience." "Everything beyond, though not less real, is an expansion of the common essence we feel burningly in this one focus." Compare with this strain in Bradley Dewey's: "Experience is the foreground of Nature"; the traits revealed in experience are traits belonging to Nature.

Yet, though the "ultimate"—Bradley's Reality or Absolute experience, or Dewey's experience as ultimately leading to all Nature—is more than "thought," more than a possible object of knowledge, still for both Bradley and Dewey it can be indicated, talked about, and in some sense "known."

All ideas in the end, if we except those of metaphysics, lack ultimate truth. They may be called working conceptions, good and true so far as they work. And, because they work, and because nothing else could work so well, there is therefore nothing better and nothing truer than such ideas, each in its own proper place; since nothing else could possibly be more relative to our needs. But these ideas are not consistent either with one another or even with themselves, and they come short of that which we demand as truth. How far and in what sense even in metaphysics that demand can be satisfied, I have discussed elsewhere.[9] (*Essays,* 267)

---

[9] Note by F.H.B.: "*Appearance,* pp. 544 ff. How far (we may ask here in passing) are the ideas used by metaphysics to be called 'working conceptions'? (i) In the first place, these ideas are not merely 'instrumental.' They are not mere means to some end outside of, or other than, understanding. And (ii) they are not means to, or elements in, the un-

For Bradley, metaphysics is "true" in a final, not merely a relative sense. For Dewey, "empirical metaphysics" is a disinterested pointing to the ultimate traits of experienced Nature; and as instrumental to the widest possible subject matter, is ultimately "true," and not selective. This is Bradley's justification for insisting that his "apprehension of the Absolute" is "Truth."

Actually, and in practice, for both Bradley and Dewey "metaphysics" serves as a "theory of criticism," and the ultimate concepts— Bradley's "Absolute Reality" and Dewey's "Direct experience"—are each primarily a critical concept, an instrument for perfecting the relative truths of various logical systems.

V

The extent to which Bradley and Dewey came in the end to approach each other—or to which Bradley's "idealism" worked itself out into a "functional naturalism," if you will—is clearest in their discussion of "instrumentalism" from 1903 to 1906. After the appearance of Dewey's *Studies in Logical Theory* in 1903, Bradley regarded Dewey as by far the best "Pragmatist," presumably because he was far more Hegelian than James. In a paper written in 1903,[10] Bradley sketches "a possible Pragmatism."

Pragmatism might have meant something which, if carried out systematically, would, so far as I am aware, be new. It might have taken truth to be mere working ideas,[11] and human interests in their entirety it might have taken as

---

derstanding merely of one limited region. On the contrary, metaphysics aims at understanding the world in principle, in general and as one whole. The ideas used for this purpose, since they work, may, if we please, be called working conceptions. They are again all imperfect, and all differ in the degree in which they approach and fall short of perfection. But the main point is this, that, in order to work metaphysically, these ideas must themselves have the character of the metaphysical end. They do not merely conduce to a foreign purpose, but are themselves the very existence in which their end and principle is realized. The phrase 'working conceptions' tends, I think, to suggest that this is otherwise, and hence it seems to me safer not to apply it to the ideas of metaphysics."

[10] Introductory Note to Chapter 4, "On Truth and Practice," *Essays*, pp. 65–74.

[11] Note by F.H.B.: "Such a position would, however, not entail downright Instrumentalism, so long as the pursuit and possession of truth is allowed to be an intrinsic human interest. All that such a position is called on to deny is the existence of a criterion of truth which is intrinsic and supreme. The criterion of truth, that is, would lie in its contribution to the aggregate of human interests, and, as so contributing, truth might be allowed a value beyond that of an external means or instrument. I am not, however, suggesting that by taking the aggregate of human interests as our end it is possible to reach a consistent view. So far as we keep to a mere collection we are without any principle of order."

the one end, and as the criterion of knowledge and reality. It might have set these interests out fully, and not merely at the dictation of prejudice and caprice, and might have made them, severally and again collectively, and perhaps even in an order, the test everywhere of truth and value, in science, in art, and in morals and religion. Such a work would indeed be welcome, and, so far as I know, it has not been accomplished. But obviously this is not the task which Pragmatism has even attempted. Obviously Pragmatism, I should say, has never even faced the above problem in earnest, and much less has it ever applied itself to reach a satisfactory solution. (66–67)

What would Dewey have said to this "possible Pragmatism"? He would have criticized its lack of specificity, its referring to "the aggregate of all human interests," rather than to a specific intellectual problem. And he would have noted Bradley's confusion between truth as a human "interest"—the *motive* for pursuing it—and the *criterion* of truth—for him a "logical" matter, not a motive. This confusion between the immediate value of truth and its test comes out as Bradley continues:

There is, indeed, a sense in which Instrumentalism, though not novel, would, as I think, be tenable. Everything in the world or in our life *can*, that is, be regarded as a means. No element apart from all the rest will retain its value, and each therefore, we may say, has worth only in so far as it conduces to the welfare of the Whole. But on the other hand the value of the Whole is not separable from that of its diverse aspects, and in the end, apart from any one of them, it is reduced to nothing. In the above sense Instrumentalism, I should say, is true, so long as you emphasize the fact that everything alike (though not to the same degree) is an instrument, and so far as you insist that there is nothing in life which, viewed otherwise, has value. The instrument, in other words, is such, only because it is *not* taken as a means to some end which fails to include itself as intrinsic and valuable. (68–69)

Bradley here oscillates between "*is* an instrument" and "*has* value"; Dewey would find him failing to distinguish between immediate value and the criterion of value, failing to catch Dewey's point that everything can be at once a means and an end.

My attitude remains the same in presence of the denial of idle or useless truths, and the assertion that a truth apart from its working is not true. If this is Pragmatism, then surely Hegel long ago was the Pragmatist *par excellence*, and I doubt if anyone who knows the facts would venture to deny this. The general view, which others and myself may be said to have inherited, is this— that the criterion lies in the idea of system. An idea is true theoretically because, and so far as, it takes its place in, and contributes to, the organism of knowledge. And, on the other hand, an idea is false of which the opposite holds good. . . . As long as we do not know what words like "practical," "action," and "working" are to mean, any claim to novelty here must remain ambiguous.

And with regard to what is called verification, the same remark holds good. . . . What is it to verify? Is it to find the object of an idea as a sensible event? Is it to envisage an ideal content clearly and convincingly, or to experience coercion from ideas and their relations? Is it to show that an idea, taken as true, makes the body of our knowledge at once wider and more consistent? . . . The only real novelty left to Pragmatism is to claim to verify truth by its practical results. (69–70)

The ambiguities clearly apply to James rather than to Dewey.

In *Mind*, no. 63 (July 1907), Dewey set forth his version of Pragmatism, and Bradley replied.[12]

Here, as with Prof. James, I find much which to myself seems ambiguous. I am again left uncertain whether in the end I am a Pragmatist, or where and how on the other hand I fail to deserve that title. . . . I myself long ago (1883) pointed out that theory takes its origin from practical collision, and again for myself theory implies a theoretical want and its satisfaction. And it is obvious that, if Pragmatism means no more than this, I, as I presume Prof. Dewey is aware, have been for many years a Pragmatist, and, however well he preaches, he is preaching here to one long ago converted.

Bradley agrees with Dewey on the "practical nature" of thinking:

Let us ask what is meant by the practical nature of thinking and truth. Let me say here at once that I have failed, I am sure, to understand what practical means for Prof. Dewey.[13] But an idea, it appears, is true only so far as it issues in behavior. . . .

If we take practical in the sense in which it is opposed to theoretical . . . objections present themselves at once. . . . Prof. Dewey . . . appears to admit that in the case of "tested" ideas we have judgments not issuing in actual behavior. . . . A large number of ideas appear in no sense to relate to my behavior either in themselves or in their results. (136–37)

This implies that for Bradley the process of verification itself is not "practical," as it is of course for Dewey. Bradley finally suggests Dewey's own answer to Dewey:

---

[12] *Essays*, Appendix I to Chapter 5, "On the Ambiguity of Pragmatism," pp. 134–42; appeared in *Mind*, XVII, N.S. (April 1908).

[13] Note by F.H.B.: "By 'practical,' he says, 'I mean only regulated change in experienced values.' But, if Prof. Dewey means no more than this, his whole article is surely one long *ignoratio elenchi*. How does such a definition exclude the existence of pure theoretical activity and practice? And if it does not, what becomes of Prof. Dewey's polemic? Pragmatism is on this understanding in agreement with even an extreme one-sided intellectualism, so long as that asserts an intellectual need and activity."

The first answer to the above objection would consist in urging that truth is the behavior of an idea rather than that of a man. When an idea acts and works in me in a certain manner, that is truth, and therefore truth in this sense is practical. I mention this view, though I do not suppose that Prof. Dewey would accept it.

It is ideas that "behave" in certain ways which warrants them, as Dewey holds.

Bradley states the extent of his agreement with Dewey, and his root objection.

So much indeed of what Prof. Dewey urges seems to me so true and so admirably stated, that I can only applaud and regret that it should seem to be directed against views which I hold. I agree that practical collision is the origin of truth, and I agree that for truth to pass into a new practical result may be called (if we speak at large) truth's natural and normal end. But that by us men theoretical truth, as well as fine art, must be cultivated, at least to some extent, independently, I am no less assured. The denial of this appears to me to violate facts and to threaten us with the mutilation of our human ideal. And if theory and fine art, or either of these, is to have no worth of its own, let us at least be informed what in the end it is which really possesses value. On such a point to state no positive doctrine, and to leave it to opponents to lose themselves in more or less mistaken conjectures, is a course, I would submit, unworthy of such writers as Profs. Dewey and James. (141)

Bradley insists, "Truth must be cultivated independently." The question that exercises him is not of the nature of truth, but of the motive for pursuing it. Dewey fully agrees as to motive, but *defines* the nature of truth functionally: "truth" is what an idea does when it does what it is intended to do, when it thus fulfills its function as "true." He states his position:

If scientific discourse is instrumental in function, it also is capable of becoming an enjoyed object to those concerned in it. Upon the whole, human history shows that thinking, in being abstract, remote and technical, has been laborious; or at least that the process of attaining such thinking has been rendered painful to most by social circumstances. In view of the importance of such activity and its objects, it is a priceless gain when it becomes an intrinsic delight. Few would philosophize if philosophic discourse did not have its own inhering fascination. Yet it is not the satisfactoriness of the activity which *defines* science or philosophy; the definition comes from the structure and *function* of subject-matter. To say that knowledge as the fruit of intellectual discourse is an end in itself is to say what is aesthetically and morally true for some persons. But it conveys nothing about the structure of knowledge; and it does not even hint that its objects are not instrumental. These are questions that can be decided only by an examination of the things in question. Impartial and disinterested thinking, discourse in terms of scrutinized, tested, and related meanings, is a fine art. But it is an art as yet open to comparatively few. Letters, poetry, song, the drama, fiction, history, biography, engaging in rites and ceremonies hallowed by time and rich with the sense of the countless multitudes that share in them, are also modes of discourse that, detached from immediate instrumental consequences of assistance and cooperative action, are ends for most persons. In them discourse is both instrumental and final. No person remains unchanged and has the same future efficiencies, who shares in situations made possible by communication. Subsequent consequences may be good or bad, but they are there. The part of wisdom is not to deny the causal fact because of the intrinsic value of the immediate experience. It is to make the immediately satisfactory object the object which will also be most fertile.[14]

Bradley states his meaning of the term "practice":

Practice is a necessary aspect of human nature and of the whole of things, but practice is not the whole of things nor is it the entirety of human nature. It is a pernicious error to set up one aspect of our being as an end by itself to which everything else is subordinate. Our nature is complex, . . . but its unity is not to be found by setting up one element as absolute, and by turning all the rest into mere external means. . . . It is wrong to conclude that within its own limits no element is to have free play, and that the whole in short is best served by the work of slaves. (*Essays*, 99–100)

"Practice" must not tyrannize. But Dewey is maintaining that every human activity is a "practice." How do Bradley and Dewey differ in their construing of "practice"? Bradley is clearly taking a very narrow view of "practice." For Dewey, the pursuit of truth for its own sake is a "practice"; for Bradley, it is an "activity." Was "practical" a good term of the Americans, Peirce, James, and Dewey, to employ? Peirce thought not; and obviously it became a source of confusion to such as Bradley. "Functional" is a far better term, for it suggests a specific "function."[15]

---

[14] John Dewey, *Experience and Nature* (Chicago, 1926), pp. 203–4.

[15] Dewey is explicit in his note to W.P. Montague, *Ways of Knowing* (cited in C.W. Morris, *Six Theories of Mind* [Chicago, 1932], p. 295): "I have never taught that all needs are practical, but simply that no need could be satisfied without action. Our needs originate out of needs that were at first practical, but the development of intelligence transforms them, so that there are now aesthetic, scientific, and moral needs. I have never said that thought exists for the sake of action. On the contrary, it exists for the sake of specific consequences, immediate values, etc. (itself and others: i.e., has a determinate function). What I have insisted on is quite a different point, viz., that action is involved in thinking and existential knowing, as part of the function of reaching immediate, nonpractical consequences."

Bradley's final statement on Dewey, when the relative autonomy of science had been explained to him by Addison W. Moore,[16] runs:

What is the good of truth? . . . On any view such as mine no one aspect of life is good ultimately by itself. . . . What is ultimately good is life itself or experience as a whole.

The question, What is the good of truth? can be asked properly, if it means, How does truth stand to, and how does it conduce to experience or life as a whole? And except as conducing, you can certainly affirm that truth is not good, and that it possesses no value whatever. . . . Truth's natural destiny is to return once more into unbroken union with Reality, and to restore at a higher level that totality out of which it has emerged. But that this destiny is accomplished, verifiably and in detail, within and throughout our experience seems demonstrably false. And within our experience truth remains and must forever remain relatively free.[17]

On his side, Dewey conducted the discussion in the article, "The Intellectualist Criterion for Truth." [18] Dewey uses a figure for Bradley's dialectic of contradiction:

It is as if we wanted to get all the cloth in the world into one garment and our only way of accomplishing this were to tear off a portion from one piece of goods in order to patch it on to another. (115)

Yet thinking, the mode of bringing existence and meaning into harmony with each other, always works by selection, by abstraction; it sets up and projects meanings which are ideal only, footless, in the air, matters of thought only, not of sentiency or immediate existence. It emphasizes the ideal of a completed union of existence and meaning, but is helpless to effect it. And

---

Dewey is also explicit in replying to Bertrand Russell, in Paul A. Schilpp, *The Philosophy of John Dewey* (Evanston, Illinois, 1939), p. 571: "In the proper interpretation of 'pragmatic,' namely, the function of *consequences* as necessary tests of the validity of propositions, *provided* these consequences are operationally instituted and are such as to resolve the specific problems evoking the operations, the text is thoroughly pragmatic." See also *Logic: The Theory of Inquiry* (New York, 1938), p. iv.

[16] *Essays*, Chapter 11, "On Some Aspects of Truth," pp. 346–47; first printed in *Mind* XX, N.S. (July 1911).

[17] Note by F.H.B.: "While denying this freedom, Prof. Moore, speaking for the 'pragmatist,' allows, as I understand, to thought a value of its own, though not in 'independence.' It is, I think, important, to have got even as far as this. But what follows is that to speak of thought, e.g., as instrumental, is not permissible. The rest of the whole process is surely also instrumental, as thought is, and may itself, by the same right, be taken as instrumental to thought. . . . However, between such a 'pragmatist' as Prof. Moore and myself, the points of difference, in comparison with the amount of agreement, seem really small. And again with regard to Prof. Dewey the same remark would, I think, hold good."

[18] *Mind*, XVI, N.S. (July 1907); reprinted in *The Influence of Darwin on Philosophy* (New York, 1910), pp. 112–47.

this helplessness (according to Mr. Bradley) is not due to external pressure but to the very structure of thought itself. (117) . . . It is expressly declared that it is the knowledge function which is responsible for the degradation of reality to appearance. . . . Thinking, self-consciousness, is disease of the naive unity of thoughtless experience. (120)

Dewey finds a fundamental contrast between Bradley's *motive* and his *method*.

Among the influences that have worked in contemporary philosophy towards disintegration of intellectualism of the epistemological type, and towards the substitution of a philosophy of experience, the work of Mr. Bradley must be seriously counted. One has, for example, only to compare his metaphysics with the two fundamental contentions of T.H. Green, namely, that reality is a single, eternal, and all-inclusive system of relations, and that this system of relations is one in kind with that process of relating which constitutes our thinking, to be instantly aware of a changed atmosphere. Much of Bradley's writing is a sustained and deliberate polemic against intellectualism of the Neo-Kantian type. When, however, we find conjoined to this criticism an equally sustained contention that the philosophic conception of reality must be based on an exclusively intellectual criterion, a criterion belonging to and confined to theory, we have a situation that is thought-provoking. The situation grows in interest when it is remembered that there is a general and growing tendency among those who appeal in philosophy to a strictly intellectualistic *method* of defining "reality," to insist that the reality reached by this method has a super-intellectual *content;* that intellectual, affectional, and volitional features are all joined and fused in "ultimate" reality. The curious character of the situation is that Reality is an "absolute experience" of which the intellectual is simply one partial and transmuted moment. Yet this reality is attained unto, in philosophic method, by exclusive emphasis upon the intellectual aspect of present experience and by systematic exclusion of exactly the emotional, volitional features which with respect to content are insisted upon! (112–13)

Dewey finds this the fundamental paradox of Bradley's thought: Logic will not bring us to Reality, yet what *is* Reality is determined by a logical criterion.

On the one hand there is a systematic discrediting of the ultimate claims of the knowledge function, and this not from external physiological or psychological reasons such as are sometimes alleged against its capacity, but on the basis of its own interior logic. But on the other hand a strictly logical criterion is deliberately adopted and employed as the fundamental and final criterion for the philosophic conception of reality. Long familiarity has not dulled my astonishment at finding exactly the same set of considerations which in the earlier portion of the book are employed to condemn things as experienced by us to the region of Appearance, employed in the latter portion of the book to afford a triumphant demonstration of the existence and character of Absolute Reality. (120–21)

What about the intellectualist criterion? The intellectualism of Mr. Bradley's philosophy is represented by the statement that it is "the theoretical standard which guarantees that reality is a self-consistent system." But how can the fact that the criterion of thinking is consistency be employed to determine the nature of the consistency of its object? Consistency in one sense, consistency of reasoning with itself, we know; but what is the nature of the consistency of reality which this consistency necessitates? Thinking without doubt must be logical; but does it follow from this that the reality about which one thinks, and about which one must think consistently if one is to think to any purpose, must itself be already logical? . . .

Those who question this basic principle of intellectualism . . . will say that the definition of the nature of the consistency which is the end of thinking and which prescribes its technique is to be reached from inquiry into such questions as these: What sort of an activity in the concrete is thinking? what are the specific conditions which it has to fulfil? what is its use; its relevancy; its purport in present concrete experiences? The more it is insisted that the theoretical standard—consistency—is final within theory, the more germane and the more urgent is the question; What then in the concrete *is* theory? and of what nature *is* the material consistency which is the test of its formal consistency? (129–30) [19]

Bradley's positive criterion runs:

"Ultimate reality must be such that it does not contradict itself; here is an absolute criterion. And it is proved absolute by the fact that either in endeavoring to deny it or even in attempting to doubt it, we tacitly assume its validity." (*Appearance*, 136–37)

Dewey goes on to ask the functional question:

We reach, I think the heart of the matter by asking, in reference to the first quotation, Absolute *for what?* Surely absolute for the process under consideration, that is absolute for thought. But the significance of this absolute for thought is, one may say, "absolutely" (since we are here confessedly in the realm just of thought) determined by the nature of thought itself. Now this nature has already been referred by considerations "belonging irremovably to

[19] Note by J.D.: "The essential point of pragmatism is that it bases its changed account of truth on a changed conception of the nature of intelligence, both as to its objective and its method. Now this different account of intelligence may be wrong, but controversy which leaves standing the conventionally current theories about thought and merely discusses 'truth' will not go far. Since truth is the adequate fulfilment of the function of intelligence, the question turns on the nature of the latter" (130).

truth's proper character," to the world of appearance and internal discrepancy. . . .

It is comical to suppose that a *special* trait of thought can be employed to alter the fundamental and essential nature of thought. The criterion of thought must be infected by the nature of thought, instead of being a redeeming angel which at a critical juncture transforms the fragile creature, thought, into an ambassador with power plenipotentiary to the court of the Absolute. (122–23)

Dewey goes on to offer his own interpretation of the autonomy of thinking, on which Bradley has so heavily insisted.

Grant that intellect is a special movement or mode of practice; grant that we are not merely acting (are we ever *merely* acting?) but are "specially occupied and therefore subject to special conditions," and the problem remains *what* special kind of activity is thinking? what is its experienced differentia from other kinds? what is its commerce with them? . . . The unquestioned presupposition of Mr. Bradley is that thinking is such a wholly separate activity that to give it autonomy is to say that it, and its criterion, have nothing to do with other activities; that it is "independent" as to criterion, in a way which excludes interdependence in function and outcome. Unless the term "special" be interpreted to mean *isolated*, to say that thinking is a *special* mode of activity no more nullifies the proposition that it arises in a practical context and operates for practical ends, than to say that blacksmithing is a *special* activity, negates its being one connected mode of industrial activity.

His underlying presupposition of the separate character of thought comes out in the passage last quoted. "Our impulse," he says, "is to alter the conflicting situation and, *on the theoretical side*, to bring its contents into peaceable unity." If one substitutes for the word "on" the word "through," one gets a conception of theory and of thinking that does justice to the autonomy of the operation and yet so connects it with other activities as to give it a serious business, real purpose, and concrete responsibility and hence testibility. From this point of view the theoretical activity is simply the form that certain practical activities take after colliding, as the most effective and fruitful way of securing their own harmonization. The collision is not theoretical; the issue in "peaceable unity" is not theoretical. But theory names the type of activity by which the transformation from war to peace is most amply and securely effected. (125–27)

And Dewey concludes:

With all our heart, then, the standard of thinking is absolute (that is, final) within thinking. The standard of blacksmithing must be absolute within blacksmithing, but what is blacksmithing? No prejudice prevents acknowledging that blacksmithing is one practical activity existing as a distinct and relevant member of a like system of activities; that it is because men use horses to transport persons and goods that horses need to be shod. The ultimate criterion of blacksmithing is producing a good shoe, but the nature of a good shoe is fixed, not by blacksmithing, but by the activities in which horses are used. The end is ultimate (absolute) for the operation, but the very finality is evidence that the operation is not absolute and self-inclosed, but is related and responsible. Why must the fact that the end of thinking is ultimate for thought stand on any different footing? (131–32)

VI

We are now in a position to state the central metaphysical paradox with which Bradley wrestled all his life. "Reality" is more than thought or truth alone, that is, it is more than T.H. Green's "logical system." Yet the knowledge of Reality, the science of reality, or metaphysics, must express the relation of "thought" and truth, of intelligibility, to its larger context or setting, in an intelligible, that is, in a "logical" way. Reality is much more than thought, truth, or intelligibility—this is Bradley's "anti-intellectualism," concretely, his protest against Green. But the science of Reality, metaphysical truth, must have an "intellectualist criterion." The subject matter is not mere thought or reason; but the method and tests for understanding it must be "rational." For Bradley, as for every intellectualist, the object of knowledge has its setting in a fundamental experience. For Bradley, Thought has its setting in "immediate experience," which started for him pretty much as the experience of the British empirical tradition, but was steadily enlarged and broadened. For Dewey, the object of knowledge has its setting in the "experience" of experimental psychology and of anthropology. In each case, as with the great Knowers of the past, and of their critics as well, the setting of intelligibility is indicated and dealt with by an intellectual method that is the same as that employed within "knowledge" in the narrower sense—perhaps inevitably so. For Bradley, the metaphysical criterion is "dialectical," freedom from contradiction. For Dewey the method and test are "experimental," verifiable through leading to further facts.

What do these facts imply? The conclusion seems to be: the nature of the method conceived to be appropriate to science or knowing determines the method of metaphysics. Since Bradley has an "intellectualist criterion" for particular "truths," he has also an "intellectualist criterion" for the nature of "Truth" itself, for the relation of intelligibility to its setting. What, then, do thinkers differ on? On the nature of "experience," and on the "right" method of exploring it.

To the paradox Dewey finds in the contrast between Bradley's conception of the nature of Reality and his criterion for truth about it, Bradley replies:

As the idea of truth's plunging us into contradictions is to Prof. Dewey obviously inconsistent with the idea of its also pointing to an end above and beyond them, and also realizing that end progressively, though always imperfectly—and as on the other hand all this to me is consistent, and was offered to and urged on the reader as consistent and true—there is really nothing to be discussed by me, and no more to be said but to leave the issue to the reader. But I am ready to admit that, though I seldom read anything written by Prof. Dewey without pleasure, when it comes to first principles I seldom succeed in understanding him.[20]

The answer Bradley would not give to Dewey, for lack of understanding him, Bradley attempted in the Appendix to the second edition of *Appearance and Reality* (London, 1897). He here states his central paradox:

The actual starting-point and basis of this work is an assumption about truth and reality. I have assumed that the object of metaphysics is to find a general view which will satisfy the intellect, and I have assumed that whatever succeeds in doing this is real and true, and that whatever fails is neither. We come against the great problem of the relation of Thought to Reality. For, if we decline (as I think wrongly) to affirm that all truth is thought, yet we certainly cannot deny this of a great deal of truth, and we can hardly deny that truth satisfies the intellect. But, if so, truth therefore is real. And to hold that truth is real, not because it is true but because also it is something else, seems untenable; for, if so, the something else left outside would make incomplete and would hence falsify the truth. But then, on the other hand, can thought, however complete, be the same as reality, the same altogether, I mean, and with no difference between them? This is a question to which I could never give an affirmative reply. It is useless here to seek to prove that the real involves thought as its *sine qua non*, for that much, when proved, does not carry the conclusion. And it is useless again to urge that thought is so inseparable from every mode of experience that in the end it may be said to cover the ground. That is, it seems to me, merely the inconclusive argument from the *sine qua non*, or else the conclusion is vitiated from another side by the undue extension of thought's meaning. Thought has now been taken, that is, to include so much more than truth in the narrow sense, that the old question as to how truth in this sense stands to reality, must break out more or less within

[20] *Essays*, Chapter 9, "On Appearance, Error, and Contradiction," p. 254*n*; first printed in *Mind* XIX, N.S. (April 1910).

thought itself. [Here Hegel is speaking.] Nor again does it seem clear why we must term this whole "thought," and not "feeling," or "will," unless we can show that these really are modes of thought, while thought cannot fall under them. For otherwise our conclusion seems but verbal and arbitrary; and again an argument drawn from the mere hegemony of thought could not prove the required conclusion. (*Appearance and Reality*, 2nd ed., 553–54)

Bradley has been so captivated by the structuralism of his teacher T.H. Green that even when he insists on the reality of feeling, he feels the compulsion to bring it "within" thought. It has not yet occurred to him, as it did in his third period, that "thought" and "reality" or "being" might be polar concepts, and that all "thought" must be about something, some subject matter, that is not thought. Things may well be what they are thought or said to be; but this is not equivalent to saying that all things are identical with "thought." Where Green reduced Substance to Form, Bradley is attempting to reduce Form to Substance. Aristotle at this point would have been of more help to Bradley than Hegel. Or, to employ another philosophical language, Bradley's paradox arises from his confusion as to the relation between discourse and its subject matter. Discourse may well find its proper function to "cover the ground," to "*express*" all modes of experience, without being under the compulsion itself to *become* those modes. Bradley might well have asked, what *is* the essential relation of language to what it is about? What *is* the function of discourse? But then he need never have written *Appearance and Reality*.

"Can thought be the same as reality?" Bradley continues:

With this we are left, it appears, in a dilemma. There is a difference between on the one side truth or thought (it will be convenient now to identify these) and on the other side reality. But to assert the difference seems impossible without somehow transcending thought or bringing the difference into thought, and these phrases seem meaningless. [Perhaps they are!] Thus reality appears to be an Other different from truth and yet not able to be truly taken as different; and this dilemma to myself was long a main cause of perplexity and doubt. We indeed do something to solve it by the identification of being or reality with experience or with sentience in its widest meaning. This step I have taken without hesitation [against Green], and I will not add a further defence of it here. . . . But this step by itself leaves us far from the desired solution of our dilemma; for between facts of experience and the thought of them and the truth about them the difference still remains, and the difficulty which attaches to this difference.

The solution of this dilemma offered in Chapter XV is, I believe, the only solution possible. It contains the main thesis of this work, views opposed to that thesis remaining, it seems to me, caught in and destroyed by the dilemma. (554–55)

So in Chapter XV, "Thought and Reality," Bradley attempts the self-imposed and impossible task of trying to "eff" the ineffable. He has adopted a "radical empiricism": "Reality" is absolute or complete experience. Is this absolute experience unintelligible? All intelligibility is "thought," and hence "appearance," necessarily incomplete.

Viewed intellectually, appearance is error. But the remedy lies in supplementation by the inclusion of that which is both outside and yet essential, and in the Absolute this remedy is perfected. There is no mere appearance or utter chance or absolute error, but all is relative. And the degree of reality is measured by the amount of supplementation required in each case, and by the extent to which the completion of anything entails its own destruction as such.(555)

Bradley has arrived at an objective relativism, or, if you prefer, an "existentialism"—all is experience—without benefit of the phenomenological analysis and path by which the Germans were to reach it. For "Reality"—what the Existentialists call "*Sein*" or "*Être*"—must have all the traits found in human experience. That Bradley is writing man large in the cosmos, and not merely, like Green, looking for God, is clear when he asks, Can we therefore facilely make the "absolute experience" or projected human traits "God" or the "Eternal Self," like Green? and gives a negative—and existentialist—answer:

And if finally I hear, Well, you yourself admit that the Absolute is unintelligible; why then object to saying that the Absolute somehow unintelligibly is self and the self is somehow unintelligibly absolute?—that gives me no trouble. For the Absolute, though in detail unintelligible, is not so in general, and its general character comes as a consequence from a necessary principle. And against this consequence we have to set nothing but privation and ignorance. But to make the self, as such, absolute is, so far as I see, to postulate in the teeth of facts, facts which go to show that the self's character is gone when it ceases to be relative.(559)

VII

The chapter on "Thought and Reality" is thus the core of Bradley's problem during his middle or "sceptical" period, before he had realized the futility of his quest.

Thought, no matter how complete, can never be the same as Reality. How then are they related? Reality is a union of a "what" and a "that"—as Bradley renders Aristotle's *synolon* or composite of a "such" and a "this," of form and matter, of meaning and existence—Reality is Substance. Thought divides this whole; it seizes on the "what" or "such," the form or universal, and is thus, in Green's sense, "ideal." Thought first distinguishes, then judgment reunites what has been torn apart. Bradley's analysis is Aristotelian:

The question is whether, in any judgment that really says anything, there is not in the subject an aspect of existence which is absent from the bare predicate. [The answer is yes.] . . . For I do not deny that reality *is* an object of thought; I deny that it is barely and *merely* so. . . . But if you admit that in asserting reality to fall within thought, you meant that in reality there is nothing beyond what is made thought's object, your position is untenable. Reflect upon any judgment. . . . See if you do not discover, beyond the content of your thought, a subject [a subject matter] of which it is true, and which it does not comprehend. You will find that the object of thought in the end must be ideal.(169)

Nothing is unintelligible; but thought, though it can "understand" anything, does not "comprehend" it. Why should it? we may well ask.

But though Bradley's analysis is Aristotelian, it is made on the basis of British empiricism. The "Other" which thought does not "comprehend" is "feeling."

Let us assume that existence is no longer different from truth, and let us see where this takes us. It takes us straight to thought's suicide. . . . In our reality we have the fact of sensible experience, immediate presentation with its coloring of pleasure and pain. . . . How it is to be exhibited as an element in a system of thought-content, is a problem not soluble. Thought is relational and discursive, and, if it ceases to be this, it commits suicide; and yet, if it remains thus, how does it contain immediate presentation? Let us suppose the impossible accomplished. . . . The delights and pains of the flesh, the agonies and raptures of the soul, these are fragmentary meteors fallen from thought's harmonious system. But these burning experiences—how in any sense can they be mere pieces of thought's heaven? For, if the fall is real, there is a world outside thought's region; and, if the fall is apparent, then human error itself is not included there. Heaven, in brief, must either not be heaven, or else not all reality. Without a metaphor, feeling belongs to perfect thought, or it does not. If it does not, there is at once a side of existence beyond thought. But if it does belong, then thought is different from thought discursive and relational. To make it include immediate experience, its character must be transformed. . . . Thought, in a word, must have been ab-

sorbed into a fuller experience. . . . It will, in short, be an existence which is
not mere truth. . . . And the question is *not* whether the universe is in any
sense intelligible. The question is whether, if you thought it and understood
it, there would be no difference left between your thought and the
thing.(170–71)

At this point the unregenerate reader—or nonidealist—is apt to ask,
Why is not Bradley content to say, thought can "express" or "formulate" reality, without having to "comprehend" or be "absorbed" in it?
Then Bradley will ask, How can we "express" the relation of "expression" to what is expressed?

No one really can believe that mere thought includes everything [except
Green]. The difficulty lies in *maintaining* the opposite. Since in philosophy we
must think, how is it possible to transcend thought without self-contradiction? . . . To maintain in thought an Other is by the same act to destroy its
otherness, and to persist is to contradict oneself.(175)

The full force of this paradox Bradley rubs in:

To think of anything which can exist quite outside of thought I agree is impossible. If thought is one element in a whole, you cannot argue from this
ground that the remainder of such a whole must stand apart and independent.
From this ground, in short, you can make no inference to a Thing-in-itself.
And there is no impossibility in thought's existing as an element, and no contradiction in its own judgment that it is less than the universe.(167)

The "Other" is intelligible; but what is unique about it? How can we
find Matter intelligible, if by definition, Form is the intelligible aspect
of what is?

If thought asserted the existence of any content which was not an actual or
possible object of thought—certainly that assertion in my judgment would
contradict itself. But the Other which I maintain is not any such content, nor
is it another separated "what," nor in any sense do I suggest that it lies outside
intelligence. Everything, all will and feeling, is an object for thought, and
must be called intelligible. This is certain; but if so, what becomes of the
Other? If we fall back on the mere "that," thatness itself seems a distinction
made by thought. And we have to face this difficulty: If the Other exists, it
must be something; and if it is nothing, it certainly does not exist.(176)

Two special characters in the subject seem to elude the grasp of
thought: sensuous infinitude, the ragged edge; and immediacy itself.
Thus every judgment really runs, "Reality is experienced as——," not
"Reality is known to be——"; and the former is more inclusive. Yet

even this implies knowledge and words! Knowledge is forever trying
to transcend its limits:

Thought seeks to possess in its object that whole character of which it already
owns the separate features. These features it cannot combine satisfactorily.
. . . And if the object were made perfect, it would forthwith *become* reality,
but would cease forthwith to be an object. It is this completion of thought
beyond thought which remains forever an Other. Thought can form the idea
of an apprehension, something like feeling in directness, which contains all
the character sought by its relational efforts. Thought can understand that, to
reach its goal, it must get beyond relations. Yet in its nature it can find no
other working means of progress. Hence it perceives that somehow this relational side of its nature must be merged and must include somehow the other
side. Such a fusion would compel thought to lose and to transcend its proper
self. . . .
  Hence in our Absolute thought can find its other without inconsistency.
The entire reality will be merely the object thought out, but thought out in
such a way that mere thinking is absorbed. This same reality will be feeling
that is satisfied completely.(181–82)

Bradley attempted to tell what this fusion of feeling and thought
would be like—he tried to paint the portrait of the Absolute.

What is impossible is to construct absolute life in its detail, to have the specific experience in which it consists. But to gain an idea of its main features—
an idea true so far as it goes, though abstract and incomplete—is a different
endeavor. And it is a task, so far as I see, in which we may succeed. For these
main features, to some extent, are within our own experience [this is Bradley's
"existentialism"]; and again the idea of their combination is, in the abstract,
quite intelligible. . . . First, in mere feeling, or immediate presentation, we
have the experience of a whole. This whole contains diversity, and, on the
other hand, is not parted by relations. . . . The relational form pointed everywhere to unity. It implies a substantial totality beyond relations and above
them. . . . We can form the general idea of an absolute experience in which
phenomenal distinctions are merged, a whole become immediate at a higher
stage without losing any richness.(159–60)

  In a famous burlesque issue of *Mind*, F.C.S. Schiller and his friends
printed a portrait of the Absolute—as a pale pink sheet of paper. Was
this fair? Is the Absolute "unintelligible"? In his 1897 Appendix,
Bradley puts it:

Certainly it is unintelligible if that means that you cannot understand its detail, and that throughout its structure constantly in particular you are unable
to answer the question, Why or How. . . . A theory may contain what is

unintelligible, so long as it really contains it; and not to know how a thing can be is no disproof of our knowing that it both must be and is. . . . And given a knowledge of "how" in general, a mere ignorance of "how" in detail is permissible and harmless.(555–56)

What Bradley is working at is really a theory of criticism, which became so consciously in the *Essays*, where the Absolute dropped out, and the degree of necessary "supplementation" is emphasized instead.

Hence if thought carried out its own nature, it both would and would not have passed beyond itself and become also an Other. And this self-completion of thought, by inclusion of the aspects opposed to mere thinking, would be what we mean by reality, and by reality we can mean no more than this. . . . Reality is above thought, and above every partial aspect of being, but it includes them all. Each of these completes itself by uniting with the rest, and so makes the perfection of the whole. And this whole is experience, for anything other than experience is meaningless [here is Bradley's existentialism, his generalization of human experience to characterize being].(555)

Bradley's "totality" is the natural implication of his theory, set forth in detail in the *Logic*, that every judgment really runs, "Reality is experienced as thus and so."

VIII

Again a comparison with Dewey proves fruitful. Thought, for Bradley and Dewey alike, arises in an experience that is not thought. For Bradley, it aims to know what is there experienced—what the experience is. And to know what experience really is, we must experience experience as known. For Dewey, to "know" what experience is *is not* equivalent to "having" the experience. Reality is reached by "having" experiences as meaningful and known; but it is not "known" that way. That is, for Dewey, "reality" is not the object of knowledge, but the object of "enjoyment." For Bradley, knowledge is larger than logic or "thought." For Dewey, known reality is smaller than experienced reality. For Bradley, the test of thought is, does it *include* the experience from which it started? Bradley is still holding on to a version of the empiricist assumption that its "origin" is the ultimate criterion of knowledge. For Dewey, the test is, does thought come to include a *different* experience from that with which it started? Does it include the one intended? Dewey's test is functional or teleological, the achievement of an end. For Bradley, thought is not active: it is *theoria*, it grasps being, it is mystical—it grasps what is there to begin with. For Dewey, thought grasps the intelligible part of what is there in order to get *more*.

To use a metaphor, Bradley was trying to get the whole of life expressed in a book, to express all aspects of everything in words. A book *about* life never succeeds in doing that, it always falls short, it remains one-sided and incomplete. So Bradley was driven toward the Perfect Book—an *Encyclopedia Britannica* more glorious. But he tried to write it as James Joyce would have written it: he follows the method of *Ulysses*, not of the *Encyclopedia Britannica*—technically, the method of Hegel's *Phenomenology*. He is driven on: the book ought really to be a play, like Eugene O'Neill's *Strange Interlude*, where the characters express all their private feelings, in their contradictions, all at once. The Perfect Play would include and express everything. This effort would end in more than a book or even a play: it would be life itself. Bradley is trying to write the drama of life as it is, with all the stage directions, to express, not only what the actors do, say, think, and feel, but also, what they are expressing. If one could succeed, the result would be life itself, completely known. We would see why, we would understand—and also, we would feel the very tang of life itself!

Or one can resort to a literary analogy familiar to Bradley's brother, the critic A.C. Bradley. The world of Shakespeare is there. We can write about it, but there is always more. One gets a sense of futility—how can one express *all* it really means? We are always trying to, but the attempt always remains incomplete. Or take Plato's philosophy—how can we express it all in words, say flatly all it means? Some things remain inexpressible: Bradley calmly asks, how then can we express the inexpressible? How can we "eff" the ineffable?

If Dewey set out to write a book about life, he would write a guidebook to life: how to get there, what is worth seeing, what the prices of admission are. Writing about Chartres Cathedral, he would tell all about it: how it was built, why it was put up, the symbolism embodied, which are the best windows and statues, and why they are so. He would write his guidebook so that when you *see* it you will see it better, understand it, enjoy it more completely. Dewey would state what a cathedral is, how to see and appreciate one, how perhaps to build one. Bradley wants to write what a cathedral is, how it feels to

see one, indeed, how it feels to be one! For Bradley, it is all there, in
the Book of Life, and thus really irrelevant to time—it is an eternal
story. Dewey's book has it not all there, only the maps and diagrams
and descriptions, so that his guide must be revised periodically—time
is real. For Bradley, philosophy is not a way of living, but a substitute
for living: we can know without living. For Dewey, philosophy *is* a
way of living, it is instrumental to living, we know in order to live
better; living well must include knowing and understanding, but is
not exhausted by them.[21]

IX

Bradley's conception of philosophy as a substitute for life is expressed in a famous passage:

At the entrance to philosophy there appears to be a point where the roads
divide. By the one way you set out to seek truth in ideas, to find such an ideal
expression of reality as satisfies in itself. And on this road you not only endeavor to say what you mean, but you are once for all and for ever condemned *to mean what you say*. Your judgments as to reality are here no less or
more than what you have expressed in them, and no appeal to something else
which you have failed to make explicit is allowed. When, for example, you
say "this," the question is not as to what you are sure is your meaning if only
you could utter it. The question is as to what you have got or can get, in an
ideal form into your actual judgment. And when you revolt against the conclusion that "this" appears to be a mere unspecified universal [Bradley is
thinking of Hegel], when you insist that you know very well what "this"
meant, and protest that your object was something other than such illogical
trifling and child's play—our answer is obvious. What are you doing, we ask,
with us here on this road? You were told plainly that on this road what is
sought is ideas, and that nothing else is here current. You were warned that,

---

[21] See Dewey, "Philosophy and Civilization," in the volume of that title (New York,
1930), p. 5: "In philosophy we are dealing with something comparable to the meaning
of Athenian civilization or of a drama or a lyric. Significant history is lived in the imagination of man, and philosophy is a further excursion of the imagination into its own
prior achievements. All that is distinctive of man, marking him off from the clay he
walks upon or the potatoes he eats, comes in his thought and emotions, in what we have
agreed to call consciousness. Knowledge of the structure of sticks and stones, an enterprise in which, of course, truth is essential, apart from whatever added control it
may yield, marks in the end but an enrichment of consciousness, of the area of meanings. Thus scientific thought itself is finally but a function of the imagination in enriching life with the significance of things; it is of its peculiar essence that it must also submit to certain tests of application and control. Were significance identical with
existence, were values the same as events, idealism would be the only possible philosophy."

if you enter here, you were committed to this principle. If you did not understand, whose is the fault? . . . Our whole way doubtless may be a delusion, but if you choose to take this way, your judgment means what ideally it contains; and, contrariwise, what you have not explicitly expressed and included in it is not reckoned. And, if so, no possible appeal to designation in the end is permitted. . . .

This I take to be the way of philosophy, of any philosophy which seeks to be consistent. It is not the way of life or of common knowledge, and to commit oneself to such a principle may be said to depend upon choice. The way of life starts from, and in the end it rests on, dependence upon feeling, upon that which in the end cannot be stated intelligibly. And the way of any understanding of the world short of philosophy still rests on this basis. . . . Outside of philosophy there is no consistent course but to accept the unintelligible, and to use in its service whatever ideas seem, however inconsistently, to work best. . . . For worse or for better the man who stands on particular feeling must remain outside of philosophy. . . . And hence the way of life, and of ordinary knowledge, obscurely conscious of its own imperfection, for ever seeks to complete itself by that which, if it aimed to be consistent, would be philosophy. (*Essays*, 234–35)

And so Bradley sat, apart from life, in his chambers in Merton College—he had been appointed Fellow in 1876, but did no teaching—striving desperately to get the whole of life, with its tang of immediacy, into the pages of an article in *Mind*. The volumes piled up on the floor about him, but each succeeding piece he wrote failed to include the literal "every aspect" he was resolved to express in words.

With his aim clear, Bradley started on his version of *Ulysses*. He might instead have started to write the *Encyclopedia Britannica:* instead of, with the present-day Existentialist, beginning with human experience, he might have begun with Nature and proceeded to include other elements in it, following instead the method and approach of naturalists like Samuel Alexander and Whitehead. In Chapter XXVI, "On the Absolute and its Appearances," he suggests how he might have followed this alternative.

Nature, regarded as bare matter, is a mere convenient abstraction. The addition of secondary qualities, the included relation to a body and to a soul, in making Nature more concrete makes it thereby more real. The sensible life, the warmth and color, the odor and the tones, without these Nature is a mere intellectual fiction. The primary qualities are a construction demanded by science, but, while divorced from the secondary, they have no life as facts. Science has a Hades from which it returns to interpret the world, but the inhabitants of its Hades are merely shades. And when the secondary qualities

are added, Nature, though more real, is still incomplete. The joys and sorrows of her children, their affections and their thoughts—how are we to say
that these have no part in the reality of Nature? . . . Our main principle insists that Nature, when more full, is more real. . . . The emotions excited by
Nature in the considering soul, must at least in part be referred to, and must
be taken as attributes of Nature. If there is no beauty there, . . . why in the
end should there be any qualities in Nature at all? . . . Everything there
without exception is "subjective," if we are to regard the matter so; and an
emotional tone cannot, solely on this ground, be excluded from Nature. . . .
I can accept the fresh consequence. The Nature that we have lived in, and
that we love, is really Nature. Its beauty and its terror and its majesty are no
illusion, but qualify it essentially. . . .

  The Nature studied by the observer and by the poet and painter, is in all
its sensible and emotional fulness a very real Nature. . . . For Nature, as the
world whose real essence lies in primary qualities, has not a high degree of reality and truth. It is a mere abstraction made and required for a certain purpose. . . . We must draw [the boundary] arbitrarily. . . . Only on this
ground can psychical life be excluded from Nature, while, regarded otherwise, the exclusion would not be tenable. . . . Our principle, that the abstract is the unreal, moves us steadily upward. It forces us first to rejection of
bare primary qualities, and it compels us in the end to credit Nature with our
higher emotions. That process can cease only where Nature is quite absorbed
into spirit. (493–95)

Dewey applies the same inclusiveness to those selected portions of
Nature he calls "situations," and the Existentialists follow the same
principle. It is clear how the enlarged "naturalism" of the twentieth
century developed painlessly out of such functional Idealism.

  How are we to write the separate chapters of our book of life? None
is complete, each by itself is misleading (and contradictory). Are they
then all worthless? How shall we write them? Here Bradley employs
a principle of "degrees of truth and reality."

Suppose I say in theology that all men before God, and measured by him, are
equally sinful—does that preclude me from also holding that one is worse or
better than another? . . . Suppose that for a certain purpose I want a stick exactly one yard long, am I wrong when I condemn both one inch and thirty-
five inches, . . . as equally and alike coming short? (557)

Viewed intellectually, appearance is error. But the remedy lies in supplementation by inclusion of that which is both outside and yet essential, and in the
Absolute this remedy is perfected. . . . the degree of reality is measured by
the amount of supplementation required in each case. (555)

Any categorical judgment must be false. . . . All our judgments, to be true, must become conditional. The predicate does not hold unless by the help of something else. . . . Judgments are conditional in this sense, that what they affirm is incomplete. . . . Truths are true, according as it would take less or more to convert them into reality. (361, 363)

The criterion of truth is thus "harmony" or "consistency" with other truths, and "inclusiveness," which are really identical tests. We do not know a thing "consistently" unless we know its relation to everything else, that is, its place in the total system.

Truth must exhibit the mark of internal harmony, or, again, the mark of expansion and all-inclusiveness. And these two characteristics are diverse aspects of a single principle. . . . Harmony is incompatible with restriction and finitude. For that which is not all-inclusive must by virtue of its essence internally disagree. . . . Hence to be more or less true, and to be more or less real, is to be separated by an interval, smaller or greater, from all-inclusiveness or self-consistency. (363–64)

With regard to harmony, that which has extended over and absorbed a greater area of the external, will internally be less divided. (375)

The essay on "Coherence and Contradiction" [22] is most explicit that by the contradictory Bradley means the incomplete.

If, in speaking of Reality, you say "R is *mere a*," and if then, while you say that, another qualification, *b*, appears and is accepted, you contradict yourself plainly. . . . In all predication I assume that the ultimate subject is Reality [from his *Logic*], and that in saying "R*a*" or "R*b*" you qualify R by *a* or *b*. My contention is that, in saying "R*a*," you qualify R unconditionally by *a*, and that this amounts to saying "mere *a*." For is there, I ask, any difference between R and *a*? Let us suppose first that there is no difference. If so, by saying first R*a* and then R*b* you contradict yourself flatly. For *a* and *b*, I presume, really are different, and hence, unless R is different from *a* and *b*, what you have done is to identify *a* and *b* simply. But the simple identification of the diverse is precisely that which one means by contradiction. If on the other hand, when I say R*a*, I suppose a difference between R and *a*, then once more I am threatened with contradiction, for I seem now to have simply qualified R with *a*, the two being diverse. . . .

A natural answer is to deny that the judgments R*a* and R*b* are unconditional. . . . The assertion then will really be "R(x)*a*" and "R(x)*b*," the *x* being of course taken to qualify R. But, if so, apparently "R*a*" is true only because of something other than *a* which also is included in R. . . . Contradiction so far has appeared as the alternative to comprehensiveness, and the criterion so far seems to rest on a single principle. (228–39)

[22] *Essays*, Chapter 8; first printed in *Mind* XVIII, N.S. (October 1909).

Hence all Thought, even mere imagination, has some "truth," some status in "reality." There is thus one single standard of truth:

And this standard, in principle at least, is applicable to every kind of subject matter. For everything, directly or indirectly, and with a greater or less preservation of its internal unity, has a relative space in Reality. (*Appearance*, 376)

Compare this with Dewey's universalism, his emphasis on the "continuity of analysis." For Bradley, the "most real" is, as for Hegel, the most "individual," the self-sufficient system—something completed only in the Whole.

In his application, Bradley's standard of consistency always includes the appeal to facts; for mere "thought" is incomplete, and hence inevitably inconsistent, without facts.

To suppose that mere thought without facts could either be real, or could reach to truth, is evidently absurd. The series of events is, without doubt, necessary to our knowledge, since this series supplies the one source of all ideal content. . . . There is nothing in thought, whether it be matter or relations, except that which is derived from perception. . . . The test of truth after all, we may say, lies in presented fact. (380)

Bradley's experientialism does not desert this root principle of empiricism. On the other hand, the test of facts themselves involves coherence: their consistency with other facts, and their comprehensiveness or inclusiveness. Facts must be fitted into a consistent system of all the facts: no single fact is immune to criticism on that score.

Does it follow that I have to accept independent facts? . . . Our intelligence cannot construct the world of perceptions and feelings, and it depends on what is given—to so much I assent. But that there are given facts of perception which are independent and ultimate and above criticism, is not to my mind a true conclusion. Such facts are a vicious abstraction. We have the aspect of datum, and the aspect of interpretation. Why must there be datum without interpretation any more than interpretation without datum? . . . No given fact is sacrosanct. With every fact of perception or memory a modified interpretation is in principle possible, and no such fact therefore is given free from all possibility of error.[23]

Bradley's objective relativism therefore holds to a universal fallibilism and acceptance of corrigibility.

We cannot suppose it possible that *all* the judgments of perception and memory which for me come first, could in fact for me be corrected. . . . There is

[23] *Essays*, Chapter 7, "On Truth and Coherence," pp. 203–4; first printed in *Mind* XVIII, N.S. (July 1909).

still a chasm between such admissions and the conclusion that there are judgments of sense which possess truth absolute and infallible. . . . The view
which I advocate takes them all as in principle fallible. . . . Facts for it are
true just so far as they work, just so far as they contribute to the order of experience. If by taking certain judgments of perception as true, I can get more
system into my world, then these "facts" are so far true, and if by taking certain "facts" as errors I can order my experience better, then so far these
"facts" are errors. And there is no "fact" which possesses an absolute right.[24]
(209–10)

Bradley finally gives the definition: "The truth is that which enables
us to order most coherently and comprehensively the data supplied by
immediate experience and the intuitive judgments of perception"
(215). Consistency, coherence, and comprehensiveness are thus all the
same principle for Bradley; and throughout he defines "contradiction"
in terms of incompleteness and finitude.

Does Bradley end, as he so often sounds, too "pragmatic" in the
vague Jamesian sense? No, answers Bradley; for the universe is really
working in me: man's knowing, he agrees with Dewey, is an expression of "reality" or "nature."

It is after all an enormous assumption that what satisfies us is real, and that
the reality has got to satisfy us. It is an assumption tolerable, I think, only
when we hold that the Universe is substantially one with each of us, and actually, as a whole, feels and wills and knows itself within us. For thus in our effort and our satisfaction it is the one Reality which is asserting itself, is coming to its own rights and pronouncing its own dissent or approval. (242)

Behind me the absolute reality works through and in union with myself,
and the world which confronts me is at bottom one thing in substance and in
power with this reality. There *is* a world of appearance and there *is* a sensuous
curtain, and to seek to deny the presence of this or to identify it with reality is
mistaken. But for the truth I come back always to that doctrine of Hegel, that
"there is nothing behind the curtain other than that which is in front of it."
For what is in front of it is the Absolute that is at once one with the knower
and behind him. (218)

X

It is in his analysis of "immediate experience" that Bradley is most
relevant to the "phenomenological" analyses of experience that have

[24] Note by F.H.B.: "To the question if the above principle is merely 'practical,' I
reply, 'Certainly, if you take "practice" so widely as to remove the distinction between
practice and theory.' But, since such a widening of sense seems to serve no useful purpose, I cannot regard that course as being itself very 'practical.' I answer therefore that
the above principle is not merely practical" (214*n*).

become so popular philosophically today; and it is "immediate experience" which, largely through Bradley's influence, became the way English-speaking philosophical critics referred to what later the Germans and then the French have come to call "human existence."

For Bradley, knowledge must get back to where it started from, after it has become known. This demands the analysis of the starting point, of the nature of "immediate experience." Bradley himself began, in his *Logic*, with the "experience" of the empiricists, in which perceived facts were identified as "perceptions." He originally had no consistent theory, except to assume that experience is "known" rather than "had" or "enjoyed." He began by taking experience as inherently cognitive.

Then, in *Appearance and Reality*, experience became more the psychological continuum. Writing in 1893, he had read James's *Psychology* of 1890—of which he was a foremost English champion—and he adopted a "stream of consciousness" view. Experience is perception and thought, together with will and desire, and also "feeling," which includes the aesthetic attitude as well as pleasure and pain. Experience became the "direct experience" that precedes the subject-object distinction giving rise to cognitive experience. In *Appearance* Bradley often speaks, in subjective terms, of states of "consciousness"—this was before James had lost consciousness—"To be real is to be indissolubly one with sentience." This human experience is transmuted in "Absolute experience" into a "totality" that is no longer temporal—Bradley is one of the last philosophers to fail to "take time seriously." Finally, in the *Essays*, experience is treated in terms of "uneasiness and satisfaction"—actual knowing is instrumental to a problem of securing "satisfaction." Thus Bradley was engaged in a constant criticism of his own conception of immediate experience, and continually reconstructing it.

In Chapter VI of the *Essays*, "On Our Knowledge of Immediate Experience" (*Mind*, January 1909), Bradley stated his final position. Immediate experience exhibits no explicit subject-object distinction.

We have experience in which there is no distinction between my awareness and that of which it is aware. There is an immediate feeling, a knowing and being in one, with which knowledge begins; and, though this in a manner is transcended, it nevertheless remains throughout as the present foundation of my known world. And if you remove this direct sense of my momentary contents and being, you bring down the whole of consciousness in one common wreck. For it is in the end ruin to divide experience into something on one side experienced as an object and on the other side something not experienced at all. (*Essays*, 159–60)

This direct sense can be "transcended" in knowing, in practice, and in aesthetic satisfaction; it is itself nonrelational, not subrelational. And even when "transcended" it persists as the "felt background" of relational distinctions. Hence there is needed no "reunion" with immediacy to get it included, after it has been "lost" through analysis, for it is actually never "lost." And hence there is no need to strive for a superrational "absolute experience" in which immediacy will be "restored." Immediate experience is an organic whole in which distinctions can be made and activities carried on; but it needs no further "absolute" to be completely "real." The absolute remains a totality of experience only as fostering humility in the face of limited achievement; immediate experience itself has become for Bradley pluralistic.

The solution, if I may anticipate, is in general supplied by considering this fact, that immediate experience, however much transcended, both remains and is active. It is not a stage which shows itself at the beginning and then disappears, but it remains at the bottom throughout as fundamental. And further, remaining it contains within itself every development which in a sense transcends it. Nor does it merely contain all development, but in its own way it acts to some extent as their judge. Its blind uneasiness, we may say, insists tacitly on visible satisfaction. We have on one hand a demand, explicit or otherwise, for an object which is complete. On the other hand the object which fails to include immediate experience in its content, is by the unrest of that experience condemned as defective. We are thus forced to the idea of an object containing the required element, and in this object we find at last theoretical satisfaction and rest. (160–61)

But Bradley has a new paradox. How is immediate experience to be known? Do not knowledge, attention, and introspection make any difference? Yes, but still immediacy persists and we remain aware of it.

Immediate experience is not a stage, which may or may not at some time have been there, and has now ceased to exist. It is not in any case removed by the presence of a not-self and of a relational consciousness. All that is thus removed is at most, we may say, the *mereness* of immediacy. Every distinction and relation still rests on an immediate background of which we are aware, and every distinction and relation (so far as experienced) is also felt, and felt in a sense to belong to an immediate totality. Thus in all experience we still have feeling which is not an object, and at all our moments the entirety of what comes to us, however much distinguished and relational, is felt as comprised within a unity which itself is not relational. (178)

This "felt background" of immediacy persists, and "jars" or "agrees" with the object known.

That which I feel, and which is not an object before me, is present and active. This felt element is used, and it must be used, in the constitution of that object which satisfies me, and apart from this influence and criterion there is no accounting for the actual fact of our knowledge. (171)

Immediate experience remains as the subject matter controlling all interpretation; it has, however, no "logical" relation to the object known, or to knowledge.

We cannot speak of a relation, between immediate experience and that which transcends it, except by a licence. It is a mode of expression found convenient in our reflective thinking, but it is in the end not defensible. A relation exists only between terms, and those terms, to be known as such, must be objects. And hence immediate experience, taken as the term of a relation, becomes so far a partial object and ceases so far to keep its nature as a felt totality. (176-77)

But if immediate experience cannot be "known," it can be pointed to, "denoted," in a functional and teleological relation—as for Dewey.
    What is it like?

Feeling need not be devoid of internal diversity. Its content need not in this sense be simple, and possibly never is simple. By feeling, in short, I understand, and, I believe, always have understood, an awareness which, though non-relational, may comprise simply in itself an indefinite amount of difference. . . . At every moment my state, whatever else it is, is a whole of which I am immediately aware. It is an experienced non-relational unity of many in one. . . . At any moment my actual experience, however relational its contents, is in the end non-relational. No analysis into relations and terms can ever exhaust its nature or fail in the end to belie its essence. (174-76)

How can immediate experience serve as a criterion of knowledge?

What is required is that the object should itself become qualified by the same content which was merely felt within me. . . . The feeling remains what it was, but it no longer is merely grouped round and centered in the object. The feeling itself is also before me in the object-world, and the object now confronts me as being itself satisfactory or discordant. My description is seen to come short, or to be otherwise conflicting, when compared with the corrected idea of my actual emotion. (179-80)

Bradley undertakes a subtle analysis, a beautiful case of "experimental procedure" without laboratory techniques.

> Our actual object fails to satisfy us, and we get the idea that it is incomplete and that a complete object would satisfy. We attempt to complete our object by relational addition from without and by relational distinction from within. And the result in each case is failure and a sense of defect. We feel that any result gained thus, no matter how all-inclusive so far, would yet be less than what we actually experience. Then we try the idea of a positive non-distinguished non-relational whole, which contains more than the object and in the end contains all that we experience. And that idea seems to meet our demand. It is not free from difficulty, but it appears to be the one ground on which satisfaction is possible. (188)

Here Bradley combines the idea of incompleteness as a spur with the process of trial and error.

Now at last we have Bradley's final answer to the metaphysical paradox that had plagued him for so long: How is Thought related to its Other? The setting or context of "thought" is and can be "known," because it is "had" and never "lost." It remains a fact that can be *denoted;* and Bradley turns to what Dewey calls the "denotative method" to indicate the relation of discourse to its subject matter, of thinking to what thinking is about, of Form to Substance.

PART THREE

Directions in Religious Thought

9

The Ontology of Paul Tillich

I

PAUL TILLICH stands in the classic tradition of Western philosophy, in that long line of thinkers stemming from the Greeks who have been concerned with the problem of being and wisdom. As a theologian, this distinguishes him both from the American liberals whose thought is rooted in the philosophic idealism of the last century, and from the European representatives of a purely kerygmatic theology who will have no conscious traffic with philosophizing at all. Standing, as he likes to put it, at the boundary between theology and philosophy, he has inherited the mantle of both disciplines, and is keenly aware of the long tradition of human thinking which the leaders in both have devoted to the problem of the nature of the world and of man's place in it. To any man with philosophical interests, one of the most stimulating aspects of Tillich's thought is his ability to penetrate beneath the symbolic forms of past philosophy and theology to the problem of human destiny with which they were grappling.

The immediate background of Tillich's philosophy is certain of the more ontological and historical strains of nineteenth-century German speculation. The later, post-Böhme philosophy of Schelling, the various mid-century reactions against the panlogism of Hegel, like Feuerbach and the early Marx, Nietzsche and the "philosophy of life," and the more recent existentialism, especially of Heidegger—all these have contributed to his formulation of philosophic issues and problems. In particular they have furnished him with a large part of

Originally published in *The Theology of Paul Tillich*, ed. Charles W. Kegley and Robert W. Bretall. The Library of Living Theology, Vol. I (New York: The Macmillan Co., 1952; copyright © 1952 Charles W. Kegley and Robert W. Bretall), pp. 132–61. Reprinted by permission of the editors.

the philosophic vocabulary with which he talks about the world and about earlier attempts to understand it. To express his own insights, Tillich employs the language of the existential philosophy. Whether this is the best possible language in which to put what he has to say is immaterial. Certainly he has greatly modified and clarified it since coming to this country. But it is obviously a language not too familiar to the vernacular of most American philosophizing, and hardly one with which English-speaking theologians have grown up. This circumstance creates a problem of communication with which it is hoped this volume [*The Theology of Paul Tillich*] will be able to deal.

On one occasion Tillich read a brilliant paper to a group of professional philosophers. Among the listeners was G. E. Moore, the distinguished representative of a very different philosophical tradition and language. When it came time for Moore to comment, he said: "Now really, Mr. Tillich, I don't think I have been able to understand a single sentence of your paper. Won't you please try to state one sentence, or even one word, that I can understand?"

Tillich is clearly not a Cambridge analyst. On another occasion a group were discussing that philosophical movement with John Dewey. Dewey remarked: "Well, I have had some pretty hard things to say about German philosophers in my time. But at least they were dealing with the important questions." I do not think any philosophical mind can talk with or read Tillich without being profoundly convinced that he is dealing with the important questions. To be sure, Moore had a point. Like most recent German philosophers, Tillich could profitably cultivate a little more precision of definition. But it was the one systematic philosopher to come out of Cambridge in the last generation, Whitehead, who exclaimed in understandable if not entirely accurate revulsion, "Exactness is a fake!" The precise statement of nothing of consequence is surely specious, and the meaning of human destiny can scarcely be cramped within the bounds of symbolic logic.

I suppose Tillich would say that I have set up a dialectical problem between precision and importance.[1] But I see no reason for not trying

---

[1] Cf. Tillich's analogous statement, *Systematic Theology*, Vol. I (Chicago, 1951), p. 105. Unless otherwise indicated, all quotations in this chapter are from this book. [At the time this paper was written, only Volume I had been published. However, Randall may have seen typescripts of other material. (Ed.)]

to speak as precisely as possible even about important matters, and I am afraid my own doubts begin when in the recent German fashion Tillich is inclined to leave ultimate matters to a final "dialectic." At any rate, it is his epistemology which seems the least adequate part of his thought, and raises the most questions. The one strand of the philosophical tradition which he does not take very seriously, and consequently fails to illuminate, is the empiricism stemming from Locke. This he is inclined to dismiss as the mere reflection of a transitory bourgeois culture, which for Germany and for him has already disintegrated and passed into limbo. Far be it from me to attempt to defend British empiricism, especially in its present-day decadent form, when it seems to have lost all function. But I should think that "dialectical thinking," if I understand it, might have learned more and absorbed more from it than Tillich apparently has.

It is not my purpose here to attempt anything like a genetic account of the development of Tillich's thought from his early dissertations on Schelling down to his *Systematic Theology*. Rather, I wish to consider his mature philosophy and its core of ontology, primarily from the time he succeeded to Max Scheler's chair of philosophy at Frankfurt in 1929, especially as expressed in the first volume of his superb *Systematic Theology*.

Both as philosopher and as theologian Tillich stands broadly in the great Augustinian tradition, that is, in the central tradition of Christian Platonism. For him the lesson of the *Symposium* has been well learned: the object of knowledge and the object of love are one and the same, and *knowledge* is ultimately a "participation" in true being.[2] This, I take it, is what "existentialism" primarily means for him. Immediately, as with Heidegger, this is a protest against the "bracketing" of questions of existence, and against the exclusive concern with a description of essences that was characteristic of Husserl's phenomenological analysis, the most important philosophical movement in the Germany in which Tillich grew up. But more ultimately, for him the concern with "existence" is a reaffirmation of the Platonic doctrines of *eros* and participation. Historically speaking, this sets him against the Thomism which recognizes a clear boundary between the realm of truths accessible to natural reason and the realm of truths accessible only to faith, and for him renders any natural theology strictly impos-

[2] Cf. his suggestive paper on knowledge as participation.

sible.[3] It sets him against the Aristotle who made science an integral part of wisdom; he finds only the Platonic strain in Aristotle congenial.

It is this fundamental Platonism, fully as much as his natural reaction against nineteenth-century optimism, that provokes his hostility to the Ritschlian theology that prevailed in liberal Protestant thinking in Germany down to 1914, with its sharp Kantian dualism between pure and practical reason, and its denial of any theological concern with the former, with questions of existence. It was the Ritschlian liberal theologians, Tillich points out, who in Germany ruined the term "practical" as a means of expressing the importance of human interests and ends in the intellectual life, and forced the quite different vocabulary of "existence" and "existential commitment" upon German philosophical thinking. American thought, moving in a similar direction, and much less constrained to emancipate itself from a Kantian formalism and intellectualism, in Peirce and James was able to build upon the Kantian and post-Kantian "practical reason" to express the same concern with the psychological and cultural matrix of thinking. No one familiar with the long and apparently ineradicable misunderstandings to which this use of the vocabulary of "practice" has exposed Dewey would claim that the term has been a very happy or clarifying one. To be sure, to an American at least, the whole vocabulary of "existence" seems wide open to analogous if not identical misunderstandings. But Tillich, whose concern with the problems of cultural reconstruction has been as intense and as sustained as Dewey's, in his own very different cultural situation and in his own very different philosophical language, has really been working out a philosophy that is certainly comparable to much recent American philosophizing. Perhaps the most fundamental difference is that he came upon the scene at a rather later stage of cultural change—of "the transformation of bourgeois culture," he would say. Hence his thought is to be judged not in comparison with that of Dewey's generation, but with that of men who have proceeded to build upon and modify Dewey's ideas in the light of more recent history.

I am far indeed from suggesting that the American philosophizing of the past generation is a yardstick by which to measure the penetra-

[3] Cf. his paper, "Two Types of Philosophy of Religion," *Union Seminary Quarterly Review* (1946).

tion and insights of Tillich, or of anyone coming out of so different an experience; or of intimating that the enterprise of a philosophical theologian like Tillich is identical with that of a philosopher of political education like John Dewey. Personally, I am inclined to take rather more seriously the fundamental contentions of the classic tradition than do either of these distinguished critics of that type of thinking. I find very congenial Tillich's ultimate concern with the mystery and the power of being, for I too am intensely interested in metaphysics—and I will not, with the unexpected caution of Tillich, water down the time-honored term to a mere "ontology."

One more personal word. I can of course lay no claim to theological competence, and any comments I may inadvertently make on Tillich's theology are strictly amateurish. Having no present "existential commitments" to the Christian revelation, certainly not in any exclusive sense, I believe that even in Tillich's rather generous eyes I could not possibly qualify as a theologian myself. But if, as he likes to assert paradoxically, belief in the existence of God is the worst form of atheism, I am at least free of atheism in that form.

II

Tillich stands in the great tradition of Augustinian philosophy—his relation to the intricacies of Augustinian theology is more complex. This is a way of saying that on certain crucial questions, particularly of epistemology and ontology, his thought differs from that of the equally great tradition of Christian Aristotelianism. For him, it was with Thomas Aquinas that the course of Christian thought went astray. He recognizes no neat line dividing philosophy from theology; the theologian must be a philosopher to formulate his questions, and the philosopher becomes a theologian if he succeeds in answering the ones he asks. In a real sense, for Tillich philosophy is faith seeking understanding—though faith appears now as "existential commitment." For him there can be no natural theology; any argument from the character of the world to the existence of God could never get beyond finite relativities, and God is not a being whose "existence" demands proof. Tillich rests upon a version of the ontological argument—rather, as for all true Augustinians, God (that ultimate in which the symbols of human ideas of God participate) neither needs nor can receive "proof." For that ultimate—Tillich's term is das Unbe-

dingte—is a certain quality of the world man encounters, which analysis reveals as "presupposed" in all his encountering. Whereas Augustine's Platonism, however, led him to an intellectual emphasis on the Truth or Logos implied in all knowledge, Tillich has expanded it to the "power of being" implied in all men's varied participations in the world in which they are grasped by an ultimate concern.

Now all this can mean much or little, depending upon how it is elaborated. As Tillich develops it, it becomes a suggestive reinterpretation of the Augustinian metaphysics, fertilized with many of the insights of a century of German thinking. Largely though not wholly, freed from epistemological entanglements in which classic German idealism mired Christian Platonism, his philosophy is a realistic interpretation of a world in which man can find a meaning for his life. Some of the doubts it leaves in the mind of a sympathetic seeker for wisdom arise from the baggage it carries along from a century of German philosophical engagements. Others are probably inherent in the Christian and Augustinian character of its Platonism, when viewed from the perspective either of an Aristotelian or of a modern empirical approach. But it is not Tillich's central enterprise with which I should want to quarrel: the working-out of a realism with vision and participation—what he used to call a "belief-ful or self-transcending realism." [4] I shall concentrate on the main points, the nature of philosophy, the nature of reason, and the nature of being.

In a brief paper [5] Tillich clarifies the nature of philosophy and its relation to theology:

Philosophy asks the ultimate question that can be asked, namely, the question as to what being, simply being, means. . . . [It is born from] the philosophical shock, the tremendous impetus of the questions: What is the meaning of being? Why is there being and not not-being? What is the character in which every being participates? . . . Philosophy primarily does not ask about the special character of the beings, the things and events, the ideas and values, the souls and bodies which share being. Philosophy asks what about this being itself. Therefore, all philosophers have developed a "first philosophy," as Aristotle calls it, namely, an interpretation of being. . . . This makes the division between philosophy and theology impossible, for, whatever the relation of God, world, and man may be, it lies in the frame of being; and any in-

---

[4] Cf. *The Protestant Era*, tr. J.L. Adams (Chicago, 1948), especially Chapter 5, "Realism and Faith."

[5] *Ibid.*, Chapter 6, "Philosophy and Theology."

terpretation of the meaning and structure of being as being unavoidably such has consequences for the interpretation of God, man, and the world in their interrelations.

Philosophy is thus fundamentally ontology—Tillich regards the traditional term "metaphysics" as too abused and distorted to be longer of any service. The Kantians are wrong in making epistemology the true first philosophy, for as later Neo-Kantians like Nicolai Hartmann have recognized, epistemology demands an ontological basis. The philosophies of "experience" are merely using another word for being itself. Positivists who would restrict philosophy to the analysis of the different kinds of being can never succeed with their "No trespassing" signs:

The meaning of being is man's basic concern, is the really human and philosophical question. . . . Man, as the German philosopher Heidegger says, is that being which asks what being is.

"Now, this is the task of theology: to ask for being as far as it gives us ultimate concern. Theology deals with what concerns us inescapably, ultimately, unconditionally. It deals with it not as far as it *is*, but as far as it is *for us*." Theology is "practical," not in contrast to theoretical, since truth is essential to our ultimate concern, but in that it "must deal with its subject always as far as it concerns us in the very depth of our being." But "practical" is another word ruined by being opposed to "theoretical," especially by the Ritschlians, and therefore Tillich adopts Kierkegaard's term "existential": "existential is what characterizes our real existence in all its concreteness, in all its accidental elements, in its freedom and responsibility, in its failure, and in its separation from its true and essential being."

Philosophy and theology are divergent as well as convergent. They are convergent as far as both are existential and theoretical at the same time. They are divergent as far as philosophy is basically theoretical and theology is basically existential. . . . Philosophy, although knowing the existential presuppositions of truth, does not abide with them. It turns immediately to the content and tries to grasp it directly. In its systems it abstracts from the existential situations out of which they are born. . . . Philosophy asks on the existential and concrete basis of the medieval church and civilization . . . or of bourgeois or proletarian society or culture. But it asks for truth itself. . . . This is its freedom.

In his *Systematic Theology* Tillich elaborates on his conception of ontology:

> Philosophy is *that cognitive approach to reality in which reality as such is the object*. Reality as such, or reality as a whole, is not the whole of reality; it is the structure which makes reality a whole and therefore a potential object of knowledge. Inquiring into the nature of reality as such means inquiring into those structures, categories, and concepts which are presupposed in the cognitive encounter with every realm of reality. (18)

These structures, of course—*pace* the Kantians and the positivists—include structures of values. Now philosophy deals with the structure of being in itself; it undertakes an ontological analysis of that structure. Theology deals with the meaning of being for us. Consequently, the two diverge, first, in their cognitive attitude.

> The philosopher tries to maintain a detached objectivity toward being and its structures. He tries to exclude the personal, social, and historical conditions which might distort an objective vision of reality. His passion is the passion for a truth which is open to general approach, subject to general criticism, changeable in accordance with every new insight, open and communicable. In all these respects he feels no different from the scientist, historian, psychologist, etc. (22)

In contrast, the basic attitude of the theologian is commitment to the content he expounds, is "existential." Secondly, the two differ in that the philosopher, like the scientist, is seeking a universal structure, the theologian, a structure manifesting itself in a particular historical event and religious institution. Thirdly, the philosopher deals with the categories of being in relation to the material which is structured by them, while the theologian treats them in relation to the salvation of man.

Actually, of course, the philosopher too is conditioned by his psychological, sociological, and historical situation, and if he be of any significance has his own ultimate concern. His existential situation and his ultimate concern shape his philosophical vision. To the extent that this is true, the philosopher is also by definition a theologian, as all creative philosophers are. He tries to become universal, but he is destined to remain particular.

Two points here require comment. The first is Tillich's definition of the core of philosophy: ontology. He passes easily from "being as such" to "reality as a whole," identifying two very different conceptions. The first is Aristotelian, the second is the object of nineteenth-century idealism. The first means those generic traits that can be discriminated in any subject matter; the second means a unified and unifying structure of the universe, "objective reason," what Tillich quite properly calls "the universal *logos*." The second can be, and traditionally has been, identified with God; the first, though it will be exemplified in religion as in everything else, possesses in itself no religious significance, and is not, as such, of "existential concern." "The structure of being" can hardly mean two such different things. The first is the proper object of an Aristotelian ontological inquiry; the second is the goal of Platonic and Neo-Platonic aspiration, the "Being" that is the Idea of the Good and the One.

Now Tillich clearly means the latter, and he is hence exposed to all the philosophical attacks directed against such a block universe from Peirce and James on. This conception is the core of what is usually called absolute idealism; it is the central target for the objections of all other philosophies. To English-speaking philosophers Tillich would inevitably seem to be offering merely one more variant of philosophical idealism, and to be identifying the whole philosophical enterprise with that historically conditioned existential commitment. Is he not here speaking, in terms of his own distinction, rather as the theologian than as the philosopher? The "structures of being" are the proper goal of a free metaphysical inquiry—an inquiry to which Tillich himself goes on to make significant contributions. But "reality as a whole," or "being-itself," αὐτὸ τὸ ὄν, seems rather an existential commitment—the proper goal of the theologian, or the philosopher as theologian.

To me this idea seems to have been, in the whole Platonic tradition, one of those great unifying symbols or "myths" by which men bring their encountered world to a focus in terms of their system of meanings and values—of their ultimate concern. It is a symbol by which the world unifies itself. I should say, it is a part of the task of metaphysics or ontology to *understand* such myths and the way they function. It is a part of the task of "practical" philosophy—and I should here include philosophical theology, as well as the philosophy of history—to *use* such myths for the direction of human life, to clarify and to criticize them. This task is obviously of fundamental importance. I suppose it is only natural for a professional theologian to assign it to

theology, and for a professional philosopher to include it in the philosophical enterprise. Speaking as a metaphysician, however, it seems to
me important to recognize that "reality as a whole" has the ontological
status of a myth or symbol rather than that of a descriptive hypothesis. It is, in Tillich's distinction, an existential rather than a theoretical
concept.

This brings us to the second point about Tillich's conception of the
nature of philosophy. As an Augustinian, he finds it ultimately impossible to set philosophy apart from theology, and his efforts to distinguish their emphases of course in the last analysis break down. The
distinction is relative and "existential"—it depends on the specific situation. Now, I have no particular objection to calling all the concern of
the philosophical enterprise with "practice" and values really theology, as Tillich does in his broadest extension of that discipline—the
sense in which a teacup by Cézanne is a revelation of being and of
man's ultimate concern, which makes aesthetics a branch of theology.
The difficulty arises not when I discover that as a philosopher I am a
theologian, but when I find that to be a good philosopher and answer
my questions I must be a Christian theologian. But I am not sure
whether for Tillich this is a question of philosophy, of philosophical
theology, or of kerygmatic theology.

The root difficulty in all these distinctions seems to lie in the too
sharp dualism Tillich accepts between the theoretical and the existential or "practical." It has been one of the major contributions of the
broad philosophical movement, of which both existentialism and
American instrumentalism are strands, to break down this dualism,
which goes back through Kant to Aristotle. The theoretical interest,
or "pure reason," it has been abundantly shown, is not something opposed to the practical or existential. Rather, theory and detached objectivity are moments or stages in a broader context or matrix of
"practice." Different sciences and disciplines vary in the degree to
which they attain universality and detachment; metaphysics, in seeking to embrace all possible situations, can hope to become the most
"theoretical" of all—and hence at the same time the most "instrumental" and "existential." Tillich accepts all this, but there seems still a
strong remnant of the Kantian dualism left in the way he uses the distinction. This comes out most clearly in his final position on the relation between philosophy and theology, his so-called "method of corre-

lation," in which he finds that philosophy must go to theology for the answers to its own questions. Unless this be a mere matter of terminology, it clearly does not take the "existential" character of theory seriously enough.

III

Just as Tillich develops his conception of philosophy as a preparation for theology, so he analyzes reason in order to lead up to the reality of revelation. He starts by distinguishing two concepts of reason, the "ontological" and the "technical"—Νοῦς or *intellectus*, and διάνοια or *ratio*.

According to the classical philosophical tradition, reason is the structure of the mind which enables the mind to grasp and to transform reality. . . . Classical reason is *logos*, whether it is understood in a more intuitive or in a more critical way. Its cognitive nature is one element in addition to others; it is cognitive and aesthetic, theoretical and practical, detached and passionate, subjective and objective. (72)

Technical reason is the capacity for reasoning—it is Aristotle's "deliberative reason," which calculates means to ends.

While reason in the sense of *logos* determines the ends and only in the second place the means, reason in the technical sense determines the means while accepting the ends from "somewhere else. . . ." The consequence is that the ends are provided by nonrational forces, either by positive traditions or by arbitrary decisions serving the will to power. (73)

Now this ontological reason—*Vernunft*—is capable both of participating in the universal *logos* of being, and of succumbing to the destructive structures of existence. It is partly liberated from blindness, and partly held in it. In Platonic terms, it can either turn upward to participate in true being, or turn downward to nonbeing. It is itself both subjective and objective: the human *logos* can grasp and shape reality only because reality itself has a *logos* character. To the rational structure of the mind there corresponds an intelligible structure of the world. Subjective reason both "grasps" and "shapes"; the mind receives and reacts:

"Grasping," in this context, has the connotation of penetrating into the depth, into the essential nature of a thing or an event, of understanding and expressing it. "Shaping," in this context, has the connotation of transforming a given material into a Gestalt, a living structure which has the power of being. . . .

In every act of reasonable reception an act of shaping is involved, and in every act of reasonable reaction an act of grasping is involved. We transform reality according to the way we see it, and we see reality according to the way we transform it. Grasping and shaping the world are interdependent. (76)

Ontological reason has a dimension which Tillich calls its "depth":

The depth of reason is the expression of something that is not reason but which precedes reason and is manifest through it. Reason in both its objective and subjective structures points to something which appears in these structures but which transcends them in power and meaning. . . . It could be called the "substance" which appears in the rational structure, or "being-itself" which is manifest in the *logos* of being, or the "ground" which is creative in every rational creation, or the "abyss" which cannot be exhausted by any creation or by any totality of them, or the "infinite potentiality of being and meaning" which pours into the rational structures of mind and reality, actualizing and transforming them. All these terms which point to that which "precedes" reason have a metaphorical character. "Preceding" is itself metaphorical. . . .

In the cognitive realm the depth of reason is its quality of pointing to truth-itself, namely, to the infinite power of being and of the ultimately real, through the relative truths in ever field of knowledge. In the aesthetic realm the depth of reason is its quality of pointing to "beauty-itself," namely, to an infinite meaning and an ultimate significance, through the creations in every field of aesthetic intuition. In the legal realm, the depth of reason is its quality of pointing to "justice-itself," namely, to an infinite seriousness and an ultimate dignity, through every structure of actualized justice. (79)

Reason, in other words, points to something that is one step beyond the intelligible structures it actually finds. This further step is the Source or the One of Neo-Platonism, the Imprinter of the seal, the Original of the copy, of Augustinian thought. For the Platonic tradition this stands one step "above" intellect and Noῦς; following Böhme and Schelling, Tillich locates it one step "below," in the "depths." It is the Standard by which finite, human intellectual activity ultimately judges. But though it thus manifests itself in every act of reason, it is hidden there under the conditions of existence, and expresses itself primarily in myth and ritual.

Myth is not primitive science, nor is cult primitive morality. Their content, as well as the attitude of people toward them, discloses elements which transcend science as well as morality—elements of infinity which express ultimate concern. (80)

Now actual reason, in being, in human existence, and in life, is finite, self-contradictory, and ambiguous. It is relative, and can grasp only relativities. The classic description of the *docta ignorantia,* the awareness of its own limitations, of such "reason in existence" is to be found in Cusanus and in Kant. Tillich finds three major conflicts within actual reason:

> The polarity of structure and depth within reason produces a conflict between autonomous and heteronomous reason under the conditions of existence. Out of this conflict arises the quest for theonomy. The polarity of the static and the dynamic elements of reason produces a conflict between absolutism and relativism of reason under the conditions of existence. This conflict leads to the quest for the concrete-absolute. The polarity of the formal and the emotional elements of reason produces the conflict between formalism and irrationalism of reason under the conditions of existence. Out of this conflict arises the quest for the union of form and mystery. In all three cases reason is driven to the quest for revelation. (83)

Reason which affirms and actualizes its structure without regarding its depth is "autonomous." Autonomy means the obedience of the individual to the law of reason, which he finds in himself as a rational being. There has been an endless conflict between this self-sufficient reason and the "heteronomy" which imposes upon reason a law from outside. But this "outside" is not wholly external; it also represents an element in reason itself—its "depth." "The basis of a genuine heteronomy is the claim to speak in the name of the ground of being and therefore in an unconditional and ultimate way" (84). The conflict is thus tragic, for autonomy and heteronomy are both rooted in "theonomy," and each goes astray when their unity is broken—as in the autonomy of secular bourgeois culture, and in the heteronomy of totalitarianisms.

> Theonomy does not mean the acceptance of a divine law imposed on reason by a highest authority; it means autonomous reason united with its own depth . . . and actualized in obedience to its structural laws and in the power of its own inexhaustible ground. (85)

"Theonomous reason" is thus for Tillich really a kind of higher autonomy, in the Kantian sense. As for all good Augustinians, this is not so much a statement about the dependence of knowledge upon God as an identification of God with the fullest actualization of the powers of reason—with the Platonic "truth-itself."

The second conflict is between relativism and absolutism. Now reason unites a "static" and a "dynamic" element, its structure and its powers of actualizing itself in life. The static element is expressed in two forms of absolutism, that of tradition, like the Catholics, and that of revolution, like the Communists. The dynamic element appears in two forms of relativism, positivistic and cynical. Positivistic relativism accepts the given situation with its norms, and has no means of rising above it. Tillich here groups philosophical positivism, pragmatism, and recent existentialism, all of which he finds have conservative implications—they all accept the values of the *status quo*. Cynical positivism, the product of disillusionment with utopian absolutism, produces an empty vacuum into which new absolutisms pour. "Criticism," of which Socrates and Kant are representatives, tries to unite the conflicting static and dynamic elements in reason by reducing the static element to pure form without content—as in the categorical imperative. But both the Platonism that came from Socrates and the idealism that sprang from Kant became pure absolutisms.

In the ancient as well as in the modern world, criticism was unable to overcome the conflict between absolutism and relativism. Only that which is absolute and concrete at the same time can overcome this conflict. Only revelation can do it. (89)

The third conflict within reason is between formalism and emotionalism. Technical reason, which flowers in what Tillich calls "controlling knowledge," and culminates in formalized logic, denies that any other method can attain to truth. This intellectualism, which appears in all fields, art, law, society, and so forth, provokes an "irrationalism" which sacrifices the structure of reason entirely. Pure theory strives with a practice unguided by any theory. Neither theory nor practice taken in isolation can solve the problem of their conflict with each other; only revelation can do it.

When Tillich comes to consider the cognitive function of ontological reason, and the nature of human knowledge—"cognitive reason under the conditions of existence"—he emphasizes its basic polar structure. Knowledge he takes, with the Platonic tradition, to be a form of union. "In every act of knowledge the knower and that which is known are united." But knowledge is a union through detachment and separation: in every type of knowledge subject and object are logically distinguished.

The unity of distance and union is the ontological problem of knowledge. It drove Plato to the myth of an original union of the soul with the essences (ideas), of the separation of the soul from the truly real in temporal existence, of the recollection of the essences, and of reunion with them through the different degrees of cognitive elevation. The unity is never completely destroyed; but there is also estrangement. The particular object is strange as such, but it contains essential structures with which the cognitive subject is essentially united, and which it can remember when looking at things. (94)

Union and detachment or estrangement are present in all knowledge. But there are two major types, that in which detachment is determining, and that in which union is predominant. The first type, following Max Scheler, Tillich calls "controlling knowledge." This is the product of technical, instrumental reason.

It unites subject and object for the sake of the control of the object by the subject. It transforms the object into a completely conditioned and calculable "thing." It deprives it of any subjective quality. (97)

But this is not the way of knowing human nature, or any individual personality. "Without union there is no cognitive approach to man." The type of knowledge where union predominates Tillich calls "receiving knowledge." It always includes the emotional element: no union of subject and object is possible without emotional participation. Knowledge in which there is a balance of union and detachment is "understanding."

Understanding another person or a historical figure, the life of an animal or a religious text, involves an amalgamation of controlling and receiving knowledge, of union and detachment, of participation and analysis. (98)

Modern culture has seen a tidal wave of "controlling knowledge," technical reason, which has swamped every cognitive attempt in which "reception" and union are presupposed.

Life, spirit, personality, community, meanings, values, even one's ultimate concern, should be treated in terms of detachment, analysis, calculation, technical use. . . . But man himself has been lost in this enterprise. That which can be known only by participation and union, that which is the object of receiving knowledge, is disregarded. Man actually has become what controlling knowledge considers him to be, a thing among things, a cog in the dominating machine of production and consumption, a dehumanized object of tyranny or a standardized object of public communication. (99)

Three main movements have protested: romanticism, the "philosophy of life," and existentialism. They have failed because they had no adequate criterion of truth and falsity. What does "truth" mean for "receiving knowledge"? Positivists would restrict the term either to tautologies or to experimentally confirmed sentences. But this involves a break with the whole classic tradition. Modern philosophy, following Aristotle, has taken "true" as a quality of judgments. Tillich protests by asserting the ancient Platonic and Augustinian position, that the truth of judgments depends on a prior truth in things:

The truth of something is that level of its being the knowledge of which prevents wrong expectations and consequent disappointments. Truth, therefore, is the essence of things as well as the cognitive act in which their essence is grasped. The term "truth" is like the term "reason," subjective-objective. A judgment is true because it grasps and expresses true being. (102)

This would have delighted St. Anselm.

Tillich is obviously committed to finding a method of verification for his "receiving knowledge" that is different from that of experimental science.

Every cognitive assumption (hypothesis) must be tested. The safest test is the repeatable experiment. . . . But it is not permissible to make the experimental method of verification the exclusive pattern of all verification. . . . The verifying experiences of a nonexperimental character are truer to life, though less exact and definite. By far the largest part of all cognitive verification is "experiential." In some cases experimental and experiential verification work together. In other cases the experimental element is completely absent. (102)

Controlling knowledge is verified by the success of controlling actions. . . . Receiving knowledge is verified by the creative union of two natures, that of knowing, and that of the known. This test, of course, is neither repeatable, precise, nor final at any particular moment. The life-process itself makes the test. Therefore, the test is indefinite and preliminary; there is an element of risk connected with it. Future stages of the same life-process may prove that what seemed to be a bad risk was a good one and *vice versa*. Nevertheless, the risk must be taken, receiving knowledge must be applied, experiential verification must go on continually, whether it is supported by experimental tests or not. (102–3)

This suggests that in most of those traits in which the knowledge gained by experimental science has been contrasted unfavorably with knowledge gained by more "certain" methods, "receiving knowledge" is far more "experimental" than "controlling knowledge." It is more tentative, less precise, more subject to reconstruction with further experience. Such knowledge is verified partly by experimental test, partly by a participation in the individ-ual life with which they deal. If this "knowledge by participation" is called "intuition," the cognitive approach to every individual life-process is intuitive. Intuition in this sense is not irrational, and neither does it by-pass a full con-sciousness of experimentally verified knowledge. (103)

Now, neither rationalism nor pragmatism sees the element of par-ticipation in knowledge. But the way in which philosophical systems have been accepted, experienced, and verified points to a method of verification beyond rationalism and pragmatism. In terms of control-ling knowledge, rational criticism, or pragmatic tests, they have been refuted innumerable times. But they live. Their verification is their ef-ficiency in the life-process of mankind. They prove to be inexhaust-ible in meaning and creative in power. This method of verification "somehow combines the pragmatic and the rational elements without falling into the fallacies of either pragmatism or rationalism."

Now, the fundamental logical realism of Tillich—the notion of an "objective" intelligible structure which is grasped by "subjective" human reason—is designedly not in the fashion of much recent nominalistic philosophizing. In this, Tillich is not only in the classic tradition of ontology; he is, I judge, on the side of the angels, and is to be criticized only at those points where he inadvertently allows Kan-tian epistemology to interfere with it. The difficulties in the working out of such a realism he does not face. They are, I judge, to be met only in a thoroughgoing functional realism; and Tillich remains with a purely structural realism. He defines reason as "the structure of the mind," instead of as "the power of the mind" to operate in the ways it ascertainably does.

That the mind has the power—or, more precisely, *is* the power—to do what he assigns to "ontological reason," as well as what he calls "technical reason," is undoubtedly true. Tillich himself is inclined to stop short with these facts, rather than to pursue the analysis of what is a much more complex process than he often suggests. Perhaps this is sufficient for his purpose as a theologian. Reason can and does de-termine ends as well as means, but hardly in the simple sense of the Platonic tradition, of participating in them intuitively—as he himself goes on to illustrate. There are overtones of the Greek Noῦς and the idealistic *Vernunft*, as well as of the Christian Logos, that at times ob-scure what he is really trying to point to.

That mind has and is the power of "depth" no sensitive man would care to deny, nor would he deny that it has a capacity for envisaging more ultimate perfections than it can actually achieve. That the powers of the mind are limited is likewise obvious, and the polarities and tensions Tillich points to are both historically and personally illuminating. The limitations of what he calls an "autonomous reason" that disregards its "depth" have not been exactly overlooked of late; sensitivity to other aspects of experience is certainly needed. The higher autonomy Tillich calls "theonomy": if this be one way of "defining" God, it is surely as good as any other. The polar values both of relativism and of absolutism are equally obvious. That this is a rationally insoluble antinomy, however, is by no means clear. The solution would seem to lie in an objective relativism—a position Tillich does not consider. Even if he is right in contending that "only that which is absolute and concrete at the same time" can solve the antinomy, this would still seem to be a rational answer to a rational question, and not beyond the power of reason, however difficult practically. Finally, the antinomy between formalism and emotionalism seems likewise capable of rational adjustment. In going beyond the traditional "technical" reason to the notion of "intelligence," recent philosophizing has been facing and dealing with precisely this problem.

In other words, the finite and relative character of human reason is clear, as well as that it confronts difficulties and "ambiguities." That any adequate intellectual method, however, faces ultimate self-contradiction Tillich has not established. He contends that only "revelation" can solve these contradictions. Now there is no objection to calling the power of reason to solve its difficulties "revelation," especially if the power be seen as a cooperation with the powers of the world to be understood—if "revelation" be taken as a discovery and not as a mere human invention. That only the Christian "revelation" can solve the problems, however, is another matter again. That particular revelation, philosophically considered, would be one hypothesis among others, and would have to be tested philosophically. "Revelation," that is, would seem to be a symbol for the power of reason to do what revelation notoriously does.

In treating the nature of knowledge, Tillich does not presume to offer a detailed epistemology. His distinctions are important; his language is obviously pointed in the direction of establishing theological "knowledge." But though he has the tradition on his side, there remains a doubt whether greater clarity would not come from calling his "receiving knowledge" by some other name than "knowledge." After all, it is only by a metaphor that knowledge can be called a "union" or "participation." "Love" for the object of knowledge may in many types of knowledge be essential for any real "understanding"; but does that make the love itself knowledge? "Knowing is not like digesting, and we do not devour what we mean," is an aphorism of Santayana's still worth pondering. "Union" with another personality may well be a necessary condition of adequate knowledge of that personality. But union with a text—even a religious text—is hardly necessary to its proper interpretation. Nor have many American students been able to accept the peculiar German view of historical knowledge which leads Tillich to say, "Without a union of the nature of the historian with that of his object, no significant history is possible." In what sense, for instance, does a significant history of capitalism demand "a union between the nature of the historian and the nature of capitalism"? Obviously, only by metaphor.

This may be a mere matter of terminology, and there is, of course, much precedent for identifying forms of immediate experience with "knowledge." Precedent, however, is hardly a philosophical justification. The knowledge of particular situations does involve a very complex gathering together of relevant factors, as well as a narrowly "technical" reason. The classic instance is the process of diagnosis in medicine. But the physician scarcely needs to be "united" with the disease. To strengthen his particular kind of religious "receiving knowledge," Tillich seems to have grouped together quite a variety of types of knowledge that in another connection would demand careful discrimination.

It is obvious that most of our so-called "knowledge" is verified "experientially" rather than "experimentally"—at least in the narrow laboratory sense. But like most idealists criticizing philosophies of "scientific method," Tillich in the end falls back, in language quite worthy of James himself, on a pretty crude pragmatic method of verification—"efficiency in the life-process of mankind." Actually, of course, what he carefully describes as a union of experimental verification with something more, and calls both an "experiential" and an "intu-

itive" method, is very close to what American pragmatists and in-
strumentalists have called the "method of intelligence." It is natural
for those without scientific interests themselves to conceive "scientific
method" very narrowly, to identify it with what Tillich calls "technical reason." But "intelligence" as the best American philosophic
thought has conceived it is certainly far more than his technical reason, even if it has still to learn some of the "depth" of his ontological
reason. Tillich would really do well to strike up an acquaintance with
"intelligence." He might in the end even be willing to participate in it.

IV

Ontology is the core of philosophy, and the ontological question of
the nature of being is logically prior to all others. Ontology is possible
because there are concepts less universal than "being," but more universal than the concepts that designate a particular realm of beings.

Such ontological concepts have been called "principles," "categories," or "ultimate notions." Tillich's analysis of these concepts is
the heart of his philosophy.

Such concepts, he holds, are strictly "*a priori*": they are present
whenever something is experienced, and determine the nature of experience itself. They constitute its structure, they are its *a priori* "conditions," and hence are "presupposed" in every actual experience.
This does not mean that they can be known prior to experience: they
are known rather through the critical analysis of actual instances of experience.

This Kantian language hardly seems essential to Tillich's position,
or even, indeed, ultimately compatible with it. The structure of experience is discovered *in* experience, by analysis; it is "recognized within
the process of experiencing." Why then call it a "presupposition,"
which suggests that it is brought *to* experience from elsewhere? Why
call it a "condition" of experience, "determining" its nature? Can one
really combine in this fashion ontology and the Kantian critical philosophy, an epistemological realism with a theory that the knower "determines" the object of knowledge? Taken seriously, such language
implies that the "being" to be analyzed is to be found only in the
knower, and not, except derivatively, in the known; and this is the essence of an idealistic epistemology.

Tillich has of course broken with Kant on what for him is the fundamental point: this structure of experience may have changed in the past and may change in the future. He takes time seriously. The structure of human nature does indeed change in history. But underlying all such historical change is the structure of a being *which has history:*

This structure is the subject of an ontological and a theological doctrine of man. Historical man is a descendant of beings who had no history, and perhaps there will be beings who are descendants of historical man who have no history. But neither animals nor supermen are the objects of a doctrine of man. (167)

Hence the *"a priori"* concepts are after all only relatively a priori, not absolutely static; and thus is the alternative of absolutism and relativism overcome. Tillich attaches his view to the voluntarism of Duns Scotus, which saw an ultimate indeterminacy in the ground of being. The similarity to Peirce, even in the enthusiasm for Scotus, is striking.

Tillich distinguishes four levels of ontological concepts: (1) the basic ontological structure; (2) the "elements" constituting that structure; (3) the characteristics of being which are the conditions of existence, or "existential being"; and (4) the categories of being and knowing. In setting off the "elements," which are polar distinctions that come always in pairs, from the categories, he is most illuminating and clarifying.

The ontological question, "What is being?" presupposes an asking "subject" and an "object" about which the question is asked; it presupposes the subject-object structure of being. This in turn presupposes the self-world structure as the basic articulation of being: being is man encountering the world. This logically and experientially precedes all other structures. Man experiences himself as having a world to which he belongs, and it is from the analysis of this polar relationship between man and the world that the basic ontological structure is derived. Since man is estranged from nature, and is unable to understand it in the way he understands man—he does not know what the behavior of things means to them, as he does know what men's behavior means to men—the principles which constitutes the universe must be sought in man himself. Following Heidegger's *Sein und Zeit,* Tillich finds "being there" (*Dasein*)—the place where the structure of being is manifest—given to man within himself. "Man is able to answer the ontological question himself because he experiences directly and immediately the structure of being and its elements" within himself. This does not mean that it is easier to get a knowledge of man "sufficient for our purposes" than a knowledge of nonhuman objects. This is notoriously untrue. It means that man is aware of "the structure that makes cognition possible," the conditions of knowing. Being is revealed, not in objects, but in "the conditions necessary for knowing." "The truth of all ontological concepts is their power of expressing that which makes the subject-object structure possible. They constitute this structure" (169).

The "self" lives in an environment, which consists of those things with which it has an active interrelation. Self and environment or world are correlative concepts. "The self without a world is empty; the world without a self is dead." It is within this polarity that are to be found the derivative polarities of objective and subjective reason, of logical object and subject. Pure objects, "things," are completely conditioned or *bedingt* by the scheme of knowing. But man himself is not a "thing" or object: he is never bound completely to an environment.

He always transcends it by grasping and shaping it according to universal norms and ideas. . . . This is the reason why ontology cannot begin with things and try to derive the structure of reality from them. That which is completely conditioned, which has no selfhood and subjectivity, cannot explain self and subject. . . . It is just as impossible to derive the object from the subject as it is to derive the subject from the object. . . . This trick of deductive idealism is the precise counterpart of the trick of reductive naturalism. . . . The relation is one of polarity. The basic ontological structure cannot be derived. It must be accepted. (170, 173–74)

This analysis of "the basic ontological structure," in which Tillich is following Heidegger, assumes without question that the epistemological "subject-object distinction" is absolutely ultimate, not only for knowledge, but for all being: It is not only "prior for us," but also "prior in nature," as Aristotle puts it. The analysis makes no attempt to explore the emergence of that distinction from the larger context of organic and social life, and of their natural conditions. This assumption of itself, coming at the very outset, is likely to prejudice any American philosopher against the whole "existential" enterprise: it smacks so clearly of an antiquated psychology of the knowing process. One of the striking features of Tillich's thought to Americans who have inherited the fruits of the evolutionary preoccupations of the last generation is the complete absence in his intellectual background of any serious concern for the implications, for metaphysics, of biological evolution. It may well be that "ontology cannot derive the structure of reality from things," or understand "self and subject" in terms drawn from them alone, leaving man himself out of account. Certainly an adequate metaphysics cannot be formulated by disregarding man and his ways, as illustrations of the powers of being. But God evidently knew how to turn the trick of deriving man from a world innocent of his presence; and there is still more interest in trying to discover how he did it than in denying that it could be done.

There seems to be a basic unclarity in Tillich's thought at this point. At times he follows Heidegger in looking for the structure of being "in man." This is the characteristic method of idealism, as Heidegger has more explicitly recognized since his *Sein und Zeit*. But at other times Tillich, following his own insights rather than another's thought, holds that the structure of being is found *by* man *in* his encounters with the world—that it is not the structure of man, but of man's cooperation with the world, a cooperation of which man is but one pole. This is a quite different ontology, not that of idealism, but of what I should call empirical naturalism, and should accept. It would be clarifying to have Tillich decide which position he is really maintaining—idealism, or an experiential and functional realism. *'Raus mit Kant!*

The second level of ontological analysis deals with those "ontological elements" which constitute the basic structure of being. Unlike the categories, these elements are polar: each is meaningful only in relation to its opposite pole. There are three outstanding pairs: individuality and universality or participation, dynamics and form, and freedom and destiny. These distinctions are discovered in the self's experience of the world, and then generalized for all interactions within being.

Individualization is a quality of everything; "it is implied in and constitutive of every self, which means that at least in an analogous way it is implied in and constitutive of every being." The individual self participates in his environment, or in the case of complete individualization, in his world. Man participates in the universe through the rational structure of mind and reality. When individualization reaches the perfect form we call a "person," participation reaches the perfect form we call "communion." The polarity of individualization and participation solves the problem of nominalism and realism. Individuals are real, but they participate in the universal structure, which, however, is not a second reality lying behind empirical reality.

Secondly, being something means having a form. But every form forms something, and this something Tillich calls "dynamics"—a rather unfortunate term. "Dynamics" is the *me on*, the potentiality of being, which is nonbeing in contrast to things that have a form, and the power of being in contrast to pure nonbeing" (179). This element polar to form appears as the *Urgrund* of Böhme, the "will" of Schopenhauer, the "will to power" of Nietzsche, the "unconscious" of Hartmann and Freud, the *élan vital* of Bergson. Each of these concepts points symbolically to what cannot be named literally. "If it could be named properly, it would be a formed being beside others instead of an ontological element in contrast with the element of pure form" (179).

The polarity of dynamics and form appears in man's immediate experience as the polar distinction of "vitality" and "intentionality." Vitality is the power which keeps a living being alive and growing. Intentionality is the actualizing of reason, being related to meaningful structures, living in universals, grasping and shaping reality. The two are the basis of self-transcendence and self-conservation. "Man's creativity breaks through the biological realm to which he belongs and establishes new realms never attainable on a nonhuman level" (181).

Freedom and destiny form the third ontological polarity. Destiny, and not necessity, is the polar correlate of freedom, for necessity is a category whose contrast is "possibility," not an "element."

Man experiences the structure of the individual as the bearer of freedom within the larger structures to which the individual structure belongs. Destiny points to this situation in which man finds himself, facing the world to which, at the same time, he belongs. (182–83)

Freedom is experienced as deliberation, decision, and responsibility. Our destiny is that out of which our decisions arise. . . . it is the concreteness of our being which makes all our decisions *our* decisions. . . . Destiny is not a strange power which determines what shall happen to me. It is myself as given, formed by nature, history, and myself. My destiny is the basis of my freedom; my freedom participates in shaping my destiny. (184–85)

Tillich generalizes this polarity in human experience to include every being, though it applies only by analogy to subhuman nature.

It is not clear whether Tillich really maintains that these three polarities alone "constitute the basic ontological structure." One can easily think of a good many more. But without following his discussion in detail, it is impossible to realize the richness of his treatment of the three.

The third level of ontological analysis expresses the power of being to exist, the nature of "existential being," and its difference from "essential being." This duality is Tillich's form of contrast between the ideal and the actual, between potentiality and actuality, or, as I prefer, between powers and their operation ($\delta \dot{\nu} \nu \alpha \mu \epsilon \iota \varsigma$ and $\dot{\epsilon} \nu \acute{\epsilon} \rho \gamma \epsilon \iota \alpha$).

There is no ontology which can disregard these two aspects, whether they are hypostatized into two realms (Plato), or combined in the polar relation of potentiality and actuality (Aristotle), or contrasted with each other (Schelling II, Kierkegaard, Heidegger), or derived from each other, either existence from essence (Spinoza, Hegel), or essence from existence (Dewey, Sartre). (165)

Freedom as such is not the basis of existence, but rather freedom in unity with finitude. Finite freedom is the turning point from being to existence. Finitude is hence the center of Tillich's analysis, for it is the finitude of existent being which drive men to the question of God.

Historically, the question of what it means to be anything arose from the problem of the meaning of "nonbeing," in Parmenides, and in the *Sophist* of Plato. Plato there determined that "being not" means "being other than." But Tillich, following Heidegger, takes nonbeing much more personally and portentously, as *"das Nichts," Nothingness*— the body of this death. Man

must be separated from his being in a way which enables him to look at it as something strange and questionable. And such a separation is actual because man participates not only in being but also in nonbeing. . . . It is not by chance that historically the recent rediscovery of the ontological question has been guided by pre-Socratic philosophy and that systematically there has been an overwhelming emphasis on the problem of nonbeing. (187)

The Platonists distinguished between the οὐκ ὄν which means "nothing at all," and the μὴ ὄν which meant for them that which does not yet have being but can become being if united with ideas. This Platonic "matter" had a positive power of resisting the ideas. This was what Augustine meant in calling evil "nonbeing"—not nothing at all, but something with no positive ontological standing that yet could resist and pervert being. In Böhme's *Ungrund*, Schelling's "first potency," Hegel's "antithesis," this dialectical negativity was located in God himself. Existentialism has given to nonbeing a still more positive character and power: Heidegger's "annihilating nothingness" threatens man with nonbeing in the form of death, thus giving his life its "existential" character. For Sartre, nonbeing includes the threat of meaninglessness—the destruction of the very structure of being.

Now, being when limited by nonbeing is finitude. Nonbeing is the "not yet" and the "no more" of being. Everything which participates in the power of being is mixed with nonbeing. It is finite. Experienced on the human level, finitude is nonbeing as the threat to being, ultimately the threat of death. It is *Angst*, "anxiety."

Fear as related to a definite object and anxiety as the awareness of finitude are two radically different concepts. Anxiety is ontological; fear, psychological. (191)

Psychotherapy cannot remove ontological anxiety, because it cannot change the structure of finitude. But it can remove compulsory forms of anxiety and can reduce the frequency and intensity of fears. It can put anxiety "in its proper place." (191*n*)

Anxiety expresses finitude from "inside." Anxiety is the self-awareness of the finite self as finite.

Every existence is finite, threatened with disruption and self-destruction. It also participates in what is beyond nonbeing, "being-itself." It has both "existence" and "essence." Now essence is an ambiguous term: its meaning oscillates between an empirical and a valuational sense, between the actual logical nature of the thing, and its "true" and undistorted nature, that from which being has "fallen." "Existence" is likewise ambiguous: whatever exists is more than it is in the state of mere potentiality and less than it could be in the power of its "essential" nature. Historically, the contrast between "essence" and "existence" has been both the colorless contrast between idea and fact, and the contrast of value between the ideal and the actual. For Tillich's theology, it is the contrast between the world as created, and the actual world after the Fall.

The fourth level of ontological concepts consists of the categories.

They are "the forms in which the mind grasps and shapes reality."
But they are not mere logical forms, only indirectly related to reality
itself; they are ontological, present in everything. They are forms of
finitude. They are not polar, like the "elements." For his purposes
Tillich emphasizes four main categories: time, space, causality, and
substance.

Time is the central category of finitude. In immediate experience
time unites the anxiety of transitoriness with the courage of a self-af-
firming present. The present implies space; time creates the present
through its union with space. Not to have space is not to be; thus in
all life striving for space is an ontological necessity. To have no definite or final space means ultimate insecurity. This anxiety is balanced
by the courage which affirms the present and space.

Causality affirms the power of being by pointing to that which
precedes a thing or event as its source. The cause makes its effect real.
Causality presupposes that things do not possess their own power of
coming into being. They are contingent: as Heidegger says, they have
been "thrown" into being. Causality and contingent being are thus the
same thing. The anxiety in which man is aware of this situation is
anxiety about the lack of necessity of his being. This is the anxiety
implied in the awareness of causality as a category of finitude.
Courage ignores the causal dependence of everything finite, and accepts contingency.

Substance points to something underlying the flux, something relatively static and self-contained. But it is nothing beyond the accidents
in which it expresses itself—it is no "I-know-not-what."

The problem of substance is not avoided by philosophers of function or process, because questions about that which *has* functions or about that which *is*
in process cannot be silenced. The replacement of static notions by dynamic
ones does not remove the question of that which makes change possible by
not (relatively) changing itself. (197)

Everything finite is innately "anxious" that its substance will be lost.
Courage accepts the threat.

These four categories express the union of being and nonbeing in
everything finite. They articulate the courage which accepts the "ontological anxiety" of nonbeing.

It is in this analysis of actuality or "existential being" that existential ontology is most characteristic and most original. It is here also that it is most "existential," in the sense of being most limited by the historical and cultural situation out of which it arose. It is an appropriate philosophic expression of the "age of anxiety," formulating the structure of human experience and of human nature as it has been historically conditioned by the cultural crises of Central and Western Europe since 1914. And since, by its own method, being is to be found in "being as experienced," or "being as encountered"—since the structure of being is the structure of the "self-world polarity"—the way being is encountered at any time by an historically conditioned self is the way being *is*.

This polarity or encountering can be looked at either from "outside"—the side of the world—or from "inside"—the side of the particular type of self.

There is no reason for preferring concepts taken from "outside" to those taken from "inside." According to the self-world structure, both types are equally valid. The self being aware of itself and the self looking at its world (including itself) are equally significant for the description of the ontological structure. (192)

Hence Heidegger and Tillich are justified in calling their analysis of the experience of the self in psychological terms, "ontology," and in taking as intentional, for example, what from the "outside" is finitude and from the "inside" anxiety. From his theological perspective Tillich naturally emphasizes the feel of the categories to immediate experience, rather than their function from "outside." The parallel here with the way in which Dewey, for example, describes immediate experience as shot through with values and emotionality, is striking. Indeed, Dewey's familiar "situation" that is objectively "doubtful" is a clear instance of just such existential ontology. Both Dewey and Tillich are open to the same misunderstandings and criticisms—criticisms that are hardly justified for any metaphysics that takes man as an integral part of Nature, or self and world as polar.

The real doubt is not as to whether the self or encounterer is part of the situation, or of being, but as to the character of the self that is made basic to the analysis. *Is* the immediate experience of finitude for the self "anxiety"? Rather, for what kind of self, under what cultural conditions, is this so? I remember Tillich once reporting, after an evening with a Russian, "Wunderbar! Sie hat keine Angst!" Despite the psychiatrists, I think this is still true. "The ontological anxiety of finitude" may well express the way many Continental Europeans feel these days. But in this country I seriously doubt whether for many it can mean more than the latest fashion in theological apologetics.

All existence is finite and determinate—is τόδε τι, as Aristotle puts it. And, as he also pointed out, for illustrative purposes, all men are mortal. But these finite limitations of human life in time and space have rarely provoked emotional disturbance, or "anxiety." It takes a good German Romanticist like Heidegger to get really excited over the natural conditions of human life. One trembles to think of the problems if man were *not* finite! Others have usually felt much more keenly the moral limitations of human nature than the "ontological anxiety" of metaphysical determinateness. In other words, "anxiety" seems to be for Tillich rather a religious symbol and an existential commitment than an ontological concept.

Tillich has no place for any natural theology, nor can metaphysics prove the "existence" of God.

God does not exist. He is being-itself beyond essence and existence. Therefore, to argue that God exists is to deny him. (205)

The traditional "arguments" are all invalid: they are neither arguments nor proof. "They are expressions of the *question* of God which is implied in human finitude." God is not *a* being, he is being-itself, or the ground of being. He is the power of being—the power inherent in everything of resisting nonbeing.

Being-itself infinitely transcends every finite being. There is no proportion or gradation between the finite and the infinite. There is an absolute break, an infinite "jump." On the other hand, everything finite participates in being-itself and in its infinity. Otherwise it would not have the power of being. It would be swallowed by nonbeing, or it never would have emerged out of nonbeing. (237)

"The statement that God is being-itself is a nonsymbolic statement. . . . It means what it says directly and properly" (238). However, nothing else can be said about God as God which is not symbolic. Into Tillich's penetrating analysis of symbols we cannot here go. God is the ground of the ontological structure of being without being subject to this structure himself. He *is* the structure; that is, he has the power of determining the structure of everything that has being.

What remains in doubt here is whether for Tillich "being-itself," the "ground of being," is an ontological, that is, a philosophical concept, or a theological symbol. He seems to identify "the structure of being," which he has analyzed philosophically, with the "ground of being," and both with "the power of being." Now, ontologically speaking, these seem to be three very different concepts, and, surprisingly enough, Tillich never attempts to distinguish or clarify them. The "structure" of being, as he has rationally analyzed it, seems fairly clear. The "power" of being, as the power in everything to resist non-being, is likewise clear—though I myself should take the power of being as a polar "element," and treat it in the plural, as the powers to operate in determinate ways. But a structure is hardly in itself a power. Nor is either to be intelligibly identified with a "ground." How does a "ground" differ from a "cause"? Tillich specifically insists that "causality" as applied to the relation between "being-itself" and finite beings is not a category but a symbol. It seems clear that all these notions are actually used by Tillich as symbols, and that they hence do not belong to metaphysics or ontology at all, but to theology.[6] This is especially true of "being-itself," a concept at which ontological analysis can never arrive. Ontology can find only the "being" which is common to all particular and determinate beings. "Being-itself," in any other sense, seems to be a religious myth or symbol. Hence the line which for Tillich is ultimately impossible to draw, between metaphysics and theology, I should draw more narrowly, and find some of the notions he takes as ontological concepts to be religious myths and symbols.

Tillich is not primarily the prophet—the man whose sincerity and stamp of inspiration bring immediate conviction—but rather the philosopher, whose appeal lies in his mastery of reason and rational argument. Paul Tillich seems to me not only the ablest Protestant theologian of the present day, but also by far the most persuasive exponent of the philosophy of existentialism, and, what is more to the point, a real contributor to the present-day revival of metaphysical inquiry. His is a first-rate philosophical mind.

[6] Cf. their "metaphorical" character, Vol. I, p. 79.

10

The Religion of Shared Experience

When the emotional force, the mystic force one might say, of communication, of the miracle of shared life and shared experience is spontaneously felt, the hardness and crudeness of contemporary life will be bathed in the light that never was on land or sea.
—JOHN DEWEY, *Reconstruction in Philosophy*, p. 211

SANTAYANA, that remote, aristocratic, and Olympian thinker, is credibly reported to have remarked of Dewey's little book of lectures on religion, " 'A Common Faith'? A very common faith indeed!" Doubtless he was voicing his own opinion of that deposit of earnest moral idealism, implemented in practice by a modicum of intelligence, left in many an American heart by the fading of concern with any particular religious creed, dogma, or belief. Such practical idealism directed toward human welfare and social good has indeed been characteristic of the latter-day American temper. Humanitarian zeal and a generous interest in setting the world aright, combined with a positive distaste for things intellectual, for all matters theological and speculative, are doubtless what religion has come to mean for multitudes today. That urge expresses the vague religious life of the "unchurched," of that great body of Americans who, while continuing to feel Christian sentiments, feel also a deep distrust of all institutionalized religion, all "churchianity." It has also infected, to a far greater extent than they realize, the congregations of those still faithful to our various churches, coloring even the activities of great historic communions,

Originally published in *The Philosopher of the Common Man: Essays in Honor of John Dewey to Celebrate His Eightieth Birthday*, ed. Horace M. Kallen (New York: G.P. Putnam's Sons; copyright © 1940 by Conference on Methods in Philosophy; renewed), pp. 106–45. Reprinted by permission of the publisher.

and converging on the emergence in them of what may well be called a distinctly American form of religion.

To a cosmopolitan spirit like Santayana, living much in the imaginative attempt to recapture the past, this American religion must seem not unnaturally a selection, in the present fashion and surely in the interest of present needs, from the much richer complex of values historic religions have offered. This is hardly what religion has meant and done in human experience on a less provincial scale. And to such a spirit Dewey might well appear to have given philosophic expression to all that is Protestant, provincial, and merely American in the religious degeneracy of our times.

It is hardly surprising that Dewey's central interest in religion should lie in the particular needs, conflicts, and problems that have of late been troubling so many of his compatriots, and that with a characteristic and unique clarity he should set forth the dissatisfactions felt by so many of them and the hopes so widely shared. It is true that his whole conception of religion is Christian, Protestant, and American, with all the limitation to the restricted experience of our own present culture those adjectives imply. It is focused on specific criticisms and on a specific program, on those ends in view which the religious experience of our generation has itself brought to the fore. How could it well be otherwise? For Santayana's comment is right in its perception that what is distinctive in Dewey's treatment of religion is his emphasis, not on the element of faith, but on that of common-ness. How indeed could a man who from the beginning has prized above all else whatever unites men with their fellows in joint endeavor, who has consistently protested against all that is divisive and disruptive of the continuity of every human activity with its cultural environment and with the natural conditions that generate and sustain it, fail to share and express those religious experiences and values which now bind so many Americans together in a common devotion?

The fading of sectarian differences and doctrinal divergencies in our religious scene has given particular point to the new American conviction that, as Dewey puts it, religion is empty and futile save as it expresses the basic unities of life. The whole long history of the weaving together of the most variegated threads into the web of American culture has not only, with us as with other peoples, generated a high appreciation for whatever fosters social unification. It has ingrained into the very texture of the life of the common man in his ordinary pursuits the realization that "getting together" is something good in its own right. In other and more stable cultures men have been able to take sociability for granted, and living together has produced its enjoyments through following the immemorial pattern. For a multitude of reasons both geographical and historical, in America associated activity has required a more conscious effort. Americans have not "lived together" time out of mind, they have had to "get together"; and so get together they have with a vengeance. The very effort required has made their joint activities something consciously sustained and emotionally and intellectually shared. It has converted mere working together into a real community of interest and endeavor, into a moral fact and a religious ideal. "Cooperation" has thus become a term to conjure with in our land. "Fellowship" has revived all those sacramental meanings and values which "the church" once possessed, but which were lost in the emotional wastes of our "denominations." And "community" has gathered about itself the religious connotations which characterize a passionately cherished ultimate social ideal.

It is against this background of the give-and-take of American life in countless face-to-face group relationships that Dewey has been able to speak of "shared experience" as the greatest of human goods. Life, he holds, achieves its richest significance when human beings undertake and undergo things together, with that conscious interplay of finding out each other's interests and views that attends a community of purpose. "Communication," in the sense of the power to use a vehicle of joint understanding, a common language, is the prerequisite of such shared and mutually directed activity; "communication," in the deeper sense of learning from joint experience with others how to enrich one's own understanding of things and to increase one's insight into the values to be found in living together in the human scene, is that perfected activity, that highest possible functioning of human powers, toward the achievement of which all human action should aim.

"Communication" is in truth the controlling conception in Dewey's thought. In terms of that process he understands all that is distinctively human, marking man off from the other animals and endowing him with mind and intelligence. By proper attention to its conditions are to be solved the philosophic problems of the nature and function of knowledge and appreciation, of all men's arts and sciences. And since society itself exists in and through communication, and communication is the essence of education, all Dewey's social thought and all his educational program radiate from that central idea. To develop through the give-and-take of communication an effective sense of being an individually distinctive member of a community is the never-ending end of education; to work for that form of associated living in which the widest number and variety of interests are consciously communicated and shared, is to work for the democratic life. A democratic society, in which the possibilities of sharing experience are freely developed, in which "the order of energies has been transmuted into one of meanings which are appreciated and mutually referred by each to every other on the part of those engaged in combined action," is a genuine community. Such a democratic community, Dewey is convinced, most fully realizes the possibilities inherent in man's fundamentally social nature. In such living man is at once most human and most divine. To be captured morally and imaginatively by such an ideal, to acknowledge its rightful claim over our desires and purposes, to live in its light, is to live religiously. The democratic life, pursued in a conscious unity of interaction with one's fellows, is the religious life. Democratic experience is thus for Dewey not only, with all the overtones he manages to put into the term, a *common* experience in which the common man can take part: it is literally a religious *communion* in which men find themselves at one and in unity with their fellow men and with the natural conditions of human achievement.

Now such an experience, capable of provoking its own perfecting into an imaginatively envisaged ideal life, is not anything a thinker can himself create. Faith in such an ideal, sustained by the very experience that has given it birth, is something Dewey has found shared by a wide body of his fellow countrymen. Such a faith philosophy cannot provide ready-made; only experience can beget a living faith, and what will function religiously in experience, what will provide a unifying focus and give a sense of direction to life, comes from sources in human culture that are beyond conscious deliberation and purpose. As Dewey points out, a religious faith possesses the will and is not its express product. Yet philosophy can help in that hardest of all human tasks, learning from experience; it can rationalize and criticize and clarify the faith that is in men, and help them enlarge that faith by reflection and further experience.

Now this is precisely what Dewey has long been doing for the religious faith implicit in American democratic experience. That faith has been slowly taking form, under the impact of innumerable forces and countless "communications of shared experience," within the framework of the various traditional churches in this country. Even where the shell has not been broken, it has revolutionized the content; for millions it has already cut the institutional bond. This growing American religion, which in formal terms might be called a humanistic and naturalistic humanitarianism, is still greatly confused in its thought and unclear in its direction. The impact of Dewey's long teaching upon our religious forces has unquestionably been felt chiefly in fostering this emerging faith. Cherishing the substance rather than the form, he has not been deeply concerned with the intellectual or the institutional problems generated by its tension with historic organizations of religious life. He has felt, perhaps, that little was to be gained by such rather external criticism before the time was ripe. Of late years he has paid more attention to clarifying what is really involved in this religion of shared experience, and to rationalizing what has been growing at an accelerated rate. What is implicit in the common moral idealism of the common man's life he has recently tried to make explicit and public; he has openly criticized what pass today as "religions" in the interest of freeing them from their outgrown historical baggage, the better to release the powers of a more vital and less divisive religious unification of life.

It is a matter of common knowledge that Dewey is little concerned with developing in detail an adequate theory of the nature and function of religious institutions in human culture. With that institutionalized form of inquiry that is science, and to a somewhat lesser extent with that embodiment of new meanings in natural materials in such a way as to reorganize the experience of the observer and heighten his immediate enjoyment that is art, Dewey does not limit his interest to an analysis of the function of the enterprise and its continuity with the rest of experience. He goes on to examine in detail the techniques and devices by which these functions are carried out. But with religious institutions he does not bother to examine the specific means by which their end is effectuated. He contents himself rather with setting forth the reasons for their contemporary failure to accomplish their historic function.

As a matter of fact it is clear from the suggestions toward such a theory of the nature of religion he does permit himself, that had he devoted serious attention to this theme he would have arrived at conclusions hardly different in their essentials from those of Santayana's *Reason in Religion*. The fact that Santayana in this classic portion of his *Life of Reason* had already explored in some detail the essentially imaginative function of religious beliefs in the criticism of life may well have had some bearing on Dewey's reluctance to set forth another version of the social functioning of the religious imagination. In any event, many of Professor Dewey's followers have had little difficulty in amalgamating his implicit views with those explicitly stated by Santayana. For both, the essential reconstruction of the religious tradition lies in the separation of piety, as respect for the sources of our being and our good, from spirituality, as devotion to the ends toward which we move. And for both there is a common insistence that the ideal has a natural basis and can be realized only by a proper respect for the natural conditions of its attainment.

It is not then in his theory of religion that Dewey differs most significantly from Santayana. The striking contrast lies rather in the religions the two actually cherish. Dewey stands as the representative of American liberal humanism, sharing its assumptions and its limitations. The very fact that Dewey *has* a religious faith of his own holds him back from that disinterested examination of the function of various types of religion in human experience, possible perhaps only for one who, like Santayana, has escaped further from faith in the religion he still enjoys. There is about Dewey's views on religion the kind of intolerance of other and alien religious values that springs from his own allegiance. This fact has had much to do with his lack of concern with other kinds of religious life, and has undoubtedly impeded his understanding of the social functioning of the host of institutionalized techniques the religious arts of the past have normally employed. But it has also been the source of his great influence in stimulating a nonecclesiastical religious attitude in millions of laymen, especially those serving at the altar of the classroom desk. Since so many of his criticisms of the failure of traditional religions to perform a religious function today are directed toward the various consequences of the professionalization of religion, it is hardly surprising that his influence has been felt less strongly by the professionals, by religious "leaders" among the ministry. Those of the clergy who have taken to heart his analysis of what is really implied in the religion of democracy they in fact so widely share, and of the causes of the failure of the churches to foster it more effectively, are comparatively few in number; and their leadership is still far ahead of their lagging following.

Dewey's marked preference for setting forth his own religious message without much attempt to adapt it to the practical needs of the churches is to that extent justified. But his refusal to accommodate it to the uses of the professionals has brought its own penalties. In the practice of every art there is after all something to be said for professional competence. That the religious arts in particular have in our day fallen into a stultifying academicism that defeats their own ends is doubtless largely true. But zealous amateurs have their own failings, even in religion; and the transformation of the religion of democratic experience into the religion of Teachers College poses its own questions.

II

During his long life Dewey has been remarkably consistent in his concern with religion, both on the positive and the negative side. From his early student days to the time he was finally inveigled into giving the Terry lectures specifically on religion, he has known clearly just what the religious attitude meant to him, and just what were the forces that would foster it and those that were interfering with its free expression. He had early a strong urge toward whatever savored of unifying and integrating what seemed disconnected intellectually or socially, and a marked antipathy for whatever was divisive and sectarian, leading to social gulfs and impassable intellectual dualisms. This temperamental drive attracted him as an undergraduate to Comte's idea of a synthesis of science that should be a regulative method of an organized social life. It led him later at Johns Hopkins to the deeper and more far-reaching integration of the Hegelians.

Hegel's thought . . . supplied a demand for unification that was doubtless an intense emotional craving, and yet was a hunger that only an intellectualized subject matter could satisfy. It is more than difficult, it is impossible, to recover that early mood. But the sense of divisions and separations that were, I suppose, borne in upon me as a consequence of a heritage of New England culture, divisions by way of isolation of self from the world, of soul from body, of nature from God, brought a painful oppression—or, rather, they were an inward laceration. My earlier philosophic study had been an intellectual gymnastic. Hegel's synthesis of subject and object, matter and spirit, the divine and the human, was, however, no mere intellectual formula; it operated as an immense release, a liberation. Hegel's treatment of human culture, of institutions and the arts, involved the same dissolution of hard-and-fast dividing walls, and had a special attraction for me.[1]

Dewey grew up in Vermont Congregationalism, subject, as his daughter remarks, to too much moralistic emotional pressure. His father was more easy-going than his mother; like so many in that day, though she came of a family of active Universalists, she had been early converted to evangelical orthodoxy at a revival meeting. But the theological spirit of his family and of the University of Vermont was, within the limits of that time, "liberal"; and that process, so characteristic of Protestantism and so incomprehensible to the Catholic, whereby intellectual beliefs may change and develop freely without shaking the core of moral conviction, had for him already begun.

I was brought up in a conventionally evangelical atmosphere of the more "liberal" sort; and the struggles that later arose between acceptance of that faith and the discarding of traditional and institutional creeds came from personal experiences and not from the effects of philosophical teaching. . . . While the conflict of traditional religious beliefs with opinions that I could myself honestly entertain was the source of a trying personal crisis, it did not at any time constitute a leading philosophical problem. This might look as if the two things were kept apart; in reality it was due to a feeling that any genuinely sound religious experience could and should adapt itself to whatever beliefs one found oneself intellectually entitled to hold—a half unconscious sense at first, but one which ensuing years have deepened into a fundamental conviction. In consequence, while I have, I hope, a due degree of personal sympathy with individuals who are undergoing the throes of a personal change of attitude, I have not been able to attach much importance to religion as a philosophic problem; for the effect of that attachment seems to be in the end a subordination of candid philosophic thinking to the alleged but factitious needs of some special set of convictions. I have enough faith in the depth of the religious tendencies of men to believe that they will adapt themselves to any required intellectual change, and that it is futile (and likely to be

[1] "From Absolutism to Experimentalism," in *Contemporary American Philosophy*, ed. G.P. Adams and W.P. Montague (New York, 1930), Vol. II, p. 19.

dishonest) to forecast prematurely just what forms the religious interest will take as a final consequence of the great intellectual transformation that is going on. As I have been frequently criticized for undue reticence about the problems of religion, I insert this explanation: it seems to me that the great solicitude of many persons, professing belief in the universality of the need for religion, about the present and future of religion proves that in fact they are moved more by partisan interest in a particular religion than by interest in religious experience.(15, 19)

Mr. Dewey has often remarked, à propos of such critics of his refusal to make a central issue of "religious problems"—critics both clerical and anticlerical—that he managed to "get over" those problems early in life. This has not meant that he conceives himself as having abandoned "religion"; quite the contrary. It means that he long ago arrived at that religious adjustment which has caused his more institutionally-minded fellows greater trouble, and that since it involved moral rather than intellectual commitments it has never given him further intellectual "difficulties." Indeed, he has himself been willing, in private, to claim a fair share of the "Christian spirit"; few would deny that rather ambiguous claim. His more recent concern with making explicit the complete compatibility between the religious values in experience and whatever beliefs may be intellectually warranted is a further expression of this lifelong "fundamental conviction." "A Common Faith," he points out, "was addressed to those who have abandoned supernaturalism, and who on that account are reproached by traditionalists for having turned their backs on everything religious. The book was an attempt to show such persons that they still have within their experience all the elements which give the religious attitude its value." [2]

Mr. Dewey's willingness to sign the Humanist Manifesto in 1933 was thus a matter of basic conviction as well as of good nature; it characteristically led to no association with the Humanist religion.

As to what this religious attitude and its value are, as well as to what forces within religions themselves obstruct and destroy it, Dewey has been clear from those first Hegelian days. It is the sense of being continuous with nature and with our fellows, of a unity and an at-one-ment with all that conditions our surroundings, the active adjustment to our natural and social world that used to be known as "the peace of God that passeth all understanding."

[2] The Philosophy of John Dewey, ed. P.A. Schilpp (Evanston, 1939), p. 597.

There is a composing and harmonizing of the various elements of our being such that, in spite of changes in the special conditions that surround us, these conditions are also arranged, settled, in relation to us. This attitude includes a note of submission. But it is voluntary, not externally imposed. . . . And in calling it voluntary, it is not meant that it depends upon a particular resolve or volition. It is a change *of* will conceived as the organic plenitude of our being, rather than any special change *in* will.[3]

At the midpoint of his career, in 1908, Dewey suggested that the very decay of traditional religious organizations of experience might be fostering this religious attitude.

We may indeed question whether it is true that in any relative sense this is a peculiarly irreligious age. . . . We are still, even those who have nominally surrendered supernatural dogma, largely under the dominion of the ideas of those who have succeeded in identifying religion with the rites, symbols, and emotions associated with these dogmatic beliefs. As we see the latter disappearing, we think we are growing irreligious. For all we know, the integrity of mind which is loosening the hold of these things is potentially much more religious than all that it is displacing. It is increased knowledge of nature which has made supra-nature incredible, or at least difficult of belief. We measure the change from the standpoint of the supranatural and we call it irreligious. Possibly if we measured it from the standpoint of the natural piety it is fostering, the sense of the permanent and inevitable implication of nature and man in a common career and destiny, it would appear as the growth of religion. We take note of the decay of cohesion and influence among the religiously organized bodies of the familiar historic type, and again we conventionally judge religion to be on the decrease. But it may be that their decadence is the fruit of a broader and more catholic principle of human intercourse and association which is too religious to tolerate these pretensions to monopolize truth and to make private possessions of spiritual insight and aspiration.[4]

The roots of Dewey's essentially religious criticism of the actual antireligious consequences of the traditional churches are brought out still more clearly in another passage in the same article, in which he is defending the strong American tradition of purely secular public education—"the subordination of churches to the state, falsely termed the separation of Church and State," he here calls it. His argument, he says, is not directed

[3] *A Common Faith* (New Haven, 1934), pp. 16–17.
[4] *Characters and Events*, ed. J. Ratner (New York, 1929), Vol. II, p. 515.

to those who are already committed to special dogmas of religion which are the monopoly of special ecclesiastic institutions. With respect to them, the fight for special agencies and peculiar materials and methods of education in religion is a natural part of their business: just as, however, it is the business of those who do not believe that religion is a monopoly or a protected industry to contend, in the interest both of education and of religion, for keeping the schools free from what they must regard as a false bias. Those who believe that human nature without special divine assistance is lost, who believe that they have in their charge the special channels through which the needed assistance is conveyed, must, naturally, be strenuous in keeping open these channels to the minds of men. But when the arguments for special religious education at special times and places by special means proceed from philosophic sources—from those whose primary premiss is denial of any breach between man and the world and God, then a sense of unreality comes over me.(505)

The protest against all that is monopolized, protected, private, and special, in the interest of what is public, open, and common, "communicated and tested in ordinary ways," could hardly be put more energetically. This is the common man's religion of common-ness, to which our multiplicity of churches has come to seem antireligious— though he is more apt to put it that denominationalism and the sectarian spirit are "unchristian."

To promote the social unity, therefore, out of which in the end genuine religious unity must grow, Dewey here turns from the divisive and factional churches to the public and common schools, and to the two institutions which are cardinal embodiments of shared and communicated experience. "It is the part of men to labor persistently and patiently for the clarification and development of the positive creed of life implicit in democracy and in science. . . . Those who believe in religion as a natural expression of human experience must devote themselves to the development of the ideas of life which lie implicit in our still new science and our still newer democracy" (507, 516). And these two common and public experiences have remained for Dewey the twin sources of the religious unification of life. Thirty-one years later he could still claim that all he has since written on religion has been "devoted to making explicit the religious values implicit in the spirit of science as undogmatic reverence for truth in whatever form it presents itself, and the religious values implicit in our common life, especially in the moral significance of democracy as a way of living together." [5]

III

Dewey's sense of continuity is not limited to the ties that bind men to their fellows in working and undergoing together. The human communication that can create a community of living takes one beyond mankind to those natural conditions that make it necessary to live together and possible to live together meaningfully and significantly. Men are one with nature, in fruitful as in bitter interaction with its sustaining and imperative forces. Dewey's naturalism, early developed as he pushed the Hegelian unity with society to a Darwinian union with the natural world, is equally the outgrowth of his craving for unification. Man is no weary but unyielding Atlas, sustaining alone the world that his own ideals have fashioned despite the trampling march of unconscious power. If man can perceive and pursue ideals, it is because nature has bestowed on its product the gift of imagination, and itself offers both the suggestions for vision and the media for the shadowing forth. "Nature thus supplies potential material for embodiment of ideals. Nature, if I may use the locution, is idealizable. It lends itself to operations by which it is perfected." [6]

These two unifying ties, the bond with one's fellows and the bond with nature, are alike capable of producing intense religious satisfactions in human experience. Dewey has woven them so closely together, in his imaginative feeling and emotion as well as in his thought, that he never speaks of one without the other: they are for him the two indissolubly united sources of a vital religion that is yet to be. Piety toward nature is as deep-seated for him as spiritual devotion to the community that intelligence is to create. Their objects indeed are to be clearly distinguished, not only to achieve intellectual clarity but still more significantly to intensify religious experience itself. But they are and must be fused in that integration of experience that constitutes its religious quality and function.

Infinite relationships of man with his fellows and with nature already exist. The ideal means a sense of these encompassing continuities with their infinite

[5] Schilpp, *Dewey*, p. 597.
[6] *The Quest for Certainty* (New York, 1929), p. 302.

reach. This meaning even now attaches to present activities because they are set in a whole to which they belong and which belongs to them. Even in the midst of conflict, struggle, and defeat a consciousness is possible of the enduring and comprehending whole. . . . Religion has lost itself in cults, dogmas, and myths. Consequently the office of religion as sense of community and one's place in it has been lost. In effect religion has been distorted into a possession—or burden—of a limited part of human nature, of a limited portion of humanity which finds no way to universalize religion except by imposing its own dogmas and ceremonies upon others; of a limited class within a partial group; priests, saints, a church. Thus other gods have been set up before the one God. Religion as a sense of the whole is the most individualized of all things, the most spontaneous, undefinable and varied. For individuality signifies unique connections in the whole. . . . Every act may carry within itself a consoling and supporting consciousness of the whole to which it belongs and which in some sense belongs to it.[7]

The intellectual recognition that the sources of man's being are to be found in natural processes, and are to be reached by the public and open channels of scientific inquiry, not in some inaccessible and "special" supernatural realm, is the basis of religious values doubly religious because they can be common and shared.

Religious faith which attaches itself to the possibilities of nature and associated living would, with its devotion to the ideal, manifest piety toward the actual. . . . Respect and esteem would be given to that which is the means of realization of possibilities, and to that in which the ideal is embodied if it ever finds embodiment. . . . Nature and society include within themselves projection of ideal possibilities and contain the operations by which they are actualized. Nature may not be worshiped as divine even in the sense of the intellectual love of Spinoza. But nature, including humanity, with all its defects and imperfections, may evoke heartfelt piety as the source of ideals, of possibilities, of aspiration in their behalf, and as the eventual abode of all attained goods and excellencies.[8]

It is a great temptation to quote the most eloquent passage in Dewey's most important book, that in *Experience and Nature* (1925) which begins, on page 419, "Men move between extremes." These paragraphs, a classic example of natural piety, attest that Dewey has been able to find in the perception of man's oneness with nature the sources of as deep and profound a religious feeling as others have gained from more traditional attachments. But the essential point for Dewey is nei-

[7] *Human Nature and Conduct* (New York, 1922), p. 330.
[8] *Quest for Certainty*, p. 306.

ther that natural piety is still open to those who have been led by intellectual reasons to abandon supernaturalism, nor that intellectual integrity demands that abandonment. It is rather that religious values themselves are stultified by the insistence on divorcing man from nature.

A religious attitude would surrender once for all commitment to beliefs about matters of fact, whether physical, social or metaphysical. It would leave such matters to inquirers in other fields. Nor would it substitute in their place fixed beliefs about values, save the one value of the worth of discovering the possibilities of the actual and striving to realize them. . . . An idealism of action that is devoted to creation of a future, instead of staking itself upon propositions about the past, is invincible. The claims of the beautiful to be admired and cherished do not depend upon ability to demonstrate statements about the past history of art. The demand of righteousness for reverence does not depend upon ability to prove the existence of an antecedent Being who is righteous.(304)

IV

When Dewey undertakes to treat the religious aspect of experience directly, in *A Common Faith* (1934), the various strands of his allegiance to community are brought to a focus. Experience becomes religious when all its different possible kinds of common-ness are fused together in a just sense of the common life of the common man in a common world. As he points out in the passage that best expresses the core of his own faith in common-ness,

Any activity pursued in behalf of an ideal end against obstacles and in spite of threats of personal loss because of conviction of its general and enduring value is religious in quality. Many a person, inquirer, artist, philanthropist, citizen, men and women in the humblest walks of life, have achieved, without presumption and without display, such unification of themselves and of their relations to the conditions of existence. . . . If I have said anything about religions and religion that seems harsh, I have said those things because of a firm belief that the claim on the part of religions to possess a monopoly of ideals and of the supernatural means by which alone, it is alleged, they can be furthered, stands in the way of the realization of distinctively religious values inherent in natural experience. . . . The opposition between religious values as I conceive them and religions is not to be bridged. Just because the release of these values is so important, their identification with the creeds and cults of religions must be dissolved.[9]

[9] *Common Faith*, pp. 27–28.

True to his general method, Dewey sets out to locate the distinctively religious character in human experience. Human life is a continuous action and reaction of men with each other and with their world, in the light of the meanings discerned, striven for, and enjoyed. In this unceasing and varied interaction, different phases, types, aspects, and stages can be distinguished. But what is so singled out for attention is not understood unless seen within its setting in the total process of experience. The aspects of experience so distinguished are tendencies of qualities, which can be heightened and lessened in intensity, but could not exist at all in isolation from the rest of experience. Art is one of these qualities which experience can emphasize, religion is another. Both are properly adjectives rather than nouns; they denote ways of experiencing, qualities that can on occasion become central. Art, for example, is the quality of a complete and unified experience, an experience that realizes all the special emphases and partial activities found piecemeal at other times. Religion is likewise a quality that may belong to any type of experience that produces a certain effect upon the self. Just as all experience is to some degree aesthetic in character, and has its aspect of immediate enjoyment or consummation, so any experience can become religious if it has a religious effect upon the experiencer.

Thus Dewey sets out, in this analysis of the intellectual implications of his faith in common-ness, to show that religious qualities, like artistic qualities, are to be found in the ordinary and natural processes of living. Just as science is controlled elaboration of the cognitive side of normal experience, just as art is the intensification of the immediate enjoyment in which every experience culminates, so religion is the unification and direction of the normal striving for the possibilities of action and appreciation. This view necessitates a criticism of those others, overt or implied, which refuse to find such qualities in the natural processes of living, and locate them rather in special experiences or in entities impinging from without, like God. Religious faith is not belief in a supernatural deity, nor in values transcending human life; it is the organized direction of man's life in devotion to the ideal possibilities discerned in imagination. When life is so unified, it is religious in quality. Failure to recognize the natural status of these processes and qualities brings failure to secure all that experience might offer. It leads the artist to aim at partial and incomplete values, the religious man to dispense with those intellectual and practical efforts which would bring new insight and realized ideals. The failure is ultimately in communication: the self does not learn new meanings, it does not use experience to grow and achieve further values.

The major theme of *A Common Faith* is the emancipation of religion from this divorce between man and nature. Experience does display a religious quality: it affords for many some complex of conditions that can bring an adjustment to life, an orientation giving security and peace. This organization of experience is achieved through the imaginative capture of the self by something beyond its own resources. Ideal ends so comprehensive that they unify and focus the entire self are acknowledged to have a rightful claim. The ends of ordinary life are scattered and discordant. When they are harmonized in so inclusive a way that the whole self is integrated in devotion to them, moral and practical action takes on a religious character: one has found a "justifying faith" by which to live. Dewey defines religious faith as "the unification of the self through allegiance to inclusive ideal ends, which imagination presents to us and to which the human will responds as worthy of controlling our desires and choices" (33).

Now when man is separated from nature, this direction from without is attributed to a supernatural source. It then becomes necessary to resort to rationalizing apologetics, with its stultification of intellectual method and integrity. Religious faith is then opposed to the most powerful and promising intellectual current of the day, the method of scientific thinking, and is shaken by every new scientific idea. Those unable to accept supernaturalism are deprived of the religious fruits of the unifying experiences they might enjoy. The support and confidence which have been attributed to God, and which in fact experience stands ready to offer, are then rejected because such a source violates men's intellectual habits. Moreover, when faith in a supernatural God has disappeared, and the power of an inclusive ideal has taken its place, the persisting isolation of man from nature renders that ideal a mere figment without natural roots. The mere humanist, who does not recognize the continuity of human life with nature, is led to an egotistic assertion of human powers, doomed to early disillusionment and defeat. Were men to recognize that the ideal is what natural conditions may become through human action, that nature does support our endeavors and that our success is due to cooperation with its

processes, then natural piety would replace both the assurance that
the ideal already exists in a supernatural realm, and the conviction
that man's aspirations are doomed to be forever unrealized. The religious attitude rests on a just sense of nature as the whole of which
we are parts, and of man's connection with it. To see man's true place
in the universe is to be free alike from the stupefying confidence of the
supernaturalist and the despair or defiance of the atheist.

While Dewey's thought brooks no compromise with supernaturalism, he is still reluctantly willing to use the term "God" to symbol-
ize the union of the ideal with the natural and human forces that make
its realization possible. Ideals have power and efficacy because they
are what the imagination discerns as possible perfectings of what exists. Were they already embodied in existence in a Perfect Being, they
would then cease to be ideals to strive for, besides being involved in
all the dubious web of religious apologetics. But were they not at the
same time actual human goods, experienced in brief moments in fragmentary and partial form; were they not precious values found in the
play of natural and human forces, which intelligent action can hope to
make more abundant and intense, they would have no rightful claim
to direct our lives toward their realization.

"God" as the historic object of religious faith may thus be taken as
denoting in experience both the unity of ideal ends that organizes and
gives direction to human life, and the fact that the natural conditions
of that life are perfectible and "idealizable." What man actually desires
is unified through imaginative realization and projection. But his faith
is directed to no "mere" ideals. It is directed to ideals that are generated and supported by natural and human forces and conditions,
and that human endeavor can in a measure realize. "God" may thus
be taken as meaning, when experience is truly religious, not merely
the highest human ideals, but also the conviction that man, in cooperation with the forces of nature, can work for their realization. "It is this
active relation between ideal and actual to which I would give the
name 'God' " (51). The term, Dewey feels, may well be too bound up
with supernaturalism to serve; he has made it abundantly clear that he
has no sentimental attachment to it. And the misunderstandings he
anticipated have been realized in full measure. But the conviction is
urgently needed that men can hope for some success in their highest
endeavors. It is that conviction, Dewey holds, which all spiritual

religions have really meant by "God"; and under some name that conviction must be recovered today by a humanism that has lost its roots
in nature. By emphasizing these natural roots of ideals that must yet
be realized through human striving, a sense of the partial union of actual with ideal, of a union not mystical but natural and moral, symbolized if men will by "God," will free men from bondage to defiance
or despair.

Practically, this takes Dewey to his prime conviction that it is the
natural values revealed in human intercourse and activity at its most
satisfying that are to be worked for, and that man *can* work for them.
Human experience is in itself potentially "divine": man's natural intelligence and moral power, sufficiently developed and educated, are
the resources for realizing that potentiality. To fall back on the hope
of supernatural aid, though perhaps natural enough in our present
social discontents, is the suicide of the religious function itself. For
Barthian theology or any of its diluted "neo-orthodox" versions, with
their despair of the resources of human nature, and indeed for all
theologies that wait for a revolution in society or an external conversion in man, Dewey has short shrift. It is rather to the passionate faith
in intelligence that we must look to make radical changes in human
relationships.

Such is Dewey's attempt to emancipate the religious quality and
function in experience from its historical connection with supernatural
forces and transcendent values. It is not the negative and reluctant
surrender of precious beliefs which modern ways of thinking have
made it difficult to retain. Dewey is no religious liberal forced to the
gradual abandonment of positions no longer intellectually respectable.
His is rather a positive and aggressive critique of the religious tradition, in the interest not primarily of intellectual values, of theoretical
consistency with scientific beliefs, but of the religious function itself.
The things he wishes to get rid of are not just inessential parts of the
tradition; it is essential to get rid of them if religion is to do its proper
work. They belong, that is, to a competing faith that serves false
gods. In the undogmatic, untheological, and unchurchly religious idealism that is emerging in American life, there are few so emancipated
from the hold of tradition as to see this so clearly as Dewey. Yet he is
surely right in his perception of the underlying drive back of all liberal
religion. The liberal movement has been in truth not an intellectual

but a moral and a religious protest: Dewey's insight makes his religious opposition to "religions" more representative than either he or those he is representing might care to admit.

The specific religious elements to which he is opposed are precisely those themselves in opposition to his religious faith in common-ness, those that interpose a barrier to common experience and public communication

> The objection to supernaturalism is that it stands in the way of an effective realization of the sweep and depth of the implications of natural human relations. . . . . Goods actually experienced in the concrete relations of family, neighborhood, citizenship, pursuit of art and science, are what men actually depend upon for guidance and support, and their reference to a supernatural and other-worldly locus has obscured their real nature and has weakened their force. (80, 71)

> The association of religion with the *supernatural* tends by its own nature to breed the dogmatic and the divisive spirit. . . . For, the greater the insistence by a given church body upon the supernatural, the more insistent is it bound to be upon certain tenets which must be accepted—at the peril of one's immortal soul.[10]

Any method that is not open and public is likewise in effect antireligious.

> Faith in the continued disclosing of truth through directed cooperative human endeavor is more religious in quality than is any faith in a completed revelation. . . . Religions hold that the essential framework is settled in its significant moral features at least, and that new elements that are offered must be judged by conformity to this framework. . . . But faith in the possibilities of continued and rigorous inquiry does not limit access to truth to any channel or scheme of things. It does not first say that truth is universal and then add there is but one road to it. . . . Under existing conditions, the religious function in experience can be emancipated only through surrender of the whole notion of special truths that are religious by their own nature, together with the idea of peculiar avenues of access to such truths.[11]

This protest against what is limited and special extends to that alleged source of religious knowledge advanced by a recent fashion in apologetics, "religious experience."

> The method of intelligence is open and public. The doctrinal method is limited and private. This limitation persists even when knowledge of the truth

---

[10] Schilpp, *Dewey*, p. 595.   [11] *Common Faith*, pp. 26, 33.

that is religious is said to be arrived at by a special mode of experience, that termed "religious." For the latter is assumed to be a very special kind of experience. . . . As a method, it lacks the public character belonging to the method of intelligence. . . . At present there is much talk, especially in liberal circles, of religious experience as vouching for the authenticity of certain beliefs and the desirability of certain practices. . . . It is even asserted that religious experience is the ultimate basis of religion itself. . . . Those who hold to the notion that there is a definite kind of experience which is itself religious, by that very fact make out of it something specific, as a kind of experience that is marked off from experience as aesthetic, scientific, moral, political. . . . But "religious" as a quality of experience signifies something that may belong to all these experiences. It is the polar opposite of some type of experience that can exist by itself. (39, 40, 10)

Mystical experiences indeed occur frequently as normal manifestations. But they are neither a source of knowledge nor in themselves religious in character. They would become so only if they had a religious effect; and with many of the extremely varied types the opposite is notorious.

The conception that mystic experience is a normal mode of religious experience by which we may acquire knowledge of God and divine things is a 19th-century interpretation that has gained vogue in direct ratio to the decline of older methods of religious apologetics. . . . As with every empirical phenomenon, the occurrence of the state called mystical is simply an occasion for inquiry into its mode of causation. There is no more reason for converting the experience itself into an immediate knowledge of its cause than in the case of an experience of lightning or any other natural occurrence. . . . Moreover, when the experience in question does not yield consciousness of the presence of God, in the sense that is alleged to exist, the retort is always at hand that it is not a genuine religious experience. For by definition, only that experience *is* religious which arrives at this particular result. The argument is circular. (37, 40)

Dewey's attack in the name of the religious against whatever is exclusive and uncommon culminates in his charge that the very notion of a particular religion is antireligious. "A body of beliefs and practices that are apart from the common and natural relations of mankind must, in the degree in which it is influential, weaken and sap the force of the possibilities inherent in such relations" (27).

One of the deepest of moral traditions is that which identifies the source of moral evil . . . with pride, and which identifies pride with isolation. . . . The historic isolation of the church from other social institutions is the result of this pride. The isolation, like all denials of interaction and inter-dependence, confines to special channels the power of those who profess special connection with the ideal and spiritual. In condemning other modes of human association to an inferior position and rôle, it breeds irresponsibility in the later. . . . The most corroding form of spiritual pride and isolation di-vides man from man at the foundation of life's activities.[12]

What can be done with the churches? For them as human associa-tions Dewey has only understanding sympathy: it is not the churches he finds to be anti-religious, but only their religion.

The transfer of idealizing imagination, thought and emotion to natural human relations would not signify the destruction of churches that now exist. It would rather offer the means for a recovery of vitality. The fund of human values that are prized and that need to be cherished, values that are satisfied and rectified by *all* human concerns and arrangements, could be celebrated and reinforced, in different ways and with differing symbols, by the chur-ches. In that way the churches would indeed become catholic.[13]

This theme of the proper function of the church as the celebration and reinforcement of catholic human values is one a less protestant critic might well explore.

V

Dewey's *Common Faith* sets out from the conviction that what is genuinely religious in life, once purified of all that has grown up about the idea of the supernatural, will then for the first time be "free to de-velop freely on its own account." He indulges, in fact, in much loose talk about ridding religious experience of "all historic encumbrances," an aim hardly appropriate from one usually so insistent on the conti-nuity of human institutions and cultures. To free the religious attitude from institutional embodiment in any religion sounds suspiciously like freeing art from embodiment in any particular work of art; and the religious man who never goes near a religious institution suggests the musical person who never touches a musical instrument or attends a concert. But the loose and amorphous religious feeling of America is shared by millions with just such a complete indifference to all "insti-tutionalized religion." Whether one welcomes whole-heartedly Dewey's defense of this widespread attitude, or feels rather that here

---

[12] *Quest for Certainty*, pp. 307, 308.   [13] *Common Faith*, p. 82.

he has allowed his personal faith to cut across the main features of his critical philosophy of social experience, will obviously depend on whether or not one shares Dewey's exclusive devotion to the religious values of common-ness. It will doubtless depend also on whether one approaches religion with the attitude of the layman or the professional—and with the latter will belong all those interested in the complicated techniques and mysteries of the religious arts.

One fact at least is clear. Dewey has made a deliberate effort to disentangle religious feeling and sentiment from any particular kind of institutionalized behavior. He has tried to make a fresh start and wipe the slate clean, to isolate an invariant "religious attitude." But in thus seeking the universal through cutting loose from the historical relativities of any particular religious tradition, he has bound himself all the more closely to the relativities of his own culture. He has sought the religious function in general; and he emerges as the spokesman of the habits of mind of the liberal American Protestant Christian of our generation. Could any other possibly have found the essence of religion to be a personal attitude?

The history of Protestantism from Luther down has been a succession of religious protests, by the layman and on behalf of his interest in the ordinary pursuits of life, against a professional priesthood with its claims and orthodoxies. In our day popular Protestantism has finally achieved the priesthood of all unbelievers; and this completely laicized religion, this quintessence of Protestantism, is Dewey's faith in common-ness. By emancipating itself from the past, from the "outgrown traits of traditional religions," it has shut the door to that emancipation from the provincialism of the present, from the insistence of the moment, which a great and catholic religious tradition still has the power to offer to him who seeks. Yet in its own way Dewey's faith brings its own deliverance from a too intense preoccupation with the passing present.

With responsibility for the intelligent determination of particular acts may go a joyful emancipation from the burden for responsibility for the whole which sustains them, giving them their final outcome and quality. There is a conceit fostered by perversion of religion which assimilates the universe to our personal desires; but there is also a conceit of carrying the load of the universe from which religion liberates us. Within the flickering inconsequential acts of separate selves dwells a sense of the whole which claims and dignifies them.

In its presence we put off mortality and live in the universal. The life of the community in which we live and have our being is the fit symbol of this relationship. The acts in which we express our perception of the ties which bind us to others are its only rites and ceremonies.[14]

But Dewey is giving voice to more than the permeating Protestantism of American life: one suspects the influence of the temperamental and radical Protestantism of William James and his psychologist followers. This is most apparent when Dewey touches on the nature of religion in *A Common Faith*. James's incorrigible love of variety and of exciting new types of religious consciousness could not indeed deflect Dewey's drive toward unification and common-ness. But the *Varieties* do seem to have left a distorting stamp on Dewey's approach to a theory of religion, when compared with his otherwise consistent treatment of cultural institutions. Here is not only much of James's emphasis on the immediate and personal aspects of religious experience, and much of James's impatience with its social and institutional modes of practice. There is a rather surprising individualism in the whole approach of the Terry lectures. Dewey not only postpones to the last a consideration of religion "in its social connections," though as against James he admits they come first and are of greater importance. Where James relegates the churches to a minor place in his lecture on "Other Characteristics," Dewey speaks of them as "the human abode of the religious function." One does not recall a separate treatment of the "human abode" of the cognitive or the aesthetic function. One finds Dewey saying: "The doctrinal or intellectual apparatus and the institutional accretions that grow up are, in a strict sense, adventitious to the intrinsic quality of such experiences. For they are affairs of the traditions of the culture with which individuals are inoculated." And one can only rub one's eyes. One finds the religious function focused on "changes in ourselves," changes of attitude, of will, with no reference to the communication of experience. One encounters more than a trace of James's primary interest in religion as a therapy for sick souls, and of his evangelical tendency to make religious conversion central. One notes that whereas elsewhere Dewey always brings religion into close connection with art and poetry, here the religious quality has lost touch with the aesthetic, and has cast in

[14] *Human Nature and Conduct*, p. 331.

its lot with an ethical function alone. A moral faith is to be set free from intellectual commitments; what happens to the whole aesthetic side of religion, the sheer enjoyment of the practice of the cult, the wealth of varied immediate satisfactions enshrined in religious activities, Dewey dismisses as summarily though not so disdainfully as James.

The doubts thus suggested come to a head in Dewey's attempts to define *the* function any experience must perform if it is to produce a religious effect. He wavers between taking *the* religious function as the setting up of any tolerable working *modus vivendi* with specific social and natural conditions, and taking it as the complete unification of the whole self by ends so inclusive that they are acknowledged as supreme over conduct. In the former case, such "religious" effects are indeed common enough, but "the religious" seems then to have lost any distinctive meaning. In the latter, such religious effects are so far from common that it is doubtful whether any human experience could be described in Dewey's terms. This sounds far more like the Idea of the Good or Green's Ideal Self than like any possibility of human living. One begins to wonder whether at this point Mr. Dewey may not have gone off the deep end, and sunk in the sea of psychological apologetics for a particular religion. But he comes up smiling after a page or two, to tell us reassuringly that "whatever introduces genuine perspective is religious," and that "any activity pursued in behalf of an ideal end is religious in quality."

Whatever its incidental illumination, it cannot be said that this attempt to define *the* religious quality of experience proves ultimately more successful than other attempts to isolate *the* religious experience itself. It is just as special and private, though the monopoly on its channels has been broken. There seems little point in calling any fairly satisfactory adjustment in life "religious"; certainly for the vast majority that is achieved through humbler and more common means than "inclusive ideal ends." When so achieved, adjustment, like any other experience, including extreme maladjustment, can receive expression in religious activities, practices, and techniques. But these practices will be found, one suspects, to be the institutionalized habits of some particular religious tradition, whether ecclesiastical or no.

One wonders whether it might not be more profitable to take religion not as an adjective, a quality and attitude of personal experience, but as an adverb, a way of acting overtly and publicly in communication with one's fellows. This might well make it more difficult to identify the deeply "religious" man who never does anything the mores of his culture would define as acting religiously. But it would really fit in rather better with Dewey's American religion of cooperation and shared experience, and with his faith in intelligent action, than does his "unification of the self," which he seems to have inherited from James's wholly individualistic and psychological interests, with a strong dash of T.H. Green. As a contribution to an understanding of religion as a cardinal fact in human experience and culture, Dewey's distinction between "religions" and "the religious" seems not particularly illuminating. Taken, however, in the context in which he introduces it, as a means of setting his own religion of common-ness off rather sharply from the rival traditional religions, it is useful enough. What is most dubious is the narrowness and the intensity which he at times, in his formal definitions especially, ascribes to a single religious function.

And this applies also to his view of the place of faith in religion. One does not usually think of Dewey as a philosopher of faith. What he has long been saying about religion, as well as the great bulk of what he says in his Terry lectures, seems to fall more naturally under the heads of piety and spirituality, of respect for nature and devotion to her possibilities. The sudden appearance in his argument of a single faith, in ideal ends so all-inclusive that they effect a generic and enduring change of the "organic plenitude of our being" and vanquish our active nature, without our conscious deliberation and purpose, in subjection to something so supreme over conduct that it completely unifies the self in a way that neither thought nor practical activity can attain—such a faith is hardly what we might have expected from Mr. Dewey. Nor is it evident, as we survey the present scene, that the chief need of the world is for a passionately unifying faith. Such faiths, alas, it has found in plenty, though scarcely the faith in intelligence Dewey would like to see common. One wonders whether in the desire to rid faith of all theological content he has not taken refuge a little too uncritically in a supreme and inclusive moral conviction. Mr. Dewey's sturdy defense of the layman in religion seems here to have succumbed to the blandishments of the professionals. The latter, especially if they share the vision of the prophet rather than the wisdom of the priest—and what Protestant preacher does not fancy himself a prophet?—are naturally convinced that the faith they proclaim must permeate and control the whole of life. The healthy-minded layman likes to hear this once a week, and believes it when not too busy to remember. How could such a faith ever be shared by the common man?

It would be untrue to suggest that the kind of faith Dewey describes in so sweeping terms is always a religious disease, as in James's clinical cases. But it is surely symptomatic of a sick soul or a sick nation, at best of one in partial recovery. Mr. Dewey was himself impressed, in 1928, by the "moving religious quality" of Communism in Russia, and its "living religious faith in human possibilities." He has since grown somewhat less enthusiastic about the unifying function of this particular inclusive ideal. But it is after all hard to see how any total faith could fail to be divisive and sectarian in effect, or how any ideal end erected into supremacy over conduct could avoid conflict with the religion of common-ness and shared experience. Certainly under the dubious overlordship of a consuming faith the common and ordinary relations of men stand little chance. Such a faith would be quite literally, in any operational sense, supranatural.

This dubious faith would be hard indeed to reconcile with the rest of Mr. Dewey's religion or philosophy. Fortunately, there is no real need to resort here to desperate apologetics, for he gives no evidence that he takes very seriously what he seems to be saying about it. His own religiously moving ideals are quite free from danger. The attitude he advocates would have no fixed values "save the one value of the worth of discovering the possibilities of the actual and striving to realize them." And the one faith he would like to see become religious in quality is the faith in a forceful and passionate intelligence.

Indeed, one is tempted to supplement the surprising things Dewey is led to say about faith in his Terry lectures with what he suggests elsewhere, and has recently made so clear in his *Freedom and Culture*. The faith that will unite men in cooperative action is a faith in means and methods. Devotion to certain common methods we can hope to make common among common men. We need imaginative visions such as the artists and prophets of the great religious traditions have provided, though they have had no monopoly on vision. But visions are to be seen and used for their clarification of human experience;

they are the last thing in the world to have faith in. Faith belongs rather to human methods and instrumentalities. And as Mr. Dewey has taught us, it should go out above all to the chief means in our power, the method of intelligence. We need visions of God, as many as we can get and share. But the faith that will bind us together in enduring communion, the faith that will transform our common plight into a community of effort, is the faith in the powers of men, of common men. Such a faith in the only instrument by which the community we behold in imagination can be approached is in fact widely shared by Americans. But in his religious devotion to the possibilities of such a community of shared experience, John Dewey is surely unique.

PART FOUR

Philosophy and History

II

Cassirer's Theory of History as Illustrated in His Treatment of Renaissance Thought

Die Aufgabe der Geschichte besteht nicht lediglich darin, dass sie uns vergangenes Sein und Leben kennen lehrt, sondern dass sie es uns deuten lehrt. . . . Was uns tatsächlich von der Vergangenheit aufbewahrt ist, sinde bestimmte historische Denkmäler: "Monumente" in Wort und Schrift, in Bild und Erz. Zur Geschichte wird dies für uns erst, indem wir in diesen Monumenten Symbole sehen, an denen wir bestimmte Lebensformen nicht nur zu erkennen sondern kraft deren wir sie für uns wiederherzustellen vermögen.
— *Zur Logik der Kulturwissenschaften*, pp. 85, 86

IN THE WORK of Ernst Cassirer, historical and systematic studies were not only carried on side by side, they were woven together and used to illuminate each other. From the outset he brought his great gifts for historical interpretation to bear on strengthening and extending the philosophy of humanism he found in Kant. The autonomy of reason, the creativity of the human spirit, *der Wille zur Gestaltung*—this was his central vision. It gave him a consuming interest in all the products of the human mind and in the processes by which they have been created—in what he came to call "the universe of symbols." "History as well as poetry is an organon of our self-knowledge, an indispensable instrument for building up our human universe." [1] The autonomy of thought was the lesson he learned from history; it was also the principle of interpretation he brought to the past to make it speak to us.

Originally published in *The Philosophy of Ernst Cassirer*, ed. P.A. Schilpp. The Library of Living Philosophers (Evanston, Illinois: Northwestern University Press, 1949; copyright © 1949 by The Library of Living Philosophers, Inc.), pp. 689–718. Reprinted by permission of Open Court Publishing Co.
[1] *An Essay on Man* (New Haven, 1944), p. 206.

Hence his special interest and love went out to those periods in the past when men were most keenly aware of their own productive powers and responsibility—to those periods in which a creative humanism was most alive, and was forging its weapons. Closest to his heart was the great humanistic movement in the classic literature and philosophy of eighteenth-century Germany. In Goethe and in Kant he found the culmination at once of an emancipated imagination and an autonomous reason; here poetry, science, and philosophy had at last reached maturity and begun to realize their *"unendliche Aufgabe."* Dear also was the Greek humanism of antiquity, above all of Plato, which classic German humanism had used as an instrument to build its own human universe. And dear was the emancipating thought of that Renaissance which had earlier turned to antiquity to win its liberation from the theocentric world of the Middle Ages, and to create its own *"freies weltliches Bildungsideal."* [2]

All three of these creative humanistic movements of the past, Cassirer held, can furnish inspiration and sources of power for creating further forms of culture in the future. When by careful historical study we have learned to understand their language, they can free us both from the optimism of a Hegel and from the fatalistic pessimism of a Spengler. Once we have achieved "a humanistic foundation for culture," we shall find that "action once more has free scope to decide by its own power and on its own responsibility, and it knows that the direction and future of culture will depend on the way it decides." [3]

"A humanistic foundation for culture"—thus Cassirer had come to see his task. How then can we explain the central role he always gave to natural science in human thought and in his historical studies? How can we reconcile his humanism with his major contribution to the history of philosophy, his making the history of scientific thought an integral part of it? How was it that Cassirer the humanist became one of the outstanding historians of science of our times?

This seems a paradox only so long as we remain with the conventional opposition between the humanist and the scientist. As William James pointed out, "You can give humanistic value to almost anything

---

[2] *Freiheit und Form: Studien zur deutschen Geistesgeschichte* (Berlin, 1916), p. 3.
[3] "Naturalistiche und humanistische Begründung der Kulturphilosophie," Götegorgs Kung. Vetenskaps- och Vitterhets—Samhälles Handlinger. Femte Földen, Ser. A, Band 7, No. 3 (1939), p. 28.

by teaching it historically. Geology, economics, mechanics are humanities when taught with reference to the successive achievements of the geniuses to which these sciences owe their being." Natural science Cassirer always looked upon as the highest and most characteristic expression of the powers of the human mind. Even when as a young student he was most under the spell of Kant's scientific interests, with his teacher Hermann Cohen he emphasized this humanistic import of the exact sciences. Mathematics and mathematical physics were always for him great creative enterprises of the human spirit, forms of Socratic self-knowledge. In analysing precisely the concepts and methods by which men have constructed their natural science, we are really analysing the nature of man himself. Hence from his earliest work on Leibniz down to the penetrating studies he wrote in Sweden and in this country, the history of natural science, the meaning and interpretation of its epoch-making creative achievements, formed the core of his investigation of the nature of man.

We have only to consider his interpretation of the humanistic movement of the Renaissance. Of his favorite historical periods, this is the one in which science is conventionally held to have played the most minor role. From Burckhardt down, the controlling interests of the Renaissance have been thought to be irrelevant to, if not actually opposed to the development of natural science. Historians of science, like Lynn Thorndike, have in turn even questioned the existence of any significant "Renaissance." [4] But for Cassirer, the "discovery of the individual," that humanistic task of Renaissance thought, "as the Renaissance pursued it in poetry, in the plastic arts, in religious and political life, found its philosophical conclusion and its philosophical justification" in the scientific achievement of Galileo and Descartes. [5]

But highly as Cassirer esteemed man's self-expression through natural science, the Kantian limitation of truth to mathematical physics was from the beginning far too narrow for him. As early as the *Substanzbegriff* in 1910, he attempted a further analysis of the concepts and methods of chemistry. More recently he did the same for biology. [6] But his outstanding theoretical achievement was to carry

---

[4] "Renaissance or Prenaissance?" *Journal of the History of Ideas,* IV (1943), pp. 65–74.

[5] "Descartes' Wahrheitsbegriff," *Theoria,* Vol. III (Gothenburg, 1937), p. 176.

[6] *Zur Logik der Kulturwissenschaften* (Gothenburg, 1942), pp. 100–4; see *The Problem of Knowledge: Philosophy, Science, and History Since Hegel* (New Haven, 1950).

through a similar methodological analysis of all those other "symbolic forms" which man makes and which make man known to himself. An analysis of the "logic of the cultural sciences"—of the categories and concepts, the methods and notions of truth and of objectivity by which men interpret these symbolic expressions of their life—came more and more to occupy the center of his attention. Only by sharpening these tools of interpretation can we make a knowledge of what man has created in his culture in the past into a genuine "humanistic foundation for the culture" of the future.[7]

Cassirer saw the "cultural sciences" as embracing primarily linguistics, the sciences of art, and the sciences of religion. And with them belongs history, so fundamental a part of them all. Cassirer did not attempt to formulate with precision the distinctive concepts and methods of historical investigation and interpretation until the latter part of his life. He then developed his analysis in critical opposition to most of the theories of history of the last generation in Germany, and against the background of his general philosophy of symbolic forms. But his thought is also obviously his own aims and procedures come to critical self-awareness; he tested other views by what he had already learned during his own practice as an intellectual historian. With a thinker so conscious of method as Cassirer, it is doubly important to start any examination of his actual historical work from his own statement of his theoretical views as to the nature and procedure of the historian's enterprise. "Nobody," he says, "could ever attempt to write a history of mathematics or philosophy without having a clear insight into the systematic problems of the two sciences. The facts of the philosophical past, the doctrines and systems of the great thinkers, are meaningless without an interpretation." [8] Likewise, no one can hope to understand Cassirer's historical practice without a knowledge of what he conceives to be the questions and problems the historian is trying to answer.

Consequently, the best way to understand what Cassirer has done as an historian is in terms of his own analysis of the historian's aim. This makes clear not only why he has proceeded as he has; it answers the questions as to why he has not done other things, why he has left out what many other intellectual historians would want to include,

---

[7] See *Logik der Kulturwissenschaften.*   [8] *Essay on Man*, p. 179.

and minimized what they would make central. We shall start, therefore, with a statement of Cassirer's analysis of history.

I

Cassirer belongs with those who find a sharp difference between natural science and history. Physical facts are not like historical facts, though neither are brute, "hard" data—both depend on theoretical construction, and their objectivity is established only by a complicated process of judgment. Physical facts are determined by observation and experiment; they become part of the physical order only if we can describe them in mathematical language. "A phenomenon which cannot be so described, which is not reducible to a process of measurement, is not a part of our physical world" (174). But historical facts are not established by observation and experiment, nor are they measured and expressed in mathematical terms. They have to be given "a new ideal existence." "Ideal reconstruction, not empirical observation, is the first step in historical knowledge" (*Ibid.*). A scientific fact is always the answer to a question; the object is always there to be questioned. But the historian's questions cannot be directed immediately toward the past he is trying to understand; they must be addressed rather to documents or monuments. His data, indeed, are not things or events, but symbols with a meaning; he confronts a world of symbols to be interpreted. The task of the historian is thus not the mathematical expression of observed events, but the interpretation of symbols.

Cassirer rejects, however, those distinctions between natural science and historical knowledge that have been most popular in recent discussions of historical knowledge and historical truth, especially in Germany. History has no distinctive "logic" of its own. Logic is one because truth is one. In his quest of truth the historian is bound to the same formal rules as the scientist. In his modes of reasoning and arguing, in his inductive inferences, in his investigation of causes, he obeys the same general laws of thought as a physicist or a biologist. So far as these fundamental theoretical activities of the human mind are concerned, we can make no discrimination between the different fields of knowledge. . . . Historical and scientific thought are distinguishable not by their logical form but by their objectives and subject matter. (175, 176)

But again, the difference does not lie in the fact that the objects of historical knowledge are past. Science too is concerned with the past;

the astronomer, the geologist, the paleontologist all succeed in disclos-
ing a former state of the physical world. Nor does the difference consist in the historian's concern with individuals—the view of Windelband and Rickert, who held that science aims at general laws and
universals, history at unique events and particulars.

It is not possible to separate the two moments of universality and particularity
in this abstract and artificial way. A judgment is always the synthetic unity of
both moments; it contains an element of universality and particularity. These
elements are not mutually opposed; they imply and interpenetrate one another. 'Universality' is not a term which designates a certain field of thought;
it is an expression of the very character, of the function of thought. Thought
is always universal. (186)

On the other hand, many natural sciences, like geology, determine
concrete and unique events. Thus, in distinguishing history from natural science, Cassirer avoids many of the theoretical difficulties of
those who have sharply divided the two realms. Above all, he does
not rule scientific procedures out of the historian's mind, but makes
them necessary if not sufficient conditions.

The real difference, Cassirer concludes, is that the historian's object
is human life and human culture.

History can make use of scientific methods, but it cannot restrict itself only to
the data available by these methods. No object whatever is exempt from the
laws of nature. Historical objects have no separate and self-contained reality;
they are embodied in physical objects. But in spite of this embodiment they
belong, so to speak, to a higher dimension. (176)

The historian must use the concepts of science in reconstructing the
past from its present traces, just like the geologist. But "to this actual,
empirical reconstruction history adds a symbolic reconstruction"
(177). Its documents are not dead remnants of the past but living mes-
sages from it to us. The historian must make us understand their language. Not the logical structure of historical thought, but this special
task of "interpretation," is his distinguishing mark.

What the historian is in search of is the materialization of the spirit of a
former age. He detects the same spirit in laws and statutes, in charters and
bills of right, in social institutions and political constitutions, in religious rites
and ceremonies. To the true historian such material is not petrified fact but
living form. History is the attempt to fuse together all these *disjecta membra*,
the scattered limbs of the past and to synthesize them and mold them into
new shape. (*Ibid.*)

The historian thus aims at a "palingenesis," a rebirth of the past. "An understanding of human life is the general theme and ultimate aim of historical knowledge. In history we regard all the works of man, and all his deeds, as precipitates of his life; and we wish to reconstitute them into this original state, we wish to understand and feel the life from which they are derived" (178, 184). All human works are forever in danger of losing their meaning. "Their reality is symbolic, not physical; and such reality never ceases to require interpretation and reinterpretation. . . . In order to possess the world of culture we must incessantly reconquer it by historical recollection. But recollection does not mean merely the act of reproduction. It is a new intellectual synthesis—a constructive act" (185).

The historian, consequently, is a kind of "retrospective prophet." He interprets the *meaning* of the past; and the category of meaning is not to be reduced to the category of being. It is, in fact, an *Urphänomen*, in Goethe's sense; its "origin" is an insoluble question. It is a kind of "mutation" in evolutionary development that must be accepted with natural piety.[9] "If we seek a general heading under which we are to subsume historical knowledge we may describe it not as a branch of physics but as a branch of semantics. The rules of semantics, not the laws of nature, are the general principles of historical thought. History is included in the field of hermeneutics, not in that of natural science."[10]

In this work of historical interpretation of the meaning of the past, the historian must take his point of departure from his own times. "He cannot go beyond the conditions of his present experience. Historical knowledge is the answer to definite questions, an answer which must be given by the past; but the questions themselves are put and dictated by the present—by our present intellectual interests and our present moral and social needs" (178). The questions we put to past thinkers are determined by our understanding of our own problems. Hence the need for continual reinterpretation. "As soon as we have reached a new center and a new line of vision in our own thought we must revise our judgments."

We have a Stoic, a sceptic, a mystic, a rationalistic, and a romantic Socrates. They are entirely dissimilar. Nevertheless they are not untrue; each of them gives us a new aspect, a characteristic perspective of the historical Socrates

---

[9] *Logik der Kulturwissenschaften*, pp. 109–12.   [10] *Essay on Man*, p. 195.

and his intellectual and moral physiognomy. . . . We have a mystic Plato, the Plato of neo-Platonism; a Christian Plato, the Plato of Augustine and Marsilio Ficino; a rationalistic Plato, the Plato of Moses Mendelssohn; and a few decades ago we were offered a Kantian Plato. We may smile at all these different interpretations. . . . They have all in their measure contributed to an understanding and to a systematic valuation of Plato's work. Each has insisted on a certain aspect which is contained in this work. (180)

When we turn from the history of ideas to "real" history—to the history of man and human actions, the same holds true. In political history we wish to understand not only the actions but the actors. "Our judgment of the course of political events depends upon our conception of the men who were engaged in them. As soon as we see these individual men in a new light we have to alter our ideas of these events" (181). Hence what Cassirer is emphasizing is a *personal* interpretation of history, in which the key is in the last analysis the *personality* and character of outstanding men. And history is for him "personal" in a double sense. Not only does the historian look for "a human and cultural life—a life of actions and passions, of questions and answers, of tensions and solutions." He must also give a "personal" interpretation of these other personalities, a "personal truth."

He infuses into his concepts and words his own inner feelings and thus gives them a new sound and a new color—the color of personal life. . . . If I put out the light of my own personal experience I cannot see and I cannot judge of the experience of others. Without a rich personal experience in the field of art no one can write a history of art; no one but a systematic thinker can give us a history of philosophy. (187)

Cassirer cites Ranke as his model—not the Ranke of the familiar precept of impersonality, but the Ranke who actually wrote history with a universal "personal" sympathy—a sympathy that was intellectual and imaginative, not emotional.

The procedure of the historian, therefore, is that of the interpreter of another human personality. Thus, to understand Cicero's role in the events in which he took part, and to understand those events themselves, we must first of all understand his personality and character.

To this end some symbolic interpretation is required. I must not only study his orations or his philosophical writings; I must read his letters to his daughter Tullia and his intimate friends; I must have a feeling for the charms and defects of his personal style. Only by taking all this circumstantial evidence together can I arrive at a true picture of Cicero and his role in the political life of Rome. Unless the historian remains a mere annalist, unless he contents himself with a chronological narration of events, he must always perform this very difficult task; he must detect the unity behind innumerable and often contradictory utterances of a historical character. (182)

In this delicate task he must be selective; but not necessarily of those events which have had important practical consequences, as Eduard Meyer held; he will single out those acts or remarks which are "characteristic," whose importance lies not in their consequences but in their semantic meaning, as "symbols" of characters and events.

The true historian must thus be not only a trained scientific investigator, he must be an artist as well.

But even though we cannot deny that every great historical work contains and implies an artistic element, it does not thereby become a work of fiction. In his quest for truth the historian is bound by the same strict rules as the scientist. He has to utilize all the methods of empirical investigation. He has to collect all the available evidence and to compare and criticize all his sources. He is not permitted to forget or neglect any important fact. Nevertheless, the last and decisive act is always an act of the productive imagination. (204)

I well remember a conversation with Cassirer, in which I was trying to establish some continuity between the procedures of the scientist—whom I do not take in strictly Kantian terms as the mathematical physicist alone—and of the historian. He admitted that the closest parallel in natural science to what the historian has to do is the physician's diagnosis of the ailment of his patient, in which all his scientific knowledge is brought to bear upon a particular case. But he went on to insist that the historian must proceed always like the biographer of a man. He must gather together all his evidence—evidence which is "symbolic" of the character of the man he is considering— and then try to find that unifying focus or "center" from which all the manifestations of that character can be understood—what he is at bottom trying to do. This is of course to try to interpret a thinker in terms of his central problem—in terms, as Ebbinghaus put it, of *"was er eigentlich will."* This seems, indeed, the height of wisdom in interpreting the thought of any individual. But it is significant that Cassirer used this example as the way to interpret all history. It illustrates what I have called his "personal" view of the historian's enterprise;

and it throws a flood of light on what he does not do in his historical studies—on his complete indifference to any economic interpretation of intellectual history, for example.

Cassirer's analysis of the aim and function of the historian is well summed up in the following passage from *Zur Logik der Kulturwissenschaften*:

> The task of history does not consist merely in making us *acquainted with* past existence and life, but in showing us how to *interpret its meaning*. All mere knowledge of the past would remain for us a "dead picture on a board" if no other powers than those of the reproductive memory were involved. What memory preserves of facts and events becomes historical recollection only when we can relate it to our inner experience and transform it into such experience. Ranke said that the real task of the historian consists in describing "wie es eigentlich gewesen." But even if we accept this statement, it is still true that what has been, when it comes into the perspective of history, finds there a new meaning. History is not simply chronology, and historical time is not objective physical time. The past is not over for the historian in the same sense as for the investigator of nature; it possesses and retains a present of its own. The geologist may report about a past form of the earth; the paleontologist may tell us of extinct organic forms. All this "existed" at one time, and cannot be renewed in its existence and actual character. History, however, never tries to set before us mere past existence; it tries to show us how to grasp a past life. The content of this life it cannot renew; but it tries to preserve its pure form. The wealth of different concepts of form and of style which the cultural sciences have worked out serves in the last analysis a single end: only through them all is the rebirth, the "palingenesis" of culture possible. What is actually preserved for us from the past are particular historical monuments: "monuments" in word and writing, in picture and in bronze. This does not become history for us until in these monuments we see symbols, through which we can not only recognize definite forms of life, but by virtue of which we can restore them for ourselves.[11]

II

This is Cassirer's statement of the fundamentally humanistic task of the historian. By entering into the spirit of former ages, he can reveal man to himself, and in so doing enlarge man's imaginative sympathies beyond the narrow limits of the present cultural expressions of what man is.

Like language or art, history is fundamentally anthropomorphic. . . . History is not knowledge of external facts or events; it is a form of self-

---

[11] *Logik der Kulturwissenschaften*, p. 85.

knowledge. . . . In history man constantly returns to himself; he attempts to recollect and actualize the whole of his past experience. But the historical self is not a mere individual self. It is anthropomorphic but it is not egocentric. Stated in the form of a paradox, we may say that history strives after an 'objective anthropomorphism.' By making us cognizant of the polymorphism of human existence, it frees us from the freaks and prejudices of a special and single moment. It is this enrichment and enlargement, not the effacement, of the self, of our knowing and feeling ego, which is the aim of historical knowledge.[12]

With this statement of a humanistic historical enterprise, of its emancipating function in liberating us from the provincialism of the present, and of the imaginative enrichment and enhancement it can bring, no sensitive man could quarrel. Nor could the methodologist seriously doubt that Cassirer's procedure is appropriate to this goal of his. Not even the embattled proponent of the unity of intellectual method could take real issue with that added "dimension" which Cassirer finds in history, or with the "artistic element," the final work of the "productive imagination," which he sees it demanding. Cassirer has no scorn for "mere" science. He is only too anxious to make use of all the help which "scientific method" can furnish.

Philosophic reflection upon the fact of history and upon the ways in which it can be construed and understood might, indeed, point out that these ways are many and diverse. Cassirer's humanistic enterprise is but one of many types of historical investigation, each of which has its own function and validity. Like most of those who have given thoughtful consideration to historical goals and methods, especially if they have been men who have themselves long and fruitfully pursued the interpretation of the meaning of the past, Cassirer is too ready to set up his own distinctive conceptions and working principles as the sufficient model for every approach to the past. But it is not only human existence that exhibits a "polymorphism"; so likewise does men's concern with their living past. It is doubtless a "prejudice of the moment" to identify one's own historical enterprise with the task of "history" in general. In the historian's house are many mansions; and a comprehensive analysis of the ways in which history may be understood, and in which that understanding may illuminate human life today, would have to examine the specific functions and contributions of each. That task Cassirer has not attempted.

[12] *Essay on Man*, p. 191.

What the historian, even the intellectual historian, is likely to find most questionable in Cassirer's "symbolic reconstruction" of the spirit of past ages in terms of the achievement of great men, is his almost total lack of concern with any question of historical causation. Men and ages in the past thought differently from each other, and from ourselves; to realize this elementary fact is an enhancement of our knowledge of man. But no mention is made that it might be a valid problem for historical investigation to ask why; there is not even a reasoned defense of a negative position on causation in history, as in theories like those of Croce or Collingwood. So far as Cassirer's analysis goes, thought might well be operating in a vacuum. The Hegelian cast of the passage quoted above about the nonindividual self actualizing the whole of its past experience is obvious. But there is not even the Hegelian concern with the "immanent" development of thought.[13] All those questions which are certainly central in the "spirit" of our own age, as to the "dynamics" in history, are simply omitted. There is no place at which even to raise the problem of a possible influence of technological or economic factors in determining the issues which confront thinkers. It is significant that in criticising historical determinism, Cassirer examines three forms: the physicalistic determinism of the French positivists, the psychologistic determinism of Spengler, and the metaphysical determinism of Hegel.[14] Economic determinism is not mentioned. Indeed, it is hard to ascertain whether the social sciences and their subject matters enter into Cassirer's thought at all. Certainly neither as symbolic forms nor as heuristic principles do they figure in his historical enterprise, nor are they ever mentioned as "*Kulturwissenschaften.*"

Cassirer, however, is surely right in pointing out that the questions the historian puts to the past are the questions that are central in his own philosophic understanding of the world. As he maintains, only a philosopher can write a significant history of philosophy; and what he

[13] Cf., however, *Essay on Man*, p. 180: "The history of philosophy shows us very clearly that the full determination of a concept is very rarely the work of that thinker who first introduced that concept. For a philosophical concept is, generally speaking, rather a problem than the solution of a problem—and the full significance of this problem cannot be understood so long as it is still in its first implicit state. It must become explicit in order to be comprehended in its true meaning, and this transition from an implicit to an explicit state is the work of the future."

[14] "Naturalistische und humanistische Begründung," pp. 12–14.

finds significant in past philosophies will depend on his own. Hence
Cassirer's statement of his conception of the task of the historian is so
intimately bound up with his systematic philosophy of symbolic
forms that a searching examination would have to come to grips with
that philosophy. This is not the place for such an undertaking. We
can only be grateful that any set of leading principles, when applied
by a mind with a scholar's equipment and scrupulous conscience before facts, is bound to shed a great light and reveal new relations and
meanings. It is not necessary to share Cassirer's extension of the
Kantian approach in order to appreciate his actual historical achievement.

III

But it is necessary to understand Cassirer's approach and his theory
of history in order to understand why that achievement is what it is.
Whatever our judgment of the importance of his humanistic conception of history, or of the validity of the philosophy on which it ultimately depends, it remains true that that conception does state the
aim and method he himelf pursued. It makes clear why he devoted
himself with such success to the particular historical task he undertook, and why he set about that task in the particular way he did. It
also makes clear the reasons for the self-imposed limitations of his historical work—why he disregarded the problems he did, and why he
gives no answer to many questions that have interested other intellectual historians. If his theory of history grew out of his own practice,
that practice in turn can be taken to illustrate the theory; and the
theory will furnish his own apologia, his own answer to the criticisms
that have been directed against the practice. I wish, therefore, to turn
now to an examination of Cassirer's treatment of the Renaissance, to
show how that treatment illuminates his theory and how it can be understood in terms of his systematic views.

As an historical interpreter, a "retrospective prophet," Cassirer
aimed to recreate the past, to recapture the spirit of a former age and
to understand and feel it from within. In the Renaissance as a whole,
or in any of the figures who represented its different facets, he was
consequently concerned to grasp what was most distinctive and original, not what was merely traditional and received as a legacy. In his
studies there abound phrases like "a wholly new feeling," "a com-

pletely different conception." The Middle Ages serve as the foil, the contrast; they have for him little existence in their own right as themselves expressions of the human spirit and its achievements. [15]

Cassirer was not a medievalist, and when he first embarked on his pioneer studies of Renaissance thought the later Middle Ages were, as he has pointed out, largely a *terra incognita*. [16] That a closer first-hand acquaintance with the complex currents of fourteenth- and fifteenth-century thought—an acquaintance won only during the past generation, and still in great need of enlargement—would have led to some modification of his interpretation of Renaissance figures, especially of the scientists, is certainly true. But it is doubtful whether that knowledge would have altered fundamentally his judgments. For the tracing of continuities and antecedents played a very minor part in his own historical enterprise. What interested him was rather the other side of history's shield, its novelties and new achievements; this concern is implicit in his whole enterprise of "palingenesis." He had a genius for seizing on what was genuinely original in a thinker, and lifting it out of its context in what was merely traditional. The traditional he freely

[15] For Cassirer, the fundamental trait of medieval thought, which sets it off sharply from that of the Renaissance, is its subjection of reason to an external standard and authority. "In order to find an unchangeable, an absolute truth, man has to go beyond the limit of his own consciousness and his own existence. He has to surpass himself. . . . By this transcendence the whole method of dialectic, the Socratic and Platonic method, is completely changed. Reason gives up its independence and autonomy. It has no longer a light of its own; it shines only in a borrowed and reflected light. If this light fails, human reason becomes ineffective and impotent. . . . No scholastic thinker ever seriously doubted the absolute superiority of the *revealed* truth. . . . The 'autonomy' of reason was a principle quite alien to medieval thought." *The Myth of the State* (New Haven, 1946), pp. 83–84, 95. "The discovery of truth and the foundation of truth [in Thomas Aquinas] is withdrawn from individual thinking and instead handed over to the Church as a universal institution." "Descartes' Wahrheitsbegriff," p. 174. Speaking of Galileo, he says: "Just this character of the completeness, the self-sufficiency, the autonomy of natural knowledge the medieval system of doctrines and beliefs could not recognize. Here there could be no possible compromise: had the Church accepted Galileo's new conception of truth and his new conception of nature, it would have been giving up its own foundation. For what Galileo is demanding, not indeed explicitly but implicitly, is the abandonment of the dogma of original sin. For him there is no corruption of human nature through which it has been led astray from its goal of the knowledge of truth and of God." "Wahrheitsbegriff und Wahrheitsproblem bei Galilei," *Scientia*, LXII (1937), p. 130; cf. pp. 191–93.

That this formulation of the "medieval conception of truth," in the light of the many different and shifting views from the thirteenth century on, is hardly adequate to the complexity or even the "autonomy" achieved by reason in medieval philosophical discussion, no impartial student of medieval intellectual life would be likely to deny.

[16] "Some Remarks on the Question of the Originality of the Renaissance," *Journal of the History of Ideas*, IV (1943), p. 50.

recognized; but that was not what he was looking for. And, having no interest in causal questions, he was not concerned to show how a man, working with traditional materials upon new problems, had managed to strike off original ideas. He loved sharp contrasts, the setting off of a "wholly new" idea against its background. Thus his symbolic reconstruction aimed ultimately at a description, an intellectual portrait of a man's ideas, not a genetic analysis.

He stated the general problem:

> Even if it were possible to answer all these psychological, sociological, and historical questions, we should still be in the precincts of the properly "human" world; we should not have passed its threshold. All human works arise under particular historical and sociological conditions. But we could never understand these special conditions unless we were able to grasp the general structural principles underlying these works. In our study of language, art, and myth the problem of meaning takes precedence over the problem of historical development. . . . The necessity of independent methods of descriptive analysis is generally recognized. We cannot hope to measure the depth of a special branch of human culture unless such measurement is preceded by a descriptive analysis. This structural view of culture must precede the merely historical view. History itself would be lost in the boundless mass of disconnected facts if it did not have a general structural scheme by means of which it can classify, order, and organize these facts. . . . As Wölfflin insists, the historian of art would be unable to characterize the art of different epochs or of different individual artists if he were not in possession of some fundamental *categories* of artistic description.[17]

For Cassirer, it is clear, the "spirit of a former age" is caught in a descriptive analysis, not in a causal or genetic explanation.

Cassirer kept in touch with all the major secondary interpretations of the medieval background of Renaissance thought. He did not dream of questioning these discovered antecedents. But he brushed them aside with some impatience; they did not affect the fundamental question, as he saw it. Typical is a statement about Galileo:

> The antecedents of Galileo's science are now much more precisely known than they were a few decades back. When I began my studies in Galileo forty years ago, this field was largely a *terra incognita*. A turning-point here came with the investigations of Duhem. . . . The antecedents of Galileo's theory of method have also been thoroughly and intensively examined. . . . But can all this historical evidence seriously shake our conviction of the incomparable sci-

[17] *Essay on Man*, pp. 68, 69.

entific originality of Galileo? I believe that it can only serve to strengthen this conviction and to support it with new arguments. . . . A work like the dynamics of Galileo could not come to birth all at once, like Athene from the head of Zeus. It needed a slow preparation, empirically as well as logically and methodologically. But to all these given elements Galileo added something completely new. . . . All this is wholly new and unique—and unique not only as a particular discovery, but as the expression of a scientific attitude and temper.[18]

Or take his judgment of Descartes:

That between Descartes' philosophy and the scholastic systems there are close relations, that the break between the two is by no means so sharp as it often appears in the traditional conception and presentation of his ideas: this cannot be contested after the fundamental investigation of Gilson. But no matter how many points of contact we may find between medieval and Cartesian thought, the whole *accent* of knowledge still changes when we pass from one to the other. The scholastics and Descartes can agree completely in assuming and establishing definite particular "truths"—as in the ontological proof of God—but in the conception of truth itself, in the explanation of its "nature" and its real meaning, there is an ineradicable, a radical difference. . . . The new in Descartes is not that he used doubt as the means by which alone we can arrive at truth. In this respect Augustine had preceded him. But Augustine's maxim: "Noli foras ire, in te ipsum redi, in interiore homine habitat veritas" had another significance from Descartes' return to the "Cogito." The inner experience that is here denoted is not that of pure knowledge, but that of the will and of religious certainty. . . . The principle of doubt become for Descartes the real synthetic constructive principle of knowledge.[19]

Or, in another field, take Cassirer's illuminating distinction between Luther and medieval mysticism:

Here there is the closest connection between Luther and the religious individual of the Middle Ages, as it is expressed in mysticism in particular. But on the other hand it is clear that the conception in which this connection is above all presented contains also the decisive difference. . . . Together with the dependence on objective things, mysticism destroys at the same time every principle of objective imposition of form: the "self" that it seeks is

[18] "Question of the Originality of the Renaissance," pp. 50, 51. Cf. his comparison of Galileo with Machiavelli: "Recent research has taught us that both Machiavelli and Galileo had their precursors. . . . They needed a long and careful preparation. But all this does not detract from their originality. What Galileo gave in his *Dialogues* and what Machiavelli gave in his *Prince* were really 'new sciences'. . . . Just as Galileo's Dynamics became the foundation of our modern science of nature, so Machiavelli paved a new way to political science." *Myth of the State,* p. 130.

[19] "Descartes' Wahrheitsbegriff," pp. 173–75, 178–79; cf. *Individuum und Kosmos* (Leipzig and Berlin, 1927), p. 135.

wholly without form, it is a "self" that has divested itself of all finite measure
and limitation. . . . In contrast, Luther's conception of freedom and of individuality contains not the mere principle of the denial of the world, but in
that principle and because of it the principle of world transformation. The
value of "working" itself is not destroyed along with the intrinsic value of particular works.[20]

The Platonism of the new age, as it appears in the Florentine Academy,
remains in its beginnings still completely bound up with Augustinianism and
as it were merged in it. Relying on the authority of Augustine, Ficino himself
acknowledges, he first dared to combine Christianity with Platonism. Hence
it is not the *discovery* of the "self" that is distinctive for the Renaissance, but
rather the circumstance that a fact and content which the Middle Ages acknowledged only in its religious psychology the Renaissance removed from
this connection and exhibited in independence.[21]

IV

These instances make clear just what Cassirer meant by "recreating
the spirit of a former age." They also illustrate the way in which
another of his historical principles entered in to modify and give direction to his aim of symbolic reconstruction. This recreation is to be no
mere passive act of reproduction, we recall.[22] It is rather a new intellectual synthesis, a new *Gestaltung*, a new creative, constructive act.
For though the answers to the historian's questions must come from
the past, the questions themselves depend on his own interests and
systematic problems.[23] Cassirer's central concern with the autonomy
of thought, the creativity of the human spirit, not only directed his attention to the Renaissance in the first place, and made him devote to
its thinkers a detailed study which he gave only in a derived sense to
the medieval philosophers, but it also determined the creative achievements and ideas he would single out.

This is most apparent in his great *Erkenntnisproblem*. The first volume includes a careful and penetrating analysis of almost all the major
Renaissance thinkers, beginning with Cusanus. Its successive editions
(1906, 1910) brought to light a great wealth of material then nearly
unknown. The problem of knowledge is very broadly construed, and
upon it is hung an analysis of most of the major themes of Renaissance

[20] *Freiheit und Form*, pp. 19–21.
[21] *Das Erkenntnisproblem*, Vol. I (Berlin, 1906; 3rd ed., 1922), p. 78.
[22] *Essay on Man*, p. 185.   [23] *Ibid.*, p. 178.

thought.[24] The store of otherwise inaccessible quotation from the sources has made it for a generation one of the most useful books for the student of the period.

But the volume is unmistakably the work of a neo-Kantian philosopher. The reader gets at times the impression that the Renaissance was populated largely with *Vorkantianer*. It is not that Cassirer actually distorts the thought of the men he is dealing with; he is too honest and scrupulous a scholar, and too largely endowed with a vivid historical sense. His interpretations have stood up remarkably well. It is rather that the problems he singles out for analysis are those which interest the Kantian.

For the *Erkenntnisproblem*, of course, was undertaken to furnish historical confirmation of "the power and the independence of the mind." It was designed to exhibit all scientific concepts "as the means by which thought wins and makes secure its dominance over appearances." It belongs with the learned and penetrating historical studies of that other "critical idealist," Leon Brunschvicg, as an historical proof that science is a construction and creation of "reason"—the reason embodied in the concrete social enterprise of science. By an analysis of the development of scientific thought it establishes the same position which the *Substanzbegriff* reaches by its systematic analysis. "In regarding the presuppositions of science as *having come about*, we are at the same time recognizing them as *creations* of thought; in discovering its historical *relativity* and conditions, we are opening up the prospect of its never-ending progress and its ever-renewed productivity." [25]

History becomes the completion and the touchstone of the results which the analysis and reduction of the content of the sciences gives us. . . . The analytic task imposed on modern thought finds its logical conclusion in the system of Kant. Here is taken the final and conclusive step; knowledge is based completely on itself, and nothing further in the realm of being or of consciousness is prior to its own legislative activity. (6, 13)

---

[24] Cf. *Erkenntnisproblem*, Vol. I, p. 13: "In general, the history of the problem of knowledge will mean for us not so much a *part* of the history of philosophy—for with the way in which all the elements in a philosophical system are internally and mutually determined, any such separation would remain an arbitrary limitation—as rather the total field from a definite point of view and a definite approach."

[25] *Erkenntnisproblem*, Vol. I, p. vi.

As Cassirer moved beyond the limits of a narrow Kantianism—he came to be provoked that the label was still attached to him—this apologetic aim and direction of his historical studies became less intrusive. He had reached "a new center and a new line of vision." But his fundamental humanism remained, and continued to dominate his interpretation of the Renaissance, and of what in it was of significance and importance. The *Individuum und Kosmos* is not a neo-Kantian book, in the same sense as the *Erkenntnisproblem*. If anything, as its very title suggests, it is Burckhardtian.[26] But it is uncompromisingly "humanistic" in Cassirer's sense.

That Cassirer should have interpreted Renaissance thought from the standpoint of his own philosophic vision was inevitable. What is more important, it is also completely consistent with his considered conception of the very nature of historical interpretation. If it be a shortcoming, it was an intentional one. Like all perspectives, to be sure, it is a limitation: it excluded other aspects of the Renaissance from the center of his attention. From a less partial point of view— perhaps merely from a different perspective, one that I happen to find more illuminating—Cassirer was prevented by his Kantian humanism from realizing the full significance of at least one of the major currents of Renaissance thought. He appreciated its Humanism, and he analysed brilliantly its Platonism. But he failed to see the role of its Aristotelianism. He did not, like other great students of Renaissance thought—like Gentile, for instance—dismiss that Aristotelianism as a mere survival of "scholasticism." His analyses of Pomponazzi[27] are suggestive; and he was the first to call attention to the great importance of Zabarella.[28] But he naturally saw in Renaissance Aristotelianism primarily its new humanistic element—which was great— and not its still greater naturalism. And since he did not adequately bring out the significance of that Aristotelianism, he did not contrast it effectively with the Platonistic movement, and thus reveal the full significance of the latter.

[26] This is also especially true of the brief sketch of the Italian Renaissance in the Introduction to *Freiheit und Form*, with its emphasis on the "new relation to politics," and "the state as a work of art."

[27] *Erkenntnisproblem*, Vol. I, pp. 105–17; *Individuum und Kosmos*, pp. 85–87, 108–12, 143–49.

[28] *Erkenntnisproblem*, Vol. I, pp. 117–20, 136–44.

The contrast between the Platonism and the Aristotelianism of the Renaissance is at bottom between a modernistic and a naturalistic humanism. Both focused attention on man and his destiny; both emphasized individual and personal values.[29] In this sense both were humanistic. But where Ficino and the Platonists, to support their religious modernism and "liberalism," went back to the Hellenistic world, to Plutarch and Alexandria, Pomponazzi and the greater Zabarella went to ancient Athens to find inspiration in its naturalistic and scientific thought. Their scientific humanism is much more original than the religious humanism of the Florentines. Where the Platonists vindicated the dignity of the individual soul by elevating it in freedom above nature, the Aristotelians made the soul a natural inhabitant of an orderly universe. Not until Spinoza and the eighteenth-century Newtonians is there another figure who effects so "modern" a blend between humanism and scientific naturalism as Pomponazzi and Zabarella. They are, in fact, the spiritual fathers of Spinoza's religious naturalism. The historical influence of the Platonists was great. But the Renaissance Aristotelians have a more original as well as a much sounder philosophy, and one which much more closely foreshadows later modern thought.

This is hardly the place to substantiate this interpretation, made from another perspective than Cassirer's, or to maintain—as I think can be done—that it is closer to the problems of Renaissance thought itself. It is easier to show that Cassirer overemphasized the influence of Platonism and underemphasized that of the Aristotelian tradition on points of detail, especially in the development of science. Galileo, for instance, was much closer to the scientific Aristotelianism of the Italian schools, and much farther from Plato, than Cassirer realized.[30]

---

[29] Cf. *Individuum und Kosmos*, p. 148: "Both men, Pomponazzi as well as Ficino, are wrestling with the problem of individuality; both are trying to make the phenomenon of the 'self' the center of psychology. But they pursue this goal in ways that are completely separate. For Ficino it is the purely intellectual nature of man which can alone form him into a 'self' in the strict sense, and elevate him above the realm of all that is merely corporeal. . . . For Pomponazzi, on the contrary, individuality is not to be asserted against Nature, but is to be derived and proved *from* Nature. . . . Just as Ficino in his fight for the rights and the uniqueness of the individual self calls for help upon supernaturalism and transcendence, so Pomponazzi in the same fight calls upon naturalism and immanence."

[30] For Cassier's view of Galileo's "Platonism," see *Individuum und Kosmos*, p. 178; "Galileo: a New Science and a New Spirit," *American Scholar*, 12 (1943), p. 10; "Descartes' Wahrheitsbegriff," p. 168. Cassirer has been very cautious in asserting the Pla-

And Cassirer likewise fails to give due importance to the Aristotelian
background of the Nature philosophies of the Italian Renaissance. On
the development of both science and Nature philosophy he underes-
timates the influence of the tradition of Ockhamism. And he undoubtedly overestimated that of his favorite Cusanus, as he came reluctantly
to admit.[31]

---

tonism of Galileo's thought. It is mentioned only once in the *Erkenntnisproblem* (Vol. I,
p. 389), and does not appear in "Wahrheitsbegriff und Wahrheitsproblem bei Galilei" at
all. In contrast to A. Koyré, e.g., who speaks of Galileo's work as "an experimental
proof of Platonism," and identifies any mathematical science of nature with "Platonism"
("Galileo and Plato," *Journal of the History of Ideas*, IV [1943], p. 428; cf. also his *Études
Galiléennes* [Paris, 1940]), Cassirer emphasizes instead the differences between Galileo's
and Plato's views. "Galilei had still another dualism to overcome before he could found
a science of nature. Plato had based his philosophy upon the presupposition that we
cannot speak of a science of nature in the same sense as we can of a science of mathematics. . . . It was most difficult for Galilei to combat the authority of Plato. . . . But
he was convinced that in his own work, in the new science of dynamics, he had removed the barrier Plato had erected between mathematical and natural science; for this
new science proved nature itself a realm of necessity rather than of chance." "Galileo: a
New Science," p. 10. Cf. also "Descartes' Wahrheitsbegriff," p. 168: "So long as the
philosophical orientation was directed toward Plato *alone*, and to a certain extent committed to him, there was a weighty obstacle opposed to the carrying through of the
ideal of an exact science of nature." And Cassirer distinguished sharply between the
"mathematical mysticism" of much of the Pythagoreanizing Platonism of the Renaissance, and the "mathematical science of nature." Cf. "Mathematische Mystik und
Mathematische Naturwissenschaft," *Lychnos* (Upsala, 1940). In his final judicious analysis ("Galileo's Platonism," *Studies and Essays in the History of Science and Learning offered in
homage to George Sarton* [1947]), Cassirer identifies Galileo's very novel "physical Platonism" primarily with the hypothetical *method* of "problematical analysis" he found in
the *Meno* as well as in Euclid and Archimedes, and best described in his letter to Car-
caville.

But if, as Cassirer emphasizes, Galileo insists that the subject matter of knowledge is
not an intelligible, "ideal" world dubiously related to the world of natural events, but is
rather the intelligible structure of that world, and if he also insists that it is arrived at by
the intellect through the careful analysis of instances of it encountered in sense experience, as Aristotle had suggested and the Italian methodologists more precisely formulated—how can this be called a "Platonism" rather than an "Aristotelianism"? There is
no evidence that Galileo was in any sense touched by Platonic metaphysics, or that he
is any more of a Platonist than Aristotle himself. On the fundamental issue in any philosophy of science, the relation of discourse to knowledge and to the subject matter of
knowledge, Galileo was one with the Italian tradition of realistic Aristotelianism. Galileo's distinction was his startling illustration that the best human knowledge is mathematics, and that the intelligible structure of things which that knowledge when clearly
formulated is able to grasp, is mathematical in character. Cf. my "Development of Scientific Method in the School of Padua," *Journal of the History of Ideas*, I (1940), pp.
204–6.

[31] "I avail myself of this opportunity to revise a former statement made in my *Individuum und Kosmos*. In the second chapter I tried to show that Nicholas of Cusa's philosophy exerted a strong influence on the general development of Italian thought in the
Quattrocento. I still think this to be highly probable, but I should perhaps have spoken
with more caution. I quite agree that, on the strength of new historical evidence, we

But when all this has been pointed out it remains true that, in importing the issues of a later day into his study of the Renaissance, Cassirer had instruments with which to ask questions. Even should we end by drastically modifying his interpretation of Renaissance thought, his questions have taught us an immense amount. What he learned forms the basis on which we have asked our own questions. And in the course of putting his problems to the Renaissance, Cassirer was led much nearer to the problems of the Renaissance itself. There is a vast difference between the *Erkenntnisproblem* and late studies like those of Pico, Ficino, Galileo, and Descartes.[32] The closer we can get to the problems of the Renaissance itself, and the farther we can get away from viewing them in terms of problems of a later incidence, the more likely we are to arrive at a genuine historical understanding. May our perspectives give us an equal chance to learn!

V

The illustrations already given show also how Cassirer himself followed his third major principle, that historical interpretation must always center on individual persons, and understand events in terms of such personalities. His analyses are always carried out as the intellectual portraits of men, even when those men have been selected as "symbols" of an age, or of characteristic answers to a problem.[33] His interest in intellectual personalities is so great that it quite bursts the frame of the context for which an idea has been introduced. It is the

---

can not give a direct and definite proof of this thesis. It is possible that Ficino conceived his general theory independently of Nicholas of Cusa. In this case the close relationship between the two thinkers would be all the more important and interesting from the point of view of the general history of ideas. For it would show us the common background of the philosophy of the fifteenth century—the general intellectual and religious atmosphere of the Renaissance." "Ficino's Place in Intellectual History," *Journal of the History of Ideas*, VI (1945), p. 492n.

[32] "Giovanni Pico della Mirandola," *Journal of the History of Ideas*, III (1942), pp. 123-44, 319-46; "Ficino's Place in Intellectual History," pp. 483-501; "Wahrheitsbegriff und Wahrheitsproblem bei Galilei," pp. 121-30, 185-93; "Galileo: a New Science," pp. 5-19; "Descartes' Wahrheitsbegriff," pp. 161-87.

[33] This is true of the one book Cassirer wrote specifically about the Renaissance, *Individuum und Kosmos*. After quoting the major criticisms of the "concept of the Renaissance," Cassirer goes on: "What is needed is the universality of a systematic point of view and a systematic orientation, which by no means coincides with the universality of merely empirical generic concepts, commonly used to divide history into periods and to delimit conveniently its individual epochs. Toward this goal the following considerations are directed. . . . They remain within the history of philosophical problems, and seek to find an answer there to the question whether and in how far the intellectual movement of the fifteenth and sixteenth centuries, in all the multiplicity of its ways of

history of "thinking," of *Denken*, that he definitely gives us, not of
ideas divorced from the minds that have entertained them. His analyses of ideas are beautifully lucid, but they aim to convey the feel of
those ideas to the men expressing them—he is true to his "personal"
interpretation. He is at his best in such a "contextual" analysis, in
pointing out how an idea in one man's thinking differs from what
seems to be the "same" idea in another's. All this, of course, lends
added value to his work, and makes the reader quite forget the limitations originally suggested by his own intellectual framework. Thus
whatever his shortcomings in appraising the significance of the Aristotelian movement as a whole, he cannot help but do a great measure
of justice when he comes to individual Aristotelians like Pomponazzi
or Zabarella. This is reinforced by the wealth of judiciously selected
quotations—quotations which are always "symbolic" of far more than
the point for which they are introduced.

In this art of portraiture, Cassirer's method is clear. He seeks above
all for that "central focus" in terms of which everything the man says
will form an "organic whole." His comment on the work of another
historian, P.O. Kristeller, states this well. In the last article he wrote,
he quotes Kristeller:

If we are to understand Ficino's metaphysics, he declares, we must start from
the phenomenon of 'internal experience.' Here we find the real clue to Ficino's philosophy—the fundamental fact and principle on which all his special
doctrines depend. . . . If we accept this starting-point of Kristeller's interpretation—and to my mind he has proved his point by conclusive arguments—
we have won a new perspective, a vantage-point from which we may see the
whole of Ficino's system in a clearer light. Many questions that were highly
controversial can now be answered in a better and more satisfactory way.
. . . He gives us a much more 'organic' view of Ficino's philosophy than we
find in other writers. Kristeller makes no attempt to conceal the contradictions
inherent in Ficino's doctrine. But he shows convincingly that in spite of all its
discrepancies Ficino's work preserves its systematic unity. It is centered
around a few fundamental problems which complete and elucidate each
other.[34]

---

putting problems and all the divergence of its solutions, forms a self-contained unity."
Individuum und Kosmos, pp. 5, 6.
   But the book itself is far from a unity. It is a collection of studies of the views of different men grouped around a few central problems—ultimately, as the title suggests,
those raised by Burckhardt. Its organization is far from clear, it is full of digressions,
and its enduring value is undoubtedly its presentation of the "intellectual portraits" of
men looking at these problems.
[34] "Ficino's Place in Intellectual History," pp. 485–87.

What Cassirer thus praises in the method of Kristeller he himself tried to do in his own. Thus, facing the apparent contradictions in the thought of Pico della Mirandola, he says:

> Pico . . . was trying to assert the validity of his own *principle of knowledge*. . . . The distinctive category under which he subsumed his doctrine of God, of the world and of man, his theology and his psychology, is the category of *symbolic thought*. Once we ascertain this central point of his thinking, the different parts of his doctrine immediately coalesce into a whole. . . . Pico is no longer trying to exhibit the Many as the *effect* of the One, or to deduce them as such from their cause, with the aid of rational concepts. He sees the Many rather as *expressions*, as *images*, as *symbols* of the One.[35]

Cassirer's method appears in a little different form in connection with Galileo:

> If we wish to comprehend Galileo's nature and activity, we confront the same problem we encounter in almost every portrayal of one of the great geniuses of the Renaissance. We cannot remain within a single area of his activity, however significant and consequential it may appear, and we cannot take our standards from this area *alone*. We must rather proceed, as in concentric circles, from the center of his intellectual activity to its ever wider and more comprehensive expressions. Here is revealed a definite scale: the extent of the problem becomes greater and greater, and embraces a richer and richer area, while the typical form in which the question is put as such remains the same. The following consideration has to do with no special content of Galileo's science, but rather with this universal type of his investigation and questioning.[36]

This procedure is clearly applicable to the thought of a single intellectual personality, where something like an "organic unity" with a discoverable "center" may reasonably be expected. Even here, one sometimes suspects, there may be more of conflict and tension, even in a great thinker, than Cassirer allows for; his heroes emerge uniformly as intellectually integrated. For many philosophers, especially those facing problems of reconciliation, one could find equal illumination in an interpretation that took the strife of incompatibles as central.

But the difficulties are greater when the method is extended to a group of men, and greatest of all in attempting to characterize an entire "age." Cassirer applies it to the Cambridge Platonists:

[35] "Giovanni Pico della Mirandola," pp. 137–38.
[36] "Wahrheitsbegriff und Wahrheitsproblem bei Galilei," p. 125.

With all this we have won only partial aspects; we have illuminated the *work* of the Cambridge School from different sides, but we have not grasped the real intellectual principle it represents, in setting forth and carrying through which it alone deserves a place in the history of the modern mind. To lay bare this principle and in it the real ideal center of the intellectual work of the Cambridge School is the task of the following investigation. . . . It is a unified and total view that is represented by the Cambridge circle: a view which is maintained and carried through as a constant basic theme amidst all the individual differences of the particular thinkers and all its extension to the manifold and disparate areas of problems. . . . What is embodied in it is a definite type of thinking of independent power and significance.[37]

The applicability of this search for a unifying "type of thinking" grows more doubtful when we begin to seek for the "center" from which to interpret an entire age. In the *Erkenntnisproblem* Cassirer is aware of the difficulties:

In Jacob Burckhardt's portrayal, which first made the total picture of the Renaissance live once more in its individual traits, philosophical efforts and achievements recede completely into the background. While everywhere else they represent the structure and the real measure of the intellectual progress of a period, they here stand as it were outside the common pattern. Nowhere does there appear at first glance a recognizable unity, nowhere a fixed center about which the different movements are ordered. The conventional traits and formulae with which we are accustomed to indicate the character of the Renaissance fail us when we honestly consider the individual philosophical currents and their multiplicity.[38]

This raises the question whether we can hope to find any unifying formula in structural or morphological terms for the thought of the Renaissance as a whole—the entire problem of "styles" of thought, a conception German *Kulturgeschichte* has taken over from the historians of art. As a conscientious scholar, Cassirer's attitude is very cautious and reserved.

That in a mere chronological sense we cannot separate the Renaissance from the Middle Ages is obvious. By innumerable visible and invisible threads the Quattrocento is connected with scholastic thought and medieval culture. In the history of European civilization there never was a break of continuity. To seek for a point in this history in which the Middle Ages 'end' and the mod-

---

[37] *Die Platonische Renaissance in England und die Schule von Cambridge* (Leipzig and Berlin, 1932), p. 4. Tr. F.C.A. Koelln and James P. Pettegrove as *The Platonic Renaissance in England* (Austin, 1953).

[38] *Erkenntnisproblem*, Vol. I, p. 74.

ern world 'begins' is a sheer absurdity. But that does not do away with the necessity of looking for an *intellectual* line of demarcation between the two ages.[39]

At times Cassirer was willing to use this notion of "style" in a definite nontemporal sense.

Our controversy as to the originality of the Renaissance and as to the dividing-line between the "Renaissance" and the "Middle Ages" seems to me in many ways rather a "logical" dispute than one about the historical facts. Ideas like "Gothic," "Renaissance," or "Baroque" are ideas of historical "style." As to the meaning of these ideas of "style" there still prevails a great lack of clarity in many respects. They can be used to *characterize* and *interpret* intellectual movements, but they express no actual historical *facts* that ever existed at any time. "Renaissance" and "Middle Ages" are, strictly speaking, not names for historical periods at all, but they are concepts of "ideal types," in Max Weber's sense. We cannot therefore use them as instruments for any strict division of periods; we cannot inquire at what temporal point the Middle Ages "stopped" or the Renaissance "began." The actual historical facts cut across and extend over each other in the most complicated manner.[40]

The meaning of these ideas of "style" Cassirer tried to clarify and analyse in his *Zur Logik der Kulturwissenschaften* (Gothenburg, 1942). In view of the inaccessibility of this volume we quote at length:

Jacob Burckhardt gave in his *Kultur der Renaissance* a classic portrait of "the man of the Renaissance." It contains features that are familiar to us all. The man of the Renaissance possesses definite characteristic properties which clearly distinguish him from "the man of the Middle Ages." He is characterized by his joy in the senses, his turning to nature, his roots in this world, his self-containedness for the world of form, his individualism, his paganism, his amoralism. Empirical research has set out to discover this Burckhardtian "man of the Renaissance"—but it has not found him. No single historical individual can be cited who actually unites in himself all the traits that Burckhardt considers the constitutive elements of his picture. "If we try" says Ernst Walser in his *Studien zur Weltanschauung der Renaissance*,[41] "to consider the life and thought of the leading personalities of the Quattrocento purely inductively, of a Coluccio Salutati, Poggio Bracciolini, Leonardo Bruni, Lorenzo Valla, Lorenzo Magnifico or Luigi Pulci, it is regularly found that for the particular person being studied the traits set up absolutely do *not* fit. . . . And if we bring together the results of inductive research, there gradually emerges a new picture of the Renaissance, no less a mixture of piety and

[39] *Myth of the State*, p. 130.
[40] "Question of the Originality of the Renaissance," pp. 54–55.
[41] Ernest Walser, *Studien zur Weltanschauung der Renaissance*, now in *Gesammelte Studien zur Geistesgeschichte der Renaissance* (1920; Basel, 1932), p. 102.

impiety, good and evil, longing for heaven and joy in earth, but infinitely more complicated. The life and endeavor of the whole Renaissance cannot be derived from a *single* principle, from individualism and sensualism, just as little as the reputed unified culture of the Middle Ages."

I agree completely with these words of Walser's. Every man who has ever been concerned with the concrete investigation of the history, literature, art or philosophy of the Renaissance will be able to confirm them from his own experience and add many further instances. But does this refute Burckhardt's notion? Shall we regard it, in the logical sense, as a null class—as a class into which no single object falls? That would be necessary only if we were here concerned with one of those generic concepts which are arrived at through the empirical comparison of particular cases, through what we commonly call "induction." Measured by this standard, Burckhardt's notion could indeed not stand the test.

But it is just this *presupposition* that needs logical correction. Certainly Burckhardt could not have given his portrait of the man of the Renaissance without relying for it on an immense amount of factual material. The wealth of this material and its reliability astonishes us again and again when we study his work. But the kind of "conspectus" he draws up, the historical synthesis he gives, is of a wholly different kind in principle from empirically acquired natural concepts. If we want to speak here of "abstraction," it is that process which Husserl has characterized as *"ideirende Abstraction."* That the results of such an *"ideirende Abstraction"* could ever be brought to cover any concrete particular case: this can neither be expected nor demanded. And "subsumption" also can never be taken here in the same way as we subsume a body given here and now, a piece of metal, under the concept of gold, because we find that it fulfills all the conditions of gold known to us. When we indicate that Leonardo da Vinci and Aretino, Marsiglio Ficino and Machiavelli, Michelangelo and Cesare Borgia are "men of the Renaissance," we do not mean that there is to be found in them all a definite particular trait with a fixed content in which they all agree. We shall perceive them to be not only completely different, but even opposed. What we are asserting of them is only that regardless of this opposition, perhaps just because of it, they stand to each other in a definite ideal connection; that each of them in his own way is cooperating to construct what we call the "spirit" of the Renaissance or the culture of the Renaissance.

It is a unity of *direction*, not a unity of *existence*, that we are thus trying to express. The particular individuals belong together, not because they are alike or resemble each other, but because they are cooperating in a common *task*, which in contrast to the Middle Ages we perceive to be new, and to be the distinctive "meaning" of the Renaissance. All genuine notions of "style" in the cultural sciences reduce, when analysed more precisely, to such notions of "meaning." The artistic style of an epoch cannot be determined if we do not bring to a unity all its different and often apparently disparate artistic expressions by understanding them, to use Riegl's term, as expressions of a definite "artistic will." [42] Such notions indeed *characterize*, but they do not *determine;* the particular that falls under them cannot be derived from them. But it is equally incorrect to infer from this that we have here only intuitive description, not conceptual characterization; it is rather a matter of a distinctive manner and direction of this characterization, of a logico-intellectual work that is *sui generis.* [43]

This passage hardly possesses the clarity we are accustomed to expect from Cassirer. Is it only an elaborate way of saying that we "perceive" certain common "tendencies" running through Renaissance thought, though fidelity to facts demands that we recognize its wide diversity? Or is Cassirer trying to indicate something deeper by his "ideal types," his "unities of direction," his "common task" and "will"? In saying that such "unities" are not historical *facts* discoverable in the web of history, that they can be used to "characterize" and "interpret" the facts, but do not "determine" them, Cassirer is of course being faithful to his general Kantian epistemology. "Unities" in that theory of knowledge are applied to the materials of knowledge, they are not discovered in those materials. In Kantian terms, Cassirer is saying that these "unities," these concepts of historical "style," are not constitutive but regulative principles. They are closest, perhaps, to the idea of teleology as it appears in the *Critique of Judgment.* In any event, we should remember that for Cassirer the act of "interpreting" any symbolic forms is creative, productive of a new synthesis; the historical "meaning" that results from it is as much a creation of the historian as a deliverance of the past. It is a genuinely new *"Gestaltung."* In less Kantian phraseology, all such unities are working hypotheses employed to explore the facts.

Cassirer's labored distinctions are thus involved in all the dubieties of his philosophy of symbolic forms. That there are discoverable unities in history, and in the thought of the Renaissance in particular, I should myself maintain. That thought, I should suggest, is unified in the light of the problems men were then facing. And there is much in Cassirer that points to such a unification in terms of problems, rather than in terms of the vague and indeterminate notion of "meaning." To be sure, his further notion of a common "task" is rather blind. In the

[42] Alois Riegl, *Stilfragen* (Berlin, 1893; 2nd ed. 1923) and *Die spätromische Kunstindustrie nach den Funden in Österreich-Ungarn,* 2 vols. (Vienna, 1901–23; Vol. I, 2nd ed., 1927).
[43] *Logik der Kulturwissenschaften,* pp. 79–81.

Erkenntnisproblem, however, he puts the matter much more precisely. "It is the fight against 'substantial form' that is above all characteristic of the Renaissance." [44] This suggests that the problems of the Renaissance were primarily negative: intellectually, men were seeking to escape from earlier views, just as in their social life they were seeking to escape from the forms of medieval society which had outlasted their usefulness and were now felt to be constricting rather than directing. The vexed question of Renaissance "individualism" also, I think, is soluble if that "individualism" is construed in terms of the specific social organizations from which men were seeking to escape, rather than in terms of any positive content. Like the Romantic movement, the Renaissance is to be understood in the light of what it was revolting against. Being, like Romanticism, a reaction and a revolt, it naturally expressed itself in a wide variety of alternatives.

Such a "functional" interpretation, I submit, is really closer to Cassirer's own fundamental position than the "structuralism"—the attempt to find some common structural or morphological "meaning"—into which he was occasionally seduced. Cassirer is at his best when he insists that the originality and novelty of a period, or a thinker, lies not in the statement of *"eine neue Thematik,"* but in the serious confrontation of *"eine neue Problematik."* [45]

Whatever weight Cassirer was inclined to give to "styles" or unities as he reinterpreted them as regulative principles, in his last statement on this problem he returned to his fundamentally "personal" conception of history. "What we learn from this discussion," he says in his final paper on Ficino, referring to the symposium on the originality of the Renaissance,[46] "is only the fact that the period of the Quattrocento and Cinquecento is too subtle and too complicated a phenomenon to be described by any simple term or abstract formula. All such formulae are bound to fail. When we come to the real question, when we begin to deal with any special problem or any individual thinker, we must forget them. They turn out to be inadequate and misleading. In every particular investigation the question must be raised anew and answered independently." [47]

[44] *Erkenntnisproblem*, Vol. I, p. 76.
[45] "Die Platonische Renaissance in England," p. 5.
[46] *Journal of the History of Ideas*, IV (1943).
[47] "Ficino's Place in Intellectual History," pp. 483–84.

The question of novelty and originality, so important in all of Cassirer's studies of the Renaissance, remains. What is it which in that period can be called really "new"? Surprisingly enough, in view of his sharp distinction between the concepts of the natural and the cultural or symbolic sciences, in good Kantian fashion Cassirer often uses metaphors drawn from the science of mechanics—"forces," "center of gravity," new "equilibrium." Thus in speaking of Machiavelli he says: "When Machiavelli conceived the plan of his book the center of gravity of the political world had already been shifted. New forces had come to the fore and they had to be accounted for—forces that were entirely unknown to the medieval system." [48]

The fullest and most illuminating use of such a mechanical figure occurs in his discussion of the originality of the Renaissance:

Nevertheless the distinction [between Middle Ages and Renaissance] has a real meaning. What we can express by it, and what alone we intend to express, is that from the beginning of the fifteenth century onward the *balance* between the particular forces—society, state, religion, church, art, science—begins to shift slowly. New forces press up out of the depths and alter the previous equilibrium. And the character of every culture rests on the equilibrium between the forces that give it form. Whenever therefore we make any comparison between the Middle Ages and the Renaissance, it is never enough to single out particular ideas or concepts. What we want to know is not the particular idea as such, but the importance it possesses, and the strength with which it is acting in the whole structure. "Middle Ages" and "Renaissance" are two great and mighty streams of ideas. When we single out from them a particular idea, we are doing what a chemist does in analyzing the water of a stream or what a geographer does in trying to trace it to its source. No one denies that these are interesting and important questions. But they are neither the only nor the most important concern of the *historian of ideas*.

The historian of ideas knows that the water which the river carries with it changes only very slowly. The same ideas are always appearing again and again, and are maintained for centuries. The force and the tenacity of tradition can hardly be over-estimated. From this point of view we must acknowledge that there is nothing new under the sun. But the historian of ideas is not asking primarily what the *substance* is of particular ideas. He is asking what their *function* is. What he is studying—or should be studying—is less the *content* of ideas than their *dynamics*. To continue the figure, we could say that he is not trying to analyse the drops of water in the river, but that he is seeking to measure its width and depth and to ascertain the force and velocity of the current. It is all *these* factors that are fundamentally altered in the Renaissance; the dynamics of ideas has changed.[49]

[48] *Myth of the State*, p. 133.
[49] "Question of the Originality of the Renaissance," p. 55.

More often, however, Cassirer employs not a metaphor drawn from the natural science of dynamics, but the more appropriate conception that a new *problem* has been insistently posed. This conception of a new *"Problematik"* dominates his major treatments. In the *Erkenntnisproblem* he says "The philosophical character of an epoch cannot be judged merely by its achievement in fixed doctrines; it announces itself no less in the energy with which it conceives and maintains a new intellectual goal. The unity of the different directions which stand opposed to each other in the thinking of the Renaissance lies in the new attitude which they gradually come to take toward the problem of knowledge." [50] In *Freiheit und Form* he says: "In destroying the whole medieval system of religious beliefs, the system of religious mediation through fixed, objectively communicable means of salvation, Luther imposed upon the individual an immense new task. Union with the Infinite must now be accomplished in himself without the aid of any assistance in material means." [51] The *Individuum und Kosmos* "remains within the history of philosophical problems and seeks to find there an answer to the question whether and in how far the movement of thought in the 15th and 16th centuries, in all the multiplicity of its ways of putting problems and in all the divergence of its solutions, forms a self-contained unity." [52]

What characterizes and distinguishes the Renaissance is the new *relation* in which individuals place themselves toward the world and the form of community which they establish between themselves and the world. They see themselves facing an altered conception of the physical and the intellectual universe, and it is this conception that imposes upon them a new intellectual and moral demand, which requires of them an inner transformation, a *reformatio* and *regeneratio*. [53]

VI

When Cassirer goes beyond the attempt to analyse the intellectual personality of an individual thinker to essay the portrait of an age, to try to reconstruct its spirit as a whole, he wavers between two rather different conceptions. On the one hand, he tries to introduce a unity into a mass of divergent currents of thought by constructing a synthesis in terms of a characteristic "style" or "ideal type" of thinking. On

[50] *Erkenntnisproblem*, Vol. I, pp. 75–76.
[51] *Freiheit und Form*, p. 18.
[52] *Individuum und Kosmos*, p. 6.
[53] "Wahrheitsbegriff und Wahrheitsproblem bei Galilei," p. 122.

the other, he finds unification in terms of the new problems forced on men—forced primarily, in his interpretation, by the advance of scientific knowledge and the new conceptions of truth to which that advance leads. Combining something of both conceptions is the notion he most commonly employs, that the unification can be constructed in terms of a new "task," a new *"Aufgabe."* The first idea is morphological, a descriptive analysis, though of a sort Cassirer claims to be not "merely empirical," but *sui generis,* appropriate to the human universe of symbolic forms. The second idea is equally appropriate to a human world: it finds understanding in terms of ends, goals, and purposes, it is teleological and functional. Is it too much to say that the first was impressed on Cassirer by Burckhardt and Dilthey, while the second came from his own more original thought? The first can be called, in his own terms, a "substantial" or "structural" conception; the second is "functional."

The structural unification has the disadvantage that when worked out with complete honesty in the face of facts, as Cassirer had to work it out, it leads to a conception that is unique and without parallel—a conception, furthermore, that Cassirer has great difficulty in trying to formulate. It is a conception that by definition eludes public confirmation; it depends on the "productive imagination" of the historical interpreter not only for its discovery, as do all hypotheses, but also for its validity. And it opens the way to no further inquiry as to its causes and conditions. The functional unification in terms of new problems forced on men by their changing social experience introduces nothing that is not already familiar in human life. It is clear and precise, and it can be confirmed by public evidence. It suggests the further investigation of the many and complex causes, intellectual and social, which have led men's social experience to change.

Cassirer quotes from Kant, in speaking of Plato: "It is by no means unusual, upon comparing the thoughts which an author has expressed in regard to his subject, . . . to find that we understand him better than he has understood himself. As he has not sufficiently determined his concept, he has sometimes spoken, or even thought, in opposition to his own intention." [54] Cassirer himself adds:

[54] *Critique of Pure Reason* (2nd ed., 1787). Tr. N.K. Smith (London, Macmillan, 1929) p. 310.

The history of philosophy shows us very clearly that the full determination of a concept is very rarely the work of that thinker who first introduced that concept. For a philosophical concept is, generally speaking, rather a problem than the solution of a problem—and the full significance of this problem cannot be understood so long as it is still in its first implicit state. It must become explicit in order to become comprehended in its true meaning, and this transition from an implicit to an explicit state is the work of the future.[55]

Is it not possible that we may be able to understand the idea of a truly functional interpretation of history better than Cassirer understood it, and that we may hope to make the problem which he introduced more explicit than he was able to do himself?

[55] *Essay on Man*, p. 180.

12

Dewey's Interpretation of the History of Philosophy

I

JOHN DEWEY has written no volume dealing primarily with the history of philosophic thought. Nor, unless in some now long-forgotten youthful indiscretion, did he ever elect to set before a class the simple record of objective and impartial knowledge of the past. He left to others that breed of scholarship that rests content to display in nice articulation the thoughts that have thrilled the search of uneasy and inquiring minds, and mount them in some museum piece so plausibly arranged as to convey the illusion of a kind of timeless life forever frozen into immobility—that perfection of a past recovered for eternity which German *Gelehrten* have so often sought in vain, and French *savants* so often captured, none better than M. Gilson in our generation. In practice as in theory history has meant for Dewey more than the mere chance to enjoy such fruits of esthetic contemplation. For him it has not been enough to weigh precisely the compulsions that have made great minds what they forever are, so that from their centers of vision the world must even now appear not otherwise than as it presented itself to them.

Not that Dewey has been blind to the appeal and significance of the comprehensive intellectual visions that make the record of what philosophy has seen so revealing a key to human nature and the rich variety of cultures it has created. These imaginative visions—more often he prefers to call them "shared meanings"—he finds indeed the no-

Originally published in *The Philosophy of John Dewey*, ed. P.A. Schilpp. The Library of Living Philosophers (Evanston, Illinois: Northwestern University Press, 1939; copyright © 1939 by The Library of Living Philosophers, Inc.), pp. 77–102. Reprinted by permission of Open Court Publishing Co.

blest fruits of thought, the goal of the busy labors of all man's cunning arts and contrivings. "Scientific thought itself is finally but a function of the imagination in enriching life with the significance of things. . . . Significant history is lived in the imagination of man, and philosophy is a further excursion of the imagination into its own prior achievements." [1] And as every reader knows, Dewey's pages are sprinkled with brief but often eloquent sketches of these visions—like the insight into Spinoza in *The Quest for Certainty*, or the portrait of Bacon in *Reconstruction in Philosophy*, or the many passages in which he pays tribute to what the Greeks saw.

No one has been more insistent than Dewey that the ultimate function of knowing is to contribute to the widest possible diffusion and sharing of such meanings—provided they be seen for what they are, visions of man's imagination and not revelations of eternal truth. [2] And surely no one has been more impressed by the power and appeal of vision in human life—a power so great and so seductive that men have been forever tempted to rest in vision without seeking to understand it or the conditions of its enhancement. Seek visions and distrust them, is the counsel born of reflection on the tragic yet magnificent history of the philosophic mind. For visions are not understood by vision, but by the use of another and more laborious intellectual method; and they can be neither generated nor shared save by the practice of intelligence, of the most critical and scientific ways of thinking.

Hence Dewey has found no time to tell, like Santayana, the story of the human imagination, or to repaint at second hand the marvels it has beheld. Even the men of vision and aspiration he has been more anxious to catch in travail than to contemplate their serene achievement. The insights that constantly occur in his writings into the great philosophies and movements of ideas in the past are concerned far more with the intellectual methods whereby they were arrived at than with praise of their fruits. Where Dewey approaches most closely to the narration of a history—as in the *Reconstruction in Philosophy*—it is in following the thread of the development of method. For him, it is

---

[1] *Philosophy and Civilization* (New York, 1931), p. 5.

[2] "Poetic meanings, moral meanings, a large part of the goods of life are matters of richness and freedom of meanings, rather than of truth. . . . For, assuredly, a student prizes historic systems rather for the meanings and shades of meanings they have brought to light than for the store of ultimate truths they have ascertained." *Experience and Nature* (Chicago, 1926), p. 411.

method rather than vision that is fundamental in the history of philosophy, that reflective and critical method that aims to reorganize and reconstruct beliefs.

Yet Dewey has given no straightforward account of the history of intellectual method comparable to the studies of men like Cassirer or Brunschvicg. Here too he has been more interested in making history than in writing it. He has used his wealth of historical knowledge, not for a display of brilliant erudition, but as material to be brought to bear upon the present-day problems of the logic of inquiry. Just because of his deep concern with the immediate future, he has tried to make the most of the successes and the mistakes of the past. Profoundly convinced of the continuity of human thinking, he has seen prior thought always as an instrument which with the proper reshaping might be used to help us in our present discontents. The past is enormously significant; but to be significant is to be significant for something, and that something is the intellectual problems the envisaged future insistently poses for us today. Praise for the past Dewey is content to leave to others; he sees his task rather as to appraise it, as a weapon for the morrow's fight. Toward the history of philosophy his attitude thus differs little from that of the chemist or the biologist: all alike view the chronicle of man's intellectual achievement as an arsenal, or as a warning, but not as an ancestral mansion to be lovingly explored.

Indeed, if Dewey's whole philosophy be taken as he would have it, as scientific method at last come to self-consciousness, as experimentalism aware of itself, its meaning and its implications, developed as a critical instrument and a constructive tool, it might well seem that concern with past thinking deserves to hold as small a place for him as for any scientist. To dwell on the record of history may be a harmless and satisfying luxury, but it can scarcely be a major or essential preoccupation of the philosophic mind. To master what inquiry has achieved that we may inquire further, would be all that wisdom could demand. Should not a scientific philosophy really in control of the best intellectual methods win us emancipation from the sterile historicism of the romantic and backward-looking nineteenth century? Scientific thought has no further interest in the scaffoldings by which it was constructed: it has plenty of work of its own to do. An experimental philosophy, wedded at last to the methods of science, should resolutely face the future with an open mind and an earnest heart. If it think of the past at all, should it not, like our latest fashion in scientific philosophizing, rejoice that it has finally escaped those centuries of bondage to darkness, and put boldly behind it all temptation to traffic with the meaningless nonsense of their unconfirmable speculations?

Now Dewey himself has dwelt so long and so vigorously on the need of just such liberation from persistent tradition that it is not irrelevant to ask these questions about the true implications of an experimental philosophy. Many who have found that basic drive congenial have indeed raised them. They have been sadly puzzled to find his works overloaded with references to the outworn ideas of thinkers they would themselves prefer to forget. Why all this beating of dead asses? For years it was possible to reach his most penetrating analysis of the logic of inquiry, in *Essays in Experimental Logic,* only through a thick tangle of Lotze, a logician whom it is safe to say no one has seriously read for a generation. And of even his fundamental *Experience and Nature,* it has been not unfairly pointed out that each page is made up half of a fresh grappling with pressing problems worthy of the best laboratory approach, and half of a wrestling with the vagaries of ancient tradition. Why does Dewey insist on conducting his original inquiries in the musty atmosphere of a historical museum? Why does he not throw open the windows to let the fresh breezes of the present blow these dusty cobwebs away? Why, to go forward a step, must he look backward on the whole course already traversed? For all but the most learned of his readers Dewey has seemed weighed down by an obsession with the past. This burden of historical baggage has inordinately increased the difficulties of his pages. What might have been so clear on the authority of a successful scientific method has been obscured by the painful resolve to win every step of the way by ceaseless polemic with the whole long course of philosophical thought. Dewey may never have written specifically on the history of philosophy; but he has rarely set forth his own position save in detailed and lengthy critical opposition to the views and methods of his many predecessors.

There is more than the mere matter of rhetorical effectiveness here at stake. It is, to be sure, not hard to conceive an easier path of persuasion for those who come, without knowledge of philosophy's past, in search of light and power for today. From Dewey's historical analyses such men have gained little enlightenment; they have scarcely yearned to cast off shackles by which they never felt themselves bound. The present emancipation they do need he might well have granted more directly. And there would not then be so many, especially among teachers, whose sole exposure to the career of philosophy has come from Dewey's critically selective treatments, with results a little too weird and painful to narrate. Even for the less unsophisticated one may venture to doubt the wisdom of Dewey's strategy. It is possible the hard-boiled professionals themselves might have been more easily won over to a philosophy of the experimental method, had not their sentimental pieties been so repeatedly and so insistently violated. There is some point in making even a revolutionary philosophy appear the culmination of the great traditions of the past: experimentalism might even have been dressed up as twentieth century certainty. The point is all the clearer when one realizes that even the most significant revolutions are not quite so revolutionary as they at first appear, and that tradition is wanting chiefly in failing to remember how rapidly it has changed.

This vexed question of Dewey's rhetoric is raised only because it alone can explain how many honest readers can quite misconceive his intentions. Intelligent interpreters have asserted that his only interest in the past is to free us from its clogging and stultifying assumptions. Greek thought we must understand, but only because it is the source of all our errors. And others, like the ancient Caliph, have judged it better to forget that past entirely: what is of value has been taken up in Dewey, what he has omitted deserves to be forgotten. Alas, a teacher's worst enemies are often his professed admirers. Such a reading does little credit to Dewey, and less to the readers. Fortunately the danger of falling into it is not today what it was a decade ago. For just such a view, put forth in the name of physical science, has been expressed almost beyond the possibility of caricature by some of the logical positivists; and even the most blind can see that Dewey's experimentalism is hardly of that stripe.

There are places, especially in *The Quest for Certainty*, where Dewey turns to past thought only to criticise its assumptions. But it would be both an insult to Dewey's intelligence, and a confession of sad ignorance in the asker, to request him to repeat once more what he has so often made clear, that the value and importance of the philosophical tradition is not exhausted by the assumptions it has transmitted that need altering. It would be much more to the point to single out that basic element in Dewey's thought which makes constant concern with the great intellectual traditions of our civilization not only compatible with his experimentalism, but actually an essential and integral component of it.

For despite all his analysis of the procedure of the natural sciences, Dewey's experimentalism is not primarily based on the methods of the laboratory. It is at once the experimentalism of practical common sense, and the coming to self-awareness of the best and most critical techniques and concepts of the social sciences. In the broadest sense, it is the experimentalism of the anthropologist, of the student of human institutions and cultures, impressed by the fundamental role of habit in men and societies and by the manner in which those habits are altered and changed. Like any honest social scientist, he finds the presence and the influence of natural science in Western culture today both its distinctive trait and its greatest achievement. But for him that science is primarily a cultural phenomenon: it is an institutionalized habit of thinking and acting, a way whereby that culture conducts many of its tasks and operations. It is essentially a social method of doing and changing things, a complex technique that has proved both extraordinarily successful and extraordinarily disruptive of the older pattern of life. It is a method of inquiry, of criticising traditional beliefs and instituting newer and better warranted ones. It is the best intellectual method our culture, or any culture, has constructed; and as such it must furnish the basis on which any philosophy must build. But it is not a sheer method in isolation, it is a cultural method whereby a society operates on its inherited and traditional materials.

It is just this combination of a critical anthropology and social psychology with his experimentalism, this permeating sense of scientific method and of all inquiry as working in and through and upon a complex social heritage of accustomed ways of believing and acting, that sets Dewey's development of the philosophic implications of scientific method off so sharply from others of the present day. Most of our fashionable "scientific philosophies" are socially far from sophisticated. Arrived at by reflection primarily upon the state of the physical sciences, they are quite innocent of the knowledge gained by a century of biological and social inquiry. For Dewey the task of a scientific philosophy is not confined to the formulation of a consistent system of the entities disclosed in sense-awareness. Nor is it limited to the analysis of the linguistic expressions that constitute science considered as a body of ordered knowledge. Even today, it seems, in the midst of the most thoroughgoing revolution in physical theory and concepts since the seventeenth century, it is possible to erect philosophies based on mathematics and mathematical physics which may recognize the interesting fact that science has had and may well continue to enjoy a history, but scarcely find that fact relevant to the understanding of what science is and does. For such theories the history of human thinking is indeed of no serious moment. Philosophy is reflection upon what is—in all probability. It has little to do with what men who were mistaken thought, and why they thought that way. But if, as Dewey has learned from the social sciences, knowledge in general and science in particular are rather the ability of a society to do what it must and can, if they are primarily a matter of the intellectual methods whereby a culture solves its specific versions of the universal human problems, then the history of that culture and its problems, and the historical criticism of its methods of inquiry and application, become of the very essence of any philosophy with a claim to scientific inspiration. If science be an institutionalized method of trial and error, or, as James Harvey Robinson put it, of fumbling and success, then the trials, the errors, and the successes are equally instructive for the refinement and improvement and extension of scientific method, of experimentalism.

For Dewey, science is ultimately a conscious and reflective method of guiding the process of changing beliefs, of using the digested lessons of past experience to clarify and learn from fresh inquiry. Indeed, the natural sciences, as a great cultural enterprise, are the best illustration of an institutionalized technique for actively initiating social change. In them has been worked out the way in which originality may be intentionally, critically, and habitually combined with the cumulative preservation of the past's achievements. The scientist does not light-heartedly enter his laboratory to try anything once; if he is worth his salt, he knows what has been slowly built up in the way of accredited techniques and tests and warranted scientific knowledge; and it is that body of laboriously certified tools and materials which both raises his problems and offers him the methods and tests with which to solve them. The history of science is the history of a never-ending reconstruction of ideas and concepts. And it is as just such an enterprise of reconstruction that Dewey regards the criticism that is philosophy, the criticism that makes the philosopher at his best the statesman of ideas, effecting some new synthesis, and at his humblest the politician of the mind, bringing about through his analysis some working agreement to live and let live.

II

More fundamental than any particular interpretation of the history of philosophy is Dewey's view of the historical function of philo-sophical thought itself. Philosophy is basically a phenomenon of human culture. Its very nature is the role it has played in the history of civilization.[3] The philosophical tradition of the Western world took form in Hellas, and Greek thinkers laid its foundations. "Even if these foundations are not always built upon, it is impossible to understand departures and innovations apart from some reference to Greek thought." [4] But the problems the Greeks thus formulated and trans-mitted to the West did not evolve in the consciousness of lonely though brilliant thinkers. Rather was Greece, and especially Athens, the intellectual mirror in which men first saw clearly reflected the es-sential difficulties and predicaments that arise in the collective relation of man to nature and to his fellow man. "These origins prove that such problems are formulations of complications existing in the mate-rial of collective experience, provided that experience is sufficiently free, exposed to change, and subjected to attempts at deliberate con-trol to present in typical form the basic difficulties with which human thought has to reckon." (*Ibid.*) Greek life offered both the typical

---

[3] "Take the history of philosophy from whatever angle and in whatever cross-section you please . . . and you find a load of traditions proceeding from an immemorial past. . . . The life of all thought is to effect a junction at some point of the new and the old, of deep-sunk customs and unconscious dispositions, brought to the light of attention by some conflict with newly emerging directions of activity. Philosophies which emerge at distinctive periods define the larger patterns of continuity which are woven in effecting the longer enduring junctions of a stubborn past and an insistent future. . . . Thus phi-losophy marks a change of culture. In forming patterns, to be conformed to in future thought and action, it is additive and transforming in its role in the history of civiliza-tion." *Philosophy and Civilization*, pp. 6–8.

[4] "Philosophy," in *Encyclopedia of the Social Sciences* (New York, 1934), Vol. XII, p. 119.

conflicts of man's social experience, and the intellectual freedom (born of the absence of a priestly power and a poetic rather than a dogmatic formulation of religious beliefs) to reflect on them, rationalize them in general terms, and endeavor to deal with them intelligently. Aware of their society as in rapid flux, and imbued with the sense of the power of human art to manipulate its materials, the Greek thinkers worked out programs of moral and political conduct in a natural setting they could hope to fathom and understand.

The Greeks built an intelligible world: they invented the ideas, concepts, and distinctions in terms of which they could create an ordered intellectual life. Since their achievement there have been successive attempts to use Greek thought to interpret a novel and alien experience, to deal with new social problems and new schemes of value. The Oriental peoples employed it to express a religious theocracy, the Christians, to rationalize the Hebrew-Oriental religious tradition, the Schoolmen, to organize medieval society and culture, the moderns, to understand and make rationally consistent a scientific method that has persisted in remaining unintelligible, and to adjust somehow their inherited wisdom to the secular and industrial values of the modern world. Each episode involved a reconstruction of Greek thought, and each a striking off of original ideas. The consequence has been a piling up of confusion, yet at the same time of an extraordinarily rich and fertile mass of intellectual resources. Always it has been the conflicts between old ideas and new ways of acting that have led men to the searching thought that is philosophy; the impingement of novel experience upon traditional beliefs and values that has impelled them to construct their systems and programs; the emergence of new ideas irrelevant to or logically incompatible with the old, which yet had somehow to be adjusted to them, and worked into the accustomed pattern of living and thinking. Philosophic problems arise whenever the strife of ideas and experience forces men back to fundamental assumptions in any field; such problems are to be understood only as expressions of the basic conflicts within a culture that drive men to thoroughgoing criticism. Philosophy is the expression in thought of the process of cultural change itself: it is the intellectual phase of the process by which conflicts within a civilization are resolved and composed. A civilization that has grown stable and static may have inherited a philosophy, but it produces no philosophic thought.[5]

It is clear how such a view of the historic function of philosophy in human culture makes questions of value integral to its very essence. The changes in philosophic problems and thought are all inherently bound up with new emphases and new redistributions in the significance of values. "For each philosophy," points out Dewey, "is in effect, if not in avowed intent, an interpretation of man and nature on the basis of some program of comprehensive aims and policies. . . . Each system . . . is, implicitly, a recommendation of certain types of value as normative in the direction of human conduct. . . . It is a generic definition of philosophy to say that it is concerned with problems of being and occurrence from the standpoint of value, rather than from that of mere existence" (122).

In the light of this interpretation, it is not hard to see why "reconstruction" is so dear a word for Dewey. The life of thought, in its humblest as in its most exalted reaches, is a reconstruction of the material it finds at hand. Now reconstruction first involves criticism, the careful appraisal, the exact determination of powers and potentialities, with their limits and their promise, the verification and testing of the values which tradition transmits and emotion suggests. But it also demands a freedom of speculation, a search for new hypotheses and more fertile principles. In its long history philosophy has again and again pruned away accepted beliefs, confined them within new and narrower limits, determined their function more effectively and precisely. But it has also brought fresh and original ideas to birth. The mere piling up of observations unfertilized and unguided by theory is to be found in neither the history nor the procedure of scientific inquiry. "The origin of modern science is to be understood as much by the substitution of new comprehensive guiding ideas for those which had previously obtained as by improvement of the means and appli-

---

[5] "The conception of philosophy reached from a cultural point of view may be summed up by a definition of philosophy as a critique of basic and widely shared beliefs. For belief, as distinct from special scientific knowledge, always involves valuation, preferential attachment to special types of objects and courses of action. . . . Thus philosophies are generated and are particularly active in periods of marked social change. . . . The chief role of philosophy is to bring to consciousness, in an intellectualized form, or in the form of problems, the most important shocks and inherent troubles of complex and changing societies, since these have to do with conflicts of value." *Ibid.*, p. 124.

ances of observation. By the necessity of the case, comprehensive directive hypotheses belong in their original formulation to philosophy rather than to science" (125). This is true not only of scientific notions like the mathematical interpretation of nature, the idea of evolution, of energy, or of the atom; it is still clearer in political and social theory, which have derived all their concepts from philosophies that started as battle-cries in some human struggle. "As long as we worship science and are afraid of philosophy we shall have no great science; we shall have a lagging and halting continuation of what is thought and said elsewhere. This is a plea for the casting off of that intellectual timidity which hampers the wings of imagination, a plea for speculative audacity, for more faith in ideas, sloughing off a cowardly reliance upon those partial ideas to which we are wont to give the name of facts." [6]

Dewey's view of philosophy as the intellectual instrument whereby a culture reconstructs itself, in whole or in part, is itself of course a reconstruction of tradition. Like everything touching the social sciences, it owes much to the Hegelian vision of history, and to the long line of idealists who built upon it in their analysis of human culture. It owes much also to the left-wing Hegelians like Marx who bent Hegel's idealism of social experience to the active service of changing the world. But the obvious points of contact should not be taken, as they have sometimes been, to obscure the essential differences. If Dewey escapes the naive provincialism of the philosophies of physics, according to which past thinkers have merely wasted their time in a fruitless search for mistaken truths about reality, he differs also from the idealists who have passively appreciated philosophy as the expression of the collective spirit and imagination. For him thought is still thinking, and human, not an unrolling of the divine plan. It is active, efficient, and constructive, not in that wholesale fashion that makes it irrelevant to any human problem, but in that specific and piecemeal way that suits the needs of intelligent organisms. It is neither the mere passive reflex of material interests and conditions, nor the slave of an immutable absolute dialectic. Philosophy is the human instrument of groups of men acting as wisely as they may on specific programs and problems. And its imaginative vision has been successful only when

[6] *Philosophy and Civilization*, p. 12.

disciplined by responsibility to the exacting tests of scientific method. For all their power and insight, the idealists failed to appreciate the liberation that comes from conformity to the regulative principles of scientific inquiry.

But if the ultimate context within which philosophy operates is cultural change, and if that social function defines its nature, Dewey is far from therefore taking its value as merely instrumental. Science too is science because of its proper function, because it enlarges our power to act and do what we have intelligently chosen; but that need not prevent the greatest good it brings being the immediate enjoyment of the power of sheer knowing. Just so the great philosophies, born as the programs for some particular task of adjustment, have yet raised themselves some little way above the conflict to a more comprehensive view of life; and those eternal visions glimpsed by men struggling in the circumstances of time may well be now their chief claim to our attention. Philosophy is an art, one of the noblest; and like every art it is at once the instrument for performing a specific function, and an immediate good to be possessed and enjoyed. With Santayana, Dewey agrees that the history of philosophy contains poetry as well as politics. But he urges us to beware lest we confuse the two.

Nor does Dewey follow the Hegelians and Marxians in taking the historical function of philosophy as unilinear and monistic. Rather he finds it inexhaustibly pluralistic in the problems from which it takes its start. There is no one type of conflict that is fundamental and controlling. Dewey is no Marxian; important as is the strife of economic groups, especially in modern times, philosophic thought has played a role far richer than that of a mere class ideology. The importance of conflict Dewey learned from Hegel as well as from the facts of history. But the conflicts that have given rise to philosophy he sees not merely as economic, but as in the broadest sense psychological and cultural—for him the two must ultimately coincide. The inertia of habitual ways of acting and believing is forever opposed to the power of new ideas. The specific historical function of philosophy is ultimately to get men to act and believe together in new ways: it is political and educational. That is why he finds the intellectual method of reorganizing and reconstructing habits of belief and action, the method of political education or "cooperative intelligence," of such basic importance.

Yet in modern times there has emerged one central conflict as the

focus for understanding all Western philosophies. It is the ever re-
peated struggle between the active force of scientific knowledge and
technical power and the deflecting force of the lag and inertia of institutionalized habits and beliefs, generating the insistent problem of political education if the potentialities of the new knowledge are to be re-
leased.

The conflict is between institutions and habits originating in the pre-scientific
and pre-technological age and the new forces generated by science and technology. The application of science, to a considerable degree, even its own
growth, has been conditioned by the system to which the name of capitalism
is given, a rough designation of a complex of political and legal arrangements
centering about a particular mode of economic relations. . . . Institutional
relationships fixed in the pre-scientific age stand in the way of accomplishing
this great transformation. Lag in mental and moral patterns provides the
bulwark of the older institutions. . . . Change in patterns of belief, desire
and purpose has lagged behind the modification of the external conditions
under which men associate. Industrial habits have changed most rapidly;
there has followed at considerable distance, change in political relations; al-
terations in legal relations and methods have lagged even more, while changes
in the institutions that deal most directly with patterns of thought and belief
have taken place to the least extent. This fact defines the primary, though not
by any means the ultimate, responsibility of a liberalism that intends to be a
vital force. Its work is first of all education, in the broadest sense of that term
. . . I mean that its task is to aid in producing the habits of mind and character, the intellectual and moral patterns, that are somewhere near even with
the actual movements of events. . . . The educational task cannot be accomplished merely by working upon men's minds, without action that effects
actual change in institutions. . . . But resolute thought is the first step in that
change of action that will itself carry further the needed change in patterns of
mind and character.[7]

This is not the place to question or to defend the adequacy of
Dewey's program for our present conflicts. If he be right, if it be true
that history itself generates change in the method of directing social
change, then surely the most insistent problem today is precisely this
one of political education. And the achievement of the political intelligence to persuade men to use the intelligence we do as a society
possess must be the conscious focus of our philosophies. Instead of
many fine generalities about the "method of cooperative intelligence,"
Dewey might well direct attention to this crucial problem of extend-

[7] *Liberalism and Social Action* (New York, 1935), pp. 75–76; 58–62.

ing our political skill. For political skill can itself be taken as a technological problem to which inquiry can hope to bring an answer. It is obviously dependent on our acquiring the knowledge of how to get men to apply the techniques already available for dealing with our social problems, how to enlist the cooperative support of men in doing what we now know how to do. Thus by rights Dewey's philosophy should culminate in the earnest consideration of the social techniques for reorganizing beliefs and behavior—techniques very different from those for dealing with natural materials. It should issue in a social engineering, in an applied science of political education—and not merely in the hope that someday we may develop one.

But whatever our needs and resources in this crucial field, it is the cultural conflict that generates this problem of political education, the strife between new knowledge and power and the lag of institutionalized habit, that gives Dewey the key to his psychological interpretation of history in general and the history of philosophy in particular. In that history philosophy has functioned as an instrument of reconstruction, and the philosopher has ever played the role of the adjuster and compromiser, the mediator between old and new, the peacemaker who consciously strives to blend both in a novel pattern which, added as a further deposit, becomes the starting-point of further change.

It may be that Dewey has developed his conception of the essentially critical and reconstructive function of philosophy out of his study of the record of the past. It may be that, himself a critic, he has found his own image in all who have come before. Doubtless both factors were present. But whatever the source of his views, it remains true that he approaches his heritage always as a critic and reconstructor of tradition. And in his constant historical analysis of the materials that have come down to him, it is as a critic of the past that he is to be understood. He is forever bringing men's past experience with ideas to the test of present experience. "It is difficult to avoid reading the past in terms of the contemporary scene. Indeed, fundamentally it is impossible to avoid this course. . . . It is highly important that we are compelled to follow this path. For the past as past is gone, save for esthetic enjoyment and refreshment, while the present is with us. Knowledge of the past is significant only as it deepens and extends our understanding of the present" (74).

In the twelfth chapter of his *Logic* Dewey has a brilliant analysis of
the historian's method, which makes plain why historical judgments
must be centered on the problems of the present. It is his most penetrating statement of the theory that lies behind his own practice.

As culture changes, the conceptions that are dominant in a culture change
. . . History is then rewritten. Material that had formerly been passed by,
offers itself as data, because the new conceptions propose new problems for
solution, requiring new factual material for statement and test. . . . All historical construction is necessarily selective. . . . If the fact of selection is acknowledged to be primary and basic, we are committed to the conclusion that
all history is necessarily written from the standpoint of the present, and is, in
an inescapable sense, the history not only of the present but of that which is
contemporaneously judged to be important in the present. . . . Intelligent
understanding of past history is to some extent a lever for moving the present
into a certain kind of future. . . . Men have their own problems to solve,
their own adaptations to make. They face the future, but for the sake of the
present, not of the future. In using what has come to them as an inheritance
from the past they are compelled to modify it to meet their own needs, and
this process creates a new present in which the process continues. History
cannot escape its own process.[8]

But the details of this functional conception of historical understanding, suggestive as they are, are not so important as the insistence
that historical knowledge *has* a function. It presents us with material
to be criticised and used. This fact has far-reaching implications for
Dewey's treatment of the history of philosophy. That treatment is
carried through consistently with an eye to what is significant and important for the problems he judges to be significant today. This explains why he singles out for attention what he does, and neglects
other things, why certain figures are emphasized, certain problems
stressed, why method is taken as more controlling than vision. It
explains why what he does select he treats as material to be critically
reconstructed, rather than as achievement to be enjoyed. While the
Greeks and the empiricists of the liberal tradition figure prominently
in his pages, the fact that they appear only to have certain of their assumptions drastically attacked is no longer a paradox. The Greeks and
the empiricists would not appear at all were their thought not so important a part of our own instrumentalities. And it helps to explain
why, for all his insight and suggestiveness, Dewey seems so often to

---

[8] *Logic: The Theory of Inquiry* (New York, 1938), pp. 233, 235, 239.

do less than justice to the great achievements of the past. He is far from denying those achievements; but his concern is with power and not justice, for he fears that in their complacent celebration we today will rest in their triumphs, instead of building further on the foundations they have laid.

III

In certain quarters Dewey still figures as the iconoclast seeking to destroy utterly the idolatrous worship of the past. Nothing could be further from the truth; and it is difficult to see how any perceptive reader could fail to discern in him the greatest traditionalist among the leading philosophical minds of today. For the true traditionalist does not merely repeat the familiar shibboleths, he understands how to use tradition in facing our present problems. In his discriminating employment of the historical resources of philosophy, Dewey has no rival.

There are two quite different ways of using a method that is essentially critical, two ways well illustrated by two students whom Dewey has taught. One, a brilliant Chinese, despite the fact that Chinese thought exhibits much of the temper of Dewey himself, took Dewey's experimentalism to mean that the state must be wiped clean for a fresh start. The Chinese past was utterly mistaken, and must be forgotten: men must build anew from scratch, and by assiduous cultivation of the scientific method, develop for China a philosophy embodying all those values which Dewey has found the permanent deposit of the Christian and individualistic West. The other was a Hindu, confronted by a culture far different from that in which Dewey has operated, and therefore tempted to sweep it too away. But he took the method of Dewey to indicate rather that one should manipulate reflectively the material at one's disposal; and so he tried to arrive at what the peculiar Hindu values might mean when critically examined in the light of the demands of today. He emerged, not with the scheme of beliefs which Dewey has rebuilt for the West, but with a translation of Hindu spirituality into terms that could stand up in the presence of scientific criticism. To him Dewey offered a method for dealing with his own inherited materials. There is little doubt but that he understood Dewey better than the Chinese, and had a firmer grasp on the spirit of his experimentalism. For he knew that Dewey meant not destruction but reconstruction; he knew that criticism demands a tradition as the material on which to work.

So, however penetrating his criticisms of traditions in the plural and in detail, it is fundamental for Dewey that tradition remains the subject matter within which the critical method that is philosophy must operate. Material and critical instrument—both are alike essential to any valid and fruitful experimental art. Nowhere has Dewey made this more explicit than in an essay in which he was most anxious to emphasize the need of working also with the present.

A philosopher who would relate his thinking to present civilization, in its predominantly technological and industrial character, cannot ignore any of these movements [eighteenth-century rationalism, German idealism, the religious and philosophic traditions of Europe] any more than he can dispense with consideration of the underlying classic tradition formed in Greece and the Middle Ages. If he ignores traditions, his thoughts become thin and empty. But they are something to be employed, not just treated with respect or dressed out in a new vocabulary. Moreover, industrial civilization itself has now sufficiently developed to form its own tradition. . . . If philosophy declines to observe and interpret the new and characteristic scene, it may achieve scholarship; it may erect a well equipped gymnasium wherein to engage in dialectical exercises; it may clothe itself in fine literary art. But it will not afford illumination or direction to our confused civilization. These can proceed only from the spirit that is interested in realities and that faces them frankly and sympathetically.[9]

The great traditions and "present realities"—they are equally indispensable materials for philosophic reflection, in our present or in any past present; and the philosophic task, ever old and ever new, is to bring them together significantly and fruitfully. From this follow several of the most characteristic traits of Dewey's treatment of the intellectual record. In the first place, there is the thoroughgoing historical relativism with which he views the figures and movements of the past—an objective relativism, to be sure, for the ideas of previous thinkers must be understood as specifically and objectively relative to the particular conditions and conflicts to which they were the answer. Before we can assay the worth of an idea today, we must first find its meaning in terms of the issues faced by the man who formulated it. Traditional concepts are not to be judged by the measure in which

[9] "Philosophy," in *Whither Mankind: A Panorama of Modern Civilization*, ed. Charles Austin Beard (New York, 1928), pp. 313–31.

they fall short of an illusory eternal truth; the ultimate test in terms of their availability for our problems can come only after we have understood their adequacy for the past problems they were devised to meet.

This is well illustrated in Dewey's most recent examination of the Aristotelian logic. This intellectual instrument he is peculiarly tempted to judge by our needs rather than by those of the Greeks. "For Aristotelian logic enters so vitally into present theories that consideration of it, instead of being historical in import, is a consideration of the contemporary logical scene." Yet he is careful to make clear:

It would be completely erroneous to regard the foregoing as a criticism of the Aristotelian logic in its original formulation in connection with Greek culture. As a *historic* document it deserves the admiration it has received. As a comprehensive, penetrating and thoroughgoing intellectual transcript of discourse in isolation from the operations in which discourse takes effect it is above need for praise. . . . Generically, the need is for logic to do for present science and culture what Aristotle did for the science and culture of his time.[10]

Or take his acute statement of Spinoza's essential problem:

An unqualified naturalism in the sense in which he understood the new science was combined by a miracle of logic with an equally complete acceptance of the idea, derived from the religious tradition, that ultimate reality is the measure of perfection and the norm for human activity. . . . A scientific comprehension was to give, in full reality, by rational means, that assurance and regulation of life that non-rational religions had pretended to give. . . . There have been few attempts in modern philosophy as bold and as direct as is this one to effect a complete integration of scientific method with a good which is fixed and final, because based on the rock of absolute cognitive certainty.[11]

Like so many of Dewey's most suggestive historical insights, these analyses occur in the midst of appraisals of our resources for meeting present problems. There is hardly need to single out professedly historical studies, like his illuminating paper on "The Motivation of Hobbes's Political Philosophy," [12] in which by viewing Hobbes in terms of his own controversies he brings him into the line of "the protagonists of a science of human nature operating through an art of social control in behalf of a common good"; or his "Substance, Power

[10] *Logic*, pp. 81; 93–95.

[11] *The Quest for Certainty* (New York, 1929), pp. 53–55.

[12] In *Studies in the History of Ideas* by the Department of Philosophy of Columbia University (New York, 1918), Vol. I, pp. 88–115.

and Quality in Locke," [13] in which he is extraordinarily successful in brushing aside conventional views and penetrating to Locke's own difficulties with the certainty of knowledge; or his analysis of Newton in the *Quest for Certainty*. Mention might be made of a somewhat different type of historical analysis that recurs in Dewey's pages, the attempts to characterize the complex cultural features that have generated and sustained certain great movements of ideas. This type of thing is extraordinarily difficult to carry through in detail, as the Marxians and other German historians have discovered to their peril; and at best the keenest insight can hope to attain only shrewd guesses which would take a lifetime of research to verify and refine. Dewey would be the first to admit that his own suggestions are far too simple; yet ever since his essay on "The Significance of the Problem of Knowledge," published in 1897,[14] he has been remarkably fertile in throwing out such leads. The two central works, *Experience and Nature* and *The Quest for Certainty*, contain enough suggestions of this sort for further investigation to keep a whole historical school going for a generation.

Secondly, out of this objective historical relativism there develops the conception of philosophic thought as cumulative and additive, like the body of science with which it is so closely allied. Especially is this true of intellectual method, which grows in flexibility and power as its problems vary and as new technical devices and skills are built up. Each time an instrument is applied to fresh circumstances, it is itself enhanced and enriched. Greek thought remains the core of the classic tradition; yet the very diversity of the movements and cultural factors on which it has been employed, especially during the modern period, has subjected it to one illuminating criticism after another. Since for Dewey the process of criticism is emphatically the addition of further knowledge and not subtraction, since it reveals the larger context within which ideas are able to function validly and dualisms are disclosed as functional distinctions, these successive critical episodes have added precision of meaning and a delimitation of range of applicability, as well as new hypotheses and suggestions to be criticised in turn. The fortunes of Greek thought under the impact of eighteenth-

---

[13] *Philosophical Review*, XXXV (Jan. 1926), pp. 22–38.
[14] Reprinted in *The Influence of Darwin on Philosophy and Other Essays in Contemporary Thought* (New York, 1910), pp. 271–304.

century empiricism, of the Kantian and post-Kantian movements, and of the new techniques and concepts of nineteenth-century natural and social science, are a cardinal illustration of the cumulative character of a vital intellectual tradition. Another is the building of the liberal tradition in social affairs, the gradual bringing to bear of scientific thought upon men's social relations. And still a third is exhibited in the growth, expansion, and ultimate adjustment of the conceptions of human liberty, as set forth in "Philosophies of Freedom." [15]

In the third place, this objective relativism and cumulative character of the philosophical traditions make possible an intellectual tolerance and comprehensiveness that can find a place for every philosophy and every way of life. No single one can claim exclusive domination; each can be welcomed with understanding appraisal when once its particular and appropriate function has been historically understood. As vision, as the imaginative expression of a definite culture, each has its own unique worth. As method, as a means for composing our own conflicts, each has a *prima facie* claim to be considered—though each must pass the stern test of its fruits. None is immune to philosophic criticism: each, stripped of its assumed unlimited validity, must abide within the bounds its historic operations have revealed. But each great belief of the past has some core of value from which we can learn and which we can use. Breadth and not narrowness of vision, generous reception and not intolerant single-mindedness, mark the spirit of Dewey's recurrent appeals to the past. If we are to assimilate its varied insights, we face a never-ending problem of harmonization and adjustment. And if all are to live in peace, none must be so stiff-necked, as to refuse submission to the necessary reconstruction.

At only two points does Dewey's tolerant welcome stop short. The cardinal philosophic sin has been to shrink from practical action to take refuge in an unshakable higher realm of fixed and antecedent Reality. Afraid to seek a shifting and relative security by the efforts of intelligence, men have found consolation in the exaltation of pure intellect and the eternal intelligible perfection it has beheld. This cowardly choice, to accept a world understood instead of trying to change it, Dewey connects, by a somewhat dubious logic, with the quest for an absolute and immutable certainty in the things of the

---

[15] Reprinted in *Philosophy and Civilization*, pp. 271–98.

mind. Whatever has appeared in past thought of such a craven yearning for the eternal and unchanging must be dissolved forever in the
relativities of time. For complete fixity or absolute certainty there can
be no place.

And the great vice of practice has been an equally illiberal and
inhumane choice. Men have cultivated the so-called higher values, and
disdained the homely goods of common experience. From the
poverty-stricken Oriental lands they have inherited despair of ever
making widespread the natural and social goods of living. Leaving the
latter to the avarice of the worldly, they have aspired to a Good Life
located in a far different "spiritual" realm. With righteousness and pu-
rity of heart, the great moral faiths of renunciation, they have con-
soled the penniless beggar, the lame, the halt, and the blind—even
such can attain the Highest. Such counsels of despair Dewey not
unwisely finds irrelevant today. But with them he also dismisses all
selection, all concentration on certain values to the inevitable exclusion of the rest. When confronted by the apparent necessity of choice,
intelligence must insist that both courses are valuable, and impel an
active and aggressive manipulation of conditions until both are made
compatible. To reject any values completely is to accept defeat. In his
ethical and educational theory Dewey has stood for the Romantic
ideal. The richest possible variety of goods must be included, but this
very choice of inclusion has excluded the historic values of selection
and single-minded devotion. There is no place for any ascetic or Puritan ideal.

IV

What has been here set forth is an attempt to catch the fundamental
drive of Dewey's position on how philosophy's past is to be understood and used. Yet men have not always read him thus. These persistent variations raise doubts as to whether he has always consistently
practiced his own essential teaching. We may well conclude by formulating these doubts for his adjudication.

First, the equal necessity of tradition, present experience, and reconstructive criticism is intellectually clear. But it is also beyond dispute that the very terms he uses again and again suggest a loading on
the side of deep emotional feeling for liberation from the past. In
Dewey's lifetime America has emancipated itself from restricting pro-

vincialism and narrow and fossilized religious and moral codes. His leadership in that emancipation has been effective and mighty: but it has determined his task and defined his own historic problems. This is both understandable and inevitable. But the warm sympathies so generously enlisted in the struggles of what is now his and not our generation have left their train of misconceptions. The question they raise is, are we to trust his obvious feelings, or his considered words? Are we to approach the past as revolutionaries who would fain forget as much of it as we can, and make a wholly fresh start? Or are we to analyse and use it in the interests of experimental reconstruction?

Secondly, there is the method whereby the value of past ideas is to be judged. Again Dewey's basic position is clear: we must summon all our resources of intellectual analysis to ascertain how those ideas have operated, in their generating conditions, in their subsequent career, in our own adjustments. The test must be wholly functional: ideas are to be evaluated by their consequences in experience. Yet here too Dewey's practice has created misconceptions: to critics he has seemed to commit the genetic fallacy, and to admirers, to justify the discrediting of ideas by an account of their origins. For instance, it has not helped for him to say: "The more adequate [Aristotelian] logic was in its own day, the less fitted is it to form the framework of present logical theory." [16] It is not the fact but the method that raises the question. Is the bare discovery of the genesis of beliefs in some past epoch enough to dispose of them? Or is such a genetic analysis only a preliminary to determining the conditions to be satisfied by a genuinely functional test?

Thirdly, there is the unceasing polemic against any traffic with "certainty" that runs as a thread through all Dewey's historical criticisms. To friend and foe this has often appeared the most characteristic feature of his treatment of the history of philosophy. I have deliberately avoided emphasizing it. For though it be essential in his own mind, I doubt whether the future will judge it a very significant part of his contribution to our knowledge of the past. We have thoroughly learned that ideas are relative to a context, and that neither history nor science reveals any fixed absolutes. Those who have not are not likely to learn it from Dewey. He has played his part, and it would be

[16] *Logic*, p. 82.

ungrateful to forget it; but Dewey scarcely gave our age its relativism. The constant harping on its previous absence sounds a little like the advice to remember the schoolmen were Christians, or the moderns dwellers in an era of capitalism.

The question is rather about the sources of this ancient illusion. Does the utmost devotion to changing the world through action exclude as a cardinal sin all attempt to change the self in emotion and idea? To be intelligent, must one renounce all wisdom of renunciation? Are there no vital and strengthening arts of consolation? Is not vision itself a power over the passions? Dewey's reasoned answer is clear, and might be abundantly cited. But there are those passages like the one about ideal friendship and the unreality of space and time.[17] Classic thought beheld the vision of the communion of the saints. But moderns have done better: they have invented the telephone and the radio. Is Dewey seriously advising the bereaved to get a medium and ring up their dead? The illustration, I fear, is symbolic. Would Dewey dismiss out of hand all that imagination has done to make existence endurable, just because the world has not yet through action been made quite wholly new?

And finally, there is the judgment of the classic tradition, of Greek thought, of Aristotle. Here Dewey's procedure is more revealing than his words. *Experience and Nature* is not unique, but typical: again and again on every major philosophic issue he first displays the dualisms, the wrenchings apart, the messy confusions of modern thought, only to turn to the Greeks in admiration for their clarity of perception. It is their ideas he deems fruitful material for further critical development. And in contrast to the whole of modern philosophy, save where it in turn has most powerfully felt Greek influence, Dewey himself seems to be working primarily with the conceptions of Aristotle. In his naturalism, his pluralism, his logical and social empiricism, his realism, his natural teleology, his ideas of potentiality and actuality, contingency and regularity, qualitatively diverse individuality—above all, in his thoroughgoing functionalism, his Aristotelian translation of all the problems of matter and form into a functional context, to say nothing of his basic social and ethical concepts—in countless vital matters he is nearer to the Stagirite than to any other philosopher. Where he has

---

[17] *Reconstruction in Philosophy* (New York, 1920), pp. 119–20.

used the instruments of a century of critical effort—the empiricists' analysis, the post-Kantian appeal to a more human experience, the biological and social conceptions of human nature, the lessons of a rapidly changing culture—it has been to carry the Aristotelian attitude still further in the direction in which Aristotle criticised Platonism. It would not be difficult to exhibit Dewey as an Aristotelian more Aristotelian than Aristotle himself.

Yet one would hardly realize this from his words. His use of Aristotelian ideas has been remarkably fruitful. But however effective in developing his own position, most of what he has explicitly said about Aristotle has conveyed little real historical illumination: it has been far more relevant to Saint Thomas than to the Greek. Much of what he points to is there; much is not, and is to be found only in the scholastic tradition. It would scarcely be proper and pertinent, even if true, to maintain here that the total impression he gives of Aristotelian thought is nevertheless false. It would be more to the point to ask: Why should Dewey view Aristotle through the eyes of the Neo-Thomists? Why should he not see Aristotle for what he is, the greatest functionalist in the philosophical tradition? For Dewey of all thinkers today can best claim to be the representative of Aristotelian thought, the truest follower of him who likewise in his time most effectively and suggestively brought the criticism of the best scientific thought to bear on the classic tradition.

APPENDIX

French Spiritualism and Idealism

WE HAVE SEEN HOW, under the Second Empire, Comtean Positivism came to express the philosophy of most of the better minds in France, leaving the official teaching positions in the hands of second-rate followers of Cousin's Eclecticism; and how even Vacherot, who had succeeded to Cousin's chair, had developed a comprehensive philosophical system with a heavy emphasis on positivistic and scientific elements. The two figures who emerged under the Empire as philosophers of European reputation, Taine and Renan, were driven by the unfavorable atmosphere—the teaching of philosophy had been forbidden in the lycées, and Vacherot was removed from his chair in 1858—to turn to independent literary pursuits, although Renan was appointed Professor of Hebrew at the Collège de France in 1861. After the establishment of the Third Republic, the official academic Eclectics lingered on through the 1880s, doing their most effective work in historical studies.

At this time two new currents came to the fore, destined, along with the continuing stream of Positivism, which developed into a psychological branch with Ribot and a sociological one with Durkheim, to dominate French philosophizing down to the Second World War. Both were French forms of the idealistic protest against the exclusive worship of natural science. The first of these was a newly invigorated Spiritualism and idealism, that partly continued the tradition of Maine de Biran, and partly turned for inspiration to the classic German Idealists of the post-Kantian period, chiefly Schelling and Hegel. The second current was a form of the return to a Kantian critical idealism that was coming to dominate German philosophizing, and that appeared in England with T.H. Green. The new Spiritualism was

Originally intended as part of Book VII.

first proclaimed in France in the ringing manifesto of 1867 of Ravaisson; it had been preceded by the Swiss thinker Secrétan. It was carried on by the most influential academic philosopher of the last generation of the century, Ravaisson's pupil Lachelier, and perpetuated in turn by his own pupil Émile Boutroux. Neo-Kantianism was given a strong impetus in France by the "neocriticism" of Renouvier; after 1890 it produced a spate of critical analyses of science known as the *Critique de la Science*, of which perhaps those of Pierre Duhem and Henri Poincaré are the best known outside France itself. These same two currents continued to monopolize French philosophizing between the two World Wars, the Spiritualism being represented by Léon Brunschvicg, the Neo-Kantianism by Émile Meyerson.

Both currents were essentially idealistic protests against science. But the impact of science on French culture was somewhat different from its incidence in England and Scotland. In these Protestant countries it was the religious tradition that felt the critical force of the so-called "scientific world view." In France the main stream of French Catholicism, after the encyclical *Aeterni Patris* of 1879, turned for its philosophic support to the medieval figure who had been able to come to working terms with Aristotelian science during a similar crisis, Thomas Aquinas; though there appeared also a strong minority who drew on the philosophic idealism of the century, and led to the Modernist movement within the Church, continuing even after their condemnation in *Pascendi Gregis* in 1907. Hence what the non-Catholic philosophers in France had to defend against the new science was not an organized religious tradition, as in English-speaking lands, but that form of "liberal Deism" that had been taught in the schools by the followers of Cousin, and above all the independent morality that had taken in public education the place of religious teaching. It was not the religious tradition but the moral life that thoughtful Frenchmen found undermined by the new scientific ideas. It was the determinism of a mechanistic science that seemed the major threat; hence it was the problem of moral freedom, indeed, the very existence of genuine morality, that seemed the most pressing philosophic issue. Both French Spiritualism and French neocriticism were philosophies that culminated in the vindication of man's moral freedom. God and immortality, so central in the English and American idealistic protest, were pushed into the background. It was thus the problem of freedom that became central for all three major French schools, Positivists, Spiritualists, and critical philosophers.

Partly because in France it was not theological and religious thinkers who felt the need of new philosophical defenses against science (such men had Neo-Thomism to turn to) but more secular humanists and even scientists themselves; and partly because any serious criticism of the reigning monistic determinism demanded some acquaintance with scientific thought, French idealism is much more closely associated with science than is the idealism of the religiously oriented English-speaking idealists. French idealism was not carried on in a different universe from the thinking of the scientists. On the contrary, most of the French idealists had received an excellent scientific training themselves. One consequence of this different situation in France is that in that land it was idealists of the Spiritualistic variety that were the popularizers of the new Romantic faith in Evolution. Since Positivism was essentially an eighteenth-century, certainly a pre-evolutionary philosophy, the French Positivists, while accepting the biological hypothesis, never found in it the emotional salvation of a new scientific faith that it awakened in England. It was left for one branch of the Spiritualistic idealists—Durand de Gros, Fouillée, and Guyau—to popularize Evolution as a substitute religious faith; and for one of this group, Bergson, a pupil of Boutroux, to be the first French philosopher to give the new philosophy of human freedom, set forth in terms of creative evolution, a world-wide influence.

I

The founders of the new Spiritualism that appealed to Maine de Biran were Secrétan and Ravaisson. As students they had heard together the lectures of the older Schelling in Munich; and both represent a fusion of ideas from Schelling and Biran, with Leibniz as a forerunner. Biran is more fundamental to Ravaisson, Schelling to Secrétan. The latter announces his views as "an attempt at positive philosophy, founded on the independence of morality."

Charles Secrétan (1815–95) was a Swiss who taught at Lausanne. He brought out in 1848–49 his *Philosophie de la Liberté* in two volumes. This can be taken as a "Spiritualistic" counterpart to Spencer's cosmic evolution, though its "positive" principles are derived from Schelling rather than from physical science. But there is the same task of proceeding from the first principles of the universe to their culmination in human morality, from the Absolute to multiplicity and heterogeneity. Metaphysics must furnish a sound basis for human conduct. And for Secrétan as for Schelling, morality reaches its goal in religion, so that his Philosophy of Liberty he calls an apologetic for Christianity. He tries to mediate between pantheism and fideism through a "Christian reason."

Absolute Being is pure freedom, self-activity. To be truly self-active is to be spirit. Secrétan follows Biran in defining spirit as the ability to determine the kind of one's activity, to be *causa sui*. Inner experience confirms the reality of such spirit. We are ourselves the cause of our activity, the cause of the way in which we are cause, cause of the laws in which we create ourselves. We are the cause of our causality and its law. In a word, we are free. Spirit and freedom are one. Thus Secrétan pushed the Spinozistic *causa sui* in the direction of the Leibniz-Biran-Schellingian dynamism of "force." Reality, spirit, will, activity, are synonymous.

Secrétan thus proclaims moral freedom as the essence both of life and of reality. Morality is the art of regulating man's free activity, it is the perfecting of life. The whole of morality lies in the imperative, "realize your freedom." Man can only do so by loving God, or absolute freedom, and thus creating his own personality.

Here is the French answer to the mechanistic determinism of nineteenth-century science. Here too is the century-old background to the "absolute freedom" of the more recent Sartre and French existentialism.

II

Spiritualism was proclaimed, as against both Cousin's eclecticism and Comte's positivism, by Félix Ravaisson-Mollien (1813–1900), in his manifesto of 1867, *Rapport sur la Philosophie en France au XIXe Siècle*. In 1838 Ravaisson had written a careful thesis, *De l'Habitude*, an analysis in the spirit of Biran; he had also produced a detailed study of Aristotle's *Metaphysics* (1837–46). His manifesto was prepared, at the request of the Ministry of Education, for the Exposition of 1867. Among his pupils were Lachelier, Boutroux, and Bergson. He called for a valid idealism combining Aristotle's emphasis on thought with the Christian insistence on love, based on Biran's analysis of inner life, and leading to a positive philosophy in Schelling's sense. Looking ahead, he prophesied:

Many signs permit us to foresee in the near future a philosophical epoch of which the general character will be the predominance of what may be called spiritualistic realism or positivism, having as generating principle the consciousness which the mind has of itself as an existence recognized as being the source and support of every other existence, being none other than its action.[1]

This spiritualism, which included the creative evolutionists Durand de Gros, Fouillée, Guyau, and Bergson, remained through Léon Brunschvicg a central strand in French philosophizing until it was reconstructed by Sartre in the 1930s into existentialism. It was a voluntaristic idealism, emphasizing after Biran the active spiritual force of "life," and opposing Schelling's realism and contingency to the deterministic idealism of Hegel. Ravaisson, though like Bergson a poet, was a careful analyst of consciousness. In habit he found the continuity of matter and spirit: habit remains a purposeful action, though become unconscious.

To reflection, which traverses and measures the distances of the contraries, the course of the oppositions, succeeds by degrees an immediate intelligence, in which nothing separates the subject and the object of thought. . . . Habit is more and more a *substantial idea*. The obscure intelligence which in habit succeeds reflection, that immediate intelligence in which the object and the subject are confused, is a *real* intuition, in which are confused the real and the ideal, being and thought.[2]

Habit is thus the clue to the character of nature: "In the bosom of the soul itself, in that inferior world which it animates and which is not itself, there is thus discovered as the limit to which the progress of habit makes action redescend, the unreflective spontaneity of desire, the impersonality of nature" (54). Nature is thus not a blind and mechanical power; it is to be found in a desire which immediately perceives its object; and there it is united to Freedom: "In everything, the necessity of nature is the chain which weaves freedom, but it is a moving and living chain, the necessity of desire, of love and of grace" (59).

Ravaisson had already emphasized Aristotle's criticism of Platonic ideas. Nature, he finds, is for Aristotle a movement and a life which

[1] *Rapport sur la Philosophie en France au XIXe Siècle* (Paris, 1867; 3rd ed., 1889), p. 275.
[2] *De l'Habitude* (Paris, 1838; ed. Baruzi, 1927), pp. 36–37.

desire pushes toward *Nous*, Intelligence, a true reality, and not the empty abstraction of the Ideas. And to Aristotle's nature, which desires a Good which does not know it, Christianity adds a Love which goes out to that which loves it; thus real and ideal, potentiality and act become one and inseparable, though distinct. Kant and the Scottish school relied on the understanding; but Biran has shown that the soul is will and effort, which presupposes a feeling of union already begun with the Good. That union is Love, which forms the true substance of the soul.

There are no psychological "events," for the essence of thinking is self-activity, under which lies no "substance." True philosophical method is hence not that of the understanding, but the living reflection which calls on all our powers, heart and reason, feeling and intellect together. Understanding looks at things from outside, intuition tries to seize them from within. The heart, in Pascal's sense, has the last word. Thus Ravaisson is a forerunner of Bergson's "intuition" and of recent anti-intellectualism.

III

The influential teacher who established the new Spiritualism in the academic teaching of philosophy, and brought it closer to the Kant of the Neocriticists, was Jules Lachelier (1832–1918). A student at the École Normale from 1851 to 1854, when philosophy was well-nigh suppressed in France, he taught there himself from 1864 to 1875. He installed Spiritualism in place of the tradition of Cousin, and supported it in his later administrative posts. His influence came from his teaching, as he wrote little: his thesis, *Du Fondement de l'Induction*, of 1871, and article, *Psychologie et Métaphysique* (1885), several studies on the syllogism, and *Notes sur le Pari de Pascal* (1901).

To Lachelier, Cousin's thought "sets on one side thought with its own internal determinations, and on the other the object, of which thought is but the image, but which consciousness does not attain and envelop." This is to accord to the sceptic all he wants; just as does sensationalistic empiricism. There can be certainty only if reality lies in thought itself. In the *Foundations of Induction* Lachelier demonstrates the law of causality by the arguments of the Transcendental Analytic, and the principle of teleology by those of the Critique of Judgment, giving to both equal value. "If the conditions of the existence of things are the same as the conditions of the possibility of thought, . . . we can determine these conditions absolutely a priori, since they follow from the very nature of our mind." [3] Mechanism differs from teleology in that it deals with an abstract and impoverished reality, while teleology points to a reality rich with directions and with aspiration. Thought, besides being the condition of the objectivity of the world, is a tendency toward the Good and toward the fulness of Being.

Hence Lachelier prefers to the Kantian analytic method a synthetic "reflexive" method. We are sure of the existence of thought when we see it generating its objects by a synthetic operation. Thought first posits time and mechanical necessity; then it creates the heterogeneity of sensations, and space. Thirdly, by reflecting on itself as the source of being, thought becomes sovereign freedom, of which nature, with its necessity and its finality, is only one moment.

Direct perception, "by which phenomena are given to us primitively and before all reflection," [4] is productive of reality. Extension is indeed externality; "but the question is always of knowing whether that existence is outside ourselves by itself, or whether it is we who have put it there by perceiving it" (128). "There is no other extension possible but an ideal and perceived extension" (130).

Lachelier practices a subtle psychological analysis of consciousness. "Consciousness of a pain is not painful, it is true." Intellectual consciousness "liberates it, in thinking it, from the subjectivity of sensible consciousness. . . . It converts simple subjective states into facts and beings which exist in themselves and for all minds; it is the consciousness, not of things, but of the truth or the existence of things" (155). "The final point of support of all truth and all existence is the absolute spontaneity of mind" (103). Lachelier thus in his own way is following the philosophical development of the classic idealists out of Kant. It is for him all the work of reason; he has no use for any method of "intuition." By the side of the anti-intellectualism of Ravaisson and Bergson, Lachelier stands for a thoroughgoing intellectualism, like Brunschvicg.

The principle of efficient causality leads to an idealistic or phenomenalistic materialism; that of final causation, to spiritualistic realism.

[3] *Du Fondement de l'Induction* suivi de *Psychologie et Metaphysique* (Paris, 1898), p. 41.
[4] *Psychologie*, p. 127.

Hence nature possesses two existences, which have their foundation in the two laws that thinking imposes on appearances: one existence identical with science, which rests on the necessary law of efficient causation, and one concrete, identical with the simultaneous aesthetic function, which rests on the contingent law of final causation.[5]

What we call Freedom is just the consciousness of the necessity by which a purpose grasped by our mind in the series of our actions determines the means which for its part is to determine its existence. (101)

On moral problems Lachelier published nothing, but in his lectures he taught an ethical religion close to that of Ravaisson.[6]

IV

Among the students of both Ravaisson and Lachelier was Émile Boutroux (1845–1921). His most influential writing was his thesis, *De la Contingence des Lois de la Nature* (1874), dedicated to Ravaisson; in 1894 he followed this up with his Sorbonne lectures, *Sur l'Idée de Loi Naturelle*, dedicated to Lachelier. Boutroux studied under Eduard Zeller in 1869, and most of his many works were historical studies. He began teaching at the École Normale in 1877; in 1885 he taught at the Sorbonne, where from 1888 to 1902 he held the chair of the history of modern philosophy.

Boutroux may be compared with the American critics of the cosmic materialistic and mechanistic philosophies of the nineteenth century, Chauncey Wright and Charles S. Peirce. He attacked their monistic determinism through a careful study of scientific thought itself. He pointed to the hierarchy of the sciences, established in France in Comte's scheme of classification, in which each increasingly complex and "concrete" subject matter exhibits laws not reducible to those on a lower level, and in that logical sense contingent. But even in the laws of conservation, is the permanence of quantity really necessary? It is a purely empirical conclusion, and it does not explain change itself. On the level of life, vital energy is almost impossible to measure, and it introduces historical or evolutionary change. Still less is it possible to find conservation in consciousness.

The law tends to approach mere fact. Moreover, the conservation of the whole no longer determines the acts of the individual; it depends on them.

[5] *Du Fondement*, p. 81.
[6] See Gabriel Séailles, *La Philosophie de Jules Lachelier* (Paris, 1920), pp. 109 ff.

The individual, having become himself the whole genus to which the law applies, is its master. It turns the law into an instrument; and it dreams of a state in which, in each instant of its existence, it would be thus the equal of the law.[7]

Thus science understood agrees with Spiritualism. We must not be deceived by the fact that its finished form is deductive: the necessity is not in the principles, but in the deduction. Positive science deals with what is stable and permanent in phenomena; "it still remains to know it in its creative source." The historical aspect of things is left out, everything in being that is unpredictable action impossible to deduce. Only in the moral life, in the tendency toward the Good, can a complete and final explanation be found.

If it should be the case that the given world manifests a certain degree of really irreducible contingency, there would be room to think that the laws of nature are not sufficient in themselves and have their reason in the causes that dominate them: so that the point of view of the understanding would not be the definitive point of view of the knowledge of things. (4–5)

Boutroux led directly to that movement of critical thought known as *La Critique de la Science*, which drew on Neo-Kantianism and Renouvier. But he also continued the Spiritualism of Ravaisson and Lachelier, and forms a link between them and Bergson. Like Peirce, he combined a careful analysis of scientific thought with an appreciation of the metaphysical tradition. And he saw them both in historical terms, illuminated by his careful study of the great minds of the past.

[7] *De la Contingence des Lois de la Nature* (Paris, 1874; 2nd ed., 1895), p. 130.

German Idealism:
The Problem of Man and Nature

IN GERMANY, philosophic idealism had been made the major national tradition. It had already, with Schelling, become a philosophy of cosmic evolution. It could loom larger than the materialism of Büchner and Moleschott, and it could easily win out among the academics and the sophisticated over Haeckel's monism. The religious reconstruction had already been effected, if not completed, and Newtonian determinism had been transcended. Hence German philosophy after 1848 did not face the religious problem that confronted England, of defending religion against the encroachments of an imperialistic science; nor did it face the problem of the French, of defending moral freedom against mechanism. The Germans had to assimilate science in an idealism that would include but transcend it. They had to analyze it carefully. And above all they had to adjust the tide of natural science to *Kultur* and to the rising *Geisteswissenschaften*.

About the middle of the century appeared a group of philosophies aiming primarily to adjust human beings to the new material and scientific order in which they were beginning to live. This movement may be called a "materialistic idealism": it is idealistic and post-Kantian in the structure of its thought, but not in what it tries to come to terms with. Here belongs the Marxism that has abandoned the humanism of the early Marx for a "materialistic" stamp. Here fits in Haeckel himself, with his open arms for Darwin. Here is to be found Fechner, combining his careful analysis of psycho-physics with a very Romantic and imaginative panpsychism. And here is Lotze, the major system-builder among the idealists of the second half of the century, carefully preserving the principles of an idealism going back to Leib-

Originally intended as part of Book VII.

niz, yet struggling to provide a place for physical facts and the material order within their framework.

The analysis of natural science on the whole dominated the period, initiated by F.A. Lange's critical *History of Materialism* (1866), with its concluding plea for a methodological as opposed to a substantial materialism. This initiated the "empirio-criticism" of Mach and Avenarius, which led on to the Vienna school of Logical Positivists. It also started the movement of *Zurück auf Kant!* which led to the Marburg school of Herrmann Cohen, Natorp, Stammler, and Cassirer.

Other thinkers carried on the devotion of the Romantic idealists to forms of experience other than natural science. Here are Windelband and Rickert and the "Southwest German school." And here is the great philosopher of the *Geisteswissenschaften*, Dilthey. Meanwhile there had begun a critique of the organized intellectualism of the universities, led by the great prophet-critic Nietzsche, and prolonged into what was called *Lebensphilosophie*.

Toward the end of the century there took form, out of a loosening Marxism, a philosophy of social evolution, whose leaders were Max Weber and Karl Mannheim. And against the formalism of the Neo-Kantians there came the protest, stemming from the Austrian Brentano, of Husserl and his phenomenological analysis.

I

Lotze's is the most imposing idealistic system of the second half of the nineteenth century. But it had a predecessor which, though created during the earlier period of Romantic idealism, did not begin to win adherents until the fifties, and thereafter remained an alternative for those dissatisfied with the methodological and formalistic analyses of Kant.

Arthur Schopenhauer (1788–1860) gave an idealistic rather than a "critical" interpretation of Kant, and thus fits in with Fichte, Schelling, and Schleiermacher. He was not wanting in self-confidence, and regarded himself as the only significant successor to Kant; the others were all wind-bags. But he pushed the nineteenth-century philosophy of development, as found in Schelling and Hegel, in a direction which makes his version the idealistic counterpart of the later philosophies of cosmic evolution. Instead of, like Spencer or Haeckel, generalizing the notion of "force" and finding it at the heart of man's life, he found in human experience "will" which he generalized into the foundation of the cosmos. Where he differed from Spencer, and from his fellow-Romanticists, was in the "pessimistic" conclusion he was supporting. The innermost kernel of existence is a blind, undisciplined, never-resting and never-satisfied wanting. Not reason but desire is primary; and it is in essence doomed to frustration or boredom.

It was this pessimism and emphasis on the limitation and impotence of reason which prevented his masterpiece from having any influence on the optimistic Romantic generation when it first came out in 1819. It was not till the disillusionment following the abortive revolutions of 1848 that readers could make sense of his temper of thought. Thereafter, disillusionment with the scientific "alien world" as well as with the hopes for a rising industrial society kept alive his appeal to the alienated. Schopenhauer became the philosophical symbol of the pessimism which many poets from Byron and Leopardi down were beginning to feel with the new world.

Schopenhauer was the son of a rich merchant who had moved from Danzig to Hamburg, and of a vivacious mother who wrote novels. After a disillusioning experience in business, into which his father had forced him, he studied under Schulze-Aenesidemus at Göttingen, and under Fichte at Berlin. His thesis was on *Die Vierfache Wurzel des Satzes vom Zureichendem Grunde* (1813), a fairly Aristotelian study of the four causes, in which he broke down Kant's sharp distinction between perception and understanding. He worked out his own system in *Die Welt als Wille und Vorstellung* (1819). The support of the natural sciences he brought to his thesis of the cosmic will in *Der Wille in der Natur* (1836); his way of salvation he elaborated in *Die beiden Grundprobleme der Ethik* (1841). For ten years he tried to teach as a Dozent at Berlin, but without success: he had selected the hour at which Hegel gave his most popular lectures. In his mind, a conspiracy of envious professors of philosophy joined his mother as sources of his dissatisfaction with the world. The latter part of his life in Frankfurt brought a certain satisfaction and success.

In Book I, the world as *Vorstellung*, Schopenhauer simplifies the Kantian apparatus of interpretation, abolishing the sharp difference between the forms of intuition and the categories of the understanding. He emerges with three transcendental forms, space, time, and causality: these in conventionally idealistic fashion bring a merely

phenomenal interpretation of the world. In denig
penhauer seems to be close to the Romantic think
he had studied under Fichte, that apostle of the p
reason. For him, reality was directly accessible in "
he included striving, impulse, instinct, interest, des
In this will, subject and object are one, for the self th
the object known. Schopenhauer admits that even her
cape the transcendental forms completely, for in will w
time. But the veil is here thinner than elsewhere.

Intelligence is secondary to the will, and cannot form
ends. There is an incipient pragmatism in this *Lebensphiloso*
penhauer. Will objectifies itself in Platonic Ideas, *Urp*
Goethe's sense. Since they are eternal, nothing essentially
happens, history is but ceaseless change. Schopenhauer
Darwin, but not Schelling. He accepted the emergence of hig
higher forms of existence, with a doctrine of emergence antici
Boutroux, as well as the later emergent evolutionists Lloyd Mor
and Alexander. Yet time is ultimately an illusion, and evolution ca
scarcely be "creative." Schopenhauer drew on the Hindu vision of the
Upanishads, the first major Western philosopher to establish connections with Oriental thought.

The good is the object of desire. But desire is itself painful, a lack,
and aims to abolish itself. The good is negative, a getting rid of what
creates it. Man is either frustrated or bored; there is a soul of evil in
things good. Music alone is the image of emotion and desire itself; it
expresses joy, but not the object of joy, or longing, but not its end.
The other arts express the objectification of the will in Platonic Ideas.
In their contemplation man can for a moment forget the striving of the
will. But only through sympathy with others, and asceticism, can
man still his desire more permanently. Schopenhauer was himself far
from an ascetic; but, he insisted, the moralist need no more practice his
good than the aesthetician need be beautiful. He made no effort to al-
leviate the miseries of men, nor did he evince patriotic or civic feeling.

There are many brilliant insights in Schopenhauer. But his influence came not from his arguments, but rather from his expression
of a mood and temper that emerged in the later nineteenth century. It
was greatest on musicians, artists, and literary figures. He had one
arch-evangelist, Julius Frauenstädt, his editor; and one disciple,

Appendix

d von Hartmann. Elsewhere he touched the thought of Wagner,
arzer, and Tolstoy. He inspired Nietzsche to reaction, Hans
inger to his view of the fictitious character of intellect; and the
ich idealistic evolutionists down to Bergson.

Outline (1969)

The Career of Philosophy in Modern Times
Volume III: The Hundred Years Since Darwin

BOOK VII
COMING TO TERMS WITH NATURAL SCIENCE

BOOK VIII
PHILOSOPHIES OF SCIENCE

BOOK IX
CRITICAL PHILOSOPHIES OF EXPERIENCE

Index

The Library
University of Saint Francis
WITHDRAWN
Fort Wayne, Indiana 46808